Sustainable Development Goals Series

The **Sustainable Development Goals Series** is Springer Nature's inaugural cross-imprint book series that addresses and supports the United Nations' seventeen Sustainable Development Goals. The series fosters comprehensive research focused on these global targets and endeavours to address some of society's greatest grand challenges. The SDGs are inherently multidisciplinary, and they bring people working across different fields together and working towards a common goal. In this spirit, the Sustainable Development Goals series is the first at Springer Nature to publish books under both the Springer and Palgrave Macmillan imprints, bringing the strengths of our imprints together.

The Sustainable Development Goals Series is organized into eighteen subseries: one subseries based around each of the seventeen respective Sustainable Development Goals, and an eighteenth subseries, "Connecting the Goals", which serves as a home for volumes addressing multiple goals or studying the SDGs as a whole. Each subseries is guided by an expert Subseries Advisor with years or decades of experience studying and addressing core components of their respective Goal.

The SDG Series has a remit as broad as the SDGs themselves, and contributions are welcome from scientists, academics, policymakers, and researchers working in fields related to any of the seventeen goals. If you are interested in contributing a monograph or curated volume to the series, please contact the Publishers: Zachary Romano [Springer; zachary.romano@springer.com] and Rachael Ballard [Palgrave Macmillan; rachael.ballard@palgrave.com].

Stefano Bianchini
Federica Bandini • Daniela Bolzani
Editors

Social Entrepreneurship and Migrants' Inclusion

Insights from the Adriatic-Ionian Region

palgrave
macmillan

Editors
Stefano Bianchini
Department of Political and
Social Science
Alma Mater Studiorum-University
of Bologna
Bologna, Italy

Federica Bandini
University of Bologna
Forli, Italy

Daniela Bolzani
University of Bologna
Forlì, Italy

ISSN 2523-3084 ISSN 2523-3092 (electronic)
Sustainable Development Goals Series
ISBN 978-3-031-55790-3 ISBN 978-3-031-55791-0 (eBook)
https://doi.org/10.1007/978-3-031-55791-0

This Palgrave Macmillan imprint is published by the registered company Springer Nature Switzerland AG.
The registered company address is: Gewerbestrasse 11, 6330 Cham, Switzerland

Paper in this product is recyclable.

Preface

This volume collects theoretical and empirical contributions regarding the inclusion of migrants through social entrepreneurship—covering everything from antecedents, processes, and outcomes to approaches, policies, and practices. Grounded in a multi-disciplinary approach, the book aims to foster debate and exchange on key issues in social entrepreneurship, including the innovative approaches of various initiatives, their potential transferability to other contexts, and the participation of beneficiaries in decision-making processes. More specifically, the book strives to provide insights into projects and practices in the Adriatic-Ionian region, which includes three EU countries (Greece, Italy, and Slovenia), EU candidate countries (Albania and Serbia) and one potential EU candidate country (Bosnia and Herzegovina). To that end, the book analyzes factors that are driving and hindering the development of the social economy, as well as offers a comparison with countries not belonging to the Ionic area (Austria and Spain). Given the scarcity of national and comparative evidence of migrants' inclusion and entrepreneurship in the Adriatic-Ionian context, and on social entrepreneurship more broadly, the book should be of interest to a wide audience: not only academics and policymakers but also a non-technical audience interested in the social and economic inclusion of migrants.

Forlì, Italy — Stefano Bianchini
Forlì, Italy — Federica Bandini
Forlì, Italy — Daniela Bolzani

Acknowledgments

This book is partly a result of the Refugees' Economic Integration Through Social Entrepreneurship (REInSER) project. The REInSER project geographically covers the ADRION[1] area, whose common societal developments and challenges call for more cooperation and shared initiatives. This is especially true if the region hopes to achieve a common future in the EU. The main goal of the REInSER project is to improve the economic and social integration of migrants and refugees in their host societies of the ADRION Programme area. REInSER brings together eight project partners from academia, business support organizations, and local authorities who can lend their varying expertise, knowledge and skills to research on the social economy—and particularly social entrepreneurship approaches. The project's long-term objectives are twofold: first, boosting refugees' possibilities of becoming active economic actors and agents of their own integration in a given host society; and second, helping migrants contribute to local and regional sustainable economic development by

[1]The Interreg V-B Adriatic-Ionian program, better known as ADRION, is one of the instruments dedicated to the implementation of the EU Cohesion Policy. ADRION supports cooperation and solidarity across borders through project funding between eight Partner States within the Adriatic-Ionian region, including Albania, Bosnia and Herzegovina, Croatia, Greece, Italy, Montenegro, Serbia, and Slovenia. https://www.adrioninterreg.eu/index.php/about-program/

generating employment and supporting the creation of new socially responsible businesses. The authors would like to thank all project partners for their input, support, and critical suggestions.

Competing Interest The authors have no conflicts of interest to declare that are relevant to the content of this book.

Ethics Approval This study was performed in line with the principles of the Declaration of Helsinki.

About This Book

The book is divided into two parts, developed after the introductory Chap. 1 authored by Bandini, Bianchini, and Bolzani. The first part of the book provides an overall framework to interpret international migration and social entrepreneurship dynamics.

In Chap. 2 Bianchini, Cittadini, and Zoppi offer a comprehensive exploration of the Adriatic-Ionian region, with a specific focus on current and potential collaborative endeavors. The analysis of socio-demographic trends reveals shared challenges, including depopulation and declining fertility rates, which underscore the need for coordinated policy responses. However, effective cooperation hinges on political factors, notably the ongoing EU enlargement process and the unresolved issues of Balkan reconciliation. Notably, civil society organizations play a central role in promoting inter-ethnic dialogue and reconciliation, often surpassing official leadership in driving social and political transformation. Addressing these political issues is crucial for both regional development and meeting the societal needs of the Adriatic-Ionian population.

In Chap. 3, Bianchini, Cittadini, and Zoppi explore the evolving governmental responses to migration in the Adriatic-Ionian region, which gained heightened political significance due to mass migration along the Balkan Route in the 2010s. The study, drawing on research from the Interreg-ADRION project REInSER, employs a combination of literature review, document analysis, and interviews with key stakeholders. Beyond humanitarian and security concerns, there are pressing questions regarding the reception and integration of asylum seekers, refugees, and migrants.

Cooperation with the EU in migration management has become crucial in light of these perceived challenges. The chapter also aims to identify trends, points of convergence, and gaps among countries, while considering potential future collaborations based on the experiences of neighboring nations.

Afterward, the book deals with social enterprises and their role in the integration of refugees and other migrants. In Chap. 4, Savoia, Bandini, and Preite explore the legal recognition and structural conditions for social entrepreneurship growth in the Adriatic-Ionian countries, emphasizing their significance in promoting sustainable development. The study investigates the evolution of entrepreneurial ecosystems across Adriatic-Ionian countries from 2006 to 2019, revealing notable improvements in entrepreneurial ecosystems in Slovenia and Italy, even as Balkan countries have remained relatively stable. The primary challenge in the region lies in addressing unstable institutions and risky environments. The research identifies areas for improvement, especially with policy frameworks, and offers insights for creating a more favorable environment for entrepreneurship and economic growth. These findings hold implications for advancing Sustainable Development Goals within the macro-region.

Subsequently, in Chap. 5, Grassi, Bolzani, and Bandini provide an overview of the potential role of social entrepreneurship in addressing the challenges and exploiting the opportunities deriving from international migration, both in migrants' homes and in host countries. The authors review the growing but fragmented academic literature linking social entrepreneurship and international migration, identifying the antecedents, processes, and outcomes of social entrepreneurial initiatives undertaken by or for migrants. The authors derive theoretical and practical implications informing future developments in academic research and managerial and public policies.

The second part of the book includes case studies and empirical evidence about the policies and practices of social entrepreneurship as they relate to migrants from the Adriatic-Ionian area.

In Chap. 6, Mujanović, Simić, Marković, and Abdi analyze the conditions for refugees' socio-economic inclusion in Bosnia and Herzegovina, also through practices of social entrepreneurship. Their work underscores the challenges faced by state authorities in enabling refugees to integrate into society and thereby access social benefits and employment opportunities. The research, conducted within a refugee camp, reveals a notable contrast between refugees' immediate survival-driven desire to remain in

Bosnia and Herzegovina and their long-term aspiration for improved integration within EU countries. This chapter emphasizes the critical importance of addressing the disparities in refugee perspectives and aspirations.

In Chap. 7, Cittadini studies both the advantages and challenges of using social entrepreneurship to facilitate the integration of refugees and asylum seekers. The chapter addresses the dual nature of social enterprises in aiding economic integration while potentially reinforcing existing social exclusion patterns. The discussion encompasses the role of racial privilege and critiques of social entrepreneurship initiatives. The study also underscores the broader socio-psychological benefits for individuals involved in social enterprises. Focusing on Serbia, a country grappling with both the transition to a capitalist economy and a significant influx of migrants, the article examines the nascent phenomenon of social entrepreneurship dedicated to refugee and asylum-seeker integration. Through fieldwork and interviews conducted in late 2022 and early 2023, the study analyzes the experiences of a specific social enterprise, Women on the Way, which provides job opportunities for refugee women in the tailoring sector. This research contributes to the broader discourse on social entrepreneurship's potential in refugee integration, offering insights that are specific to the complex migratory context of Serbia.

In Chap. 8, Gombač delves into the potential to leverage social entrepreneurship for emancipatory outcomes—namely, empowering asylum seekers in Slovenia through participatory methodologies. Grounded in a series of workshops convened at the asylum residence on Kotnikova Street in Ljubljana during 2021, the study explores an array of practices, interventions, and techniques that arose in collaboration between diverse stakeholders and asylum seekers. Informed by antecedent research and experiences at the Slovenian Migration Institute ZRC SAZU, the study highlights an imperative to nurture the entrepreneurial aspirations of asylum seekers and refugees, particularly in Slovenia and in light of the post-2015–16 "crisis of the EU border regime". Through its methodology, the research offers information that would have been difficult or impossible to obtain otherwise. While all participants found the workshops useful, they also encountered constant methodological, theoretical, and content discords that led to a complex process and slow progress.

In Chap. 9, Perković, Lenarčič, and Zadel focus on the under-explored subject of refugee employment within the context of social entrepreneurship in Slovenia. While prior studies have indirectly touched upon refugees' employment vulnerability, none have specifically delved into their role within social enterprises. The chapter offers a comprehensive examination of Slovenia's socio-economic landscape, including the legal, systemic, practical, cultural, and economic factors that influence refugee employment within this sector. Notably, the paper underscores that refugee employment in social enterprises transcends mere economic gains; it serves a pivotal role in the integration of refugees into host societies. This engagement helps counteract stigmas surrounding their contributions and challenges preconceptions that refugees do not enrich their host communities.

Next, in Chap. 10, Sejdini and Shyti study the economic integration of refugees and migrants through social entrepreneurship, with a specific focus on Albania. The chapter examines the relevant national policy and legislation regarding social entrepreneurship and provides an overview of social enterprises' characteristics, legal structures, size, sectors, governance and stakeholders networks, support from public institutions and private entities, and their sources of financial backing. Furthermore, the article explores both exemplary approaches and forthcoming challenges specific to Albania in these areas, with a special emphasis on the impact of migration. The central objective of this chapter is to indicate the motivating factors and hurdles of social entrepreneurship and, from there, to recommend strategies to aid migrants' integration into host societies. The chapter presents insights that may guide the formulation of public policies that would facilitate economic integration and broaden access for refugees and migrants alike.

In Chap. 11, Mantzos, Theodosiou, and Kameas explore the context of Greece, where the social economy has gained traction in the last decade, thanks in part to the debt crises that began in 2009. The chapter provides an overview of the social and institutional changes that culminated in a significant expansion of the social economy in Greece over the past decade, encompassing grassroots movements in civic associations and institutional shifts aligning with the European trend toward social economy. Nevertheless, this work indicates that the so-called third sector has not yet established a firm foothold in Greece's broader financial and entrepreneurial landscape. It remains at an ideological perimeter, endeavoring to chart an independent course. This assertion is exemplified by a detailed examination of a local association of social enterprises in northwest Greece. The chapter aims to illuminate both the ideological foundations and practical challenges confronting the social and solidarity economy, particularly in the Greek periphery, and its relationship with more conventional entrepreneurial and economic activities.

In Chap. 12, Martinelli, Serpente, and Bolzani bring the attention to the role of entrepreneurial support organizations, such as incubators and accelerators, as important pillars of entrepreneurial ecosystems that can foster equal and inclusive entrepreneurship practices. This chapter provides evidence about how two neglected types of support organizations, namely social incubators and accelerators, support migrant entrepreneurs. Analyzing explorative data collected through semi-structured interviews with specialists from one social incubator and one social accelerator in Italy, the authors highlight the pivotal role of governance and organizational structures, targeting and selection processes, and services provided. The work provides insights that contribute to the literature on entrepreneurial support organizations, along with practical recommendations.

Lastly, in Chap. 13, Zafošnik and Zavratnik study and compare the integration of refugees into the labor markets of Slovenia, Spain, and Austria. The research underscores the significance of well-defined integration policies, particularly for the most vulnerable migrant group—refugees. Employing a comparative approach, the study draws on semi-structured interviews with 25 refugees who have successfully integrated into these countries' labor markets since 2015. The findings reveal that countries with greater migration experience face fewer integration barriers. Early integration emerges as a pivotal factor, expediting labor market entry and enhancing overall integration. The chapter emphasizes that gaining employment and financial independence significantly contribute to refugees' self-sufficiency within their host societies.

Contents

Notes on Contributors

Tariku Ayana Abdi holds a PhD in Sciences of Mind (Work and Organizational Psychology) from the University of Campania "Luigi Vanvitelli", Italy. Previously he received an Erasmus Mundus Joint Master's Degree in Work, Organizational, and Personnel Psychology from the University of Valencia, Spain (home), and the University of Bologna, Italy (host). In addition, he also holds a Bachelor's Degree in Psychology and a Master's Degree in Developmental Psychology, both from Addis Ababa University, Ethiopia. Tariku has extensive teaching and professional work experience in Ethiopian higher education, and also worked as a counselling psychologist at the Johns Hopkins University, Bloomberg Public Health Center for Communication Program, for several years. Since July 2023, Tariku has been working as a research fellow in the Department of Management Science at the University of Bologna. Currently, he is conducting research on the entrepreneurship patterns and pathways of migrant entrepreneurs in Italy. Tariku's teaching interests include different psychology courses such as general psychology, developmental psychology, organizational psychology, and research methods. His research interests, which led to publications in academic journals and presentations at international conferences, include employability, career success, entrepreneurship, and well-being in the workplace, especially looking at minorities.

Federica Bandini is Associate Professor of Social Enterprises Management and Accounting. She achieved an International Teachers Programme (ITP) at London Business School, UK, and a PhD in Management for Public and Nonprofit Organizations at University of Parma, Italy. She has been the director of the Master of Science in Management for Social Economy at the University of Bologna, and director of the Social Enterprise and NGO Master at Bocconi School of Management. She has been teaching in the Department Public Policy and Management at the Bocconi School of Management, and doing research at CERGAS (Centre for Research on Health and Social Care Management) of the same University. She has been the director of the Executive Master in Management and Impact Finance for Social Entrepreneurship. Her main research interests are on public management, change management, social impact, and business administration studies, with a focus on social enterprises, hybrid, NGO, and public health. She is a founder and member of the steering committee at the Yunus Social Business Center, Bologna University, Italy.

Stefano Bianchini is Professor of East European Politics and History at the University of Bologna, Italy. From 2015 to 2021 he was Rector's delegate for relations with Eastern Europe. Previously, he was the director of the two years' Interdisciplinary Master of Arts in East European Studies (MIREES), a joint diploma of the Universities of Bologna, St Petersburg, Vytautas Magnus at Kaunas, and Corvinus of Budapest. He is a visiting professor at the St. Petersburg State University and holds a HD in Humanities from the Vytautas Magnus University, Kaunas. From 2001 to 2018 he was also the co-director of the European Regional Master in Democracy and Human Rights for SEE (ERMA) awarding a double diploma from the Universities of Sarajevo and Bologna. He is a member of the Executive Committee and former vice-president of the Association for Studies of Nationalities (ASN) based at the Harriman Institute, Columbia University, New York, and an executive editor of the blind peer-review journal *Southeastern Europe*, published by Brill, Leiden, and other academic journals. As an expert of Balkan issues, he was an adviser of the International Criminal Tribunal for the Former Yugoslavia (ICTY), Hague. He has written and co-edited 36 books and more than 200 articles in Italian, French, English, and other languages.

Daniela Bolzani obtained a PhD in Business Management in 2013, after 5 years of work in the domain of financial audit and of development cooperation in Europe and Africa. She was a postdoctoral fellow in the Departments of Business and Educational Sciences at University of Bologna (UNIBO) and Junior Assistant Professor of Management at the Università Cattolica, Milan, and at the University of Bologna (2020–2023).

She is Associate Professor of Management at the University of Bologna. She was a visiting scholar at Leeds School of Business, University of Colorado, and HEC Paris; and visiting professor at JUNIA-ISA Lille. Her research concerns entrepreneurial decision-making with a focus on diversity (e.g., culture, gender) and social inclusion. She coordinates and is a member of numerous European and national projects on these topics and has been a consultant for the OECD and UN-IOM.

Silvia Cittadini is a young researcher and expert in the fields of social rights, minorities, and diversity. She obtained a PhD in Politics, Human Rights, and Sustainability at the Sant'Anna School of Advanced Studies, Pisa, in 2019. Between 2021 and 2023, she was a research fellow in the Department of Political and Social Sciences at the University of Bologna, where she worked on the social integration of refugees and asylum seekers in the Adriatic-Ionian region. Before that, she was a post-doctoral fellow in the Romani Studies Program at the Central European University in Budapest and a research fellow at the European Centre for Minority Issues, Flensburg, Germany, where she worked on the social rights to housing and the inclusion of the Romani minority. She is an alumna of the European Regional Master in Democracy and Human Rights in South-East Europe (ERMA)—Universities of Sarajevo and Bologna—and a member of The Institute for Central-Eastern and Balkan Europe (IECOB). In her publications, she especially focused on the analysis of racial and gender diversity and discrimination through qualitative methods and adopting a feminist approach. In this area, she conducted field research in Italy and Bosnia and Herzegovina. She is the author of *Social Justice and Adequate Housing: Rights, Roma Inclusion and the Feeling of Home*, published by Routledge in 2021.

Jure Gombač holds a PhD in Sociology. He currently works as a researcher at the Slovenian Migration Institute ZRC SAZU. His main field of work is migration and border studies. He is involved in several national and international projects that focus on the social inclusion of migrants and their inclusion in the labour market. He is also a lecturer at the University of Nova Gorica.

Eleonora Grassi is a post-doctoral fellow in the Department of Management at the University of Bologna, Italy. She researches social movements, with a particular interest in the processes aimed at promoting alternative forms of organizing and fair and sustainable futures. She is also collaborating with the Yunus Social Business Centre of Bologna, with a project exploring the potentialities of social entrepreneurship for migrants' integration.

Achilles Kameas is Professor of Pervasive Computing Systems at Hellenic Open University (HOU), Greece, and holds various leadership roles, currently serving as the dean of the Faculty of Science & Technology and as a board member for HOU's Managing Board, Lifelong Learning Center Board, and Gender Equality Committee. Additionally, he directs the Internal Evaluation Unit, the MSc course "Pervasive and Mobile Computing Systems", and the Ubiquitous and Mobile Computing, Quality, and Ambient Intelligence Laboratory. Internationally, Achilles contributes to the Board of ALL DIGITAL, having served as chair and vice-chair. He actively engages in the EADTU Working Group on Diversity & Inclusion, with a focus on migrant inclusion in European Higher Education. He was a member of the ESCO Committee on ICT skills. At the national level, Achilles participates in initiatives such as the ELOT Standardization Committee on Resilient and Smart Cities, the National Digital Skills and Jobs Coalition, the ReBrain Greece initiative, and the UNHCR Working Group in Higher Education. Achilles has a prolific academic record, having been involved in over 100 EU and national R&D projects, authored numerous scientific articles and books, and received substantial citations. His commitment to fostering an inclusive society through digital transformation is evident in his teaching, MOOCs, and research interests, which span digital and green skills, technology-enhanced learning, STE(A)M education, smart environments, zero-energy buildings, digital cultural heritage, and digital social innovation.

Blaž Lenarčič is a research associate and an assistant professor employed at the Science and Research Centre of Koper, Slovenia. As a sociologist, he is mainly interested in research topics related to the impact of ICT on broader society and migration studies. He was a member of research teams in several national and international research projects on migration topics. He was also a visiting academics at the University of Canterbury in Christchurch, New Zealand. Between 2007 and 2016 he was a lecturer at the University of Primorska. He presents his work in scientific publications at scientific conferences in European countries and wider.

Konstantinos Mantzos is a social anthropologist. He holds a Degree in Social Anthropology from Panteion University of Social and Political

Sciences, Athens, followed by an MA in History and Anthropology from the University College London. Konstantinos has contributed to anthropology, particularly in the areas of migration and borders, combining his research interest with a commitment to education through teaching engagements at the Konitsa Summer School of the Border Crossing Network, where he imparted knowledge on these critical subjects. Currently, Konstantinos is a research associate at KETHEA (Center for Addicted Individuals) actively engaged in its transformative work, demonstrating his commitment to addressing societal challenges. Simultaneously, he holds a research position in the DAISSy group at the Hellenic Open University, contributing to various projects. His extensive experience includes participation in numerous EU-funded initiatives, spanning programs such as Erasmus+, European Social Fund, CERV, and Creative Europe. Konstantinos Mantzos's research interests focus on exploring the dynamic interplay of social and solidarity economy with social innovation. He assumes a dual role as both a practitioner, being a member of a social enterprise, and a dedicated researcher. This multifaceted approach underscores his commitment to understanding and enhancing the symbiotic relationship between social and economic dynamics, contributing to advancements in the field of social innovation.

Branko Marković is a leading expert and lecturer in the area of digital transformation and SDG in Bosnia and Herzegovina. He has many years of experience in the field of designing and developing software and services for various government bodies. Also, he has extensive experience in the transformation of state and private organizations and systems according to the requirements of digital transformation or energy transition. As an international consultant he worked in numerous countries of the Western Balkans and has carried out a large number of projects in the fields of energy transition, smart cities, ICT systems, and electronic administration and services. In the last few years, he deals with issues of sustainable development (SDG), and also in the field of social responsibility. In response to the challenges of migration and climate change, he worked on the preparation of documents and strategies for public institutions in Bosnia and Herzegovina. He worked and cooperated with several international organizations and multinational companies in the region and worldwide. He worked on projects sponsored by the World Health Organization and the EU. He is the author and co-author of a large number of professional and scientific works in the field of GDPR, digital transformation, smart city, IoT, corruption, international conflicts, as well as several books in the field of literature and film—prose and poetry.

Giulia Martinelli is a PhD student at the Gran Sasso Science Institute, L'Aquila, Italy. Her current research focuses on the analysis of factors underlying the well-being of individuals from the perspective of health and labour economics. Previously, she collaborated with tsm (Trentino School of Management) in the field of culture, tourism, and local development, and with the Ministry for Economic Development in innovation for SMEs. She was a research fellow in the Department of Management at the University of Bologna, where she worked on a project about migrant entrepreneurship and incubators. During her Master's, she did an internship at the OECD Trento Centre for Local Development, working on a project on local spatial productivity. She holds a Bachelor's Degree in International and Diplomatic Sciences from the University of Trieste and a Master's degree in Economics from the Scuola Superiore Sant'Anna and the University of Pisa.

Erol Mujanović is a reliable leader and economic development expert with a rich experience in transformation of organizations, including the digital transformation. He is also an assistant professor, marathon runner, and Ironman triathlon finisher. He currently works as deputy director in the Economic Growth Office of USAID Mission to Bosnia and Herzegovina. He holds an Undergraduate Degree in Business Administration in France, an MA Degree in Business Intelligence, and a PhD in Economics, specialized in social entrepreneurship. He continued professional development through numerous diplomatic and business skills training in Paris, London, Brussels, and Washington DC. He is a co-founder of the Association of Business Service Leaders in Bosnia and Herzegovina (BiH) (ABSL). Erol led teams and projects for top-level governments and international organizations in Western Balkans, implementing complex economic and business development projects. Within the diplomatic missions he worked for, all roles required deep understanding of high-level goals of the US, UK, or French Government and translating them into actionable ideas and projects on the ground in a rapidly changing environment. The same was with the World Bank Group and the UNDP high-level goals and development visions.

Ksenija Perković is a researcher at the Science and Research Centre Koper, with a special interest in social and spatial integration, (regional) identity, multiculturalism, and interethnic relations. As a young researcher she gained several months of research experience abroad at various institutes and departments of geography and social sciences (UK, Netherlands, Finland, Austria, Serbia). She is involved in the implementation of ongoing projects and coordinates different types of surveys at the Institute of Social Studies. She was the coordinator of the project REInSER—Refugees' Economic Integration through Social Entrepreneurship, funded by the Interreg Adrion programme.

Daniela Preite is Professor of Business Administration and Management at the University of Milan, Italy, and Rector's Delegate on Strategies for Financial Sustainability. She is Affiliate Professor of Financial Accounting in the SDA Bocconi School of Management at Bocconi University. She holds a Degree in Economics and Banking, cum laude, at the University of Lecce and a PhD in Business Administration and Management at the University of Bari Aldo Moro. She is a Chartered Accountant and is a member of the Registry of Auditors Accountants.

Her research activities focus on various fields, including financial accounting & analysis, planning and control, internal auditing, performance management and measurement, corporate governance, risk assessment and management, sustainable accounting and finance, accountability and reporting, business government relations, and change management.

She is the author of several books and articles on her topics of interest. Her works have been published in important journal, such as *Cities*, *Administration & Society*, *Socio-Economic Planning Sciences*, *Journal of Management Control*, and *Economia & Management*. She has taken part in many national and international conferences and she is a member of the Italian Academy of Business Administration and Management (AIDEA) and Italian Society of Accounting and Business Administration (SIDREA).

Francesco Savoia is a research fellow at the University of Milan and research affiliate at the Yunus Social Business Centre, University of Bologna, Italy. His research interests lie primarily in empirical applications to regional development issues at the macro and micro levels, including economic inequality, technological change, and financial development. He was a visiting PhD fellow at the Joint Research Centre (JRC), European Commission. Before joining the University of Milan, he was a research fellow at the University of Bologna, the University of Modena and Reggio Emilia, and the University of Naples Federico II. He also worked as a policy analyst at the Italian Ministry of Economic Development.

Imelda Sejdini, born in 1978, graduated from the University of Elbasan “Aleksandër Xhuvani”, Albania, in 2001 in business administration, with study profile in “Management”. After the Executive Master Studies in Management, in 2012 she completed the doctoral studies, receiving the scientific degree “Doctor of Science in Management”, from the Faculty of Economics, University of Tirana, Albania. In March 2015, she was promoted with the academic title “Associate Professor” by the University of Elbasan “Aleksandër Xhuvani”, Albania. She started her academic career immediately after graduation, during the academic year 2001–2002, initially as a part-time lecturer in the Department of Business Administration at the University of Elbasan “Aleksandër Xhuvani”, and in February 2004, as a full-time lecturer in the Department of Business Administration. Actually she is the dean of the Faculty of Economy, elected in 2016, after holding the position of vice-rector of the University of Elbasan “Aleksandër Xhuvani” during 2013–2016. She teaches courses in business ethics, reward management, risk management and insurance, and theories of organizations and management. She is the author of *Business Ethics*, text book for students (1st edition in 2014). During her academic career she has written on a lot of topics related to business administration with a special focus in business management in various economics, business, and management journals. She is fluent in English and Italian.

Greta Serpente is a PhD candidate in Management from the Alma Mater Studiorum-University of Bologna, Italy, since 2019. Prior to entering the doctoral program, she obtained the Master’s Degree in Economics and Management from the University of Pescara. Her research interests include entrepreneurship education, innovation, and entrepreneurial support organizations (e.g., incubators, accelerators). During her Master’s degree, she conducted research on innovative start-ups in the fashion industry and on the role of human capital trust during an M&A between a start-up and a temporary industry agency.

Bederiana Shyti, born in 1970, graduated in mathematic sciences from the Faculty of Natural Sciences, University of Tirana, in 1992, with study profile in applied mathematics. After the Executive Master in Mathematics, direction “Probability and Statistics”, Faculty of Natural Sciences,

University of Tirana, Albania, in 2004, she completed the doctoral studies in 2009, receiving the scientific degree Doctor in Mathematics, direction "Probability and Statistics", from the University of Tirana, Albania. In March 2013, she was promoted with the academic title "Associate Professor", by the University of Elbasan "Aleksandër Xhuvani", Albania. She started her academic career, during the academic year 1996, initially as a part-time lecturer in the Department of Mathematics at the University of Elbasan "Aleksandër Xhuvani", and in April 1999, as a full-time lecturer in the Department of Mathematics. Since 2016 she is the head of the Mathematics Department in the Faculty of Natural Sciences at the University of Elbasan "Aleksandër Xhuvani". She teaches courses in probability and statistics, applied mathematics, and financial mathematics. She is the author of *Applied Mathematics*, text book for students (1st edition in 2015). During her academic career she has written a lot of topics related to mathematical statistics, with a special focus in application of mathematics in daily life, in various scientific journals. She is fluent in English and Italian.

Slavko Simić is a leading expert and lecturer in the area of controlling in Bosnia and Herzegovina. He is the founder and president of the Association for the Promotion of Controlling—ICV in Bosnia and Herzegovina since 2012 in front of the Internationaler Controller Verein—ICV Wörthsee, Germany. He is a full-time professor and lecturer at a number of domestic and foreign higher education institutions, and authored a number of professional and scientific works in the field of management and controlling. Since 1996, he has embarked on entrepreneurship and successfully runs his own company engaged in production, wholesale, and business consulting, for which he was awarded the prestigious award "Manager of 2009 in Bosnia and Herzegovina". In 1999, he entered the world of business education, improving himself as a consultant, trainer, and lecturer in the fields of controlling, organizational management, quality management, marketing, sales, balanced scorecard, lean, project management, and soft skills. He was educated both at home and at prestigious academies and universities in the Netherlands, Germany, Austria, England, and others. Among others, he obtained the prestigious (CMC) international certificate from the ICMCI in Vienna for the provision of consulting services in the field of management. He consulted several international organizations and multinational companies in the region. He held more than 950 trainings and over 250 consulting activities in micro, small, medium, and large enterprises in Bosnia and Herzegovina and abroad.

Aspasia (Sissie) Theodosiou, a social anthropologist with a PhD from the University of Manchester, currently holds the position of an associate professor at the University of Ioannina, Greece. Alongside her academic role, she serves as a Teaching Fellow at the Hellenic Open University and holds the position of a senior researcher in the DAISSy research group since 2011. Her extensive research affiliations include the University of Manchester and Helsinki University. Over the years, she has actively contributed to various EU and national R&D projects, including those under the Lifelong Learning and Erasmus+ programs. Theodosiou's research interests encompass diverse areas such as the anthropology of music, anthropology of education and learning, borders, European "minorities", and their integration, particularly focusing on Roma and refugees. Her work extends to issues of sovereignty and national identities on the web, examining communities of practice and learning practices in technologically enhanced study environments, particularly in online platforms. Furthermore, she has delved into the impact of the Greek crisis on civil society organizations and disadvantaged populations. In her recent research endeavours, Theodosiou explores themes like intercultural mediation for migrants, hate speech, and social innovation, shedding light on the experiences of outsiders in contemporary European societies.

Maja Zadel is a research associate at the Institute for Social Studies, Science and Research Centre Koper (ZRS Koper), Slovenia. She is mainly engaged in the study of ethnicity and nationalism, transculturation, identities, migration, and integration. She has been involved in national and international projects and at the moment she is concluding her postdoctoral project on the topic of migrant integration in schools. In 2013 she was a visiting academics at the University of Canterbury, Christchurch, New Zealand; in 2022 at the University of Southern Denmark, Odense, Denmark; and in 2023 at University of Barcelona, Barcelona, Spain.

Anja Zafošnik received her Master's degree from the Faculty of Social Sciences, University of Ljubljana, Slovenia, where in recent years she has focused on the topic of integration and employment of refugees. In 2019 and 2020, she conducted field interviews for her Master's thesis in Spain,

Austria, and Slovenia. She currently works in a pharmaceutical company in the field of human resources and focuses on the employment of foreigners in Slovenia and the inclusion of people with disabilities in the work process. In 2021, she co-authored the publication of a monograph titled *#Stayathome. Migration, Refugees and COVID-19*, together with other authors who gathered reflections on migration and social margins in the COVID-19 era. In the past, she attended several international conferences in Europe on the topic migration.

Simona Zavratnik is Associate Professor of Sociology and a researcher at the Faculty of Social Sciences, University of Ljubljana, Slovenia. Her research areas include migration and refugees, global mobilities, social minorities, marginalized groups and vulnerabilities, human rights and human trafficking, gendered migration, and lately climate change and its effects on migration. She is the author of numerous scientific and professional articles in social science journals and anthologies, editor of the anthology *Women and Trafficking* (2004) and co-editor of the anthology *Migration—globalization—the EU* (2003). In the latest book *Digital Refugees* (2020), co-authored with Sanja Cukut Krilić, they investigate social transformations in the field of international migration, with focus on new information technologies and connected migrants in transnational space. She was a visiting researcher at the University of Frankfurt Institute for Social Research (2013) under the DAAD Fellowship; a guest lecturer at the Panteion University of Social and Political Sciences, Athens (Erasmus programme), and Ohio State University, Columbus (bilateral Slovene-USA programme); and a participant in numerous international conferences at universities in Europe and abroad. Currently (2023) she is a guest teacher at the Universidad de Antioquia, Medellin, Columbia.

Marco Zoppi is a post-doctoral research fellow in the Department of Political and Social Science at the University of Bologna, Italy. In this position, he was involved in several international research projects dealing with the topics of migration, diaspora, and integration of asylum seekers, refugees, and migrants in Europe and across the Adriatic-Ionian macro-region. Marco is also a board member of IECOB—The Institute for Central-Eastern and Balkan Europe, which carries out research and training on a wide range of topics, including peace and reconciliation. Marco's research interests focus primarily on migration, diaspora, and integration issues, which he analyses also through interviews and quantitative data. He is the author of about forty academic publications, among which journal articles, book chapters, and monographies. He has authored the recently published book *Futures of the Western Balkans: Fragmentation and Integration in the Region and Beyond* (Springer, 2022), and he is the editor of a forthcoming volume titled *Contested Heritage in Europe and Africa: Representation, Commemoration and Memorialization of a Connected Past* (Routledge, 2024).

List of Figures

List of Tables

List of Tables

PART I

An Overall Framework to Interpret the Relationship Between International Migration and Social Entrepreneurship in the Adriatic-Ionian Region

CHAPTER 1

An Introduction to Social Entrepreneurship and Migrants' Inclusion in the Adriatic-Ionian Region

Federica Bandini, Daniela Bolzani, and Stefano Bianchini

The twenty-first century has been called the "century of migration"[1] thanks to a notable increase in intercontinental movement. Indeed, the last decade has seen escalating numbers of migrants, asylum seekers, and

[1] Ian Goldin, Geoffrey Cameron and Meera Balarajan (2011), Exceptional People: How Migration Shaped Our World and Will Define Our Future, Princeton, NJ: Princeton University Press; Stephen Castles, Hein de Haas and Mark J. Miller (2014), "The Age of Migration: International Population Movements in the Modern World," Ethnic and Racial Studies, Volume 38, Issue 13.

F. Bandini (✉) • D. Bolzani
Department of Management, Alma Mater Studiorum-University of Bologna, Bologna, Italy
e-mail: federica.bandini@unibo.it; daniela.bolzani@unibo.it

S. Bianchini et al. (eds.), *Social Entrepreneurship and Migrants' Inclusion*, Sustainable Development Goals Series,
https://doi.org/10.1007/978-3-031-55791-0_1

refugees[2] that have substantially elevated the overall immigrant demographic. This trend could transform societies across the globe: On the one hand, migration is emblematic of the modern open society and thus a top priority on international agendas (Massey et al., 1993); on the other, it poses significant social and economic concerns. For instance, Greece experienced an influx of more than one million refugees, asylum seekers, and migrants in 2015 and early 2016—a number that declined after the closure of the Balkan border in March 2016. However, the Eastern Mediterranean route remains active, with many individuals entering Europe annually for various reasons, including international protection, family reunion, economic opportunities, and education. Frontex,[3] the European Border and Coast Guard Agency, reported that the Western Balkan route was the second-most-used path to Europe in 2021, with detections of illegal border crossings more than doubling to a total of 61,735. Consequently, the arrival and inclusion of refugees and other migrants in host societies represent significant challenges for both EU member states and non-member (transition) states, especially those in the Adriatic-Ionian region.

[2] According to the United Nations High Commissioner for Refugee (UNHCR) and International organization for Migration (IOM), the terms "refugee," "asylum seeker," and "migrant" have distinct legal definitions and implications, although they are often used interchangeably. Refugee is a person who has been forced to flee their country because of persecution, war, or violence. Refugees have sought and been granted asylum in another country or have been recognized as refugees through a formal legal process. An asylum seeker is an individual who has left their own country and applied for asylum (protection) in another country, but has not yet received a decision on their application. The term "migrant" is a broader category that includes anyone who moves from one place to another, often for economic reasons, family reunification, or other reasons not necessarily related to seeking protection from persecution. The legal definitions and protections associated with these terms vary internationally. The distinction is crucial for understanding the rights and legal status of individuals in different circumstances. Additionally, within the category of migrants, there are different subcategories such as economic migrants, seasonal migrants, and others.

[3] Frontex (2022), Western Balkan Route. https://frontex.europa.eu/we-know/migratoryroutes/western-balkan-route/

S. Bianchini
Department of Political and Social Science,
Alma Mater Studiorum-University of Bologna, Bologna, Italy
e-mail: stefano.bianchini@unibo.it

Refugee integration and resettlement are not only key policy objectives but also subjects of intense public discourse within the EU. In order to successfully integrate refugees, policymakers need to consider the various barriers along with the appropriate strategies for overcoming them. Recognizing refugees as "individuals with special needs,"[4] European governments emphasize the importance of close links and multisector alliances between social actors involved in refugee issues, such as public institutions, nongovernmental organizations (NGOs), and social enterprises.

Notably, policymakers have shown growing interest in managing increased migration into Europe to address labor market shortages and the challenges of an aging population. Consequently, national governments must grant refugees employment rights and access to work permits, along with training and other programs that promote their labor participation.

Migration is a global issue requiring cooperation and common initiatives that account for regional disparities. Migrants need to be empowered to leverage their resources and skills in order to actively participate in EU and non-EU states. Transnational cooperation facilitates the sharing of best practices around social entrepreneurship (SE), which can help address challenges and opportunities in refugees' economic inclusion. Self-employment and entrepreneurship play a crucial role in achieving labor market inclusion, particularly in the context of SE, which is gaining increasing attention for its ability to integrate refugees and asylum seekers in host societies.

SE encompasses all entrepreneurial activities aimed at achieving social objectives, regardless of organizational form, including both for-profit and non-profit organizations. Social enterprises, operating in the broader field of Social Economy, exemplify an "economy that works for people," that is, they work toward the social and economic inclusion of disadvantaged groups. As a form of inclusive business, SE has proven vital in addressing the challenges posed by the refugee crisis, providing assistance in economic and social inclusion, temporary housing, health, psychological support, language, and education. Consequently, social enterprises are pivotal players in the process of inclusion.

[4] European Council on Refugees and Exiles (2002) Position on the Integration of refugees in Europe. https://ecre.org/wp-content/uploads/2016/07/ECRE-Position-on-the-Integration-of-Refugees-inEurope_December-2002.pdf

While many EU countries have adopted legislation and policies to support social enterprises and the Social Economy, there are both definitional and practical obstacles that persist. Public institutions still need to design and implement policies that can foster social enterprise development, as well as assess their impact and transferability potential. These challenges are particularly relevant amid political debates on migration and inclusion dynamics in Europe. Therefore, further discussions on these themes are crucial and timely.

The Adriatic-Ionian macroregion presents an intriguing yet overlooked area for research on interconnected phenomena such as migration and inclusion, SE, and territorial development. This context is unique insofar as it involves non-EU countries at various stages of the EU enlargement process, connected by cooperation programs and initiatives intended to foster policy and practice convergence. Despite the recent political relevance of the Balkans in migration dynamics, these countries appear less equipped to develop migration and inclusion policies, along with the strategies to address potential challenges. The region's legislation and reforms related to SE are also lagging compared to EU countries.

Reference

Massey, Douglas S., et al. (1993). Theories of International Migration: A Review and Appraisal. *Population and Development Review, 19*(3), 431–466. JSTOR.

CHAPTER 2

A Socio-political Perspective on the Adriatic-Ionian Area

Stefano Bianchini, Silvia Cittadini, and Marco Zoppi

Introduction

The Adriatic-Ionian area, the geographical focus of this volume, represents an interesting yet overlooked field of research for what concerns several human phenomena that interconnect the political, social and economic spheres. This is especially the case of migration and integration; social entrepreneurship; and territorial development, since they impact directly on the stability of these societies, which in most cases rests on flimsy foundations. While the three phenomena just mentioned may not be unique to the Adriatic-Ionian area, addressing them within the lens of

S. Bianchini
Department of Political and Social Science, Alma Mater Studiorum-University of Bologna, Bologna, Italy
e-mail: stefano.bianchini@unibo.it

S. Cittadini • M. Zoppi (✉)
IECOB—Institute for Central Eastern and Balkan Europe, Forlì, Italy

S. Bianchini et al. (eds.), *Social Entrepreneurship and Migrants' Inclusion*, Sustainable Development Goals Series,
https://doi.org/10.1007/978-3-031-55791-0_2

a "macro-regional Europe" can shed light on unexplored opportunities and untapped potential for cooperation within this specific context (Gänzle & Kern, 2016).

The Adriatic-Ionian territory embraces that portion of Southern Europe ranging from Italy and reaching to all the countries outlining the "coastal arc" eastwards, going down through the Balkan coastal lines to end up in Greece, where the Adriatic and Ionian seas merge one with the other. The area finds also a clear geopolitical dimension in the European Union Strategy for the Adriatic-Ionian Region (EUSAIR), which groups countries that agreed to work together on the areas of common interest for the benefit of each country and the whole region (Belloni, 2020). EUSAIR partly overlaps with the geographical focus of this volume, as it incorporates four EU Member States (Croatia, Greece, Italy and Slovenia) and six non-EU countries (Albania, Bosnia and Herzegovina, Montenegro, North Macedonia, San Marino and Serbia). Here the focus will be narrower as this chapter is inspired by the findings of the project REInSER, financed by the Adrion Interreg Programme (see the Preface and Introduction of this volume).[1] Still, what the countries contemplated in this chapter and the broader EUSAIR space have in common is that the realization of cooperation initiatives in this area is oftentimes perceived to be a difficult task, due to geomorphological diversity, political tensions, different EU statuses, dissimilar administrative and governance capacity as well as different levels of economic development (European Commission, 2019a; OECD, 2019, p. 5).

This chapter will, firstly, reflect on the existing cooperation and political processes ongoing in the Adriatic-Ionian, underlining both positive factors and shortcomings. A specific attention will be devoted to the EU, which is one of the key actors involved at many levels in the area. Secondly, the chapter will show that pursuing and strengthening cooperation among countries in the Adriatic-Ionian is meaningful, despite challenges, and will illustrate on which common basis such cooperation should take place. In fact, the area is experiencing convergence in some key socio-economic trends, such as demographic changes: depopulation and ageing stand out as two clear, common processes affecting countries in the

[1] Compared to EUSAIR, at the time of writing this chapter the Adrion Interreg Programme's cooperation does not include San Marino. Moreover, it is important to underline that the said cooperation area incorporates only parts of Italy, namely 12 regions and 2 provinces (Abruzzo, Molise, Puglia, Basilicata, Calabria, Sicilia, Provincia Autonoma di Trento, Provincia Autonoma di Bolzano/Bozen, Veneto, Friuli-Venezia Giulia, Lombardia, Emilia-Romagna, Umbria and Marche).

Adriatic-Ionian that will become more and more significant for societal dynamics in the next decades and thus require urgent strategies and policy remedies in the present.

Therefore, the analysis of social and demographic dynamics aims to highlight the common challenges in order to stimulate reflections on the necessity to strengthen existing instruments and policy frameworks, and also to develop new ones based on existing good practices in the area. In this framework, the interconnection mentioned above between migration, social entrepreneurship and territorial development will turn particularly useful. Moreover, the data collected describes trends that are in line with what has been recorded also in the other regional countries, and can be considered therefore representative of the entire EUSAIR region (cf. the findings contained in Espon, 2018). The sources backing up the analysis presented here are the statistics retrieved from European, national and international statistical databases, and were in large part included in the deliverables of the project REInSER. When available, datasets have been updated with the latest figures.

Against this backdrop, the reader will find in this chapter a much needed socio-political perspective on the Adriatic-Ionian area, and the information presented will prove useful for the deeper analysis of the single case studies that will follow in the second part of the volume. The next section provides a description of the subject area focused on the various aspects contributing to the definition of the Adriatic-Ionian as an area of cooperation and common interests despite variety.

The Adriatic-Ionian Area: Common Interests Despite High Variety?

"Variety" is certainly a key concept to any analyses of the Adriatic-Ionian area. This statement holds true in many respects: at the environmental level, the area includes in fact continental, Alpine and Mediterranean habitats endowed with a unique biodiversity in the European continent. The sea and its multiple uses represent the pillar of the so-called Blue Economy: seas allow maritime transportation, which is already fundamental for present macroregional economy and is expected to grow further in the future thanks to the increase of container shipping and the intensification of good trades (Bocci et al., 2021, p. 6). The activities that gravitate around the oil and gas extraction and processing, as well as fishing and aquaculture, are likewise significant for the national economies included in the area. While the sea(s) may seem at first to be the dominating element, the area features also high mountains and valleys, where inner territories and a constellation of small, depopulating villages are found. In most cases, these territories are characterized by economic stagnation, although they have natural resources employable for tourism, biodiversity, wood supply chain, organic agriculture and clean energy that could be valorized and provide employment opportunities (Espon, 2018). Mountains leave then the ground to large plains, such as the Pannonian plain and the Po Valley, where agricultural production thrives. Large, connected and easy-to reach cities, such as Athens, Milan, Belgrade and Zagreb, exert an attractive, centripetal force on young individuals, because they tend to concentrate more and more opportunities, services and wealth. Therefore, diversity is replicated also at the social level, since in the Adriatic-Ionian area large urban centres coexist with many rural and remote territories, contributing to shaping very diverse societal contexts. Islands are numerously present in front of the Balkan Peninsula: on the one hand, these are territories struggling to move beyond high seasonality and to attract workers and residents all year round, with specific socio-economic implications to take into account. Yet on the other, they represent a great economic opportunity for the tourism sector.

This industry represents in fact an important share of the Adriatic-Ionian GDP and employs a share of the active population that is higher that the EU average. Venice, Dubrovnik, the Greek islands are mass (or over-)tourism destinations that have developed a thriving economy on their own. The economic opportunities linked to tourism extend also in the field of cultural tourism: the presence of several UNESCO sites indicates that this is also an area with a rich historical and cultural heritage, product of centuries during which the Balkan societies prospered and bridged Central Europe with the Adriatic and the Eastern Mediterranean space. Culture represents a key asset for tourism in the area, as it helps creating distinctiveness on the global marketplace as well as promoting the unique features of the Adriatic-Ionian socio-natural environment, especially in connection with sustainability approaches. The European Commission (2019b, p. 8) has defined sustainable cultural tourism as "the integrated management of cultural heritage and tourism activities in conjunction with the local community, creating social, environmental and economic benefits for all stakeholders in order to achieve tangible and intangible cultural heritage conservation and sustainable tourism development". The six countries making up the so-called Western Balkans[2] can especially benefit from a joint effort to sustainable tourism, as its approach is still "fragmented", not complementary and based on excluding competition (Niented & Shutina, 2020).

Even more so, since the pandemic crisis has had severe consequences on the economy of these countries: the tourism industry was indeed among the most affected sectors, since its dependency on international demand exposed it to the negative effects of bans on travels (as reported in REInSER, 2021b; see also Adrion, 2022). These and other studies agree in suggesting that the post-pandemic economic recovery will require a transition in tourism approaches, based on a balance between economic, cultural, social and environmental sustainability. Long-term investments and innovative services to intercept and manage future tourists flow will be essential as well (Perretti et al., 2022). Lockdowns and containment measures have affected also the industrial production, leading to raising unemployment and to a rapid decline of aggregate supply and demand. It is also true on the other hand that most supply chains have quickly recovered after that COVID-19 restrictions were lifted (De Vet et al., 2021; World Bank Group, 2021).

At the political level too, it is possible to observe a number of challenging differences. All non-EU countries in the area are involved in the EU enlargement process, but they are not in the same stage presently (Economides, 2020). More specifically, we can differentiate between countries that hold an EU "candidate" status and countries that have only "potential candidate" status. The former group includes Albania, Montenegro, North Macedonia, Serbia and, since December 2022, also Bosnia and Herzegovina. Currently, only Kosovo is left with the status of "potential candidate", but it has sent a formal application to become EU member on 14 December 2022. Kosovo's position in relation to EU membership is far more delicate though because, besides the need to reform and converge with the EU legislation, it also needs to normalize relations with Serbia. Moreover, many countries presently do not recognize its independence, including Serbia and five EU members.

[2] This term intends to refer to the area including: Albania, Bosnia and Herzegovina, Montenegro, Kosovo, North Macedonia, Serbia. This same term is used to refer to the migration route passing through these countries (Western Balkan Route) and, for this reason, it is used in this study.

Membership negotiations have so far started only with Montenegro and Serbia; in the case of the former country, after eight years of negotiations, all the screened chapters have been opened, but only three have been "provisionally" closed. By contrast, twenty-two chapters have been opened with Serbia and only two closed until now. Albania and North Macedonia have only recently received the green light to start negotiations, after solving resistance primarily from France and Bulgaria, respectively. The area, and especially the Balkans, is also traversed by recurrent tensions, which create patterns of uncooperative attitudes and diversification of stances on various matters. Reconciliation in the Balkans seems to exert not sufficient weight and attraction on local leaders, and is not perceived as a potential game changer for both the further development of the region and EU accession. At the same time, the different pace of EU negotiations and statuses is not always conducive for stimulating more fruitful and relaxed relations between Balkan neighbours. We will come back to these issues in the next section.

In socio-economic terms as well, the Adriatic-Ionian area is best described as uneven and unbalanced, due to disparities between countries. It could not be otherwise, considering the different size of the countries themselves, or the recent and problematic transition to market economy experienced by the former socialist and communist Balkan economies (see also Chap. 3 in this volume). The Montenegrin GDP, for example, is not even comparable to Italy's, just as the unemployment rate of Albania is much higher than the Croatian one. The same argument can be made for the companies' different ability to exploit the potential of international trade and globalization, of innovation and research, not to mention the uneven development of social economy across the area. Most countries share similar critical issues regarding barriers to entrepreneurship (REInSER, 2021a). These include: common institutional weaknesses hindering the development of a healthy business-environment and the access to financing instruments; the lack of information and business support for entrepreneurial initiatives. Imbalances exist of course also within countries. For example, the employment rate in 2020 in Italy ranges from 41%, the lowest value registered in Region Sicilia, to the highest reported for the autonomous Province of Bolzano: 72.2%. The same pattern can be recognized also in Greece, where Dytiki Ellada's employment rate in 2020 stood at 55.3%, against the highest performance of Peloponnisos (68.3%). Socio-economic imbalances create push-pull mechanisms of migration that penalize low-income and poor performers. As we shall see below, emigration is depleting large parts of the area of young people, and of qualified workers that decide to go work elsewhere in the country or abroad, contributing to the "brain drain" phenomenon. The Adriatic-Ionian is traversed by important migration routes, for which a systematic and structural system for societal integration is still missing (cf. Chap. 3).

All countries in the Adriatic-Ionian area find though a connection point around the EU enlargement perspective, which has favoured already many cooperation programmes and institutional initiatives aimed at fostering convergence in policies and practices, encouraging in particular non-EU countries to implement decisions on equal footing as the EU member states. The latest example of this was provided by the mass migration dynamics that have interested the area, and particularly the countries along the Balkan Route (see Chap. 3): after enacting a chaotic and uncoordinated set of early measures attempting at "managing" migrants and asylum seekers, EU and non-EU countries have developed in short time a more harmonized and agreed response to what was perceived as a challenge and as a security threat to Europe. Although the outcome of such inter-governmental coordination is highly questionable, due to the concerns for human rights and specifically for the violation of rights to liberty and to seek asylum, the point here is to underline that cooperation in the area does happen when a common challenge and a set of incentives for collaborating countries are identified.

Despite geomorphological, economic, societal and institutional diversity, transnational cooperation is thus turning into a necessary and convenient effort, because the pooling of resources, skills and practices can help to address and solve common challenges more efficiently. A proof of the need for joint actions was recently provided by the COVID-19 pandemic, against which the area discovered itself to be unprepared to deal with complex emergencies and its implications. This need to pool resources, to develop common legal and operational frameworks and, ultimately, to unlock the untapped potential characterizes also the field of social entrepreneurship being explored in this volume. It is, in addition, an urgent task, since the energy crisis that has followed the Russian invasion of Ukraine may increment the population share living in poverty and social exclusion against countries' limited possibilities to increase public expenditures. However, transnational cooperation does not rely only on the functionalist credo emphasizing effective integration as the simple result of joint geographical and territorial features. Historical legacies, political dynamics and disputes are essential ingredients for determining the fate of cooperation initiatives. The next section attempts thus to put forward some reflections in this direction, highlighting in more detail the main political dynamics currently traversing the Adriatic-Ionian area, especially in relation to the EU enlargement and its implications.

EU "Unfinished" Enlargement and Post-war Reconciliation in the Area

The Adriatic-Ionian area contains at once elements of integration and disunion, opportunities and obstacles to cooperation, which call into question the recent traumatic past of the Balkan region. In the 1990s, the dissolution of Yugoslavia led to ethnic tensions, armed conflicts and huge civilian casualties throughout the region. If Slovenia managed to secede more or less peacefully, the other constituent republics became involved in a much more violent conflict along marked ethnopolitical identities. Thirty years later, the memory of war and violence is still vivid and, in most cases, politically contested, consequently jeopardizing the strenuous process of post-war reconciliation (Meka & Bianchini, 2020). Searches for missing persons is still going on, and the prosecution of individuals responsible for human rights violations is not yet completed (Fischer, 2016; Haider, 2021). Moreover, most of the area bears the visible consequences of wars: to mention but one, there are still more than 300,000 Internal Displaced People (IDPs) in Bosnia and Herzegovina and Serbia, with a number of challenges attached to that, such as housing, labour access and ultimately their right to return home (REInSER, 2021b). While regional governments have formally committed to reconciliation and have taken some steps in this direction, nationalist and revisionist rhetoric from politicians and public figures are a stable feature of debates and narratives, and there have been several moments of high tension in the region. Above all, the issues of the recognition of Kosovo and the fragile institutional arrangement of Bosnia and Herzegovina keep exerting a toll on the stability of the entire Balkan region, and also on the economic performance of these countries: foreign direct investments remain low in comparison with other world areas, there is a lack of intermodal integration and intra-regional trade too is limited (Haase, 2015; Grieveson et al., 2020).

The EU is one of the actors that has invested more in the Balkan area diplomatically and economically, with the ultimate goals of achieving stability and englobing these countries into the Union. The relations of the

EU with the six Western Balkan states trace back at least to 1999, when the former launched the Stabilization and Association Process (SAP), its official policy for the region. The EU then significantly reiterated that "the future of the Balkans is within the European Union" at the Thessaloniki 2003 Summit. Nevertheless, only Slovenia and Croatia have managed so far to become EU Member States, in 2004 and 2013, respectively. For the other non-EU countries in the area, accession is still ongoing under a stiff negotiation process. Accession is conditional on satisfying the so-called Copenhagen criteria, adopted in 1993, that require candidate countries to progress with respect to the following matters: stable and democratic institutions; functioning market economy; and the implementation of the European *acquis*, that is the accumulated legislation of the EU. The EU Commission reviews annually the progress achieved by the Western Balkans in democratization, rule of law, fight against corruption, freedom of the press and many other sectors, and this assessment is directly linked to enlargement possibilities. The accession negotiation methodology is subject to changes over time: two prominent examples are the reorganization of chapters from 31 to 35 and the adoption of a new accession negotiation methodology in March 2020, which both have made negotiations more demanding and tougher for the candidate states (Petrovic, 2022).

To increase its political leverage, Brussels has also imposed political dialogue, the overcoming of bilateral issues and reconciliation as prerequisites for accessing the EU (European Parliament, 2019). Reconciliation represents "a necessity after a violent conflict or regime change in which human rights were grossly violated", and should be intended as the re-establishment of friendly neighbourly relations between states and, at the societal level, between former adversarial groups (Meka & Bianchini, 2020, p. 20). The notion of reconciliation goes deeper "vertically", within societies, where it incorporates the restoration of trust among different ethnic groups, institutions and societies at large; the attainment of forms of settlement for contested issues; and of justice for the victims.

Clearly enough, EU accession is ultimately a political process that reflects also the levels of agreement and solidarity between involved countries. As for EU Member States, the latter's attitude towards accession can, and in fact did, change over time due to the backlash of international events, political disputes and perceptions of the candidate countries. This has occurred several times in the history of EU-Western Balkans relations, leading many observers to talk of an enlargement "fatigue". By the same token, also the Western Balkans' aspiration to join the EU should not be taken for granted, as polls show that it oscillates over time and, in Serbia specifically, it remains generally low and at times even below the 50% (Dartford, 2022). To explain Belgrade's swinging attitudes, it should take into account also the historical memory of the sanctions and bombardment by the North Atlantic Treaty Organization (NATO) in 1999, as well as the issue of Kosovo's independence and its partial recognition by some EU members.

The enlargement perspective thus affects a big part of public and political discourses, in both positive and negative ways, and is therefore one of the main political hallmarks to be incorporated in the analysis of the Adriatic-Ionian area. Although it may often appear to be suspended between an overly technical and bureaucratic approach on the part of the EU, and the Western Balkans' sluggish reform pace and reluctance in engaging in deeper regional cooperation (Richter & Wunsch, 2020), the enlargement process presents also a number of other shortcomings and unintended consequences. For example, it should be mentioned that the different speeds of integration so far have not necessarily translated into "constructive competition" between Western Balkan countries, and between the latter and the EU: quite the contrary, "multi-speed" European integration fosters the views that countries in the region are at the bottom rung of membership and engaged in a second-tier process (cf. Economides, 2020).

Another implication often debated in the literature is the relation between EU enlargement and state capture in the Western Balkans (Vachudova, 2018; Soyaltin-Colella, 2022). Summarizing here an argument that presents in reality many facets and aspects, observers argue that the EU's actions in the region can sometimes aid indirectly a process of democratic backsliding in the six countries. In fact, in their activities EU bureaucrats and leaders may be met by regional governmental elites that are only formally committed to stability, democratic reforms, reconciliation, EU integration, and that can instead use their position as privileged EU interlocutors to entrench their more or less authoritarian rule. In doing so, the EU is thus inadvertently stabilizing authoritarian and corrupted regimes.

A final aspect worth mentioning here is the double-standard attitude displayed by EU member countries towards non-EU members: an example of that was seen with the Ukrainian-Moldavian case in 2022, when the Union promised them a fast-track procedure for accession, subsequently frustrating Western Balkan countries (Siebold & Melander, 2022). This happened again when the EU granted Ukraine candidate status after Russia's invasion. Earlier, the same dynamics occurred when Bulgaria vetoed the decision to open EU accession negotiations for North Macedonia, after that the latter had laboriously agreed to change its country name, ending the long dispute with Greece. These are examples of attitudes and approaches that have increased Balkans' popular distrust of the EU and frustrated their efforts. It is perhaps no coincidence that the 27 EU members recently showed a renewed interest for strengthening ties with the region, and agreed to accept the candidacy of Bosnia and Herzegovina at the EU-Western Balkan summit held in Tirana in December 2022.

Hence, the enlargement process is today still unfinished and unpredictable, as it has been characterized by delays, postponements and unintended consequences that have also undermined EU's credibility and influence in the region (Pètrovic & Tzifakis, 2021). In order to achieve a proper understanding of the Adriatic-Ionian area, it is thus a fundamental task to take into account all these interconnected dynamics. Key considerations on enlargement and reconciliation come also from civil society actors, but their voice is too often left unheard despite the fact that they represent not just beneficiaries of top-down strategies but also proposers of valid, bottom-up initiatives at various levels. In a recent, jointly produced document, a number of civil society organizations from across the Western Balkans have denounced that "reconciliation has regressed" and has "disappeared from the EU agenda", calling their governments and especially Brussels to develop a far more ambitious strategy in this regard.[3]

Addressing the lack of reconciliation seems even more desirable since the several cooperation initiatives and programmes are increasingly shedding light on the need for a shared macro-space that can enhance concerted, transnational development beyond hard and soft borders, for the benefit of all involved societies. It is though important to emphasize that cooperation depends on, and at the same time can be instrumental for achieving post-war reconciliation. The next section provides the reader with a state-of-the-art description of such cooperation initiatives involving various multi-level governance actors.

[3] Read the full document here: https://www.mzv.cz/file/4768915/WB_CivSoc_Call_to_Action___Outcome_from_Prague_Roundtable_Final.pdf

An Overview of the EU-Promoted Territorial Cooperation Initiatives in the Adriatic-Ionian Area

Against the challenging and non-linear enlargement process described above, cooperation initiatives have been established for the realization of new institutional configurations within the panorama of multi-level governance in Europe, coming to play a crucial role to preserve the achievements of the EU engagement in the region despite its political delays. They encourage in fact innovative approaches, the transferability of best practices in other contexts, and the participation of the beneficiaries in decision-making processes. When it comes to cooperation on territorial governance, the EU's policy platform to realize joint initiatives is the European Structural and Investment Funds (ESIF), which covers two major funds: the European Regional Development Fund (ERDF) and the Cohesion Fund (CF). The goal of this tool is to promote and strengthen economic and social cohesion in response to the imbalances existing between countries and regions. The ERDF provides financial support that is then transformed into operational programmes to enable investments in a smarter, greener, more connected and more social Europe that is "closer to its citizens".[4] The CF targets Member States whose Gross National Income per inhabitant is less than 90% of the EU average, providing them with financing instruments in the fields of transport, environment, energy efficiency and renewable energy.

The ERDF supports also the Interreg Programs, the Union's instruments supporting cooperation across regions and countries that contribute to realize the goal of European Territorial Cooperation. More specifically, Interreg provides funding for projects of cross-border cooperation, transnational cooperation and interregional cooperation, and not just within the EU: they also cover in their programme area EU outermost regions, the EU acceding countries and the neighbourhood countries. Of specific interest here are the so-called Interreg IPA (which stands for Instrument of pre-accession), which target candidate countries and potential candidate countries (thus also those in the Balkans) to make political and economic reforms, preparing them for the rights and obligations that come with EU membership. Importantly, these actions improve also building trust between neighbouring territories, societies and bureaucratic apparata. Among these programmes, it is worth mentioning the Interreg

[4] https://ec.europa.eu/regional_policy/funding/erdf_en

VI-B IPA Adriatic-Ionian programme, known as Adrion, which involves four European Union Member States (Croatia, Greece, Slovenia and Italy's eastern regions[5]), five IPA III beneficiaries (Albania, Bosnia and Herzegovina Montenegro, North Macedonia, Serbia), and a third country, San Marino.

Another significant example of initiative for territorial cooperation is the EU's macroregional strategy, which seems to represent a much-appreciated tool for participating countries (EU and non-EU) to achieve specific goals in certain strategic areas such as growth of economic and employment; improvement of transportation and energy supply; natural environment protection; increase of tourism attractiveness, of security in the area concerned, and support to research and innovation. The EU defines a Macroregion (strategy) as "a policy framework which allows countries located in the same region to jointly tackle and find solutions to problems or to better use the potential they have in common". The area in focus in this volume falls within the EU strategy for the Adriatic–Ionian Region,[6] the third to be established after the EU Strategy for the Baltic Sea Region[7] and the EU Strategy for the Danube Region,[8] and before the latest EU Strategy for the Alpine Region.[9] All strategies share the same rule known as "3 No's": no new institutions, no new EU funding and no new regulations. This framework for implementation provides limitations, yet also flexibility for participating countries (OECD, 2019, p. 9).

EUSAIR provides a cooperation framework to address a set of common challenges and opportunities. As for the challenges, these are largely related to the marked socio-economic disparities that characterize the countries involved and create an uneven and unbalanced context. This extends also to the ability of entrepreneurships to exploit the potential of the transnational dimension of trade, innovation or research. Other common challenges are the infrastructure deficit, in particular the limited road and rail connections between and within these countries, and the congestion of maritime traffic. The environment, too, shows a clear need for actions safeguarding the ecosystems, supporting the transition to

[5] Friuli Venezia-Giulia, Veneto, Lombardia, the two autonomous provinces of Trento and Bolzano, Emilia-Romagna, Marche, Umbria, Abruzzo, Molise, Puglia, Basilicata, Calabria and Sicilia (for a total of 12 regions and 2 provinces).

[6] EUSAIR, established in 2014.

[7] EUSBSR, established in 2009.

[8] EUSDR, established in 2011.

[9] EUSALP, established in 2016.

sustainable forms of tourism, and for actions against marine pollution and supporting the sustainability of fishing and aquaculture. For what concerns the opportunities that the macroregional framework of cooperation can offer, the EU Commission mentions four aspects: the blue economy (the seas); transport and energy networks connectivity; environmental quality (biodiversity); and finally sustainable tourism (including cultural heritage). These four recognized strength points constitute the four pillars of EUSAIR around which the action plan is structured, while capacity building, research and innovation and SME development run through all pillars as crosscutting themes. Other organizations linked to EUSAIR and representing civil society platforms are UniAdrion (the association of universities and research centres of the Adriatic-Ionian area), established in 2000 to promote international cooperation; AIC Forum (Forum of the Adriatic and Ionian Chambers of Commerce); and FAIC (the Forum of Adriatic and Ionian Cities), a non-profit international association open to municipalities of the Adriatic-Ionian basin (European Commission, 2022, p. 5).

Socio-demographic Trends in the Adriatic-Ionian Area

This section provides a description of the Adriatic-Ionian area from the point of view of the main socio-demographic trends. The latter helps clarifying what are both the challenges and opportunities for social entrepreneurship, migrants' integration and territorial development. In general terms, during the last decade the Adriatic-Ionian area has experienced a convergence in the trends related to socio-demographic changes. As result, depopulation and ageing stand out as two clear processes which these countries all are already facing and that will become more and more significant in shaping societal dynamics in the next decades. The selection of statistics and graphs offered in this section will help visualizing these phenomena.

Let us start from the data on the total population. The Adriatic-Ionian area has overall undergone a decline of more than 2% only in the last decade (from 89,609,220 total inhabitants in 2012, to 87,620,900 in 2022)[10]. However, the decline has not affected the countries equally. In

[10] If we consider Italy's 12 Regions and 2 Provinces actually included in Adrion, and thus not the country in its entirety, the decline amount instead to almost 5%, with a total population estimated at 32,305,000 in 2022.

fact, Slovenia has even increased the total population (+2.5%) in the period under consideration, while the decline is instead considerable in almost all the other countries: Italy (-0.7%); Greece (-4.3%); Serbia (-5.8%); Croatia (-9.2%); and Bosnia and Herzegovina (-10.0%). Clearly enough, the diversity emerging in the trends above does not depend only on natural factors (e.g., mortality rate) but is highly influenced by im- and e-migration. In Italy, for example, the number of foreign citizens has increased by around one million in the last decade, reaching 5,190,000 in 2022 (72% are non-EU foreigners), that is, 7.4% of the total population.[11] This has counterbalanced the declining number of Italian citizens caused by emigration, decrease of the fertility rate and natural decrease.

By the same token, the loss of population in the other area countries is often associated with the emigration rates of the younger cohorts of the population. Let us consider another, different example. The declining population in Serbia is largely due to emigration in the absence of significant return or immigration in the country. As stated by the Commissariat for Refugees and Migration (2020, p. 47), Serbia "is traditionally an area of emigration. Albeit incomplete, data on emigration show considerable outmigration from the Republic of Serbia towards more developed countries in the EU, North America, Australia and New Zealand. Today it records a clear negative migration balance. Childbearing crisis and its effects related to population ageing and open depopulation will continue and become more profound in the times to come". In the latest report issued, the Commissariat (2022, p. 64) added that "Serbia is in advanced stages of demographic transition, with profound biological depopulation, developed all forms of modern internal and international migration, biological ageing, marriage, family and household transitions".

Importantly, most national statistical offices in the area agree in projecting further population decline in the next decades. The statistics of the United Nations Department of Economic and Social Affairs (UNDESA) suggest as well a population shrinking of around 10% in Bosnia and Herzegovina, Croatia, Greece and Serbia, and of around 5% in Italy and Slovenia by year 2041 (according to the medium variant, which excludes stark changes in natural change rates). As a consequence, by 2051 the regional population may drop below 80 million. The implications of these long-term changes are various and significantly impacting on the societies concerned. It is worth recalling that part of the emigration dynamics

[11] Information retrieved on ISTAT database.

mentioned above are linked to the phenomenon known as "brain drain", the outflow of graduated and/or high-skilled individuals that afflicts the entire area and especially the Western Balkan countries,[12] from where hundreds of qualified and educated young people depart each year to find employment elsewhere, creating in the long run skill gaps in their homelands (Russell & Oruc, 2019). Addressing brain drain requires ameliorating employment conditions and improving employment opportunities for the motivated and highly educated, as well as overcoming the territorial mismatch between the needs of the labour market and the skills available, or again the skills that can be acquired through higher education. In the absence of long-term reform and strategies, affected countries may face massive repercussions. Differences in the demographic performance are also visible within each country (i.e., between sub-state regions) and will be addressed later, in the section specifically devoted to the analysis of territorial dynamics.

Besides depopulation trends, we can observe at least another crucial, transformative process taking place at the societal level: ageing. On the one hand, an ageing population can be interpreted as the positive result of increasing health levels, of the development of healthy lifestyles and more in general of enhanced life conditions. On the other hand, an ageing society may develop new needs and new challenges to be tackled by state institutions, enterprises and citizens. Think of elder care services, yet also about the implications of having fewer people in working age, or again the lack of innovation deriving from emigrating, talented and educated young individuals. To better grasp this trend, it is possible to refer to the figures on median age in the project countries.[13] Since 2010, it has risen on average from 39.1 to reach 42.8 in 2021, the latest year for which there are statistics available. Greece and Italy are the countries recording the highest median age of their population, while Albania displays the lowest values in the area, although the indicator is getting higher at a comparatively fast rate. Among the other countries, Montenegro, North Macedonia and Serbia remain below the EU-27 average, while Croatia and Slovenia are placed slightly above (both at 44.4 in 2021) (Fig. 2.1).

[12] A recent study suggests though that in Serbia, Montenegro and North Macedonia there has been also "evidence of brain gain" (Leitner, 2021).

[13] Data for Bosnia and Herzegovina are not available on Eurostat.

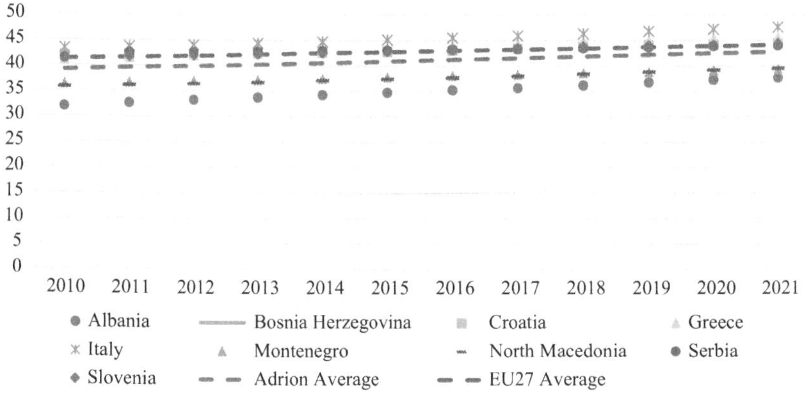

Fig. 2.1 Evolution of median age, 2010–2021

Strictly connected to ageing is the change of the fertility rate.[14] The direct comparison of 2010 and 2020 figures for the project area indicates -4.2%, which in the graph below is represented by the red, cone-like column most right. As with the previous cases, there are interesting differences in the performance of the countries to underline: Italy, Greece and North Macedonia are reporting the highest decreases. However, it is important to note that fertility rates are fluctuating up and down every year, and therefore it is a bit more difficult to talk about trends precisely. Still, it is possible to remark that for Croatia, Greece, Italy and North Macedonia, 2010 was the year in the entire decade examined when the highest rate was recorded, and for Bosnia and Herzegovina it was 2012. Hence, and in connection with the other statistics explored so far, we may take this as an indication that the fertility rate is declining overall, too. Out of the group of countries, only Montenegro (dark blue in Fig. 2.2) appears to be on an opposite trend: the highest rates were all recorded in the last 6 years, with 2020 being the highest of the decade (1.8). National statistical offices across the project area have acknowledged the decline of the fertility rate and its consequences. Albania's Instat, for example, describes

[14] Defined by Eurostat as: the mean number of children that would be born alive to a woman during her lifetime if she were to pass through her childbearing years conforming to the fertility rates by age of a given year, and surviving. All data are from Eurostat, except for Bosnia-Herzegovina, for which we have resorted to the statistics of the National Statistical Office.

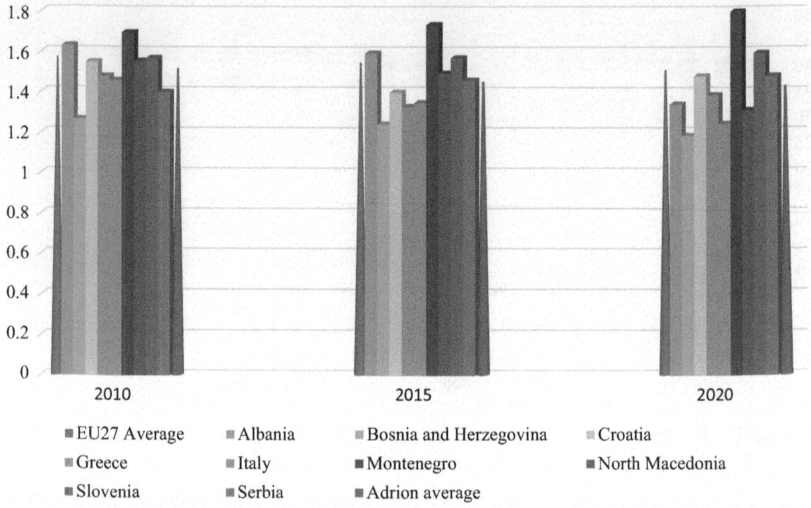

Fig. 2.2 Fertility rate change, 2010–2020

that the decline of average fertility "can be reflected in the number of population in the next decades and have impact, not only in decreasing the population, but more at the effects that derivate from that situations, which can be social or economic, such as: decreasing the purchasing power, increasing the old dependency ratio, putting in risk the scheme of pensions, etc."[15]

Finally, an important indication of socio-demographic developments comes from the statistics on the old-age dependency ratio, which expresses the number of persons aged 65 and over (age when they are generally economically inactive) and the number of persons aged between 15 and 64. In other words, this indicator in combination with the other helps completing the picture of societal change, in terms of future sustainability and generational turnover. The findings are very similar to those of the figures previously analysed. The overall Adrion ratio for the number of 65+ every 100 of working age (15–64) has risen over time, from 24.0 to 30.6. Italy (coloured in orange) and Greece (green) are firmly above both Adrion and EU-27 averages and this on the upper part of Fig. 2.3, yet the sharpest increase recorded in the period is that of Slovenia, which in 2021 reached very close to the EU average (from 23.8 to 32.1). Albania and

[15] See here: http://www.instat.gov.al/en/statistical-literacy/the-population-of-albania/

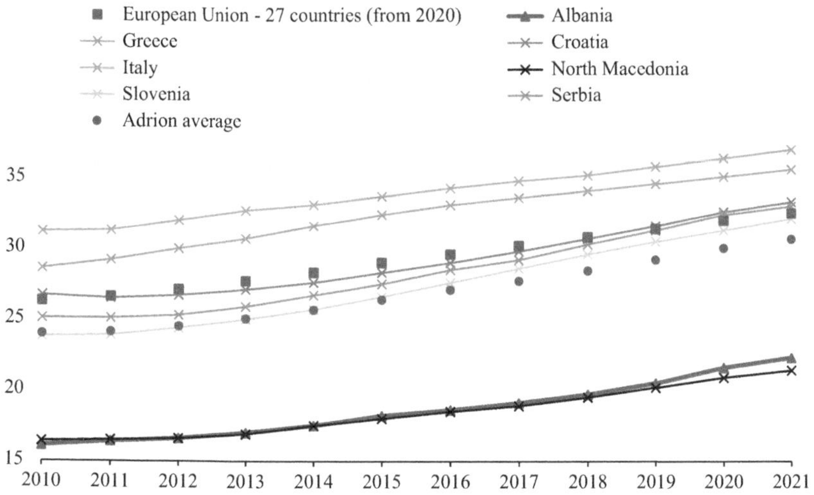

Fig. 2.3 Evolution of old-age dependency ratio, 2010–2021

North Macedonia presents the lowest values during the observer period, with the ratio increasing a bit more quickly in the former country in the past few years. Figures for Bosnia and Herzegovina, not included in the graph for methodological reasons, are available on the World Bank database[16]: according to the latter, the ration has increased from 42.2 in 2010 to 46.8. While it is not possible to establish a correlation between the data of the two different datasets, it can be still concluded that Bosnia and Herzegovina too follow the general trend we have retrieved in the other project countries.

Territorial Analysis of Socio-demographic Trends

This section extends the analysis of the socio-demographic and economic trends, focusing on the sub-national level in the Adriatic-Ionian area. The aim is to move beyond the generalizing country overviews, underlining instead regional territorial imbalances. With this goal, the following section presents different graphs showing how some of the main indicators considered in this study have varied since 2010 at the sub-state level.

[16] See: https://data.worldbank.org/indicator/SP.POP.DPND?end=2019&locations=BA&start=2010

Depopulation Trend at the NUTS2[17] Regional Level

As already highlighted in the socio-demographic section above, depopulation concerns most of the countries included in this study. Figure 2.4 shows the variation of the population across regions between 2010 and 2020[18]: at the sub-national territorial level as well, it emerges that depopulation trend is a common challenge. In fact, the only regions that have registered a growth in the total resident population are part of Northern

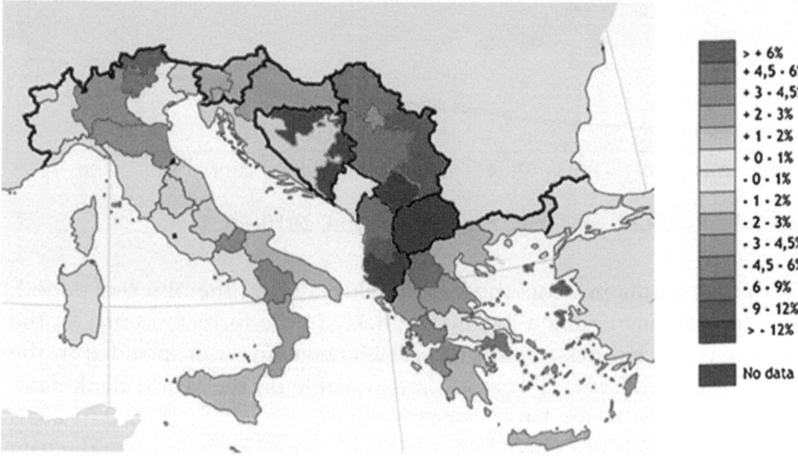

Fig. 2.4 Variation of the regional population in NUTS2 region, 2010–2020

[17] "NUTS" stands for *Nomenclature of Territorial Units for Statistics*, namely the hierarchical system for dividing up the economic territory in use at Eurostat. There are three levels of classification (NUTS1, 2 and 3). NUTS2 corresponds to sub-state units, usually regions, counties according to each state's own administrative terminology.

[18] With some exceptions: Bosnia and Herzegovina, where data on the two entities (Federation of Bosnia and Herzegovina and Republika Srpska) have been retrieved within local statistical databases that did not present data for all the years. In the Federation, data on the resident population were available between 2013 and 2019, while in Republika Srpska between 2010 and 2018. In addition, Slovenia does not collect data according to NUTS2 regions, and, therefore, the national level was considered in filling the map. Montenegro, for which NUTS regions do not exist due to the country's limited extension (data for the entire country are presented in Fig. 2.4). North Macedonia, for which NUTS regions have not been yet established (for this reason, the country appears grey in Figs. 2.4 and 2.5).

Italy, the Eastern Islands of Greece, the region of Belgrade and Slovenia. All the others have experienced a more or less intense population decline.

Greece is the state that presents major internal unbalances between territories: while Dytiki Makedonia and Attiki are among the regions that overall have lost more population in the last decade (respectively -7.6% and -6.6%), the regions of Notio Aigaio and Voreio Aigaio are among the ones that have known major increases (respectively +4.5% and + 14.7%). Particularly interesting is the case of the region of Voreio Aigaio that is by far the one featuring the largest population growth in the entire Adriatic-Ionian area, followed by the province of Bolzano, in Italy, where the variation of the resident population registered a +7% growth. As it will be further shown also in the analysis of the other indicators, the region of Voreio Aigaio[19] is a case where socio-demographic indicators present a sharp deviation compared to the trends registered in other regions. The reasons behind this phenomenon are not perfectly clear: while there is some evidence that the arrival of asylum seekers and refugees on the Greek islands might have impacted the socio-demographic and economic trends, there are not enough studies on this matter to conclude that migration has played a major role, and that this phenomenon does not have other origins (Espon, 2019; Petropoulou, 2021).

In Italy, the map highlights the difference between Northern and Southern regions: the latter are the ones traditionally suffering from depopulation processes—in particular Basilicata, -4.8%, and Molise, -5.1%. In the Italian case, the difference can be explained by the still relevant economic gap between the two areas, which keeps pushing many young people from Southern regions to look for better economic opportunities in the North of Italy, or abroad. The lack of economic opportunities and the consequent mass emigration of labour force abroad may also partly explain the degrowth of the population in the Western Balkans, where only Slovenia and the region of Beograd registered a positive trend in the period considered. In this sub-area, the regions marked by major negative variations are Šumadija and Western Serbia (-7%), Southern and Eastern Serbia (-10%) and Republika Srpska (-19.9%).

[19] The Greek region of Voreio Aigaio includes 9 islands that are located in front to Turkey. They include the islands of Lesvos, Chios, Samos, Ikaria and Lemnos.

Ageing Processes at the NUTS2 Regional Level

Figure 2.5 shows the old-age dependency ratio. It reveals that all regions are going through a quite sharp increase of this indicator, with the sole exception of the Greek region of Voreio Aigaio that, as already mentioned, deviates in relation to all the trends that affect the rest of the region.[20] The old-age dependency ratio is defined as the number of individuals at an age when they are generally economically inactive (65 and over), per 100 people of working age (i.e., 15–64 years old). Higher ratios indicate a greater level of dependency on the working-age population, which represents a societal challenge in terms of sustainability and provision of services to the elderly throughout the country. The major increases of this indicator are registered in the regions of Šumadija and Western Serbia (+35%), Attiki (+33.3%) and Slovenia (+31.5%), here considered as the whole country since data on NUTS regions are missing. The regions that, instead, have gone through minor increases of the old-age dependency ratio are Emilia-Romagna (+ 7.9%), Sterea Ellada (+9.9%) and the Autonomous province of Trento (+11.6%). In Bosnia and Herzegovina, data on the old-age dependency ratio are not available at the entity level and only for the years

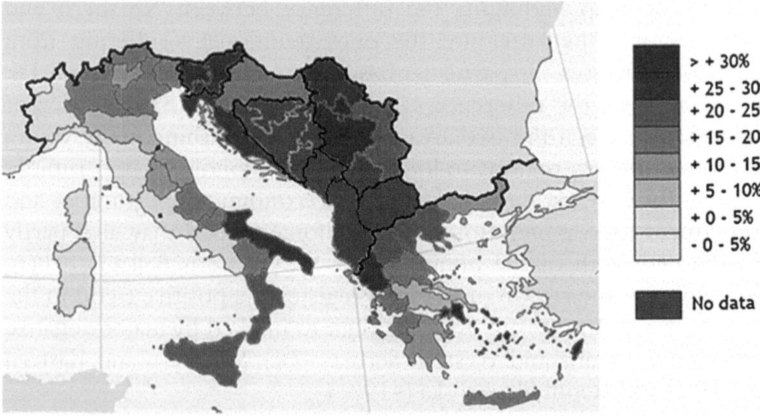

Fig. 2.5 Variation of the old-age dependency ratio in NUTS2 regions, 2010–2020

[20] Data for Albania, Montenegro and North Macedonia were either not available or not applicable (cf. footnote 14).

between 2010 and 2014 at the national level (indicating a slight decrease of this ratio: -1.4%). Because of the lack of data for all the years, that would allow a proper comparison with the other regions, Bosnia and Herzegovina has been left blank in this map.

Regarding the variation of the median age in the Adriatic-Ionian region, this trend is in line with the ageing process already highlighted. All regions considered, with the exception of Voreio Aigaio where median age has decreased (-5.2%), have registered an increase of the population's median age. The three regions that have recorded major increases are Dytiki Makedonia (+12.1), Puglia (+11.6%) and Basilicata (+11%), while the Serbian regions of Beograd, Southern and Eastern Serbia and Vojvodina are the ones where the population's median age increased the least (respectively, +1.9%, +3% and +3.1%).

Fertility Rate at the NUTS2 Regional Level

Surely connected with the increase of the old-age dependency ratio is the generalized decrease of the fertility rate. The only regions that have registered an increase of this rate are Serbian and Slovenian regions, the Autonomous Province of Trento and the islands of the Greek regions of Voreio Aigaio and Notio Aigaio. Among the others, the ones that have registered a major decrease are the Greek regions of Sterea Ellada (-26.3%), Thessalia (-20%) and Anatoliki Makedonia (-19.8%). In Italy, the regions that have suffered from major decreases of the fertility rate are Marche and Umbria (both -16.2%) and Lombardia (-15.9%), while southern regions such as Calabria and Basilicata have registered minor decreases, similarly to Croatian and Bosnian territories.

Final Reflections and Conclusion

This chapter has provided an overview of the Adriatic-Ionian area centred on political and socio-economic aspects. The analysis reveals that the Adriatic-Ionian area is increasingly characterized by cooperation initiatives, most of which have in the EU a key actor for its promotion and financing. The Adriatic-Ionian area and broader EUSAIR have become institutionalized spaces that through the already existing initiatives are now further incentivizing the exchange of knowledge and the elaboration of common strategies. The chapter has underlined that such cooperation is indeed useful, as there is a number of common challenges entangling the Adriatic-Ionian countries into a functional macro-space in which sharing good and best practices can indeed help achieving better results as well as a convergence also in policy structures and legislation in the area, for the common good. In these regard, the REInSER project has looked especially into social entrepreneurship and instruments of social economy as means for achieving these goals.

However, this chapter has also underlined the implications of the enduring political divisions in the area, an issue that risks being overshadowed by the trans-regional, functionalist cooperation euphoria. Especially in the Balkans, the legacy of the war atrocities occurred in the recent past is still vivid. Moreover, nationalist rhetoric and ethnic polarization are being regularly used by political elites: in other words, there is an enormous, dangerous potential for dividing countries politically, and for sparking inter- and intra-societal tensions and fuelling non-cooperative behaviours. This is a matter of serious concern that appears to be still on the margins of states' and suprastate's activities and interests, including those promoted in the EUSAIR framework.

In this respect, the notion of "exceptional diversity" that is often acknowledged as an added value in the Adriatic-Ionian area can also contribute dramatically to instability and to the exacerbation of socio-economic trends, jeopardizing the future of the region (Haase, 2015). Therefore, the limitations coming with the over-emphasized functionalist approach to cooperation and (macro-)regionalism should be compensated with a specific, renewed attention to political reconciliation. In doing so, states and institutions in the area should look at the various initiatives on reconciliation and inter-ethnic dialogue started by civil society organizations, which seem to be often much more well-disposed to transform the social and political context of the Adriatic-Ionian than their leaders (Mastrorocco, 2020; Meka & Bianchini, 2020; Bakić, 2021). An example of such commitment is the Initiative for RECOM, initiated by a coalition of NGOs and aimed at the putting in place a regional commission to establish facts of the victims of war crimes and violation of human rights in the territory of the former Socialist Federal Republic of Yugoslavia. By the end of 2014, more than 580,000 people from all over former Yugoslavia supported the initiative with their signatures.[21] A greater involvement of these organizations in participatory planning can be then extremely beneficial to elaborate need-based initiatives, foster community building and

[21] See here: https://www.recom.link/en/sta-je-rekom/

call for governments' accountability, while containing illiberalism and democratic backsliding. Importantly, the implementation of social economy measures that target vulnerable groups, stimulate territorial development and reduce societal inequalities can strongly support the achievement of these goals.

References

Adrion. (2022). *Sustainable Development of the Tourism Sector in the ADRION Macro Region a Strategic Proposal for the Programming Period 2021–2027.* Policy Paper by the ADRION 3rd Thematic Sub-cluster "Innovation through New Methodological Approaches and Models and ADRION Branding". https://www.adrioninterreg.eu/wp-content/uploads/2022/01/Policy-Paper-Cluster-3-action-6-1.pdf

Bakić, S. (2021). Different Voices and Luminosities Encouraging Reconciliation through Museum Practices. *Southeastern Europe, 45*(3), 341–360.

Belloni, R. (2020). Assessing the Rise of Macro-regionalism in Europe: The EU Strategy for the Adriatic and Ionian Region (EUSAIR). *Journal of International Relations and Development, 23*, 814–839.

Bocci, M., Ramieri, E., & Marković, M. (2021). *Pan Adriatic Scope.* UNEP.

Commissariat for Refugees and Migration. (2020). *Migration Profile of the Republic of Serbia for 2019.* CRM.

Commissariat for Refugees and Migration. (2022). *Migration Profile of the Republic of Serbia for 2021.* CRM.

Dartford, K. (2022). For First Time, a Majority of Serbs are against Joining the EU—Poll. *Euronews*, 22 April.

De Vet, J. M., Nigohosyan D., Núñez, F. J., Gross, A., Kuehl, S., & Flickenschild, M. (2021). *Impacts of the COVID-19 Pandemic on EU Industries.* Study Requested by the ITRE Committee. European Parliament.

Economides, S. (2020). *From Fatigue to Resistance: EU Enlargement and the Western Balkans.* Dahrendorf Forum IV Working Paper No. 17. eprints.lse.ac.uk/104393/1/Economides_from_fatigue_to_resistance_published.pdf

Espon. (2018). *MIGRATUP—Territorial and Urban Potentials Connected to Migration and Refugee Flows.* Final Main Report. https://www.espon.eu/migration

Espon. (2019). *MIGRARE—Impacts of Refugee Flows to Territorial Development in Europe.* Final Report. https://www.espon.eu/refugee

European Commission. (2019a). *Orientation Paper, Transnational Cooperation Programme Adriatic-Ionian (ADRION) 2021–2027.* Ref. Ares(2019) 7164059.EC.

European Commission. (2019b). *Sustainable Cultural Tourism.* Report of the Omc (Open Method of Coordination) Working Group of Member States' Experts. EC.

European Commission. (2022). *Report from the Commission to the European Parliament, the Council, the European Economic and Social Committee and the Committee of the Regions on the Implementation of EU Macro-regional Strategies.* COM(2022) 705 Final. EC.

European Parliament. (2019). *Reconciliation in the Western Balkans. The Difficulty of Emulating the EU Model.* Briefing of the European Parliamentary Research Service. https://www.europarl.europa.eu/RegData/etudes/BRIE/2019/637964/EPRS_BRI(2019)637964_EN.pdf

Fischer, M. (2016). Dealing with the Past from the Top Down and Bottom Up—Challengers for State and Non-state Actors. In M. Fischer & O. Simic (Eds.), *Transitional Justice and Reconciliation: Lessons from the Balkans* (pp. 3–21). Routledge.

Gänzle, S., & Kern, K. (2016). Macro-regions, 'Macro-regionalization' and Macro-regional Strategies in the European Union: Towards a New Form of European Governance? In S. Gänzle & K. Kern (Eds.), *A 'Macro-regional' Europe in the Making Theoretical Approaches and Empirical Evidence* (pp. 3–22). Palgrave Macmillan.

Grieveson, R., Holzner, M., & Vukšić, G. (2020). *Regional Economic Cooperation in the Western Balkans: The Role of Stabilisation and Association Agreements, Bilateral Investment Treaties and Free Trade Agreements in Regional Investment and Trade Flows.* wiiw Research Report, No. 450. Vienna Institute for International Economic Studies (wiiw).

Haase, D. (2015). *Research for Regi Committee—Adriatic and Ionian Region: Socioeconomic Analysis and Assessment of Transport and Energy Links.* EP.

Haider, H. (2021). *Transitional Justice and Reconciliation in the Western Balkans: Approaches, Impacts and Challenges.* K4D Helpdesk Report. Brighton. Institute of Development Studies. https://doi.org/10.19088/K4D.2021.033

Leitner, S. M. (2021). *Net Migration and its Skill Composition in the Western Balkan Countries between 2010 and 2019: Results from a Cohort Approach Analysis.* The Vienna Institute for International Economic Studies.

Mastrorocco, R. (2020). OSCE and Civil Society in the Western Balkans: The Road to Reconciliation. In A. Mihr (Ed.), *Transformation and Development: Studies in the Organization for Security and Cooperation in Europe (OSCE) Member States* (pp. 83–100). Springer.

Meka, E., & Bianchini, S. (2020). Introduction. In E. Meka & S. Bianchini (Eds.), *The Challenges of Democratization and Reconciliation in the Post-Yugoslav Space* (pp. 9–33). Nomos.

Niented, P., & Shutina, D. (2020). Tourism in Transition, the Post COVID-19 Aftermath in the Western Balkans. *Annual Review of Territorial Governance in the Western Balkans, 2*, 46–60.

OECD. (2019). *Multi-level Governance and Cross-Sector Practices Supporting EUSAIR. EUSAIR Synthesis Report*. OECD.

Perretti, B., Pinto, P., & Marani, S. (2022). Cultural Tourism in the Adriatic Ionian Macro Region: Understanding the Impact of COVID-19 and the Potential for a Sustainable Restart. In A. Trono, T. Duda, & J. Schmude (Eds.), *Tourism Recovery from COVID-19* (pp. 311–327). World Scientific.

Petropoulou, C. (2021). Local Economies and Socio-Spatial Segregations in the Aegean Islands: Touristic Development versus Refugee Arrivals? The Case of Lesvos Island. In J. Dominguez-Mujica, J. McGarrigle, & J. M. Parreño Castellano (Eds.), *International Residential Mobilities: From Lifestyle Migrations to Tourism Gentrification* (pp. 331–338). Springer.

Petrovic, M. (2022). *EU Enlargement into the Western Balkans: A Gloomy Prospect Gets Gloomier*. ZEI Discussion Paper C271. ZEI. https://d-nb.info/1258954346/34

Petrovic, M., & Tzifakis, N. (2021). A Geopolitical Turn to EU Enlargement, or Another Postponement? An Introduction. *Journal of Contemporary European Studies, 29*(2), 157–168.

REInSER—Refugees' Economic Integration through Social Entrepreneurship. (2021a). *Comparative STA Report on the Assessment of Main Challenges in the Partners' State*. Deliverable T1.2.2. https://reinser.adrioninterreg.eu/news/comparative-sta-report-on-the-assessment-of-main-challenges-in-the-partners-state

REInSER—Refugees' Economic Integration through Social Entrepreneurship. (2021b). *Comparative STA Report on the Assessment of Societal Change in the Partners' State*. Deliverable T1.1.2. https://reinser.adrioninterreg.eu/news/comparative-sta-report-on-the-assessment-of-societal-change-in-the-partners-state

Richter, S., & Wunsch, N. (2020). Money, Power, Glory: The Linkages between EU Conditionality and State Capture in the Western Balkans. *Journal of European Public Policy, 27*(1), 41–62.

Russell, K., & Oruc, N. (2019). Editorial Introduction: Migration in the Western Balkans—Trends and Challenges. *Journal of Balkan and Near Eastern Studies, 21*(1), 1–10.

Siebold, S., & Melander, I. (2022). EU Grants Ukraine Candidate Status, 'Beginning a Long Journey Together'. *Reuters*, 24 June. https://www.reuters.com/world/europe/wind-change-europe-path-eu-opens-ukraine-2022-06-23/

Soyaltin-Colella, D. (2022). The EU Accession Process, Chinese Finance and Rising Corruption in Western Balkan Stabilitocracies: Serbia and Montenegro. *Europe-Asia Studies*. https://doi.org/10.1080/09668136.2022.2115013

Vachudova, M. A. (2018). EU Enlargement and State Capture in the Western Balkans. In J. Džankić, S. Keil, & M. Kmezić (Eds.), *The Europeanisation of the Western Balkans* (pp. 63–85). Palgrave Macmillan.

World Bank Group. (2021). *Greening the Economy*. Western Balkans Regular Economic Report 20, Fall 2021. World Bank Group.

CHAPTER 3

Socio-economic Inclusion of Migrants in the Adriatic-Ionian Area: Dynamics, Policies and Challenges

Stefano Bianchini, Silvia Cittadini, and Marco Zoppi

Introduction

In the last 10 years, migration towards and through the Adriatic-Ionian region has been one of the most important phenomena that has marked the area at the socio-economic, political and legislative levels. Although countries like Italy and Greece were already experiencing economic immigration, and the Western Balkans had managed internal migrations for economic reasons during the Yugoslav period and on humanitarian grounds after its fall, the whole area has always been considered more a land of

S. Bianchini
Department of Political and Social Science, Alma Mater Studiorum-University of Bologna, Bologna, Italy
e-mail: stefano.bianchini@unibo.it

S. Cittadini (✉) • M. Zoppi
IECOB—Institute for Central Eastern and Balkan Europe, Forlì, Italy

S. Bianchini et al. (eds.), *Social Entrepreneurship and Migrants' Inclusion*, Sustainable Development Goals Series,
https://doi.org/10.1007/978-3-031-55791-0_3

emigration, rather than immigration. In this context, the arrivals witnessed in the years 2013–2017 were unprecedented because of the diversity of the countries of origin and of the reasons behind these movements—the majority of the new arrivals, indeed, were asylum seekers and refugees fleeing from the conflicts inflaming Middle Eastern and African countries. The main routes that have shaped the migratory context and political response have been the Central Mediterranean route from Northern Africa to Italy by boat and the Balkan Route that from Turkey crossed the whole Balkan Peninsula to reach Western Europe. The international and national response to this new phenomenon diverged in many aspects because of the different political and social conditions. However, the existing similarities between the different social and migratory contexts, as extensively reported in the previous chapter, highlight the importance of comparing the legislative and political responses to the migratory phenomenon to seek for potential common trends and convergences between countries.

In this context, the main difference that shaped the evolution of these routes and the governments' responses is the different EU membership status of the countries directly concerned by these routes. Italy, Greece and Slovenia are full EU and Schengen members, representing thus the main doors to the most important European free movement area. Croatia is an EU member that has just entered the Euro and Schengen area in 2023, and had therefore the interest to demonstrate its reliability as a border country. Concerning the non-EU Western Balkan countries considered in this study, Serbia is an EU "candidate state" since 2012, while Bosnia and Herzegovina has been recognized as such only in December 2022, and although the interest to enter the EU might trigger political cooperation also in matters concerning migrations, the slowness of the accession process is surely increasing disillusionment among political institutions and citizens. The different status of the countries not only has shaped the route itself, since entering the EU and Schengen area is certainly the ultimate goal of the great majority of asylum seekers and refugees crossing this region, but also because of the impact of EU legislation on the management of these flows by its Member States. On this regard, Dublin regulation (2013) identifies which country is responsible for processing the asylum application of a person belonging to a non-EU country or a stateless person. In most cases, the country responsible for processing the application is the first country where the applicant sets foot. In addition, the regulation establishes a series of measures to ensure that the applicant receives a fair examination, although national legislations on asylum recognition still differ considerably.

Both the Mediterranean and Balkan routes have attracted the attention of numerous scholars, because of their political, social and human consequences. In the Western Balkan context, most of the publications focused on the role of the area as a new European borderland and on the impact of the securitarization of the migration management on the lives of thousands of migrants stranded in the region (Beznec et al., 2016; Bianchini et al., 2022; Bobić & Šantić, 2020; Šelo-Šabić, 2017; Webb, 2020; Zaragoza-Cristiani, 2017). Other studies have looked at the national and local levels, highlighting the lack of a comprehensive and coherent strategy for the reception and integration of asylum seekers, who are often obliged to squat abandoned buildings and navigate deprived post-war contexts where minefields are still present (Hromadžic, 2020; Milan, 2019). The lack of a strategy for integration is also due to the idea that asylum seekers are exclusively transiting the area and have no interest to stay. While this assumption might be valid, it is also true that the slowness of the status recognition process, the lack of proper reception infrastructures and the few opportunities for integration considerably hinder the possibilities to integrate (Galijaš, 2019; Minca & Collins, 2021; Vukcevic, 2020). While some of these authors have started talking of refugees' integration, the number of persons that receive the refugee status in these countries is still very low, leaving the issue of integration at the margin. However, the situation might evolve as happened in Italy and Greece, once considered only "transit zones" for migrants, and today hosting large numbers of asylum seekers and refugees. The EU accession process might speed up this evolution, especially if the arrival of asylum seekers and refugees does not decrease significantly.

Italy and Greece present a quite different situation compared to the Western Balkans, mostly because, being two of the most important EU and Schengen entrance points, they had to establish legal and institutional mechanisms to receive and process hundreds of thousand requests for asylum under Dublin regulation and, subsequently, organize and implement a strategy for their reception and integration. In addition, asylum seekers and refugees started integrating in these countries, becoming part of the hosting society and contributing to their economic and social life. As a consequence, there is a much larger scholarship regarding the reception and integration systems of refugees and asylum seekers in these contexts.

In Italy, scholarly debates often focus on the contested and evolving legislation in regard to migration and status recognition: current legislation is often criticized for perpetuating the irregularity of thousands of migrants that would be rather needed in the Italian labour market, leaving them at the mercy of black market and exploitation (Chiaromonte & Federico, 2021; Collini, 2023; degli Uberti, 2021; Dives & Rigo, 2015; Hermanin, 2017). Other scholars have criticized political institutions for the criminalization of NGOs rescuing migrants in the Mediterranean and for the securitarian approach that overlooks potential violations of the human rights of migrants (Mancuso & Signorelli, 2022; Ortensi & Kingston, 2022). There is then a large literature analysing various aspects of the integration process of asylum seekers and refugees in Italy, looking especially at the impact of a multi-level governance aimed at localizing integration processes at the rural level (Caponio et al., 2022; Dotsey & Lumley-Sapanski, 2021; Ponzo et al., 2022). In Greece, scholars have looked especially to the consequences of the EU-Turkey agreement and the evolution of Greek legislation on the matter (Bagavos et al., 2021; Kafkoutsou & Oikonomou, 2020; Mantanika & Arapoglou, 2022). Here, much attention has been paid to the system of the hotspots (Kourachanis, 2018b), defined as liminal spaces representatives of the new EU border regime (Papoutsi et al., 2019) and to the inadequacy of a integration strategy that ensures basic services to a minority of the asylum seeker and refugee population and does not ensure the necessary support to integration (Kourachanis, 2018a; Manou et al., 2021).

Also in the light of the scholarship on the reception and integration legislations and policies at the national level, this chapter aims to propose a macro-regional analysis, highlighting the main legislative and political trends emerged in the Adriatic-Ionian region. Indeed, there are no studies on the management of asylum seekers reception and integration at the macro-regional level, proposing a comparative lens of analysis of the national policies in this area. To fill this gap, this chapter intends to investigate how the governmental response to migration evolved in the Adriatic-Ionian area and what are the main trends, points of convergence and gaps between countries. Here, the objective is also to foresee possible future evolutions in light of the experiences of the neighbouring countries and in consideration of possible future reinforced cooperations. The study here presented grounds on the findings collected within the Interreg-Adrion project REInSER though literature review, document analysis and interviews to key stakeholders, and it is supported with further desk research aimed at highlighting the latest legislative evolutions in the region. With this aim, the chapter divides the analysis in two temporal frameworks, with the year 2016 as the main turning point, being it the year of the EU-Turkey deal to close the Balkan Route and of the agreement with Libya to stop new arrivals to the Italian coasts.

Migrations and Government Responses Before 2016

Italy and Greece: The Fragmented Development of a Reception and Integration System

Compared to other European countries, such as France and Germany, Italy and Greece have been for long considered lands of emigration. In Italy, first waves of immigrants arrived already during the 1970s, but only through the end of the 1980s there was a net increase of new arrivals in search for working opportunities, especially from Morocco, Tunisia, Philippines and Senegal. In Greece, as well, emigration from the country continued to be a relevant phenomenon until very recently, but, at the same time, it started receiving a considerable number of immigrants, mostly from other Balkan countries and Asia in the 1990s (Cavounidis, 2015). However, both countries continued for long to be considered land of emigration and transit. It is probably because of this that both countries started adopting laws for regulating immigration only in the 1990s and did not foresee a long-term and comprehensive strategy for the reception and integration of both economic and humanitarian immigrants (Hermanin, 2017). In Italy, the first law regulating immigration matters was adopted in 1990—the so-called Martelli law, under the name of the Minister who proposed it—also in response to the pressure of the European Institutions to ensure an adequate control of immigration to enter the Schengen area. The law defined refugee status, clarified the procedures for status recognition and expulsion, and set the first rules for programming labour immigration. However, the annual planning for issuing working permits kept underestimating the actual offer and demand, leaving the regularization of hundreds of thousands of undocumented immigrants to ad-hoc amnesties, and the management of major flow to emergency decrees. For this reason, Italian institutions have often been criticized for continuing treating the migration issues as an exception or an emergency, failing to adopt a quota system responding to the actual needs of the labour market and a legislative framework setting clear and comprehensive mechanisms for the reception and integration of both economic and humanitarian migrants (Abbondanza, 2017; Hermanin, 2017).

In 1997, the adoption of the Treaty of Amsterdam, that set stricter rules concerning immigration, and the entrance of Italy in the Schengen area pushed the Italian institutions to adopt a new legislation also in response to the increasing intolerance of public opinion towards foreigners. The law, known as Turco-Napolitano law, introduced more stringent rules for border controls and expulsion procedures, while promoting the integration of those present on the territory. Also in this case, though, the law did not manage to offer a long-lasting and structural solution to the problem of the undocumented migrants, feeding the widespread reality of the black labour market. At the end of the 1990s, the number of undocumented migrants reached its peak and the entrance of far-right parties in the government pushed the adoption of a much stricter legislation, the Bossi-Fini law in 2002, limiting considerably the possibility to access residence permits for working reasons and establishing identification and detention centres for the refoulment of asylum seekers and irregular migrants (Abbondanza, 2017; Ambrosetti & Paparusso, 2018). The Bossi-Fini law also established the Protection System for Asylum Seekers and Refugees (SPRAR) to manage the reception, protection and integration of asylum seekers and refugees. However, this system gained relevance years later as at the beginning of the 2000s, the arrival of migrants for humanitarian reasons was still marginal (Ambrosetti & Paparusso, 2018). The following years have been marked by a series of legislative decrees and measures always aimed at exacerbating the rules against undocumented immigrants, like the contested friendship agreement with Libya, signed in 2008, that ensured tighter controls on its border to stop the arrival of illegal immigrants to Italy.

However, the situation completely changed with the surge of the Arab uprises, which pushed an increasing number of economic and humanitarian immigrants to cross the Mediterranean to reach the Italian coasts, marking the beginning of what would be later named "refugee crisis" (Abbondanza, 2017). In the following years, then, political action has tried to control and limit the arrival of the over-crowded boats from Northern Africa, dangerously exposed to tragic and recurring shipwrecks, by prosecuting human traffickers and launching periodical humanitarian missions. At the same time, a series of legislative decrees has changed several times the rules on asylum procedures and on the functioning of the reception and integration system. In particular, the SPRAR system has been considerably reformed, becoming one of the most important reception and integration strategies ever implemented in Italy in 2015 by a legislative decree. The idea was to ensure the smooth passage between the different phases of the asylum procedure with the distribution and integration of asylum seekers on the whole Italian territory. With this idea, the system was divided in three phases: the hotspots, where asylum seekers were registered in the first 48 hours, the first reception centres to host new arrivals for few weeks and, at last, the SPRAR projects, where asylum seekers were hosted and supported in the path towards integration within local municipalities that could apply for funds to receive humanitarian immigrants. This system has received international mediatic attention as a best practice of asylum seekers' integration, especially for those cases in which the integration funds have been used not only to receive and support asylum seekers but also as an occasion to re-populate remote and abandoned areas (Aloïse, 2011; Tondo, 2018).

The Greek context shares some similarities with the Italian one, not only because it has become an immigration country relatively in recent times but also for the numerous changes occurred on national legislation regulating immigration in response to EU directives. Here the legislative reforms have adopted an even tighter securitarian approach to border controls and asylum procedures to limit the new arrivals, while taking some small legislative and policy's steps to favour the integration of asylum seekers, still considered largely unsatisfactory. At the same time, like in Italy, the policy action towards migration has been often directed to mitigate public discontent and anti-immigrants sentiments. The first contemporary legislation on immigration was adopted by the Greek government in 1991 and was mostly aimed at deterring immigration and favouring detention and deportation of undocumented migrants. According to this law, entering illegally the country was defined a criminal act. Consequently, the main policy instruments used to control immigration were the creation of detention centres and the deportation of thousands of immigrants. However, as in the case of Italy, strict limitations to regular immigration resulted in a sharp increase of irregular migrants, which were then regularized with a series of ad-hoc mass-measures (Tramountanis, 2022; Triandafyllidou, 2009).

In 2001, a new law was adopted with the aim to tackle the issue of the regularization of undocumented migrants and the integration of those regularly residing in the country. The law was then followed by an Action Plan for social integration which, however, as claimed by a number of scholars, it largely remained on paper (Mantanika & Arapoglou, 2022; Tramountanis, 2022; Triandafyllidou, 2009). The law adopted in 2005 moved further leading to the adoption of an Integrated Action Plan, aimed at supporting the integration of immigrants at the local level in various sectors. Also in this case, though, the ambitious programme did not find adequate funding and implementation. It must be also noted that the following years have been marked by the economic crisis that heavily impacted on Greek politics and society. The crisis did impact also the Greek migration context, increasing significantly the phenomenon of emigration, not only of Greek nationals but also of immigrants that left the country (Labrianidis & Pratsinakis, 2016).

Between 2009 and 2010, in Athens and in border areas, the increasing arrival of immigrants, more and more for humanitarian reasons, led to the creation of a series of informal encampments, initially fought by the Greek institutions through a series of police raids. It was only after 2010 that, in response to the external pressure of humanitarian and international organizations, the Greek government started developing a reception system and a legislative framework for asylum (Mantanika & Arapoglou, 2022). An important evolution in legislation occurred in 2014, with the adoption of the Social Integration Code, which simplified procedures to issue residence permits, modified terms and conditions for granting long-term residence permits and access to labour market, and ensured the legal stay of the second generation of third-country migrants (Bagavos et al., 2021). In the period 2014–2015, though, the numbers of new arrivals increased considerably, and the reception system just set in place proved unable to channel and process all of them. In those years, the Greek islands facing the Turk coast became a hub not only for Greek institutions but also for international organizations, NGOs and individual volunteers to develop a complex system of reception that would then be replicated through what is going to be called the new "Balkan Route", where hotspots and camps are the main reception facility (Mantanika & Arapoglou, 2022; Rozakou, 2017).

Western Balkans: The Evolution of the Balkan Route

As the data presented in the previous chapter show, the demographic changes of the Western Balkan countries considered in this study, with the exception of Slovenia, are marked by the phenomenon of emigration that, in some cases, became one of the most pressing issues since the wars of the 1990s. In this context, the mass arrivals of foreigners crossing the Balkan Route was something completely new and unexpected for the countries of this area that never experienced the arrival of a significant number of immigrants from other continents. However, the countries of this region are not completely new to the management of immigration and, especially, to the reception of refugees and asylum seekers. Indeed, already during the Yugoslav period, along with the phenomenon of emigration abroad, the entire area experienced relevant waves of internal immigration. After the Second World War, internal economic immigration was considerable especially towards Slovenia, where the fast economic growth during the 1970s and 1980s pushed the arrival of workforce from all other Yugoslav Republics (Dolenc, 2007). In addition, all countries of the area had to tackle the reception of asylum seekers from neighbouring countries and internally displaced persons (IDPs) during the wars of the 1990s. While many of those fleeing the wars sought refuge in other European or North American countries, a significant number remained in the region, moving to neighbouring countries or to other area of the same country.

Then, in response to this situation, and under the pressure of international community, the first laws on asylum and the first programmes for the reception of refugees were adopted in this period. Serbia, for instance, adopted the Law on Refugees in 1992, establishing the Commissariat for Refugees (KIRS) with the mandate to receive and accommodate people fleeing the wars within reception centres (Stojic Mitrovic, 2019). According to this law, refugees were provided with temporary accommodation and food assistance, health care and certain social protection rights, as well as support in the processes of return and integration by provision of support to their housing needs. Moreover, in 2002, 2011 and 2015 the Serbian authorities have adopted National Strategies for Resolving the Problems of Refugees and Internally Displaced Persons, establishing the rights and services for refugees from other Western Balkan countries and IDPs. Likewise, Croatia had adopted in 1992 the Act of Refugees and Displaced Persons, establishing the procedures for temporary stays and regulating reception centres managed by the Office for Refugees and Displaced Persons (Meznaric & Winter, 1993). In Slovenia, asylum procedures started being regulated with the Temporary Protection Act in 1997 and the Asylum Act in 1999 (Zalar, 2006). Bosnia and Herzegovina has been especially affected by the phenomenon of Internally Displaced Persons and persons fleeing the country to find refuge abroad. In this context, one of the main issues addressed after the Peace Agreement by international organizations was the safe return of displaced persons to their homes, an issue still today central in the management of migrations in the country (Ivanova, 2010; MIGREC—Migration, Integration and Governance Research Centre, 2020).

Since 2013, the situation started to radically change with the first arrivals of asylum seekers and refugees, crossing the region to reach Western and Northern Europe. The opening of this route has been probably sparked by the long-lasting war in Syria that has pushed millions of Syrian people to first find refuge in Turkey and then to move towards Europe. This flow, peaking in 2015, has caused a political and mediatic turmoil because of its supposed unpredictability and the consequent unpreparedness of the concerned countries to deal with it, and because of the high numbers of children and families that were risking their life to cross the sea between Turkey and Greece. As a consequence, in October 2015, the European Union has promoted the joint management of the Route developing a system of hotspots, while the momentary welcoming policies of some EU countries (i.e., Austria, Germany and Sweden) together with the mushrooming of civic initiatives of solidarity across the Route allowed the creation of a "formalized" channel through which asylum seekers could safely reach Europe and ask for international protection. In that period, the so-called migration flow through the region was managed with the provision of 72-hour papers to move within the country and the organization of a reception and transport system. In this sense, after the initial chaos and the cases of violence against people crossing borders along the Route, national institutions, in cooperation with EU agencies and international organizations, developed a system of humanitarian assistance to smooth what was expected to be a mere transit (Abikova & Piotrowicz, 2021; Beznec et al., 2016; Minca & Collins, 2021; Tošić, 2017).

Nevertheless, this solution did not last long as in March 2016 the European Union signed a deal with Turkey that marked the official closure of the Balkan Route, which, though, has never really ceased to exist. Indeed, although with reduced numbers, asylum seekers continued to arrive from Turkey to Greece, from where they tried to reach Europe mostly through North Macedonia and Serbia in an illegal manner and facing higher risks. In addition to this, the construction of an anti-immigrant wall along the border between Serbia and Hungary has pushed refugees to seek for other ways to reach Europe: from 2018, a considerable number started to cross Bosnia and Herzegovina, to then reach Croatia and Slovenia mostly by foot until the border with Italy. This new evolution of the Route determined a new humanitarian crisis because of the absence of reception centres able to host refugees crossing the Bosnian territory and to offer satisfactory assistance, and because of the increasing numbers of violent pushbacks reported in Croatia, Slovenia, Italy and Greece (Bogucewicz, 2020).

Refugees and Asylum Seekers' Reception and Integration Policies After 2016

Italy and Greece

In Italy, the increasing arrival of asylum seekers and refugees by boat through the Mediterranean and the consequent increase of tragic shipwrecks sparked the political and public debate, especially in relation to the possible reform of the current European legislation on asylum application, the Dublin's regulation and to the rescue work of NGOs in high sea. After 2016, government action has, on one side, tried to stop new arrivals by boat from Libya and Tunisia, and, on the other side, reformed the system of reception and integration several times. One of the most relevant and debated measure has been the deal with Libyan Government of National Accord in order to avoid the departure of boats from the Libyan coasts also through the creation of a Libyan coastguard, in 2017. The deal has surely resulted in a drop of the arrivals by sea but has also raised numerous criticisms due to the inhuman conditions of the prisons in which refugees and immigrants are kept in Libya and the apparent indifference of EU and Italian institutions towards human rights violations (Hermanin, 2017).

On the side of the reception and integration system, other two reforms occurred in 2018 and 2020. The reform of 2018, promoted by the Ministry of Interior Salvini, adopted a more restrictive approach to the protection of asylum seekers: it replaced the SPRAR system with a new one called SIPROIMI, limiting the access to the integration system only to those whose application for protection was already accepted and unaccompanied minors; it abolished the "humanitarian protection" and restricted the possibilities to recognize international protection. As a consequence, the number of asylum applications accepted drastically decreased. In 2020, a new reform of the system, adopted by the new Ministry of Interior Lamorgese, brought the system only partially back to the protection ensured before the Salvini's reform. On the one hand, it replaced the SIPROIMI system with a new one called SAI, including also those who were still waiting for a decision on their application, but ensuring full integration services only to those already entitled with a form of protection. On the other hand, it introduced a new "special protection", enlarging again the cases in which international protection can be accorded (Giovanetti, 2021; Guerrieri, 2021).

As mentioned, the SPRAR system, called SAI after 2020, has been praised as a best practice of asylum seekers and refugee integration and surely can represent an example to follow for neighbouring countries facing similar challenges. The most interesting aspect of the system is its potential capacity to tackle two different issues concerning these areas: the reception and integration of asylum seekers and refugees and the depopulation of remote areas (Mastilovic & Zoppi, 2021). However, the system is still confronted by a series of issues that have an impact on its potential, as highlighted in the findings of the research conducted within the REInSER project and presented in two comparative reports (Bianchini et al., 2021b, 2021a). The first issue concerns the fact that receiving refugees and asylum seekers is not mandatory for local authorities, which are free to decide whether to apply for funds on this purpose or not. It results that places offered within the SAI system are insufficient and the vast majority of asylum seekers and refugees are hosted in Centres for Extraordinary Reception (CAS), which were meant to be an "exceptional" measure and are today the "norm". These centres host larger numbers of immigrants for humanitarian reasons and do not offer the same services of SAI, precluding them important possibilities for social integration. The second issue concerns the effective long-term impact of the arrival of refugees and asylum seekers in remote areas: the lack of working opportunities in these areas often pushes refugees and asylum seekers to seek for working opportunities elsewhere, once the period at SAI has ended. Finally, the study conducted within the project highlighted the fact that the majority of asylum seekers and refugees would need longer periods of support as many of them, when out of the integration system, still do not have a job and the means to find a proper accommodation.

In Greece, the closure of the legal channels allowing the passage of refugees through the Western Balkans determined a change of approach towards immigration and the worsening of the living conditions of those hosted in the hotspots on the islands. Here, the Law 4375/2016 established a clear division between reception and asylum procedures for those entering the country before and after 20 March 2016—the cut-off date of the EU-Turkey deal. Asylum seekers arriving after 20 March 2016 are subject to a fast-track border procedure that determines whether they can be returned to Turkey according to the EU-Turkey statement which defines the country as "safe third country" or "first country of asylum", or if their asylum application can be considered admissible as the EU-Turkey statement does not apply to them (Greek Council for Refugees, 2017). While waiting for a decision, the applicants have to remain within the Reception and Identification Centres (RIC) in the hotspots on Greek Islands, with no possibility to move. These centres have been criticized for being over-crowded, poor in sanitation and hygiene, and with limited—if none—access to health care facilities and services (Bagavos et al., 2021). This situation, particularly critical in the Island of Lesbo, has also attracted mediatic attention for the numerous revolts and clashes that broke out among asylum seekers due to the inhuman conditions (Smith, 2020). At the same time, the law adopted in 2016 granted more rights to those admitted in mainland, namely those who applied for asylum before 20 March 2016 or those whose application was considered admissible. The main changes regarded the access to labour market, ensuring the same rights of nationals to those with residence permit or asylum seeker's card, and the access to health care services. In 2019, the legislation has been significantly reformed by Law 4636/2019, increasing the maximum detention time for rejected asylum seekers and further limiting protection standards for asylum seekers, including vulnerable groups. For this reason, the law has been criticized by national and international organizations for undermining the right to asylum as protected by international legislation (Kafkoutsou & Oikonomou, 2020).

At the moment, the main reception facility used in Greece to host asylum seekers and refugees remains the "camp", both on Greek islands and on mainland. Along with the Reception and Identification Centres located on the islands, there are a number of accommodation facilities throughout the whole Greek territory, such as the temporary accommodation facilities. These infrastructures ensure improved access to sanitary facilities and living conditions compared to the RICs, but they are mostly considered inadequate for ensuring proper social integration, as they generally consist of camps with containers or reconverted hotels, hosting large numbers of asylum seekers and refugees, and badly connected to urban areas (Greek Council for Refugees, 2022). Another measure, that potentially can provide a privileged pathway towards autonomy and independence, is offered by the ESTIA programme, implemented since 2017 by UNHCR through EU funds. The programme aimed at relocating vulnerable asylum seekers and refugees into social apartments, offering them, beyond free accommodation, an allowance for basic needs and travels. Despite the commendable objective, it has been questioned the actual capacity of the programme to lead to social integration, as the support offered to beneficiaries is often insufficient to ensure a path towards autonomy and its implementation has encountered several obstacles, starting from unstable funding (Kourachanis, 2018a). In addition, after the Greek government took over the management of the Programme between 2020 and 2021, the places available considerably decreased and the funding problems worsened (ECRE, 2022; Menegus, 2022).

In the Greek context, an important role has been played by international organizations and NGOs that not only supported local authorities in the establishment and management of the first reception structures and services, but also served as the main services' providers in the context of the reception and accommodation centres. Although the contribution of NGOs in this context is recognized, especially in terms of humanitarian aid, legal and administrative assistance, protection of human rights and dissemination of information, the capacity of these organizations to foster social integration of asylum seekers and refugees through the access to labour market has been limited. In general, it has been noted how social integration requires a structural and comprehensive approach that cannot be properly ensured through fragmented funding and short-term projects (Bagavos et al., 2019). However, the Greek public authorities have recently attempted to take a major role in the social integration of asylum seekers and refugees, as in the provision of employment services. With this purpose, since 2017 a series of projects and programmes have tried to smooth the recognition of skills and qualification, the provision of counselling and the organization of Greek and English language classes.

Western Balkans

The closure of the Balkan corridor in 2016 with the EU-Turkey statement and the following construction of the wall along the Serbian-Hungarian border changed radically the situation. Although the agreement with Turkey decreased the numbers of new arrivals, thousands of asylum seekers continued to cross the Balkan Route (see Fig. 3.1). This despite the increasing dangers due to the lack of an organized and legalized path towards Western Europe. In this context, cases of violence against asylum seekers by border police started to increase again, as well as smuggling

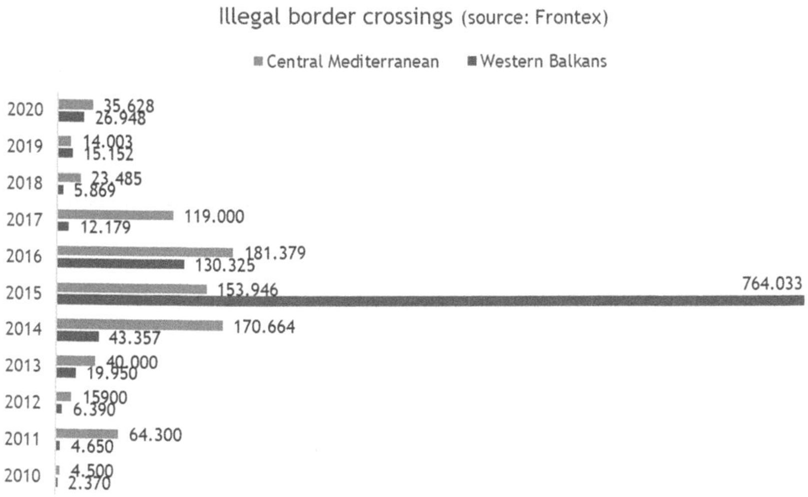

Fig. 3.1 Illegal border crossings along the Central Mediterranean and Western Balkan routes, 2010–2020

practices to cross the region (Minca & Collins, 2021; Moschopoulos, 2019). First tragic deaths of asylum seekers trying to cross borders were recorded, either drawing while crossing freezing rivers or hit by trains while walking along rails during the night (Papachristou, 2021; Zivanovic, 2017). As a consequence, the mobility from the Western Balkans to Western Europe has been considerably hindered and, despite the fact that reaching richer countries remains the main objective of the majority of asylum seekers, many of them remained stranded in the area for months or years. The humanitarian support then offered by local institutions and international organization resulted inadequate to tackle the new situation, highlighting the need to develop a new strategy going beyond the idea that Western Balkan countries were exclusively "transit countries" (Mandić, 2021; Stojic Mitrovic, 2019).

In Serbia, the main institution in charge of asylum procedures is the Commissariat for Refugees, which is also in charge of the management of the Temporary Reception Centres and Asylum Centres. Most of the services offered in these facilities, from legal information to integration services, are provided by local and international NGOs. Here, however, the relation between state's structures and NGOs has often been conflictual, as solidarity activities outside state-controlled camps have been criminalized by state institutions. Since 2016, Serbian institutional action turned from a humanitarian approach to a securitarian one, enforcing border control, criminalizing solidarity and evacuating abandoned buildings or areas where asylum seekers sought refuge. At the same time, though, the services offered in the reception centres continued to be inadequate, asylum procedures complex and prolonged and the rights for integration insufficient. This despite the new laws adopted in 2018, Law on Asylum and Temporary Protection and Law on Foreigners, which established new rules for the management of the asylum procedures and the rights of the applicants. Under these conditions, many asylum seekers continued to look for temporary accommodation within informal settings where it was easier to get in contact with smugglers and organize the continuation of the trip (Bogucewicz, 2020). However, as recognized by some scholars, integration of asylum seekers in Serbia society is already a reality, as children are attending local schools and larger number of persons are staying for prolonged periods (Vukcevic, 2020). In this context, then, the narrative that Serbia is a "transit country" might serve to assure citizens that migrants are not staying and to deresponsibilize state institutions, but it might result completely inadequate to tackle the new situation on the long term (Mandić, 2021; Stojic Mitrovic, 2019).

Croatia, with the first arrival of large numbers of asylum seekers in 2015, reacted in a quite organized way, opening in few days a reception centre and dealing with the passage of transiting people in a ordered manner (Šelo-Šabić, 2017). However, the situation changed radically once the Balkan corridor was closed, and especially when large numbers of refugees started entering the country from Bosnia and Herzegovina in 2018. Since then, Croatia has been harshly criticized by NGOs, International Organisations and scholars for the numerous violent pushbacks that have been recorded along the Bosnian border. Croatian authorities are criticized not only for violating the right to ask for asylum, as they refuse to collect asylum requests, but also for the verbal and physical violence used against asylum seekers crossing the borders[1] (Davies et al., 2022; Human Rights Watch, 2018). This practice, moreover, highlights how the humanitarian approach adopted at the beginning of the Balkan Route was backed by the fact that Croatia was only seen as a transit country. The closure of

[1] On this regard, it must be noted that pushbacks are an unfortunate practice more and more common on EU borders, including Italy, Slovenia and Greece.

the corridor and of the border, with the consequent risk of increasing numbers of asylum seekers stranded in the country, led to a radical change of approach (Župarić-Iljić & Valenta, 2019).

Currently, asylum procedures in Croatia are regulated by the Law on International and Temporary Protection adopted in 2015 to harmonize Croatian legislation with EU norms. The Ministry of Interior is in charge of asylum procedures and reception structures, which at the moment are two, located in Zagreb and Kutina. Similar to Serbia, the number of applicants granted with international protection is very low, because of the complexity of the procedures and the fact that the majority of asylum seekers leave the country before a decision is taken. Once the protection is granted, on paper the rights and services offered to asylum seekers and refugees are quite broad: a paid apartment for two years, a small allowance, Croatian language courses, support from the employment services. However, as highlighted by Rahela Jurković (2018), this assistance most of the time is insufficient and dysfunctional: most of those granted with international protection remain in the reception centre for prolonged periods, hindering significantly their possibility to integrate; Croatian language courses are fragmented and often provided by NGOs volunteers who are not language professors; the employment service does not provide any actual assistance to find a job and asylum seekers end up depending on the very little money allowance sufficient to barely survive.

In Bosnia and Herzegovina, the situation is even more difficult. Here, the general context is still deeply marked by the consequences of the war, not only because of the still ongoing social and economic reconstruction, but especially because of the administrative complexity of the state structures resulted from the Peace Agreement. Being a state composed of two entities, Republika Srpska and Federation of Bosnia and Herzegovina, one autonomous district and ten cantons, Bosnia and Herzegovina has often been defined an administrative nightmare, affecting all sectors of society and hampering the process of reconciliation and reconstruction. This situation has an impact also in the management and the asylum procedures and humanitarian assistance (MIGREC—Migration, Integration and Governance Research Centre, 2020). In 2018, when the country started being on the map of the Balkan Route, the president of Republika Srpska opposed the settlement of reception centres on his territory, fuelling tensions with the central state, while the Ministry of Security and the Service for Foreigners' Affairs (SFA), in charge of the management of the asylum procedure and reception facilities, proved unprepared to address the situation (Moschopoulos, 2019; Nezirović et al., 2021).

Along with the new arrivals from Serbia and Montenegro, Bosnian authorities had to deal also with the numerous pushbacks from Croatia that increased the number of migrants stranded in the area for prolonged periods, especially around the North-East border of the towns of Bihać and Velika Kladuša, which became a sort of migration choke point. To manage the disastrous humanitarian situation that was emerging in this context, IOM took a central role in the provision of basic services and reception infrastructures. These were mostly divided between reception centres for single men and centres for families and unaccompanied minors, offering slightly improved infrastructures and services. However, the situation continued to be very precarious, exposing asylum seekers to unbearable conditions (Astuti et al., 2020). Exemplary is the case of Lipa, a reception centre located 30 km away from Bihać, opened by IOM as a temporary structure to host single men during the COVID pandemic: after burning down in December 2020, local authorities did not find an alternative accommodation and left migrants to live in tents for the whole winter in an area affected by heavy snows and extremely low temperatures (Tondo, 2020). Currently, the SFA is taking more and more the control and management of reception centres, where, though, basic services are still ensured by international organizations and NGOs, whose action, like in other countries, is criminalized if carried out outside. Here, as well, asylum procedures, regulated by the Law on Asylum adopted in 2016, continue to be very slow and inefficient, resulting in a very restricted number of people granted with international protection (Ahmetašević, 2021).

In the last country considered by this study, Slovenia, asylum procedures and services are regulated by the International Protection Act adopted in 2016 and the Foreigners Act adopted in 2011. Here, the Government Office for the Support and Integration of Migrants (UOIM) is responsible for the reception and accommodation of asylum seekers, although many humanitarian and integration services are still provided by NGOs. Asylum seekers are accommodated in the so-called Asylum Home in Ljubljana or in one of its three branches located in the rest of the country. Here, as well, accommodation varies for single men, families or unaccompanied minors. All these structures accommodate large numbers of asylum seekers, hindering their possible social integration in the country. After being granted with international protection, asylum seekers and refugees can be accommodated in integration houses, located in Ljubljana and Maribor, up to six months (Elia, 2021). However, here as well, official services for reception and integration are reported to be largely inadequate and are mostly covered by the work of local NGOs. In addition, after a short period characterized by a humanitarian approach in 2015, government action turned to securitization, tightening border controls and asylum legislation, towards a progressive criminalization of migration. In this context, rejection and detention of asylum seekers has become a common and even institutionalized practice (Bajt, 2019).

Analysis and Conclusions

As highlighted in the analysis of the migration context in the Adriatic-Ionian Area, asylum legislation and policies are mostly pushed by EU directives and pressure. Accordingly, all countries considered have adopted regulations to ensure the right to asylum and international protection in respect to international standards. However, in all these countries, the implementation of the legislation is often inadequate and strategies for the integration of asylum seekers and refugees risk remaining only on paper, while border controls have increased, and immigration is being criminalized. The lack of proper reception and integration structures is partly due to the institutional inefficiency characterizing some of these countries and the lack of proper infrastructures and resources. At the same time, though, the recurrent idea that these are simple "transit zones" for migrants is used to deresponsibilize public institutions towards the implementation of adequate strategies for the protection and integration of asylum seekers and refugees. The tendency of underestimating the migratory context and procrastinating the implementation of structural policies, while dealing with current issue with an emergency approach, does not only affect the lives of migrants and asylum seekers entering these countries, but it also feeds the criminal markets of smugglers and black labour, as especially the Greek and Italian cases show.

Along with these similarities, the analysis highlighted also some important differences, especially in regard to the support to integration. While Italy, although with its limitations, has adopted an integration system which ensures comprehensive support outside the bigger reception centres and camps, these two facilities remain the main, if not the only, accommodation opportunity offered in all other countries. Beyond the fact that these structures hinder integration because of their segregating nature, the services here offered are very often inadequate or insufficient. In addition, in all countries here considered, including Italy, the integration system does not always manage to support the individual towards full autonomy, as many of these who exit the system of support still do not have the means to provide for themselves. This is surely due to the numerous internal and external challenges that asylum seekers and refugees face (knowledge of the language, trauma, discrimination), but also to the inadequacy of some of the services offered, such as language courses and labour services. The lack, then, of structural systems to collect refugees and asylum seekers' skills and match labour demand with offer appears an issue throughout the whole area.

One characteristic that is common in all the countries of the Western Balkans and Greece is the important role played by NGOs in the provision of essential reception and integration services. While the intervention of NGOs might support the creation of solidarity networks and ease the process of integration, the assistance needed by asylum seekers and refugees requires a more systematic and structural approach, which cannot be granted by individual NGOs. One example are the language courses, which are often carried out by volunteers of NGO professionals who are not professional teachers, hindering the possibilities for the students to properly learn the local language. Another example is the support to find employment: this service, as well, is often provided by NGOs officers or social workers who do not have the proper competences to match refugees' labour offer with demand. These examples show the importance of developing a structural system for integration, where NGOs can intervene to support, but should not replace the work of the competent structures and agencies.

One important difference, in this sense, regards the legislation regulating the possibility for asylum seekers and refugees to work. While in Italy asylum applicants can start working two months after they have applied for asylum; in Greece they have to wait for 6 months; and in Slovenia, Serbia, Croatia and Bosnia and Herzegovina for 9 months, unless a decision regarding their application is taken earlier, which is very rarely the case. This prolonged wait to start working regularly is a critical obstacle to integration because it prevents asylum seekers to earn a living and start a new life in the hosting country. The impossibility to work for a long period of time, then, might reinforce the dependence on social support, which is however often inadequate to carry on a proper life. This issue might then push asylum seekers to leave the country or not to apply for asylum, as the opportunities for integration remain too low. In countries such as Serbia,

Croatia and Bosnia and Herzegovina, the number of asylum applications is still low and those granted with protection extremely low. In light of the increasing difficulties to cross borders, the low numbers of recognized asylum seekers and refugees might correspond to higher number of undocumented migrants and asylum seekers relying on the criminal networks of smugglers and undeclared work.

References

Abbondanza, G. (2017). Italy's Migration Policies Combating Irregular Immigration: From the Early Days to the Present Times. *The International Spectator, 52*(4), 76–92. https://doi.org/10.1080/03932729.2017.1384606

Abikova, J., & Piotrowicz, W. (2021). Shaping the Balkan Corridor: Development and Changes in the Migration Route 2015–16. *International Migration, 59*(5), 248–265. https://doi.org/10.1111/imig.12828

Ahmetašević, N. (2021). *Limits to Access to Asylum along the Balkan Route.* Refugee Rights Europe. https://resourcecentre.savethechildren.net/document/limits-access-asylum-along-balkans-route/

Aloïse, S. (2011, April 26). *Dans le sud de l'Italie, un village déserté reprend vie en accueillant des immigrés.* https://www.lemonde.fr/europe/article/2011/04/26/dans-le-sud-de-l-italie-un-village-deserte-reprend-vie-en-accueillant-des-immigres_1512969_3214.html

Ambrosetti, E., & Paparusso, A. (2018). Migrants or Refugees? The Evolving Governance of Migration Flows in Italy during the "Refugee Crisis". *Revue Européenne Des Migrations Internationales, 34*(1), 151–171. https://doi.org/10.4000/remi.10265

Astuti, M., Bove, C., Brambilla, A., Clementi, A., Facchini, D., Giordani, C., Maraone, S., Pignocchi, P., Saccora, D., & Stojanova, I. (2020). *The Balkan Route. Migrants without Rights in the Heart of Europe.* Rivolti ai Balcani. https://www.asgi.it/wp-content/uploads/2020/09/The-Balkan-Route-Report-2020-by-_-Rivolti-ai-Balcani_-italian-network.pdf

Bagavos, C., Chatzigiannakou, K., & Kourachanis, N. (2019). Greece. In D. Numerato, K. Čada, & K. Hoření (Eds.), *Civil Society Enablers and Barriers. WP4 Report.* SIRIUS Project. https://www.sirius-project.eu/sites/default/files/attachments/Civil%20society%20enablers%20and%20barriers%20D4.1.pdf

Bagavos, C., Kourachanis, N., Lagoudakou, K., & Xatzigiannakou, K. (2021). Between Reception, Legal Stay and Integration in a Changing Migration Landscape in Greece. In V. Federico & S. Baglioni (Eds.), *Migrants, Refugees and Asylum Seekers' Integration in European Labour Markets* (pp. 173–192). Springer International Publishing. https://doi.org/10.1007/978-3-030-67284-3_9

Bajt, V. (2019). The Schengen Border and the Criminalization of Migration in Slovenia. *Südosteuropa, 67*(3), 304–327. https://doi.org/10.1515/soeu-2019-0024

Beznec, B., Speer, M., & Stojic Mitrovic, M. (2016). *Governing the Balkan Route: Macedonia, Serbia and the European Border Regime.* Research Paper Series of Rosa Luxemburg Stiftung, 5.

Bianchini, S., Zoppi, M., Cittadini, S., Bandini, F., Bolzani, D., & Savoia, F. (2021a). *Comparative STA Report on the Assessment of Main Challenges in the Partners' State.* REInSER Project. https://reinser.adrioninterreg.eu/wp-content/uploads/2022/03/DT1.2.2-Comparative-STA-Report-on-the-identification-of-the-main-challenges-in-the-partners-states_new-cover.pdf

Bianchini, S., Zoppi, M., Cittadini, S., Bandini, F., Bolzani, D., & Savoia, F. (2021b). *Comparative STA Report on the Assessment of Societal Change in the Partners' State.* REInSER Project. https://reinser.adrioninterreg.eu/wp-content/uploads/2022/03/DT1.1.2-Comparative-STA-Report-on-the-assessment-of-societal-change-in-the-partners-states_New-cover.pdf

Bianchini, S., Cittadini, S., & Zoppi, M. (2022). In-Securitization through Externalization? The EU and the Western Balkans "Borderlands". In *Fences, Refugee Boats, and the New Borderlands: Making Sense of the European Union's Emerging Internal and External Borders.* BordEUr. https://bordeur-project.com/wp-content/uploads/2022/11/BordEUr-Publication.pdf

Bobić, M., & Šantić, D. (2020). Forced Migrations and Externalization of European Union Border Control: Serbia on the Balkan Migration Route. *International Migration, 58*(3), 220–234. https://doi.org/10.1111/imig.12622

Bogucewicz, M. (2020). The Consequences of the Migration Crisis on the Balkan Route and Human Rights: The Current Situation and Prospects in Serbia. *Eastern Review, 9*, 149–167. https://doi.org/10.18778/1427-9657.09.10

Caponio, T., Donatiello, D., & Ponzo, I. (2022). Relational and Reputational Resources in the Governance of Top-Down Asylum Seekers' Reception in Italian Rural Areas. *Territory, Politics, Governance, 10*(3), 407–425. https://doi.org/10.1080/21622671.2021.1995479

Cavounidis, J. (2015). *The Changing Face of Emigration: Harnessing the Potential of the New Greek Diaspora.* Migration Policy Institute. https://www.migrationpolicy.org/research/changing-face-emigration-harnessing-potential-new-greek-diaspora

Chiaromonte, W., & Federico, V. (2021). The Labour Market Needs Them, But We Don't Want Them to Stay for Good: The Conundrum of Migrants, Refugees and Asylum Seekers' Integration in Italy. In V. Federico & S. Baglioni (Eds.), *Migrants, Refugees and Asylum Seekers' Integration in European Labour Markets* (pp. 193–212). Springer International Publishing. https://doi.org/10.1007/978-3-030-67284-3_10

Collini, M. (2023). Italy: The Promised Land? Journeys of Migrants, Refugees and Asylum Seekers Towards Labour Market Integration. In I. Isaakyan, A. Triandafyllidou, & S. Baglioni (Eds.), *Immigrant and Asylum Seekers Labour Market Integration upon Arrival: NowHereLand* (pp. 129–160). Springer International Publishing. https://doi.org/10.1007/978-3-031-14009-9_6

Davies, T., Isakjee, A., & Obradovic-Wochnik, J. (2022). Epistemic Borderwork: Violent Pushbacks, Refugees, and the Politics of Knowledge at the EU Border. *Annals of the American Association of Geographers*, 1–20. https://doi.org/10.1080/24694452.2022.2077167

degli Uberti, S. (2021). Unveiling Informality through Im/mobility. Conceptual Analysis of Asylum Seekers and Refugees at the Margins of the Reception system in Italy. *Journal of Modern Italian Studies, 26*(5), 528–551. https://doi.org/10.1080/1354571X.2021.1953777

Dives, N., & Rigo, E. (2015). Postcolonial Citizenships and the "Refugeeization" of the Workforce: Migrant Agricultural Labor in the Italian Mezzogiorno. In S. Ponzanesi & G. Colpani (Eds.), *Postcolonial Transitions in Europe: Contexts, Practices and Politics*. Rowman and International.

Dolenc, D. (2007). Priseljevanje v Slovenijo z območja nekdanje Jugoslavije po drugi svetovni vojni. In M. Komac (Ed.), *Priseljenci. Študije o priseljevanju in vključevanju v slovensko družbo*. Inštitut za narodnostna vprašanja.

Dotsey, S., & Lumley-Sapanski, A. (2021). Temporality, Refugees, and Housing: The Effects of Temporary Assistance on Refugee Housing Outcomes in Italy. *Cities, 111*. https://doi.org/10.1016/j.cities.2020.103100

ECRE. (2022). *Greece: ESTIA Melt Down Continues—Criminalisation, Crack-Downs and Pushbacks Still the 'Welcome' for People in Search of Protection*. https://ecre.org/greece-estia-melt-down-continues-criminalisation-crack-downs-and-pushbacks-still-the-welcome-for-people-in-search-of-protection/

Elia, C. (2021, April 21). Igor and the House in Maribor. *Snapshots from the Borders*. http://www.snapshotsfromtheborders.eu/igor-and-the-house-in-maribor/

Galijaš, A. (2019). Permanently in Transit. Middle Eastern Migrants and Refugees in Serbia. *Südosteuropa, 67*(1), 75–109. https://doi.org/10.1515/soeu-2019-0004

Giovanetti, M. (2021). I perimetri incerti della tutela: La protezione internazionale nei procedimenti amministrativi e giudiziari. *Questione Giustizia.*. https://www.questionegiustizia.it/data/doc/2883/giovannetti-su-dati-protezione-internazionale-30-04-2021.pdf

Greek Council for Refugees. (2017). *Country Report: Greece 2016*. Aida Asylum Information Database. https://asylumineurope.org/wp-content/uploads/2017/03/report-download_aida_gr_2016update.pdf

Greek Council for Refugees. (2022). *Conditions in Reception Facilities*. Aida Asylum Information Database. https://asylumineurope.org/reports/country/greece/reception-conditions/housing/conditions-reception-facilities/

Guerrieri, F. (2021, May 8). Asilo politico, protezione sussidiaria e speciale: Dati e differenze. *Le Nius*. https://www.lenius.it/asilo-politico-protezione-sussidiaria-umanitaria-quali-le-differenze/

Hermanin, C. (2017). *Immigration Policy in Italy: Problems and Perspectives*. IAI Working Papers, 17(35).

Hromadžic, A. (2020). 'Migrant Crisis' in Bihac', Bosnia and Herzegovina. *Movements, 5*(1), 163–180.

Human Rights Watch. (2018, December 11). *Croatia: Migrants Pushed Back to Bosnia and Herzegovina*. https://www.hrw.org/news/2018/12/11/croatia-migrants-pushed-back-bosnia-and-herzegovina

Ivanova, V. (2010). Internally Displaced Persons in Bosnia and Herzegovina: Policy Developments in Managing Displacements Waves. In K. Krasteva & Karabinova (Eds.), *Migrations from and to Southeastern Europe* (pp. 225–235). Longo Editore.

Jurković, R. (2018). The Integration of Refugees into Croatian Society. Ethnographies of Exercising Rights. *Etnološka Tribina, 48*(41), 102–121. https://doi.org/10.15378/1848-9540.2018.41.02

Kafkoutsou, N.-R., & Oikonomou, S.-V. (2020). *Diminished, Derogated, Denied: How the Right to Asylum in Greece is Undermined by the Lack of EU Responsibility Sharing* (Greek Council for Refugees and Oxfam Briefings, p. 24).

Kourachanis, N. (2018a). From Camps to Social Integration? Social Housing Interventions for Asylum Seekers in Greece. *International Journal of Sociology and Social Policy, 39*(3/4), 221–234. https://doi.org/10.1108/IJSSP-08-2018-0130

Kourachanis, N. (2018b). Asylum Seekers, Hotspot Approach and Anti-Social Policy Responses in Greece (2015–2017). *Journal of International Migration and Integration, 19*(4), 1153–1167. https://doi.org/10.1007/s12134-018-0592-y

Labrianidis, L., & Pratsinakis, M. (2016). *Greece's New Emigration at Times of Crisis*. Hellenic Observatory Papers on Greece and Southeast Europe, 99.

Mancuso, M. C., & Signorelli, V. (2022). Heroes or Criminals? The Legitimacy of Humanitarian Organizations Rescuing Lives in the Central Mediterranean Sea after 2017. *Journal of Italian Cinema & Media Studies, 10*(1), 37–58. https://doi.org/10.1386/jicms_00101_1

Mandić, D. (2021). A Migrant "Hot Potato" System: The Transit Camp and Urban Integration in a Bridge Society. *Journal of Urban Affairs, 43*(6), 799–815. https://doi.org/10.1080/07352166.2018.1490153

Manou, D., Blouchoutzi, A., & Papathanasiou, J. (2021). The Socioeconomic Integration of People in Need of International Protection: A Spatial Approach in the Case of Greece. *Social Sciences, 10*(12). Scopus. https://doi.org/10.3390/socsci10120454

Mantanika, R., & Arapoglou, V. (2022). The Making of Reception as a System. The Governance of Migrant Mobility and Transformations of Statecraft in Greece Since the Early 2000s. *IMISCOE Research Series*, 201–220. Scopus. https://doi.org/10.1007/978-3-031-11574-5_10

Mastilovic, J., & Zoppi, M. (2021). (In)security and Immigration to Depopulating Rural Areas in Southern and Southeastern Europe. *Southeastern Europe, 45*(2), 229–253. https://doi.org/10.30965/18763332-45020003

Menegus, G. (2022, February 18). The ESTIA Program Is a Glimmer of Hope, but It's Fading Away. *Open. Cultural Center*. https://openculturalcenter.org/the-estia-program-is-a-glimmer-of-hope-but-its-fading-away/

Meznaric, S., & Winter, J. Z. (1993). Forced Migration and Refugee Flows in Croatia, Slovenia and Bosnia-Herzegovina. *Refuge: Canada's Journal on Refugees, 12*(7), 3–5. https://doi.org/10.25071/1920-7336.21183

MIGREC—Migration, Integration and Governance Research Centre. (2020). *Mapping of Migration Related Research and Policy Development in the Western Balkan Countries—Report on Prospective Regional Networks*. https://www.eliamep.gr/wp-content/uploads/2021/03/Deliverable-1.3.pdf

Milan, C. (2019). Refugees at the Gates of the EU: Civic Initiatives and Grassroots Responses to the Refugee Crisis along the Western Balkans Route. *Journal of Balkan and Near Eastern Studies, 21*(1), 43–60. https://doi.org/10.1080/19448953.2018.1532686

Minca, C., & Collins, J. (2021). The Game: Or, 'The Making of Migration' along the Balkan Route. *Political Geography, 91*, 102490. https://doi.org/10.1016/j.polgeo.2021.102490

Moschopoulos. (2019). The "Balkan Route" Three Years after Its Closure. *IeMed*. https://www.iemed.org/publication/the-balkan-route-three-years-after-its-closure/

Nezirović, S., Durmišević, B., Hodžić, A., & Živko, A. (2021). Bosnia and Herzegovina—Transit Area or Unwanted Migrant Deposit? *Revue Roumaine de Géographie/Romanian Journal of Geography, 65*(1), 3–19.

Ortensi, L. E., & Kingston, L. N. (2022). Asylum Seekers' Experiences on the Migration Journey to Italy (and Beyond): Risk Factors and Future Planning within a Shifting Political Landscape. *International Migration, 60*(1), 228–243. https://doi.org/10.1111/imig.12849

Papachristou, L. (2021, July 14). Drowning in the Balkans: 'His Body Went Away with the Water'. *Al Jazeera*. https://www.aljazeera.com/features/2021/7/14/his-body-went-away-with-the-water-refugees-drown-in

Papoutsi, A., Painter, J., Papada, E., & Vradis, A. (2019). The EC Hotspot Approach in Greece: Creating Liminal EU Territory. *Journal of Ethnic and Migration Studies, 45*(12), 2200–2212. Scopus. https://doi.org/10.1080/1369183X.2018.1468351

Ponzo, I., Giannetto, L., & Roman, E. (2022). The Variance in Multilevel Governance of Asylum Seekers' Reception in Italy. In I. T. Caponio & I. Ponzo (Eds.), *Coping with Migrants and Refugees* (1st ed., pp. 90–119). Routledge. https://doi.org/10.4324/9781003129950-5

Rozakou, K. (2017). Nonrecording the "European Refugee Crisis" in Greece. *Focaal, 2017*(77), 36–49. https://doi.org/10.3167/fcl.2017.770104

Šelo-Šabić, S. (2017). The Impact of the Refugee Crisis in the Balkans: A Drift Towards Security. *Journal of Regional Security, 12*(2), 51–74. https://doi.org/10.11643/issn.2217-995X171SPS80

Smith, H. (2020, February 9). Crisis in Lesbos as More Refugees Arrive. *The Observer*. https://www.theguardian.com/world/2020/feb/09/tensions-refugees-and-islanders-crisis-on-lesbos

Stojic Mitrovic, M. (2019). The Reception of Migrants in Serbia: Policies, Practices, and Concepts. *Journal of Human Rights and Social Work, 4*(1), 17–27. https://doi.org/10.1007/s41134-018-0077-0

Tondo, L. (2018, March 19). 'They are Our Salvation': The Sicilian Town Revived by Refugees. *The Guardian*. http://www.theguardian.com/world/2018/mar/19/sutera-italy-the-sicilian-town-revived-by-refugees

Tondo, L. (2020, December 23). Fire Destroys Migrant Camp in Bosnia. *The Guardian*. https://www.theguardian.com/global-development/2020/dec/23/fire-destroys-migrant-camp-bosnia-lipa

Tošić, J. (2017). From a Transit Route to the "Backyard of Europe"? Tracing the Past, Present and Future of the "Balkan Route". *Facultas, 10*.

Tramountanis, A. (2022). Pathways to Integration and Dis-integration: An Assessment of the Greek Immigration Policy for the Inclusion of Immigrants, Applicants and Beneficiaries of International Protection. In M. Kousis, A. Chatzidaki, & K. Kafetsios (Eds.), *Challenging Mobilities in and to the EU during Times of Crises* (pp. 263–282). Springer International Publishing. https://doi.org/10.1007/978-3-031-11574-5_13

Triandafyllidou, A. (2009). Greek Immigration Policy at the Turn of the 21st Century. Lack of Political Will or Purposeful Mismanagement? *European Journal of Migration and Law, 11*(2), 159–177. https://doi.org/10.1163/157181609X440013

Vukcevic, N. (2020). Eventual Integration or Delayed Transit: Interaction of Residents in Reception Centres with Their New Environment in Serbia. *Stanovnistvo, 58*(1), 1–23. https://doi.org/10.2298/STNV191017003V

Webb, J. (2020). The 'Refugee Crisis' and Its Transformative Impact on EU-Western Balkans Relations. *Journal of Ethnic and Migration Studies*, 1–18. https://doi.org/10.1080/1369183X.2020.1851466

Zalar, B. (2006). The Experiences and Challenges for Adjudication on Refugee Law in Slovenia. *International Journal of Refugee Law, 18*(1), 118–181. https://doi.org/10.1093/ijrl/eei048

Zaragoza-Cristiani, J. (2017). Containing the Refugee Crisis: How the EU Turned the Balkans and Turkey into an EU Borderland. *The International Spectator, 52*(4), 59–75. https://doi.org/10.1080/03932729.2017.1375727

Zivanovic, M. (2017, November 23). Migrant Child Reported Killed on Croatia-Serbia Border. *Balkan Insight*. https://balkaninsight.com/2017/11/23/migrant-child-killed-on-the-border-between-serbia-and-croatia-msf-11-23-2017/

Županić-Iljić, D., & Valenta, M. (2019). Opportunistic Humanitarianism and Securitization Discomfort Along the Balkan Corridor: The Croatian Experience. In C. Cantat, M. Feischmidt, & L. Pries (Eds.), *Refugee Protection and Civil Society in Europe* (1st ed.). Springer International Publishing : Imprint: Palgrave Macmillan. https://doi.org/10.1007/978-3-319-92741-1

CHAPTER 4

Social Entrepreneurship in the Adriatic–Ionian Countries: Policy Background and Entrepreneurial Ecosystems Development

Francesco Savoia, *Federica Bandini*, *and Daniela Preite*

Introduction

Over the past decade, the growing number of asylum seekers and refugees has contributed significantly to increasing the overall share of immigrants in Europe (OECD and EU, 2018, 2019), leading to new social and economic concerns and political and policy challenges. Given its implications, international migration has become a priority on international agendas,

F. Savoia (✉)
Department of Historical Studies, University of Milan, Milan, Italy

Yunus Social Business Centre, University of Bologna, Forlì, Italy
e-mail: francesco.savoia@unimi.it

S. Bianchini et al. (eds.), *Social Entrepreneurship and Migrants' Inclusion*, Sustainable Development Goals Series,
https://doi.org/10.1007/978-3-031-55791-0_4

characterising the modern open society (Kourtit & Nijkamp, 2011; Massey et al., 1993).

In this context, the role of the social economy in providing innovative and concrete opportunities for vulnerable people is central to European Union (EU) policy making. Social enterprises (SEs), aligned with EU policies, exemplify an 'economy that works for people', providing services and working towards the social and economic integration of disadvantaged groups, among other objectives. The interest in boosting the social economy is driven by a broader expected contribution to both sustainability and inclusiveness.[1] In this respect, the United Nations recognises the outstanding role of social entrepreneurship as a driver of sustainable development and of the 2030 Agenda by fostering inclusive employment growth, addressing social inequalities and facing up to major social and environmental issues (United Nations, 2018, p. 12).[2]

The social economy has been revealed as a crucial response to the emergence of the refugee and migrant crises, offering practical solutions to

[1] The European Commission launched an Action Plan for Social Economy in December 2021 and, jointly with the OECD, a Global Action 'Promoting Social and Solidarity Economy Ecosystems' (https://www.oecd.org/cfe/leed/social-economy/oecd-global-action/). For other specific actions within the framework of EU policy, see the Social Business Initiative (SBI), and the Employment and Social Innovation (EaSI) programme.

[2] The social economy contributes to the implementation of the UN Sustainable Development Goals (SDGs) by addressing a wide range of societal challenges, including the social and economic integration of vulnerable people, environmental sustainability, responsible consumption and production, and the promotion of equal opportunities and civic participation (European Commission, 2020; OECD and EU, 2017).

F. Bandini
Yunus Social Business Centre, University of Bologna, Forlì, Italy

Department of Management, Alma Mater Studiorum-University of Bologna, Bologna, Italy
e-mail: federica.bandini@unibo.it

D. Preite
Department of Historical Studies, University of Milan, Milan, Italy

SDA Bocconi, Bocconi University, Milan, Italy
e-mail: daniela.preite@unimi.it

common needs such as language learning, social inclusion, education, temporary housing, basic healthcare and psychological assistance (Harima & Freudenberg, 2020). Especially during the COVID-19 pandemic, social enterprises delivered essential social services complementing the efforts of member states (European Commission, 2021).

Despite the growing effort of the EU countries to support and boost the social and solidarity economy, recognition and growth across European countries is highly uneven, especially in the Adriatic–Ionian macro-region (often, and henceforward, referred to as Adrion). In addition, definitional and practical obstacles are still present, with growing concerns over designing and implementing specific policies that vary considerably across countries (OECD, 2020). These issues are gaining relevance within the ongoing political debate on the inclusion of asylum seekers, refugees and migrants in the EU.

The Adrion region includes both EU and non-EU countries involved in various stages of the EU enlargement process, with different approaches towards the social economy. The peculiarity of this context is also determined by the high heterogeneity across and within these countries, where political, cultural and socioeconomic features are concerned, representing an interesting yet overlooked area of research. For these reasons, countries in this area are involved in many cooperation programmes and institutional initiatives that foster convergence in policies and practices.[3] Given the recent international migration dynamics and the rapid evolution of European policies for the social economy, it is relevant to analyse how structural characteristics that may stimulate this process are evolving in this area.

Making use of the existing evidence and of information collected from partners in the Refugees' Economic Integration through Social Entrepreneurship (REInSER) project, this chapter discusses the relevance of social entrepreneurship and the existing policy framework in this region, providing an overview of its coherence with the EU framework.[4] In addition, using data from the Global Entrepreneurship and Development

[3] In the past few years, the Balkans have also acquired new political relevance in the aftermath of the migration dynamics along the so-called Balkan Route, cooperating with the EU in security and migration management.

[4] The interregional REInSER project dealt with the integration of refugees through social entrepreneurship. The main project goal was to improve refugees' economic and social integration into the hosting societies of the European transnational ADRION programme area by exploiting social economy and social entrepreneurship approaches.

Institute from 2006 to 2019, our research explores how the level of the region's entrepreneurial ecosystems, measured by the Global Entrepreneurship Index (GEI), has evolved over time, investigating the specific conditions that hinder or support entrepreneurial activities.

The comparative overview provided by this research indicates that, despite the variety of approaches and legislative frameworks, there is growing recognition of the importance of social entrepreneurship. Evidence from the GEI reveals that Adrion countries are experiencing a widening of the gap in the overall level of development of their entrepreneurial ecosystems, with improvements in Slovenia and Italy and constant or declining trends in the Balkan countries. The major issue in this area concerns unstable institutions and a low propensity to take entrepreneurial risks, driving the low performance.

The study is organised as follows. The following section introduces social business and its crucial role in future development prospects. Section "The Policy and Legal Framework for Social Entrepreneurship" elaborates on the legislative framework in Adrion countries, illustrating the state of the art and some critical emerging issues. Section "The Variety of Structural Conditions in the Adrion Area: Evidence from GEI Data" illustrates how the characteristics of the entrepreneurial ecosystems have evolved over time. The concluding section summarises and discusses the findings, providing policy recommendations and implications for future research.

The Role of the Social Economy and Social Entrepreneurship in Sustainable Development

The social and solidarity economy comprises a variety of organisations pursuing activities in a wide range of sectors and with different business and organisational models but sharing the same mission and values. Typically, this sector encompasses both for-profit and non-profit entities driven by common solidaristic, democratic and inclusive principles, such as cooperatives, social enterprises, associations, foundations and mutual benefit societies.[5] Among these, social enterprises represent the most recent

[5] These principles refer to solidarity and mutuality, democratic and participatory governance, the primacy of people over capital, the combination of the individual and general interest, and the reinvestment of financial surplus into services to members or society (OECD, 2020).

legal entity understood as part of the social economy and characterised by a more developed entrepreneurial approach. Following the EU operational definition, social enterprises denote those entities whose primary purpose is to respond to social and environmental problems through business activities and inclusive governance. Specifically, a social enterprise is identified as

> an operator in the social economy whose main objective is to have a social impact rather than make a profit for [its] owners or shareholders. It operates by providing goods and services for the market in an entrepreneurial and innovative fashion and uses its profits primarily to achieve social objectives. It is managed in an open and responsible manner and, in particular, involves employees, consumers and stakeholders affected by its commercial activities. (European Commission, 2011, p. 2)

As an inclusive and sustainable form of business, social enterprises play a significant role in future development prospects. Here we report some recent outcomes from developed countries. The results from the SEFORÏS project on social enterprises revealed revenues exceeding €6 billion, provision of services and products to about 871 million beneficiaries, job creation for about half a million people (especially for those with disabilities or migrant backgrounds) and job placements for around 5.5 million people (Huysentruyt et al., 2016; Huysentruyt & Ute, 2017).[6] As if this is not impressive enough, social enterprises represent one of the largest inclusive job creation areas in European countries (European Commission, 2012) and have also displayed remarkable resilience in terms of employment generation and protection during periods of economic crisis. Between 2008 and 2014, in Italy, Belgium and France, employment in social enterprises grew, respectively, at a rate of 20%, 12% and 0.8%, while employment in mainstream or private enterprises decreased (OECD and EU, 2017).

Promoting social entrepreneurship and a social economy—in recognition of their role in creating sustainable development models of production, finance and consumption—constitutes a prominent feature of the political agenda at every level of governance, including that of international organisations, financial institutions and NGOs. Prominent among those promoting social entrepreneurship are the UN, the OECD, the

[6] The survey was conducted in 2015 within the international research project SEFORÏS. It surveyed more than 1000 social enterprises in seven EU countries (Germany, Hungary, Portugal, Romania, Spain, Sweden and the UK), as well as in China and Russia.

International Cooperative Alliance and the African Development Bank, among others. Because of their nature, these entities have an outstanding role as a driver of the 2030 Agenda for Sustainable Development by fostering inclusive employment growth, addressing social inequalities and facing up to major social and environmental issues (United Nations, 2018, p. 12).[7]

International migration flows, which constitute an ongoing and pressing social and political issue affecting the EU-wide area, present challenges and opportunities at various levels. On the one hand, migration raises questions about handling unexpected flows while providing services and support for social and economic integration. On the other hand, it also creates opportunities for local development and meets the labour market needs of hosting countries, matching the demand for skills and fostering entrepreneurship. However, it is important to note that, despite the remarkable potential of social economy entities in addressing these concerns, the Adrion countries have diverging reception and integration systems, mainly thanks to their EU membership and Schengen status, as well as differing levels of institutional and legal recognition of the social economy. This peculiarity clearly undermines the potential of social economy entities and poses challenges for the overall management of these flows.

In this context, the strategic partnership of the (now closed) REInSER project endeavoured to find a sustainable solution to the urgent issue of refugees and asylum seekers by enhancing the institutional capacity of public administrations and key stakeholders and favouring networking and knowledge transfer about transnational as well as cross-sectional cooperation among key stakeholders. The long-term policy objective of the project was to enhance the possibilities for migrants to become active economic actors and agents of their integration in the hosting society, with an expected contribution to local and regional sustainable economic development by generating employment and supporting the creation of new social and responsible businesses.[8]

[7] On this point, enterprises surveyed by the European Social Enterprise Monitor (ESEM) focused particularly on Goal 3: good health and wellbeing (51%), Goal 10: reduced inequalities (51%), Goal 8: decent work and economic growth (49%), Goal 12: responsible consumption and production (44%), Goal 4: quality education (41%), Goal 17: partnerships for the goals (39%) and Goal 11: sustainable cities and communities (38%). For additional details, see the ESEM report (Dupain et al., 2021).

[8] See Appendix 1 for further details about REInSER and the European ADRION programme.

The rationale behind an approach focused on the enhancement of institutional capacity, local innovation systems and networking, with a general emphasis on improving the social and institutional environment for entrepreneurship, is well-supported by theoretical and empirical evidence in the academic literature (for comprehensive reviews, see Urbano et al., 2019; Bjørnskov & Foss, 2016). Creating the right policy and legal framework remains a complementary challenge for a variety of reasons including, for example, the wide sectoral diversity and typology of legal forms, as emphasised in the recent Action Plan for the Social Economy (European Commission, 2021).

The Policy and Legal Framework for Social Entrepreneurship

The Adrion area includes EU member states (Croatia, Greece, Italy, Slovenia) and EU candidate countries (Albania, Bosnia-Herzegovina, Montenegro, Serbia) at the crossroads between the Mediterranean and Eastern Europe and represents a strategic area for the processes of Europeanisation and European integration (Belloni, 2020).[9]

What do we know about the policy and legal framework for social entrepreneurship in these countries? Generally, the social economy sector seems characterised by a wide diversity and rapid ongoing changes in the Adrion countries. Recent evidence from the comprehensive comparative analysis carried out by Borzaga et al. on social enterprises in European and neighbouring countries reveals, not surprisingly, a 'colourful picture' characterised by 'different traditions, a variety of public policies, diverse legal and institutional frameworks' (Borzaga et al., 2020).

Based on the existing evidence and the information collected from REInSER project partners, we have structured a summary of the main characteristics of the Adrion countries. Table 4.1 presents a comparative overview of the policy and institutional background, focusing on the degree of acceptance of social enterprises (SEs), the existence of a legal definition in relation to the EU operational definition, countries' national policies and the existence of a specific fiscal framework.

Looking at the first aspect, the degree of acceptance of the social enterprise concept varies significantly across countries, ranging from an

[9] See Appendix 1 for further details about the geographical area and the main EU policy initiatives.

Table 4.1 Social entrepreneurship in the Adrion countries: policy and institutional background

	Institutional acceptance/Legal recognition	*Legal definition of social enterprises*	*National policies*	*Fiscal framework*
Albania	Emerging acceptance	Law on Social Enterprises (65/2016) limits SEs to non-profit organisations, specific sectors and 30% of marginalised employees	No specific policy	No fiscal benefits
Bosnia-Herzegovina	Emerging acceptance	No official definition	No specific policy	No fiscal benefits
Croatia	Politically and legally accepted but narrow understanding and weak self-recognition	The Strategy for Social Entrepreneurship Development (2015) provides a definition of SEs that closely matches that of the EU (except for some minor aspects)	Strategy for Civil Society Development 2012–2016 and Strategy for Social Entrepreneurship Development 2015	No fiscal benefits
Greece	Challenged by other concepts such as social economy, and social and solidarity economy	In Law on Social and Solidarity Economy (4430/2016) the definition of social and solidarity economy largely resembles the EU definition	Strategic Pact for the Development of Social Entrepreneurship (2013)	Specific fiscal benefits for social enterprises

(*continued*)

Table 4.1 (continued)

	Institutional acceptance/Legal recognition	*Legal definition of social enterprises*	*National policies*	*Fiscal framework*
Italy	Politically and legally accepted and large self-recognition	Closely matches the EU operational definition (Law on Social Cooperatives 381/1991; Legislative Decree on SEs 155/2006; Reform of the Third Sector and SE 106/2016)	Italy Social Economy 2022 (Ministry of Economic Development) Incentives for companies to spread and strengthen the social economy (Ministerial decree 3 July 2015)	Specific fiscal benefits for social enterprises
Montenegro	Challenged by other concepts, such as corporate social responsibility, social entrepreneurship and social innovation	No official definition	No specific policy	No fiscal benefits
Serbia	Politically and legally accepted but narrow understanding and weak self-recognition	No official definition	No specific policy	No fiscal benefits
Slovenia	Politically and legally accepted but narrow understanding and weak self-recognition	Matches the EU definition (Act on Social Entrepreneurship 2018)	Strategy for Social Entrepreneurship 2013–2016 Strategy for the Development of Social Economy 2019–2029 (under development)	No fiscal benefits

Sources: The table's contents are mainly based on the European Commission's comparative synthesis report (Borzaga et al., 2020) and the country reports and country fiches from the European Union study 'Social enterprises and Their Ecosystems in Europe', available at https://euricse.eu/en/social-enterprises-and-their-ecosystems-in-europe-mapping-study/. Additional information retrieved from REInSER comparative reports, available at https://reinser.adrioninterreg.eu/library

'emerging acceptance' (Albania & Bosnia-Herzegovina) to 'large recognition' and 'full political and legal acceptance' (Italy). Acceptance seems to depend on the relevance of the phenomenon and the existence of similar concepts. It is worth noting that a further distinction relates to the coexistence of political and legal acceptance and a weak level of self-recognition from the same businesses (as in the case of Croatia, Slovenia and Serbia).

Where the existence of legal definitions in line with the EU operational definition is concerned, the comparison shows a close match in Italy, Slovenia and Croatia, while partly matching in Greece but completely missing in the remaining countries. This is not surprising as, for the national policy framework too, EU member countries (Croatia, Greece, Italy and Slovenia) have implemented specific policies, although with different degrees of development, driven by the European policies for social economy. No specific policy is reported for each candidate country, even if a growing recognition of the importance of social entrepreneurship clearly emerges in many policy documents.

Finally, fiscal measures vary across countries, and the framework is rather complex, as benefits may be granted based on the legal forms adopted or on operational activities. The nature of social enterprises means that, in all the countries we studied, they may be able to exploit some fiscal benefits existing for other social organisations. Nevertheless, Italy and Greece have introduced distinct measures for social enterprises, especially in the form of tax exemptions on retained profits (for additional information on this point, see Borzaga et al., 2020, p. 91).

To conclude, it is worth pointing out that this region is extremely varied in several respects, alongside the diversity of legal frameworks and experiences in the social economy sector. Beyond their wide socioeconomic disparities and recent histories marked by ethnic and political tensions that persist, these countries hold different EU membership and Schengen statuses. These differences have significant practical implications for transnational cooperation activities, particularly in the context of managing migrant and asylum seeker flows. On this issue, the lack of a strategy for integration, possibly stemming from limited knowledge of the migration flows, and the lack of awareness about potential growth opportunities may affect ongoing transnational cooperation programmes and the macroregional EU strategy for the Adriatic–Ionian Region (EUSAIR), potentially hindering the process of socioeconomic convergence.

The Variety of Structural Conditions in the Adrion Area: Evidence from GEI Data

Economic, cultural and institutional conditions are crucial for the development of countries' entrepreneurial activities and economic growth. In this respect, the European Commission is deeply committed to creating a conducive environment and to levelling up disparities across member states. This holds especially for the social and solidarity economy sector, as it contributes significantly to inclusive and sustainable growth. However, the level of its diffusion remains unbalanced across European countries, especially in the Adrion region.

This section provides an overview of the overall health and development of entrepreneurship ecosystems in the Adrion countries. Using data from the GEI, we analyse the conditions and structural factors potentially hindering or enabling social and traditional entrepreneurial activity in these countries and how the former have evolved over recent years. Evidence is based on data available from GEI reports and datasets, aggregated in the form of an unbalanced panel running the period 2006–2019.[10] This composite index considers both individual and institutional conditions related to the micro- and macro-level aspects of entrepreneurship, aggregated along three main dimensions indicating entrepreneurial attitudes, abilities and aspirations. As we explore in further detail below, the indicator takes into account several measures: cultural and institutional factors, economic and financial characteristics, human capital, technology and infrastructure aspects.[11]

Figure 4.1 displays the level of development of the entrepreneurial ecosystems in 137 countries measured by the GEI in 2019. Looking at the last available data for the index, two key facts emerge. First, the overall distribution displays significant variance, with about 78 points separating

[10] The assembled country dataset used in this chapter is available upon request.

[11] The index aims to measure the quality and dynamics of entrepreneurship ecosystems at the national level, elaborating individual data surveys and macro data from a variety of international sources including the World Bank, Transparency International, the World Economic Forum, UNESCO and the Global Entrepreneurship Monitor (GEM). For further details, see the GEI report 2019 (Acs et al., 2020). A regional version for the EU countries (REDI) is also available, but uniquely for 2013 (Szerb et al., 2013). Since its introduction, the GEI has gone through many smaller changes and in 2016 it was extensively reviewed and renewed. Further details are available at http://thegedi.org/global-entrepreneurship-and-development-index/.

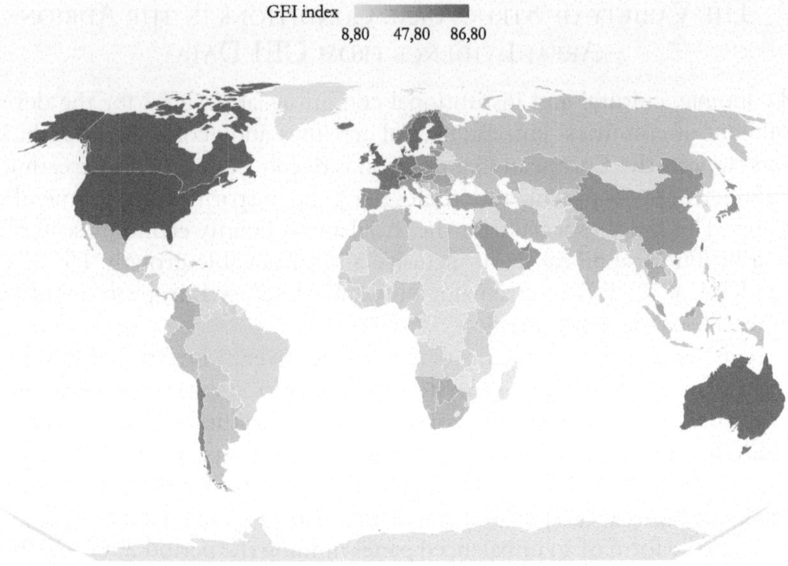

Fig. 4.1 Global Entrepreneurship Index 2019. (Source: Authors' elaboration on GEI data. Note: Light grey indicates countries with no data)

the top-performing and bottom-performing countries. Second, the Mediterranean and Balkan areas are positioned in the middle to lower tiers of the global ranking, while there is a small cluster of countries scoring high percentages in all the pillars constituting the GEI: the USA, Canada, Australia and the northern European countries.

How do Adrion countries rank globally in terms of entrepreneurial ecosystem development? Slovenia stands out among the top countries, ranking 23rd out of 137, placing in the first quintile with a GEI of 56.5. Italy falls into the second quintile with a score around ten points lower (45.1), followed by Croatia (36.1) and Greece (35.4). The remaining countries score below the global average (34): Montenegro (31.8), Serbia (28.6), Albania (22.5) and Bosnia-Herzegovina (19.5).[12]

If we look more closely at our area of interest, Fig. 4.2 further confirms a remarkable gap when restricting the comparison to Europe as a whole. Generally, Adrion countries all score below the threshold of the European

[12] To look at the full global ranking, see the GEI report 2019 (Acs et al., 2020, p. 19).

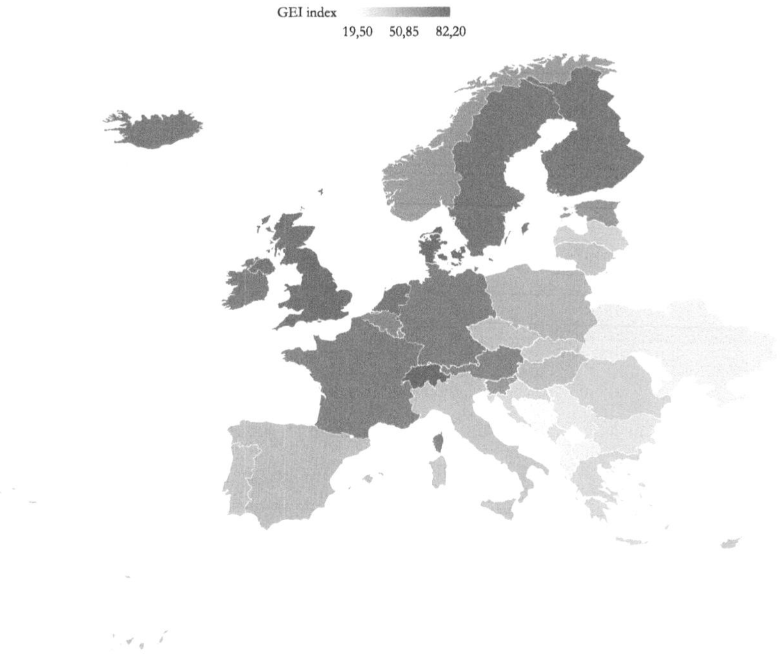

Fig. 4.2 Global Entrepreneurship Index 2019 in European countries. (Source: Authors' elaboration on GEI data)

average (50.7), except for Slovenia. In this case, in 2019 the difference between the minimum and maximum values expressing the level of development of the entrepreneurial ecosystem was about 62 points, with Eastern European and Mediterranean countries lagging well behind.

To look at how Adrion countries have evolved over time, we plot in Fig. 4.3 the GEI trends for 2006–2019. A remarkable overall gap between the top and bottom countries is immediately apparent. Although this disparity was gradually reduced from 2008 to 2009 onwards, the recent available data indicate a consistently widening gap. Three out of the eight countries showed an increase (Slovenia, Italy and Serbia), while the others remained stable or experienced a decrease (as in the case of Albania).

It is worth noting that, while the level of development of the business and entrepreneurial ecosystem in Italy falls significantly below that of the top countries and even below the EU average, the index has shown a

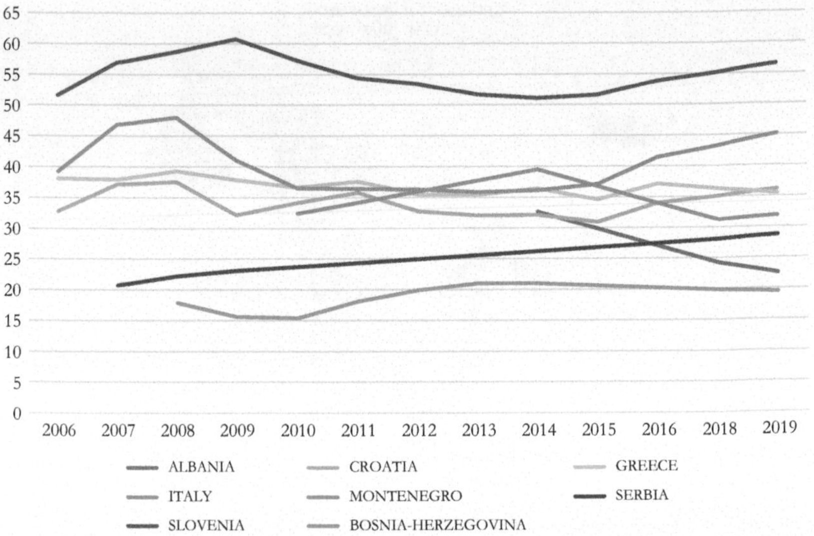

Fig. 4.3 Global Entrepreneurship Index in the Adrion countries, 2006–2019. (Source: Authors' elaboration on GEI data)

notable increase in recent years. In 2019, Italy was among the top ten countries globally in terms of the biggest gains in GEI score, indicating promising signs of catching up with the best-performing European nations.

Is the GEI Driven by Specific Factors?

The GEI is conceived as constituted by 14 pillars along three main dimensions (the sub-indexes). According to Acs et al. (2014, p. 3), country-level entrepreneurship is defined as 'the dynamic, institutionally embedded interaction between entrepreneurial attitudes, entrepreneurial abilities, and entrepreneurial aspirations by individuals, which drives the allocation of resources through the creation and operation of new ventures'. Using this definition, a multi-level index is built based on individual and institutional variables, pillars, sub-indexes and the composite GEI itself. The sub-indexes, expressing entrepreneurial attitudes, abilities and aspirations, contain different pillars, 'which can be interpreted as the quasi-independent building blocks of this entrepreneurship index' (Acs et al., 2014, p. 26).[13]

The following graphical evidence (Fig. 4.4) illustrates how the Adrion countries perform in each pillar constituting the composite GEI, allowing for an assessment of specific strengths and weaknesses over time. Radar graphs compare the 14 pillars at two data points: the first year available and 2019. In these graphs, each variable is plotted along a spoke-like axis. The distance of each data point from the centre of the graph represents

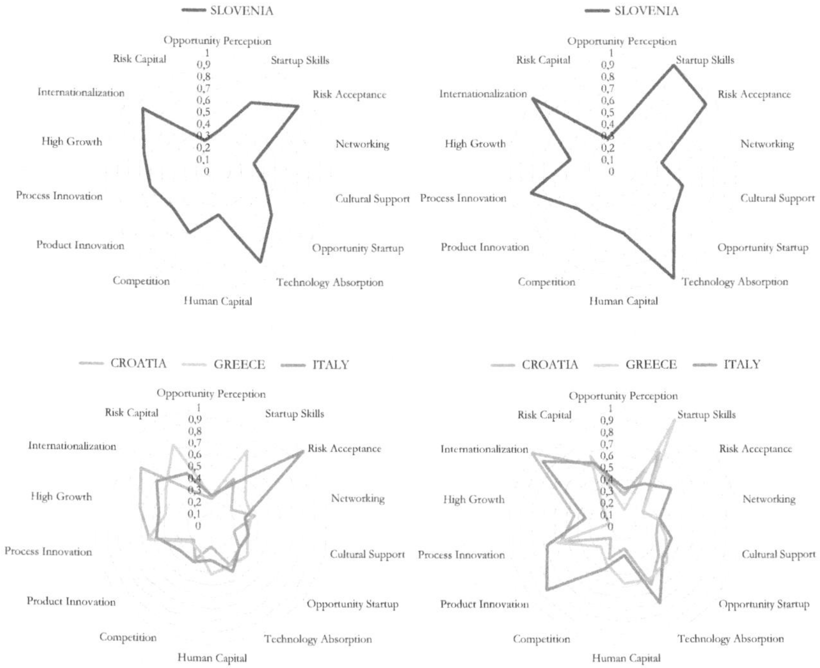

Fig. 4.4 GEI pillars in 2006 and 2019. (Source: Authors' elaboration on GEI data)

[13]Generally, entrepreneurial attitudes refer to how a country thinks about entrepreneurship; abilities refer to skills, while the third dimension refers to entrepreneurial aspirations. Appendix 2 reports the full structure of the index (Table 4.3) with additional details on the three main entrepreneurial dimensions (or sub-indexes). It also offers a comparison between the Adrion countries and other European countries (Fig. 4.7).

the value or magnitude of the corresponding variable, with points closer to the centre indicating lower values. Countries are grouped based on their common characteristics and overall performance.

The first fact emerging from Fig. 4.4 is that Slovenia is a stand-alone case for remarkable scores in different pillars embodied in all the entrepreneurial dimensions (or sub-indexes). Looking at its evolution from 2006 (left-hand graph) to 2019 (right-hand graph), one can note that Slovenia has enhanced its start-up skills, technology absorption and internationalisation, reaching the highest scores (equal to 1), while significant progress has also been achieved in process innovation. The measure of 'risk capital' remains relatively unchanged, which is a matter of concern, because the availability of risk capital is crucial for meeting growth aspirations. Overall, when considering the aggregation of pillars within the main dimensions, we can conclude that the entrepreneurial ecosystem thrives as a result of positive individual attitudes to entrepreneurship and favourable institutional embedding (start-up skills and risk acceptance); aspirations and expectations expressed through high levels of internationalisation and process innovation; and capabilities in terms of technology absorption.

Looking at the other EU member countries (Croatia, Greece and Italy), it becomes apparent that they are somewhat behind Slovenia. Overall, the development of entrepreneurial ecosystems in these countries is not harmonious, as they are characterised by various weaknesses in crucial structural conditions and specific areas with high levels of development.

When examining Italy's country profile, it stands out in the domain of entrepreneurial aspirations, showing significant advances in internationalisation, product innovation and process innovation—far exceeding the European average. This indicates that the country's entrepreneurs exhibit a strong inclination to enter global markets and confirms its vocation for international expansion with high levels of innovation in both products and processes. Furthermore, Italy reveals a distinctive strength in its technology absorption capacity, which has increased significantly above the European average. When comparing data, a significant reduction in risk acceptance is also apparent. This pillar reflects the willingness of individuals to take the risk of starting a business (the individual component) and the presence of unstable institutions (the institutional component). The major weakness concerns entrepreneurs' human capital, as measured by levels of education, training in business and ability to move in the labour market.

In the case of Greece, it is notable that the overall decreasing trend in the GEI is driven by very low levels in pillars such as opportunity perception and risk acceptance—reflecting entrepreneurial attitudes—and high growth—reflecting entrepreneurial aspirations. When comparing the variations between 2006 and 2019, these pillars have undergone considerable downward movement, and can therefore be considered critical areas needing structural interventions. However, an exceptional upward increase reaching the maximum value for start-up skills, a measure revealing adequate skills of individuals and quality of education, should be noted as specific strengths of this country. The entrepreneurial abilities dimension, including the four pillars from opportunity start-up to competition, remains a balanced area with moderate increases in all pillars, although still below the European average.

Croatia exhibits a similar trend in the overall evaluation of variables that express the quality of its entrepreneurial environment. In this case as well, the overall GEI is influenced by specific underdeveloped factors, such as the product innovation, human capital and risk acceptance pillars. These significant weaknesses reflect limitations in expanding internationally in terms of product innovation, followed by the poor quality of entrepreneurs in terms of education and training. More importantly, the low inclination to take risks when starting a business, coupled with unstable institutions, poses significant challenges for new entrepreneurship. When comparing changes between 2006 and 2019, we observe moderate shifts across different pillars. Notably, there is a remarkable increase in the internationalisation pillar, indicating an increased entrepreneurial interest in entering global markets with valuable ideas. Interestingly, Croatia aligns with the EU average in terms of entrepreneurial aspirations, especially concerning the ability to expand internationally through process innovation and the availability of risk capital.

Figure 4.5 compares the 14 pillars for the remaining two groups of countries, with the left-hand graph showing data for the first year and the right-hand graph displaying data for 2019. These nations are characterised by a similar pattern in the evolution of indicators over time and exhibit very low levels of entrepreneurial development. Note that the panel dataset is unbalanced. Data for these countries are as follows: Bosnia-Herzegovina (2008–2019), Montenegro (2010–2019), Serbia (2007–2019) and Albania (2014–2019).

However, when examining data for Montenegro and Serbia, it becomes evident that, despite their poor overall performance, these countries do

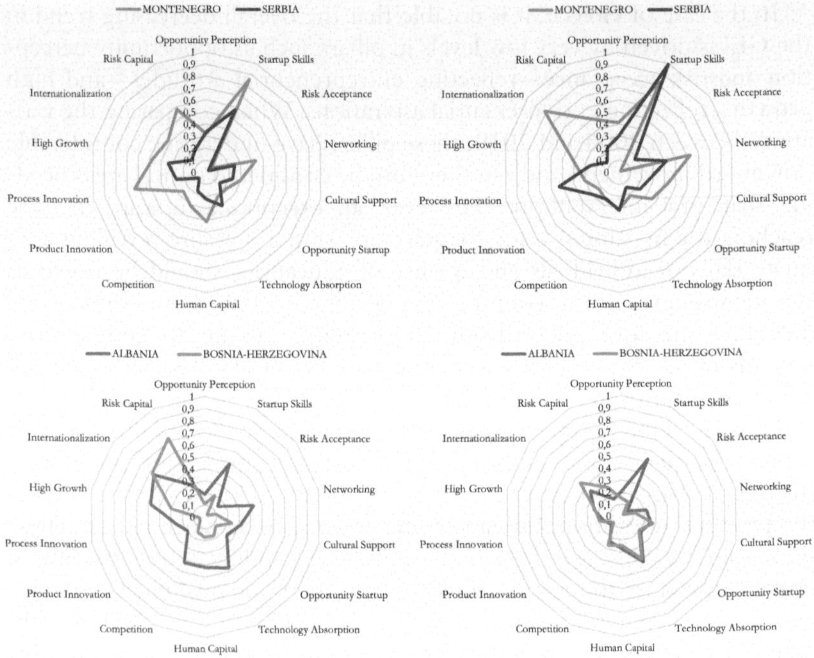

Fig. 4.5 GEI pillars in 2008 and 2019. (Note: Authors' elaboration on GEI data)

have the skills necessary to start a business, coupled with the quality of tertiary education (measured by the start-up skills pillar). Importantly, it is worth noting that this crucial factor seems to be an inherent feature of these countries, as indicated by their high scores, which aligns with the European average in the initial year and even surpasses it in 2019. In the case of Montenegro, this is accompanied by high aspirations to enter global markets with valuable ideas (internationalisation) and ability in networking. Data for Serbia confirm that the country is undergoing a general growth process, with positive variations over time across almost all pillars, except for capacity in technology absorption, which is significantly reduced.

This comparative overview concludes with Albania and Bosnia-Herzegovina, both characterised by very low levels of entrepreneurial ecosystem development. Looking at the evolution over time of the data, it is apparent that these ecosystems are still in their early stages and demonstrate an overall decrease in most pillars. However, there are some promising signs regarding the levels of start-up skills and technology absorption in Albania and in internationalisation and technology absorption in Bosnia.[14]

Summing Up

Table 4.2 presents the strongest and weakest areas for each country, using minimum and maximum values, along with the percentage of the individual and institutional components of the GEI for the most recent available year. Three key findings emerge from this analysis.

First, the Adrion countries share common strengths in the domain of entrepreneurial attitudes, revealing adequate start-up skills coupled by the quality of tertiary education (referred to as 'start-up skills'), and in the domain of entrepreneurial aspirations, showing a high propensity and capacity to enter global markets with valuable ideas (referred to as 'internationalisation').

Table 4.2 Strengths and weaknesses of the Adrion countries in 2019

	Strongest area	*Weakest area*	*Individual score*	*Institutional score*
Albania	Start-up skills	Risk acceptance	57%	38%
Bosnia-Herzegovina	Internationalisation	Risk acceptance	58%	33%
Croatia	Internationalisation	Product innovation	60%	47%
Greece	Start-up skills	High growth	56%	59%
Italy	Internationalisation	Human capital	58%	62%
Montenegro	Start-up skills	Risk acceptance	66%	45%
Serbia	Start-up skills	Internationalisation	57%	43%
Slovenia	Start-up skills Technology absorption Internationalisation	Risk capital	65%	66%

Note: Data for individual and institutional components refer to the GEI for 2018

[14] Note that for Albania individual information to construct the GEI pillars are not directly available from the GEM Adult Population Survey. The individual variable method of calculation therefore employed data from neighbouring and similar countries, in this case, the average of Macedonia and Bosnia for 2016 and 2017, respectively. See Bonyadi and Sarreshtehdari (2021) for a recent critical review of this estimation method.

Second, Slovenia stands out as a distinctive case, demonstrating substantial improvements in technology absorption capacity, internationalisation and start-up skills.

Third, the low willingness to take the risk of starting a business and the presence of unstable institutions (referred to as 'risk acceptance') emerge as major challenges in the Adrion countries. Risk aversion also represents a significant weakness in Greece, Croatia and Serbia, where scores are very low. Italy and Slovenia are exceptions, showing medium and high scores, respectively. Addressing this issue should be considered a critical priority, albeit one that requires long-run structural interventions.

Finally, it is worth emphasising that the underdeveloped entrepreneurial ecosystems in Albania and Bosnia-Herzegovina are primarily attributed to deficiencies in the institutional component. Their low institutional scores (38% and 33%, respectively) reflect the quality of the institutions supporting entrepreneurship.[15] These low scores can be seen as a key factor contributing to the overall low performance of these countries and represent a significant barrier to entrepreneurship. To further support this argument, recent research on the Italian case investigated the effect of the quality of institutions on the employment dynamics of social enterprises over time, confirming the crucial role of institutions and emphasising the importance of regional-level analysis (Savoia et al., 2023). The regional version of the GEI, the Regional Entrepreneurship and Development Index (REDI), further emphasises the importance of sub-national analysis. Unfortunately, available data only cover the year 2013, but confirm that country-level analyses may obscure striking internal disparities. For example, this is evident in Italy's historical north–south divide and in the gap between the capital region, Attiki, and the rest of Greece (Szerb et al., 2013, p. 52).

Conclusions

Economic, cultural and institutional factors play a pivotal role in fostering entrepreneurial activities and driving economic growth within nations. In this respect, EU policy making is committed to levelling disparities across member states and creating an environment conducive to entrepreneurship, especially in the social and solidarity economy. This strategic policy objective holds particular relevance for several reasons.

[15] The individual score measures the entrepreneurial quality of the people in the ecosystem.

The social economy constitutes a prominent feature of the political agenda for its significant role in driving sustainable development by fostering inclusive employment growth, addressing inequalities, promoting equal opportunities and civic participation, and facing up to major environmental and social issues. Thanks to their intrinsic nature, social economy entities also display remarkable resilience in terms of employment protection during economic crisis, representing one of the largest inclusive job creation areas in European countries. Furthermore, the social economy has been instrumental in addressing the needs of refugees and migrants, especially during the COVID-19 pandemic, by offering essential services.

These features are all gaining importance as the level of recognition and diffusion of social enterprises remains unbalanced across European countries, especially in the Adrion region. In this respect, we emphasise the need to investigate the evolution of the disparities in the institutional and business environments and the underlying dynamics of the single components of the ecosystems.

In this chapter, we have focused on the Adriatic–Ionian macro-region, an interesting yet overlooked area of research, investigating its unique diversity in relation to the development of entrepreneurial ecosystems. After discussing the importance of the social economy, we have provided an overview of the policy background for social entrepreneurship, indicating encouraging signs of acceptance of this concept and alignment with the European framework. Using a composite measure expressing the overall health and development of entrepreneurship ecosystems (i.e. the Global Entrepreneurship Index), we have concentrated on changes in the main index and in the individual and institutional factors that allow entrepreneurship to thrive, thereby exploring how the level of the Adrion countries' entrepreneurial ecosystems has evolved over time and which factors are driving these trends.

The following key findings have emerged from the foregoing analysis. Overall, the notable structural disparities affecting the Adrion countries are heavily influencing their positions in the global and European rankings. In this context, Slovenia represents an exception, being positioned above the global and European average and following the best performers, while recent evidence for Italy indicates promising signs that it is catching up with the best-performing European nations. In terms of a comparative analysis of specific factors, the Adrion countries share common strengths in the domains of entrepreneurial attitudes and entrepreneurial aspirations, revealing adequate start-up skills and good quality tertiary education and showing a high propensity and capacity to enter global markets with valuable ideas. Slovenia again stands out as a distinctive case, demonstrating substantial improvements in technology absorption capacity and internationalisation, as well as start-up skills. Finally, a low willingness to take the risk of starting a business and the presence of unstable institutions (referred to as 'risk acceptance') have emerged as major challenges in these countries. Addressing this issue should be considered a critical priority, although it requires long-run structural interventions.

Our study contributes to the broad debate on the development of entrepreneurship and the business environment. While it has adopted a descriptive approach, it provides initial comparative evidence for an overlooked area, offering some insights for further quantitative analysis along two primary research trajectories. First, it encourages firm-level studies investigating the effects of such factors on the creation and growth of entrepreneurial activities, distinguishing between for-profit and non-profit entrepreneurship. Second, it advocates an increased focus on geographical analysis, promoting a greater awareness of regional-level dynamics within countries. Entrepreneurial ecosystems are intricate socioeconomic structures that evolve over time. Understanding their functioning necessitates a close examination of how various actors operate within local ecosystems and how local institutions shape the rules. In our case, this calls for a deeper investigation of structural aspects at disaggregated level, especially in broader contexts like Italy and Greece. This nuanced approach is crucial for comprehending local phenomena and designing effective territorial development policies that can foster entrepreneurship and economic growth.

Appendix 1

The Adriatic–Ionian macro-region (Adrion) includes both EU countries and candidate members and has been targeted by different EU policy initiatives because of its strategic importance in the processes of Europeanisation and European integration. Among these, the EU Strategy for the Adriatic and Ionian Region (EUSAIR) is a macro-regional strategy and constitutes the most significant recent effort to bridge the gap between the EU and the Western Balkans in terms of economic and infrastructural development and environmental protection (Belloni, 2020);[16] the Adrion programme (known as ADRION to distinguish it from the Adrion region) is a European transnational programme that invests in regional innovation systems, cultural and natural heritage, environmental resilience, sustainable transport and mobility, and capacity building.[17]

ADRION brings together eight countries in the Adriatic and Ionian region, four EU countries (Croatia, Greece, Italy and Slovenia) and four candidate countries (Albania, Bosnia and Herzegovina, Montenegro, Serbia), and aims to act as a policy driver and governance innovator. The geographical area of each country covers its national territory except for Italy, where the programme area covers 12 regions and two provinces (see Fig. 4.6).

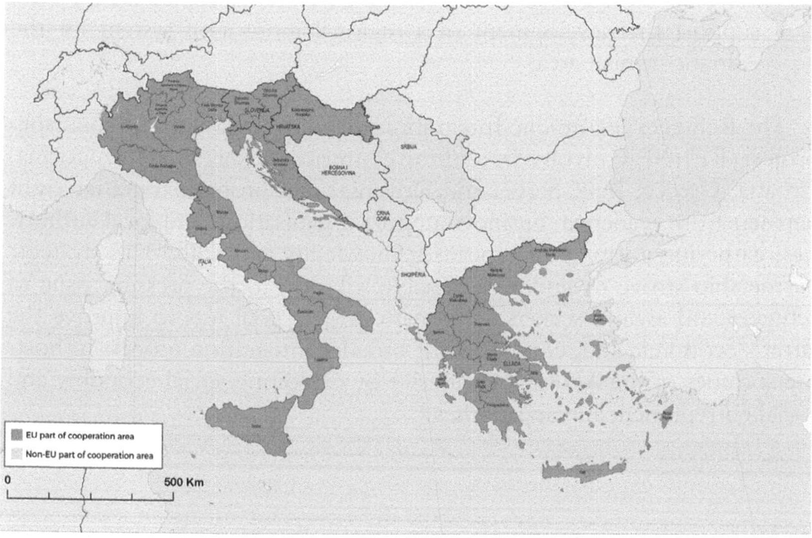

Fig. 4.6 Regional disaggregation of the Adrion countries, EU and non-EU cooperation area. (Source: https://www.adrioninterreg.eu/index.php/about-program/cooperation-area/)

[16] Official web page available at https://www.adriatic-ionian.eu/.

[17] Official web page available at https://www.adrioninterreg.eu/.

The sub-programme 2014–2020 INTERREG VB Adriatic–Ionian, including the REInSER project (see below), has a budget of €118 million funded by the European Regional Development Fund and is structured to:

- enhance capacity for integrated transport and mobility services and multimodality in the Adriatic–Ionian area;
- enhance the capacity in transnationally tackling environmental vulnerability, fragmentation and the safeguarding of ecosystem services in the Adriatic–Ionian area;
- facilitate the coordination and implementation of EUSAIR by enhancing the institutional capacity of public administrations and key stakeholders and by assisting the progress of implementation of joint priorities;
- promote the sustainable valorisation and preservation of natural and cultural heritage as growth assets in the Adriatic–Ionian area;
- support the development of a regional innovation system for the Adriatic–Ionian area.

The Refugees' Economic Integration through Social Entrepreneurship project (REInSER) involved six Adrion countries (Bosnia and Herzegovina, Croatia, Greece, Italy, Serbia and Slovenia) and brought together eight partners from academia, business support organisations and local authorities, gathering a variety of expertise, knowledge and skills. This strategic partnership strove to find a sustainable solution to the pressing issue of refugees and asylum seekers. The main project goal was to improve the latter's economic and, consequently, broader integration process in hosting societies of the ADRION initiative by exploiting social economy and social entrepreneurship approaches.[18]

[18] Official web pages available at https://keep.eu/projects/25271/Refugees-Economic-Integrati-EN/ and https://scienzeaziendali.unibo.it/en/research/research-projects/european-projects/interreg-adrion-refugees-economic-integration-through-social-entrepreneurship-reinser.

Appendix 2

Figure 4.7 reports GEI and sub-indexes for Adrion countries compared to the European average. Table 4.3 illustrates the full structure of the Global Entrepreneurship Index (GEI). This composite index considers both individual and institutional conditions related to the micro- and macro-level aspects of entrepreneurship that constitute 'pillars', aggregated along three main dimensions indicating entrepreneurial attitudes, abilities and aspirations ('sub-indexes').

Entrepreneurial attitudes reflect individuals' perspectives on entrepreneurship, encompassing aspects such as recognising opportunities, possessing start-up skills, evaluating risk and fostering networks and the cultural encouragement of entrepreneurial endeavours. Institutional embedding, on the other hand, is expressed through factors such as

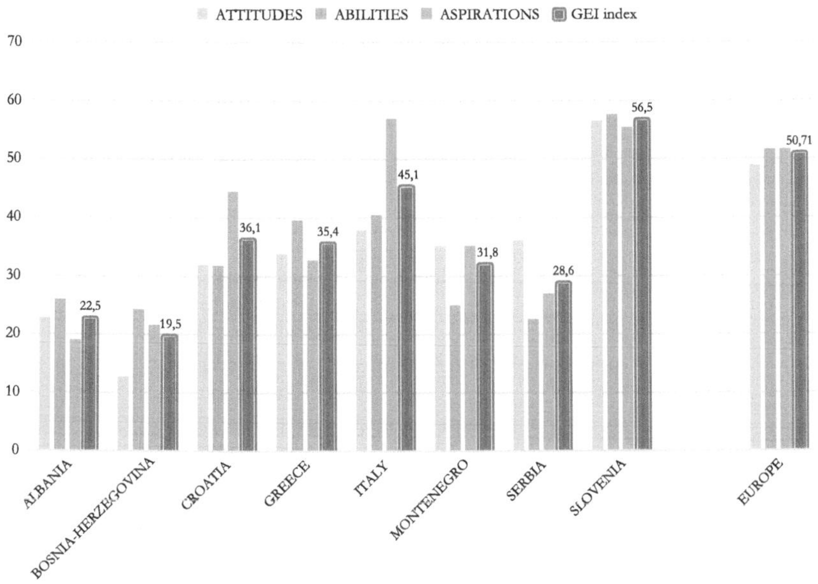

Fig. 4.7 GEI and sub-indexes compared to the European average in 2019. (Source: Author's elaboration on GEI data. Note: Data for Europe include the EU 27 plus Switzerland, Iceland, the UK, Ukraine, North Macedonia, Norway, Albania, Bosnia-Herzegovina, Montenegro and Serbia)

Table 4.3 The structure of the Global Entrepreneurship Index

	Sub-indexes	*Pillars*	*Individual and Institutional Variables*
Global Entrepreneurship Index	Attitudes sub-index	Opportunity perception	*Opportunity recognition* Freedom (Economic Freedom*Property rights)
		Start-up skills	*Skill perception* Education (Tertiary education*Quality of education)
		Risk acceptance	*Risk perception* Country risk
		Networking	*Know entrepreneurs* Agglomeration (Urbanisation*Infrastucture)
		Cultural support	*Career status* Corruption
	Abilities sub-index	Opportunity Start-up	*Opportunity motivation* Governance (Taxation*Good governance)
		Technology absorption	*Technology level* Technology absorption
		Human capital	*Educational level* Labour market (Staff training*Labour freedom)
		Competition	*Competitors* Competitiveness (Market dominance*Regulation)
	Aspiration sub-index	Product innovation	*New product* Tech transfer
		Process innovation	*New technology* Science (GERD*((average quality of scientifical institutions+availability of scientists and engineers))
		High growth	*Gazelle* Finance and strategy (Venture capital*Business sophistication)
		Internationalisation	*Export* Economic complexity
		Risk capital	*Informal investment* Depth of capital market

Source: Reproduced from Acs et al. (2020)

Note: Individual variables are in italics and institutional ones in roman type property rights, economic freedom, educational quality, a country's risk profile, connectivity potential and the prevalence of corruption.

Entrepreneurial abilities involve key attributes of an entrepreneur that influence the growth potential of new start-ups. These attributes include the entrepreneur's motivation, whether driven by opportunity or necessity, the potential technology intensity of the start-up, the level of education, the level of market competition and the digital readiness of the start-up. These individual factors align with corresponding institutional factors, such as taxation and government efficiency, technology absorption capacity, labour market flexibility and workforce training, as well as the power of influential business groups and the effectiveness of anti-monopoly regulations.

Finally, entrepreneurial aspiration pertains to the unique characteristics associated with entrepreneurial endeavours. It encompasses individual and institutional factors related to innovation in products and processes, including technology transfer, the utilisation of scientific research capabilities, ambitious growth expectations, the accessibility of venture capital, strategic proficiency in finance and strategy, international expansion and the presence of risk financing.

For the sources and a full description of the pillars, individual variables and institutional indicators, refer to the GEI report 2019 (Acs et al., 2020, pp. 28–39).

References

Acs, Z. J., Autio, E., & Szerb, L. (2014). National Systems of Entrepreneurship: Measurement Issues and Policy Implications. *Research Policy, 43*(3), 476–494.

Acs, Z. J., Szerb, L., Lafuente, E., & Márkus, G. (2020). *The Global Entrepreneurship Index 2019*. Global Entrepreneurship and Development Institute (GEDI). http://thegedi.org/downloads/

Belloni, R. (2020). Assessing the Rise of Macro-regionalism in Europe: The EU Strategy for the Adriatic and Ionian Region (EUSAIR). *Journal of International Relations and Development, 23*, 814–839.

Bjørnskov, C., & Foss, N. J. (2016). Institutions, Entrepreneurship, and Economic Growth: What Do We Know and What Do We Still Need to Know? *Academy of Management Perspectives, 30*(3), 292–315.

Bonyadi, E., & Sarreshtehdari, L. (2021). The Global Entrepreneurship Index (GEI): A Critical Review. *Journal of Global Entrepreneurship Research, 11*(1), 469–488.

Borzaga, C., Galera, G., Franchini, B., Chiomento, S., Nogales, R., & Carini, C. (2020). *Social Enterprises and Their Ecosystems in Europe*. Comparative Synthesis Report. Publications Office of the European Union.

Dupain, W., Pilia, O., Wunsch, M., Hoffmann, P., Scharpe, K., Mair, J., Raith, M., & Bosma, N. (2021). *The State of Social Enterprise in Europe – European Social Enterprise Monitor 2020–2021*. Euclid Network. https://euclidnetwork.eu/portfolio-posts/european-social-enterprise-monitor-esem/

European Commission. (2011). Social Business Initiative – Creating a Favourable Climate for Social Enterprises, Key Stakeholders in the Social Economy and Innovation. COM(2011) 682 final.

European Commission. (2012). Towards a Job-rich Recovery. COM(2012) 173 final.

European Commission. (2020). *Social Enterprises and Their Ecosystems in Europe*. Comparative Synthesis Report. [Carlo Borzaga, Giulia Galera, Barbara Franchini, Stefania Chiomento, Rocío Nogales, and Chiara Carini]. Publications Office of the European Union.

European Commission. (2021, December). Building an Economy that Works for People: An Action Plan for the Social Economy. COM(778).

Harima, A., & Freudenberg, J. (2020). Co-creation of Social Entrepreneurial Opportunities with Refugees. *Journal of Social Entrepreneurship, 11*(1), 40–64.

Huysentruyt, M., & Ute, S. (2017). *Social Enterprises, an Economic Force for Building More Inclusive Societies? Evidence from the SEFORÏS Study*. SEFORÏS.

Huysentruyt, M., Mair, J., Le Coq, C., Rimac, T., & Stephan, U. (2016). *Cross-country Report: A First Cross-country Analysis and Profiling of Social Enterprises Prepared by the SEFORÏS Research Consortium*. SEFORÏS/European Commission.

Kourtit, K., & Nijkamp, P. (2011). Strategic Choice Analysis by Expert Panels for Migration Impact Assessment. *International Journal of Business and Globalization, 7*(2), 166–194.

Massey, D. S., Arango, J., Hugo, G., Kouaouci, A., Pellegrino, A., & Taylor, J. E. (1993). Theories of International Migration: A Review and Appraisal. *Population and Development Review, 19*(3), 431–466.

OECD. (2020). *Regional Strategies for the Social Economy: Examples from France, Spain, Sweden and Poland*. OECD Publishing. OECD Local Economic and Employment Development (LEED) Papers, no. 2020/03. https://doi.org/10.1787/76995b39-en

OECD and EU. (2017). *Boosting Social Enterprise Development: Good Practice Compendium*. OECD Publishing.

OECD and EU. (2018). *Settling in 2018: Indicators of Immigrant Integration*. European Union. https://doi.org/10.1787/9789264307216-en

OECD and EU. (2019). *The Missing Entrepreneurs 2019: Policies for Inclusive Entrepreneurship*. OECD Publishing. https://doi.org/10.1787/3ed84801-en

Savoia, F., Bandini, F., Bolzani, D., & Grassi, E. (2023). Quality of Institutions and Employment Dynamics of Social Enterprises: Evidence from Italian Regions. *Finance Research Letters, 56*, 104080.

Szerb, L., Ács, Z., Autio, E., Ortega-Argiles, R., & Komlosi, E. (2013). *REDI: The Regional Entrepreneurship and Development Index – Measuring Regional Entrepreneurship*. Final Report. GEDI. https://op.europa.eu/en/publication-detail/-/publication/afc2a25c-d650-4be0-85cc-621ac9bab53c

United Nations. (2018). *Entrepreneurship for Sustainable Development: Report of the Secretary General*. Retrieved October 5, 2023, from https://digitallibrary.un.org/record/1639377?ln=en

Urbano, D., Aparicio, S., & Audretsch, D. (2019). Twenty-five Years of Research on Institutions, Entrepreneurship, and Economic Growth: What Has Been Learned? *Small Business Economics, 53*(1), 21–49.

CHAPTER 5

Social Entrepreneurship Addressing the Challenges and Opportunities of International Migration: A Review of the Literature

Eleonora Grassi, *Daniela Bolzani*, *and Federica Bandini*

Introduction

The last decades have been characterized by an increase in migration flows worldwide (IOM, 2020). International migration is a wide-ranging phenomenon "decisively shaping and reshaping the lives, the horizons, the very identities of tens of millions of actual and prospective migrants, as well as the lives, horizons and identities of those whom they encounter at their destinations" and of those left behind (Brubaker, 1991, p. 957). In

E. Grassi • D. Bolzani (✉) • F. Bandini
Department of Management, Alma Mater Studiorum-University of Bologna, Bologna, Italy
e-mail: eleonora.grassi5@unibo.it; daniela.bolzani@unibo.it; federica.bandini@unibo.it

S. Bianchini et al. (eds.), *Social Entrepreneurship and Migrants' Inclusion*, Sustainable Development Goals Series,
https://doi.org/10.1007/978-3-031-55791-0_5

this chapter, we adopt a general definition of international migrants as people moving away from their place of usual residence, "across an international border, temporarily or permanently, and for a variety of reasons" (IOM, 2019). International migration deals with dynamic social processes "linked to broader patterns of social transformation" (Castles, 2007), thus posing issues that have a transnational and interdisciplinary nature.

Many of the challenges related to international migration derive from the pressure between the expanding demands for international mobility driven by economic, ecological, social, political, technological, and cultural factors and a still limited supply of migration opportunities (Brubaker, 1991; McAuliffe & Triandafyllidou, 2021). Migrants can make sociocultural, civic-political, and economic contributions in destination and origin settings, which depend on the institutions and social structures and on migrants' characteristics (IOM, 2020). However, as international migration continues to be globally polarized towards highly developed countries (McAuliffe & Triandafyllidou, 2021), the issue of migrants' inclusion in their destination countries, together with wider social cohesion, has become a matter of public concern (IOM, 2020). Inclusion encompasses "achievement and access across the sectors of employment, housing, education and health; assumptions and practice regarding citizenship and rights; processes of social connection within and between groups within the community; and structural barriers to such connection related to language, culture and the local environment" (Ager & Strang, 2008). Inclusion is a challenging process that involves a wide array of actors, from communities to public authorities, and requires the development of new policies and organizational practices (Guo et al., 2020).

The literature has testified that migrants are likely to be subject to systemic barriers that prevent them from being fully included in local communities (Lee et al., 2020), leaving them in a marginalized position within society. In this context, social enterprises (SEs) are expected to operate as support organizations in the process of inclusion (Lee et al., 2020) since their raison d'être lies in the use of business logics to make an impact on society and communities, for instance, by increasing social cohesion or improving the situation of segments of the population that are excluded or marginalized (Saebi et al., 2019). SEs can be either for-profit or nonprofit entities (Gupta et al., 2020) and are characterized by the element of *hybridity*, since they combine a business organizational form with a social mission, therefore seeking to reach both financial sustainability and a social purpose (Battilana & Lee, 2014; Doherty et al., 2014). Thanks to their ability to create social value and their embeddedness in the local context, SEs are seen as privileged actors for the implementation of new practices aimed at responding to unmet social needs or societal grand challenges (Grimm et al., 2013; Markman et al., 2019), among which we can find the inclusion of refugees and other migrants in the host countries.

Despite the pressing challenges posed by international migration and the existence of multiple examples of how SEs can act in this regard, academic research addressing the role of SEs in catalysing migrants' contributions and addressing migrants' needs is still fragmented and lacks conceptual clarity. In this chapter, therefore, we contribute to the literature by investigating the following research question: *What is the relationship between social entrepreneurship and international migration?* We carry out a systematic literature review, bringing to light the scarcity of research in this field, the main topics addressed with respect to the antecedents, processes, and outcomes of social entrepreneurship in valuing migrants' contributions and addressing migrants' inclusion, theoretical and methodological considerations, and gaps that future studies should try to address.

Methodology

Data Collection

The first step of our literature review involved a query on Scopus and Web of Science, aimed at identifying all the academic articles related to the topic. The query included keywords related to the topic of migration ("*migrant**"; "*refugee**"; "*asyl**") matched with keywords pertaining to the field of social entrepreneurship ("*social entrepr**"; "*social business**"; "*social enterpris**") and limited to academic articles written in English and published before the end of February 2023. The results of the query consisted of a total of 83 records in Scopus and 85 records in Web of Science: once the duplicates were removed, the sample featured 92 records.

Then, we reviewed the articles' abstracts to drop from the sample those that did not address our topic of inquiry. These cases encompassed the following: the use of keywords in a different context than international migration (e.g., "*asylum*" used in psychotherapy); teaching case studies; articles focusing on SEs that do not have migrants as target beneficiaries; articles dealing with internal migrants or displaced people; articles dealing with entrepreneurship by refugees in general and not specifically on social entrepreneurship; interventions not consisting of SEs (e.g., governmental integration programmes); and articles where social entrepreneurship is not the core of the paper or is used in a different sense than business. This screening reduced the sample to 56 articles. We were not able to retrieve one article, leaving the resulting sample composed of 55 articles to be analysed.

The following step involved a careful reading of all the selected articles, which brought to the exclusion of 13 more articles from the sample because they were dealing with issues related to ethnicity or in-migration from other regions without specifying whether they were related to international migration (e.g., Xiang & Luk, 2011) and using SE working with migrants only as a research context and not as the object of the study (e.g., Longoni et al., 2019). The final sample thus consisted of 42 academic articles (listed in Appendix). Figure 5.1 summarizes the sample selection process.

Once the sample was established, we proceeded by coding the papers according to several dimensions (definitions of migrants and of SEs; research questions; theory employed; method; sample; home/host countries; etc.). This process informed us with a descriptive overview of the main characteristics and contents of the papers included in our sample.

Sample Description

The first retrieved article in the sample is dated 2010, and the trend of published articles shows an increase over time (Fig. 5.2). Confirming our initial intuition that the literature linking social entrepreneurship and international migration is fragmented, the retrieved articles were published across 37 academic outlets. By looking at the sources' subject areas,[1] the most represented one is "business, management and accounting" (43%), followed by "interdisciplinary" (24%) and "social sciences" (17%) (Fig. 5.3).

With the exception of two conceptual papers and one literature review, all the analysed articles were empirical. The vast majority of the empirical articles adopted a qualitative methodology, with only one article using a quantitative methodology and four articles implementing a mixed-method approach. Overall, single-case study research designs were the most widely used method in our sample (51%), which is not uncommon for emerging

[1] To define the subject area, we consulted the sources' profiles on Scopus, and we read the journals' descriptions when more than one subject was present.

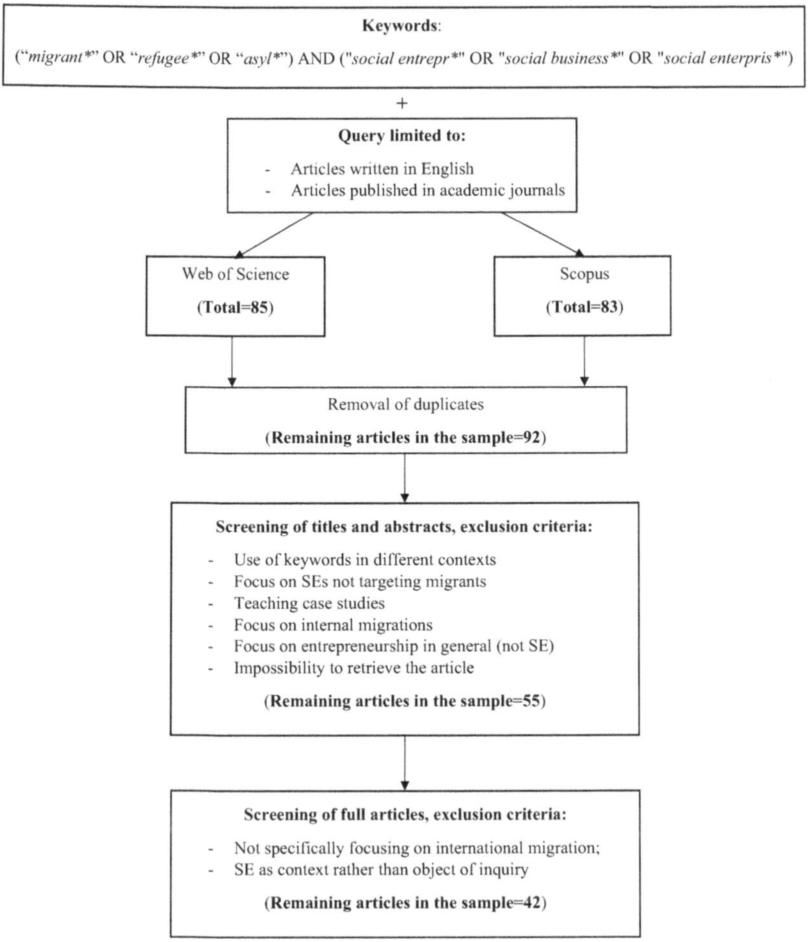

Fig. 5.1 Sample selection process. (Source: The authors' elaboration)

research topics and is characteristic of research about social enterprises (Gupta et al., 2020).

Given that studying international migrants should transcend national borders (Castles, 2007), we were interested in analysing the geographical contexts investigated in the retrieved papers. In this regard, 15 articles considered a specific migrant country of origin, while 36 articles

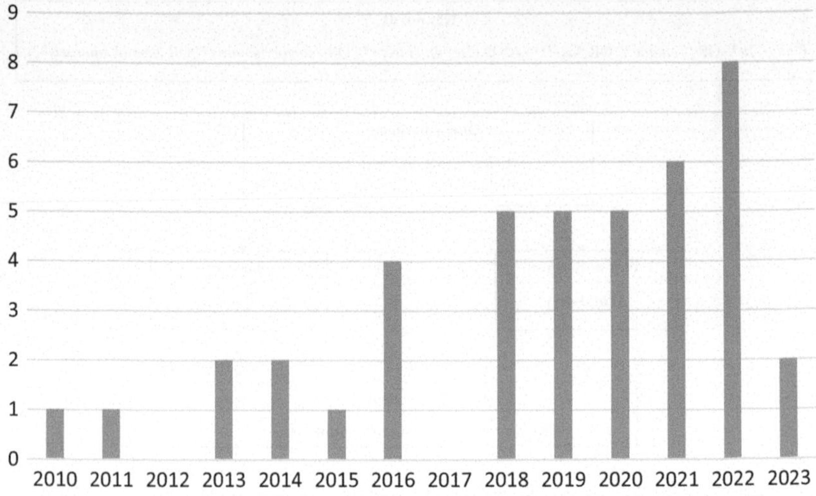

Fig. 5.2 Sampled articles: Publication year. (Source: The authors' elaboration. The number of published papers in 2023 should be interpreted considering that the data were extracted February 2023)

considered a specific host country. If we look at the macroregions in which these countries are located, we can state that the literature has been mostly concerned with migrants coming from the Middle East (27%) and East Africa (20%) (Fig. 5.4), being directed to and hosted in North America (27%), West Europe (24%), and Australia and Oceania (14%)[2] (Fig. 5.5).

Review Process

To answer our research question about the relationship between social entrepreneurship and international migration, we started by coding the objectives and findings of the articles included in the data collection stage. We proceeded by applying an input-process-output analytical framework, which is particularly useful for exploring entrepreneurial mechanisms (e.g., Bolzani et al., 2019; Saebi et al., 2019). During this phase, we categorized as "input" papers those dealing with the antecedent factors and mechanisms of social enterprise inception; as "process" articles those

[2] These proportions are computed on the number of articles considering a specific home or host country and not on the total of the sample.

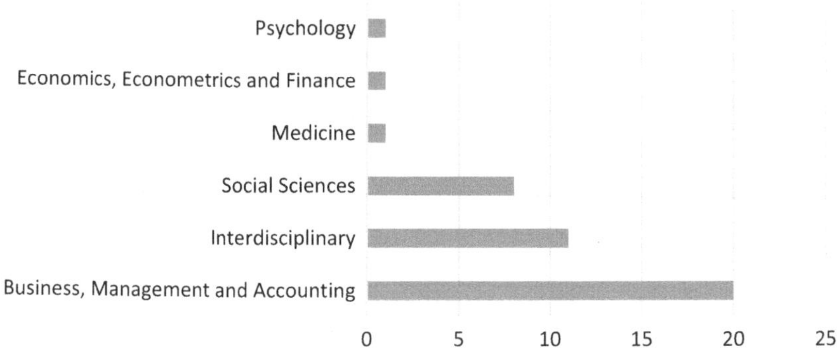

Fig. 5.3 Sampled articles. (Sources' subject area. Source: The authors' elaboration)

looking at the various angles of the developments taking place at the intersection of SE activities and international migration; and as "outputs" studies those focused on understanding the consequences of social enterprise actions.

Soon in our analysis, we realized the existence of two different kinds of SE that were analysed in regard to migrants' issues: (1) social enterprises created *for* migrants by local social entrepreneurs that want to provide means for inclusion, usually through employment; and (2) social enterprises created *by* migrants to generate social change and impact.[3] This important dimension largely influenced the objectives, topics, and findings observed in the sampled papers. We thus added this dimension to our analytical framework, categorizing the studies as regarding SEs created for or by migrants. We found that the sample is almost equally split between these two categories, with 48% of the papers relating to SE for migrants, 38% relating to SE by migrants, and the remaining 14% referring to both.

After coding the articles, we conducted our analysis by crossing the two analytical dimensions considered in the coding: (a) whether the scope of the research is to explore the input, process, or outputs of the social entrepreneurial phenomenon (*input-process-output*); and (b) whether the SE that constitutes the object of inquiry is created by migrants or by local social entrepreneurs (*for/by* migrants).

[3] Freudenberg and Halberstadt (2018) had found a similar categorization to be relevant in reviewing literature about social enterprises and refugees' workers' integration.

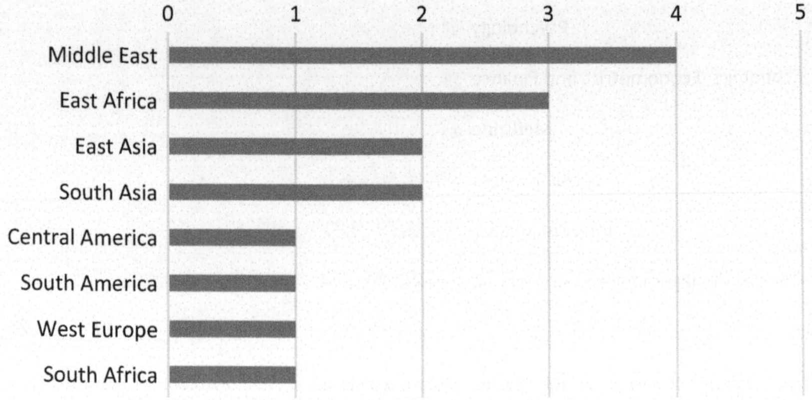

Fig. 5.4 Sampled articles: Home countries' region considered in empirical studies. (Source: The authors' elaboration. Unit of measure: number of papers)

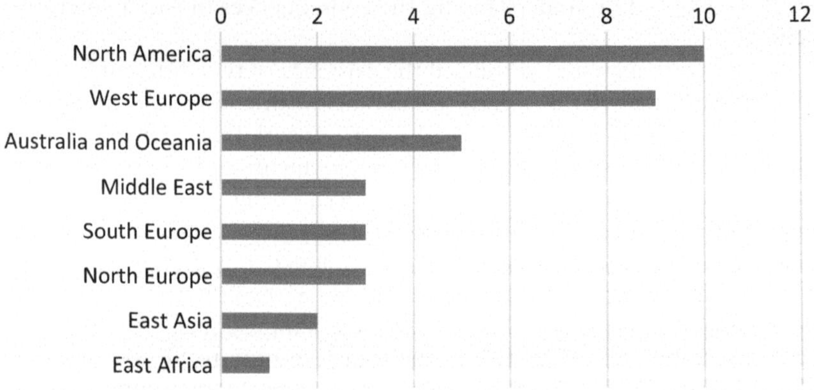

Fig. 5.5 Sampled articles: Host countries' region considered in empirical studies. (Source: The authors' elaboration. Unit of measure: number of papers)

Findings

In this section, we systematize the extant literature about SE and migrants' inclusion along the two main dimensions summarized in Table 5.1: focus of the paper in terms of inputs, processes, or outputs of SEs for inclusion; and creation of SEs by or for migrants. For each paper, we identify the

Table 5.1 Summary overview of the topics of the papers

	BY	*FOR*
INPUTS	Entry into SE (Abou Chakra & Al Jardali, 2022; Cheung et al., 2019; Modesti et al., 2020; Senthanar et al., 2021) Motivation for SE (Chen, 2021; Cruz & Fromm, 2019; Lee, 2018; Senthanar et al., 2021) Social entrepreneurship opportunities (Harima et al., 2021; Harima & Freudenberg, 2020)	Motivation for SE (Mittermaier et al., 2023)
PROCESSES	Legitimacy building (Bolzani et al., 2020; Madichie, 2016) Managing tensions (Mafico et al., 2021; Sepulveda et al., 2013) Effectiveness of social entrepreneurship practices (Schwabenland & Hirst, 2022)	Legitimacy building (Barinaga, 2013; Rivna & Gress, 2023; Tracey & Phillips, 2016) Managing tensions (Forde & Mackenzie, 2010; Leslie et al., 2023; McKay et al., 2018; Murphy et al., 2018; Rantisi & Leslie, 2021; Streuli & Lewis, 2022) Effectiveness of social entrepreneurship practices (Kidd & McKenzie, 2014; Kuckertz et al., 2023; McSweeney, 2023; Norbäck & Zapata Campos, 2022)
OUTPUTS	Impact on migrants' wellbeing (Burrai et al., 2022; Kong, 2019) Work integration (Freudenberg & Halberstadt, 2018)	Impact on migrants' wellbeing (Haines et al., 2018; Kong, 2011; Praetorius et al., 2016; Sahyoun et al., 2019) Work integration (Bidet & Jeong, 2016; Calò et al., 2022; Freudenberg & Halberstadt, 2018; Gaillard & Hughes, 2014; Idiakez et al., 2022; Walk et al., 2015)

main topic(s) and create clusters of similar papers in terms of these topics. We allowed each paper to cover and be classified across one or more topics.

As a first descriptive consideration, the literature about the antecedents to SEs tied to international migration issues (inputs) was mainly studied by scholars focusing on SEs founded by migrants; contrarily, the majority of the articles related to impacts of SEs in the domain of migrants' inclusion (outputs) have analysed SE created for migrants. Such a trend shows that, in general terms, research about SE *by* migrants is more focused on migrants as the main protagonist of SE creation, thus aiming to understand the factors that explain enterprise creation. Research about SE *for* migrants, instead, is rather focused on migrants as a subject to be served and included in host countries, thus focusing on defining SEs' impact on society. In the following, we dig deeper into the details of the different dimensions, highlighting what aspects of the relationship between SEs and international migration opportunities and challenges have been studied in the literature.

Inputs

Through our analysis, we have identified ten papers dealing with input factors investigating social entrepreneurship related to international migration issues. As anticipated above, research in this category has been mostly focused on understanding the antecedent factors leading migrants to set up SEs. In particular, the extant literature has focused on three aspects: the factors driving *entry into SE*, the *entrepreneurs' motivations* to do that, and the creation of *social entrepreneurship opportunities.*

In terms of entry conditions, the extant literature has examined the diverse factors encouraging or preventing refugees and other migrants from setting up SEs. A prominent role has indeed been recognized in the context in terms of financial and regulatory aspects (Senthanar et al., 2021), as well as the cognitive, legal and normative configurations of the institutional environment and how it is perceived (Abou Chakra & Al Jardali, 2022). Furthermore, the role of both social and psychological capital has been claimed to be of significant importance in the creation of SEs (Modesti et al., 2020), since the degree of hope, resilience, and confidence perceived by migrants, together with their social relationships, can constitute great advantages. It is important to mention here that several conditions can nuance how migrants build and develop their social capital in the host country. For example, migrants having the opportunity to study in the host country can build on the ties developed with their peers in education institutions (e.g., Amornsiripanitch et al., 2021; Modesti et al., 2020); policies allowing refugees to be placed in reception centres at their arrival can favour the creation of bridging networks with local inhabitants rather than bonding networks within their ethnic communities (Modesti et al., 2020). In regard to actively engaging in the process of venture creation, some studies have shown that practices of bricolage, meant as the "redeployment of discarded, disused, or unwanted resources-at-hand, including physical artefacts, skills, and knowledge, in ways different from those for which they were originally intended" (Jayawarna et al., 2014), can help in overcoming resource constraints that refugees and other migrants could encounter (Cheung et al., 2019).

Analysing the motivations leading migrants to set up SEs, the literature contemplates push factors such as financial needs as possible drivers of the willingness to establish new SEs (Senthanar et al., 2021). However, the motivation that has received the greatest attention in the literature regards these social businesses aimed at providing some help to the home country. Such businesses are identified as transnational social enterprises and involve "using some form of commercial activities and business principles within dual social fields (i.e., home and host country), with the goal of solving development problems in the entrepreneurs' countries of origin" (Bolzani et al., 2020). In these cases, the main motivation is the desire to help the home country (Lee, 2018), which can be driven by place attachment and sense of duty (Cruz & Fromm, 2019) or guilt when disasters happen and migrants are not there to partake in recovery efforts (Chen, 2021). On the other hand, the only paper considering the motivations to set up SEs for migrants by local entrepreneurs (Mittermaier et al., 2023) has observed two different kinds of motivations: the willingness to help others and entrepreneurial aspirations. In the first case, the primary object of social entrepreneurs consists of scaling their pro-social activities to increase their capacity to meet migrants' needs in the short term. In the second case, social entrepreneurs' efforts are directed towards building their own organization and establishing viable businesses that will also address migrants' needs in the long run (Mittermaier et al., 2023).

Another important aspect relating to the start-up of social businesses is the identification or creation of entrepreneurial opportunities. The literature provides evidence of different mechanisms at play with migrant social entrepreneurs. In transnational social enterprises, for example, the main mechanism of entrepreneurial opportunity recognition is homeland problem solving, which can benefit from a detachment from the context of the targeted country (Harima et al., 2021). In addition, multiple advantages can be achieved by exploiting the complementarity of different actors, such as when migrants and locals work together. Migrants in fact can provide direct knowledge of the issues to be approached, connections with the target community and feedback, while locals have institutional knowledge and access to key stakeholders in the territory (Harima & Freudenberg, 2020).

Processes

The articles analysing the process through which SEs intersect with migration issues explore multiple facets of organizational practices. Three topics are present in both streams of literature concerning social entrepreneurship by and for migrants: practices of *legitimacy building*, *tension management*, and *effectiveness of SE*.

Legitimacy building is an important aspect for new ventures and could be highly challenging for social enterprises (Ruebottom, 2013). In these terms, the analysed papers both in the *by* and *for* dimension have reported that for the social change to be reached, founders must engage in discursive efforts aimed at increasing the legitimacy of their organizations (Madichie, 2016) through the construction of frames that justify and legitimate their actions (Barinaga, 2013). This need comes from the fact that there is often a lack of awareness of the goals of SEs, which makes it more difficult to access finance and reach the stated objectives (Rivna & Gress, 2023). However, the legitimation of a social entrepreneurial activity poses different challenges that can be different according to whether the founder is a migrant or a local entrepreneur. In the case of transnational social enterprises founded by migrants, for example, such efforts need to be directed to key stakeholders both in the home and in the host country, addressing different institutional environments, and go hand in hand with the individual legitimacy of the founders (Bolzani et al., 2020). On the other hand, for local social enterprises, the challenge could come from a possible stigma that shifts from the beneficiaries of the organization (in this case migrants) to the organization itself and that can be addressed through a strong identity affirmation of the social mission of the venture (Tracey & Phillips, 2016).

Regarding managing tensions, the main task for both kinds of SEs lies in balancing the business and the social logics and thus refers to the hybrid nature of these ventures (Sepulveda et al., 2013). In enterprises founded by migrants, this tension is intensified by the interculturality of migrant entrepreneurs and by structural barriers such as inequality or social exclusion (Mafico et al., 2021). The way such tensions are addressed mirrors the experience of the founders: migrants who experienced low barriers to social inclusion (e.g., those with a high socioeconomic status) are more likely to engage in efforts to integrate social and commercial objectives; migrants who experienced high barriers to social inclusion and negative intercultural experiences differentiate more between the two logics; and migrants who have had neither positive nor negative experiences of inclusion have a mixed approach (Mafico et al., 2021).

On the other hand, managing hybridity in SE established for migrants' inclusion poses some questions in terms of the ethics of the practices put in use by the organization. When the enterprise focuses too much on the commercial aspect, centring its practices on profit generation and incorporation of neoliberal values, it risks alienating the same communities that it is meant to serve (Forde & Mackenzie, 2010; Streuli & Lewis, 2022). Rantisi and Leslie (2021), for example, have observed that social enterprises aimed at promoting work inclusion can instead contribute to the commodification of the labour market if their practices are too close to the market logics. However, also giving too much prominence to the social aspect can trigger negative effects, as adopting practices closer to the logics of charities could undermine the aim of promoting dignity and reinforce feelings of shame and insecurity in beneficiaries (McKay et al., 2018). To find the right balance, Leslie et al. (2023) suggest adopting a critical approach when defining the practices of the SE, which should be directed at building participant self-esteem and truly empowering their targets.

Finally, research has acknowledged the possibility for SEs to trigger social change and challenge poverty and inequality through their everyday activities (McSweeney, 2023) and has thus tried to understand which organizational practices can be more effective for this aim. The majority of studies addressing this topic in our sample refer to SEs founded by local entrepreneurs, which are often not from the community they intend to serve and thus can have problems in understanding how to take action (Murphy et al., 2018). Kidd and McKenzie (2014) observed some features that can enhance organizational effectiveness, including the personal investment and involvement of leaders, who are therefore able to recognize what is actually needed, feel problems as their own, adopt an action-oriented approach, and increase social capital by making connections. Another aspect that has been emphasized is the multiple advantages of collaboration, for example, in cross-sector partnerships, which allow the codevelopment of solutions and a deeper understanding of the context (Kuckertz et al., 2023) or the placement of participants at the centre of the innovation process to increase their ability to gain skills and confidence (Kraff & Jernsand, 2020). Similarly, Norbäck and Zapata Campos (2022) highlight the benefits of collaborative governance of SE projects by a diversity of actors coming from the private sector and civil society through the construction of spaces that allow mutual learning, participation in design and implementation of services. However, the difficulties of collaboration and coordinating multiple actors have also been noted since possible misalignments could hamper the achievement of social objectives (Kraff & Jernsand, 2020).

One paper (Schwabenland & Hirst, 2022) has analysed the processes through which a refugee-led social enterprise can generate and organize solidarity relationships with the local community and potential cultural transformation by drawing on managed impressions of both similar "dividualities" (e.g., salient professional identities) and different "dividualities" (e.g., identity as refugee, noncitizen, or marginalized individual).

Outputs

The last group of articles is focused on understanding the consequences of the activities of SEs run by or for migrants. Two main outputs are taken into consideration by these studies: the impact on migrants' wellbeing and their work integration.

In terms of improving migrants' wellbeing, studies focusing on SEs founded by migrants argue that this kind of entrepreneurial activity plays a prominent role in migrants' resettlement experience since social entrepreneurship might allow migrants to harness their prior knowledge and skills and create new skills, as well as improve financial and social conditions (Kong, 2019). For example, Burrai et al. (2022) have analysed a successful experience in the tourism sector, which has shown that SEs can help in deconstructing sociocultural barriers often existent in current societies between "westerners" (locals) and "strangers" (refugees) and that collaborating and cocreating solutions with refugees can help in increasing their integration. Similarly, the literature centred on the effects of SEs targeting migrants' inclusion has shed light on the multiple positive effects of SE interventions. Among these, there is increased decision-making capacity and food security (Sahyoun et al., 2019); heightened self-esteem, confidence and emotional security (Kong, 2011); improved self-efficacy and mental wellbeing (Praetorius et al., 2016); and increased personal connections (Haines et al., 2018).

To date, the category of studies that has received the greatest attention is the one exploring the relation between SE activities and migrants' work integration. Although inclusion is a multifaceted concept encompassing different dimensions of immigrants' resettlement experience, such as housing, education, and health (Ager & Strang, 2008), the employment dimension is the dimension that has been studied the most. Inclusion through employment is in fact one of the main concerns for both policy-makers and organizations, which are looking for successful practices to implement and can be reached through different means. In the papers covered by our analysis, Freudenberg and Halberstadt (2018) distinguished among nonrefugees' entrepreneurial activities and refugees' self-employment that aim at achieving employment integration for refugees. Among the nonrefugees' entrepreneurial activities, they contemplate social intrapreneurship, which involves entrepreneurial efforts internal to another organization, and social entrepreneurship, which either creates job opportunities for refugees or brings together refugee employees and employers, thus acting as an intermediary. On the other hand, social entrepreneurial activities by refugees are mainly aimed at fostering self-employment, but they could also be directed at employing other refugees.

This dimension of work integration has been mainly studied in contexts of SEs founded by locals, which are often referred to as Work Integration Social Enterprises (WISEs), but the potential of cooperative organizations has also been pointed out (Idiakez et al., 2022). These studies have observed that SEs could be important vehicles of inclusion, especially for the most vulnerable groups, such as refugees and asylum seekers, by "offering opportunities for socialisation and networking, as well as gaining work experience via volunteering" (Calò et al., 2022). Migrants working in SEs indeed have the chance to build working skills, and their jobs are more stable and paid than in the traditional market (Bidet & Jeong, 2016). In addition, research has shown that the benefits of working in such environments not only provide tangible outcomes such as a job, improved skills and knowledge but also intangible outcomes such as social networks, a sense of self-efficacy and personal growth (Walk et al., 2015). However, assessing the impact of these realities is not easy and requires resources and time to be deployed (Walk et al., 2015).

Discussion and Conclusion

This work has shown that social entrepreneurship is increasingly intertwined with issues related to international migration. The academic literature on this topic is fragmented and interdisciplinary, even if mostly published in business and management outlets. To date, scholarly knowledge is predominantly empirical, focusing on migration flows originating from Southern countries (e.g., Africa, Middle East, and South and East

Asia) and headed to Northern countries (e.g., North America, Europe, and Oceania). The specific definition of migrants with respect to their legal status is often not reported in the sampled papers, which include both refugees and other migrants with different motivations, entry routes, preparedness to migrate, and prospects for stay in the host country or return to the home country (Ager & Strang, 2008; Cassarino, 2004). These descriptive data suggest the need for future scholarly work to document more nuanced evidence of this phenomenon. First, considering the changing patterns of migration flows at the global level, not only directed South–North but also to other directions (e.g., Elo, 2016), and the increasing prevalence of social entrepreneurship models around the globe (United Nations, 2020), more work is needed to broaden our perspective and include geographical and institutional contexts involved in international migration all around the globe. Second, future studies should pay more attention to the subcategories of migrants emerging from increasingly complex patterns, for instance, in terms of formal identity (legal status), generation, mixed-origin, multilocation, diversity of migratory patterns, and transnationalism (Elo et al., 2022) or other intersectional categories of identity, such as gender, race, educational, and socioeconomic background (Bolzani, 2024).

Our review identified a distinction between articles studying SE started and owned by migrants and studies focusing on SE created by native entrepreneurs for migrants. In addition, our analysis distinguished across inputs, processes, and outcomes to social entrepreneurship by/for migrants.

The results of our review shed some light on the antecedent factors explaining social entrepreneurship concerned with migration issues. Migrants become or not social entrepreneurs due to personal and contextual barriers and facilitators, such as individual psychological and social capital (Modesti et al., 2020), financial and regulatory structures, and cognitive, legal and normative institutions (Abou Chakra & Al Jardali, 2022; Senthanar et al., 2021). To overcome such resource constraints (Cheung et al., 2019), migrants can implement practices of bricolage[4] (Jayawarna et al., 2014). Starting an SE can be a form of necessity entrepreneurship aimed at making a living (Senthanar et al., 2021), but the

[4] Bricolage indicates the practice of "making do by combining the resources at hand to solve problems or catch opportunities" (Baker & Nelson, 2005).

majority of studies have identified cases of opportunity entrepreneurship based on altruistic motivations towards the home country (Bolzani et al., 2020; Lee, 2018; Cruz & Fromm, 2019; Chen, 2021). The reviewed literature here has provided interesting insights into how migrant entrepreneurs can recognize opportunities based on their individually idiosyncratic migratory patterns, for instance, by formulating problem-solving business ideas based on their detachment from the home country (Harima et al., 2021) or working together with home country individuals and organizations to exploit resource complementarities (Harima & Freudenberg, 2020). While some of the factors that facilitate the entrepreneurship are overall similar to those for nonmigrant or nonsocial entrepreneurs, we suggest that future studies could be more refined in identifying inputs to entry into SE that can be more salient for migrant entrepreneurs, for instance, due to racialized labour and entrepreneurial markets (Bruton et al., 2023; Knight, 2016), inclusion in social networks, decision-making, and power structures (Senthanar et al., 2021). On the other hand, our review shows that there is a dearth of research about the antecedents to social entrepreneurship for migrants. Evidence suggests that such activities can be motivated by the willingness to help others or by entrepreneurial aspirations, having important implications in the short-term versus long-term impact of SE activities (Mittermaier et al., 2023). Future research is needed on the motivations, types of activities, and types of organizational configurations (e.g., involvement of migrants in decision-making structures and daily operations) in SEs for migrants.

Our review highlighted that racialized social structures and discrimination towards migrants, together with a limited understanding of the operations and objectives of social enterprises (Rivna & Gress, 2023), pose challenges to SEs established by and for migrants, which can be approached through legitimacy building, for instance, with discursive practices and storytelling (Barinaga, 2013; Madichie, 2016). The available studies suggest that the socially marginal position of migrants, either as entrepreneurs or beneficiaries of SEs' activities, is a key factor in driving these processes. For example, SEs run by native entrepreneurs often need to face a possible stigma that shifts from the beneficiaries of the organization (in this case, migrants) to the organization itself (Tracey & Phillips, 2016). Instead, migrant social entrepreneurs can legitimize their SEs in the eyes of key stakeholders, thus also increasing their own personal status both in the home and in the host country (Bolzani et al., 2020).

The cultural diversity of migrant entrepreneurs, together with their marginal position in home country social structures, is a factor that affects how these entrepreneurs deal with the tensions between the commercial and social logics pursued by SEs (Mafico et al., 2021). The reviewed studies suggest that migrants who experienced low barriers to social inclusion (e.g., those with a high socioeconomic status) are more likely to navigate the hybridity of SEs (Mafico et al., 2021). To date, there is a need to better understand how migrants' individual diversity affects these processes, for instance, due to their different cultural understanding of the meaning of social or commercial goals or their privilege in terms of identity categories, such as class, race, and gender. It is also important to better understand how SEs deal with hybridity through their strategies and activities. In fact, when SEs are established for vulnerable groups such as migrants, focusing too much on the commercial aspect brings about the risk of alienating the same communities that it is meant to serve (Forde & Mackenzie, 2010; Streuli & Lewis, 2022; Rantisi & Leslie, 2021). In contrast, emphasizing social aspects can degenerate in a charitable approach towards beneficiaries, undermining the promotion of their dignity and self-esteem (McKay et al., 2018). In this regard, balancing the two different logics could derive from a move of SEs towards policies and practices of equity, diversity, and inclusion based on a critical appraisal of privilege in and around the organization (e.g., Leslie et al., 2023).

Several studies included in our review have focused on how SEs can be effectively managed to generate an impact and trigger social change (McSweeney, 2023). Effectiveness might be impaired in SEs established for migrants by native entrepreneurs, since they might have a weak understanding of the problems and needs of their target group (Murphy et al., 2018). Effectiveness might also be impaired for SEs established by migrant entrepreneurs due to their lack of connections and trust on behalf of the local community (Schwabenland & Hirst, 2022). Some solutions to these issues can be found in the personal investment and involvement of SE leaders (Kidd & McKenzie, 2014), storytelling and impression management (Schwabenland & Hirst, 2022), engagement in multistakeholder collaborations and collaborative governance (Kuckertz et al., 2023; Norbäck & Zapata Campos, 2022), or involvement of beneficiaries in service codesign or codelivery (Kraff & Jernsand, 2020). Future studies should provide more empirical evidence about the processes fostered across different solutions, highlighting both their benefits—such as providing a deeper understanding of the context, mutual learning across actors, participation, and codevelopment of solutions—and their costs—related to collaboration and coordination (Kraff & Jernsand, 2020). In addition, future studies could provide evidence of configurational approaches when SEs' solutions are more or less effective in producing impact and social change, identifying boundary conditions at multiple levels of analysis (e.g., individual, team, organizational, and environmental).

In terms of outcomes of SEs run by or for migrants, the reviewed studies have taken into account migrants' wellbeing and work integration. Becoming social entrepreneurs can allow migrants to harness their prior knowledge and skills or create new ones, as well as improving financial and social conditions (Kong, 2019), also by deconstructing or changing institutions and norms (e.g., Burrai et al., 2022). Additionally, SEs established to foster migrants' inclusion can generate multiple positive effects in terms of psychological and emotional wellbeing (e.g., Kong, 2011; Praetorius et al., 2016) and material wellbeing (e.g., Sahyoun et al., 2019; Haines et al., 2018). The majority of studies have considered the impacts of SEs established for migrants' work integration, which can offer not only work experience, improved skills and knowledge, and stable salaries but also opportunities for socialization and networking and personal growth (Bidet & Jeong, 2016; Calò et al., 2022; Walk et al., 2015). To date, as in general for the studies aiming at assessing the impact of social entrepreneurship, it is still difficult to measure the impact of SEs' solutions, as they involve a complex set of objectives and long-term approaches that are difficult to standardize and, consequently, to compare (Kroeger & Weber, 2014; Rawhouser et al., 2019).

We believe that there is an exciting and relevant space to be addressed by scholars in intersecting the domain of social entrepreneurship and migrants' engagement and integration in home countries, host countries, and transnational domains. We hope that this space of scholarly contribution will also be pushed by increased collaboration not only with SEs established by and for migrants but also with the wider entrepreneurial and social ecosystems involved in such activities—such as governments and policymakers, investors and financers, entrepreneurial support organizations, universities and other education institutions, and social and community organizations.

Appendix

Table 5.2 Sampled paper (ordered by publication year)

Authors	*Title*	*Year*	*Source title*
Forde C., Mackenzie R.	The ethical agendas of employment agencies towards migrant workers in the UK: Deciphering the codes	2010	*Journal of Business Ethics*
Kong E.	Building social and community cohesion: The role of social enterprises in facilitating settlement experiences for immigrants from non-English speaking backgrounds	2011	*International Journal of Interdisciplinary Social Sciences*
Barinaga E.	Politicising social entrepreneurship: Three Social Entrepreneurial Rationalities Toward Social Change	2013	*Journal of Social Entrepreneurship*
Sepulveda L., Syrett S., Calvo S.	Social enterprise and ethnic minorities: Exploring the consequences of the evolving British policy agenda	2013	*Environment and Planning C: Government and Policy*
Gaillard D., Hughes K.	Key considerations for facilitating employment of female Sudanese refugees in Australia	2014	*Journal of Management & Organization*
Kidd S., McKenzie K.	Social entrepreneurship and services for marginalized groups	2014	*Ethnicity and Inequalities in Health and Social Care*
Walk M., Greenspan I., Crossley H., Handy F.	Social return on investment analysis: A case study of a job and skills training program offered by a social enterprise	2015	*Nonprofit Management and Leadership*
Bidet E., Jeong B.G.	Social enterprise and work integration of North Korean migrants in South Korea	2016	*Contemporary Politics*
Madichie N.O.	The business of saving lives in Sub-Saharan Africa (SSA)—a social imperative? Insights from "The Global Soap Project"	2016	*Journal of Enterprising Communities*
Praetorius R.T., Mitschke D.B., Avila C.D., Kelly D.R., Henderson J.	Cultural integration through shared learning among resettled Bhutanese women	2016	*Journal of Human Behavior in the Social Environment*

(*continued*)

Table 5.2 (continued)

Authors	*Title*	*Year*	*Source title*
Tracey P., Phillips N.	Managing the consequences of organizational stigmatization: Identity work in a social enterprise	2016	*Academy of Management Journal*
Freudenberg J., Halberstadt J.	How to integrate refugees into the workforce—different opportunities for (social) entrepreneurship	2018	*Problemy zarzadzania—Management Issues*
Haines B.C., McKay F.H., Dunn M., Lippi K.	The role of social enterprise in food insecurity among asylum seekers	2018	*Health and Social Care in the Community*
Lee S.K.	From political activists to social entrepreneurs: Burmese refugees in South Korea	2018	*Journal of Refugee Studies*
McKay F.H., Lippi K., Dunn M., Haines B.C., Lindberg R.	Food-based social enterprises and asylum seekers: The food justice truck	2018	*Nutrients*
Murphy P.J., Smothers J., Novicevic M.M., Humphreys J.H., Roberts F.B., Kornetskyy A.	Social enterprise in Antebellum America: the case of Nashoba (1824–1829)	2018	*Journal of Management History*
Cheung C.W.M., Kwong C., Manzoor H., Rashid M.U., Bhattarai C., Kim Y.A.	The co-creation of social ventures through bricolage, for the displaced, by the displaced	2019	*International Journal of Entrepreneurial Behavior & Research*
Cruz A.D., Fromm I.	Understanding the emergence of a social enterprise by highly skilled migrants: The case of Honduras Global Europa	2019	*International Journal of Entrepreneurial Behavior &Research*
Green K.R.	Social return on investment: a women's cooperative critique	2019	*Social Enterprise Journal*
Kong E.	Harnessing and advancing knowledge in social enterprises: Theoretical and operational challenges in the refugee settlement experience	2019	*Journal of Social Entrepreneurship*
Sahyoun N.R., Jamaluddine Z., Choufani J., Mesmar S., Reese-Masterson A., Ghattas H.	A mixed-methods evaluation of community-based healthy kitchens as social enterprises for refugee women	2019	*BMC Public Health*

(*continued*)

Table 5.2 (continued)

Authors	*Title*	*Year*	*Source title*
Bolzani D., Marabello S., Honig B.	Exploring the multi-level processes of legitimacy in transnational social enterprises	2020	*Journal of Business Venturing*
Harima A., Freudenberg J.	Co-creation of Social Entrepreneurial Opportunities with Refugees	2020	*Journal of Social Entrepreneurship*
Kraff H., Jernsand E.M.	The roles of social enterprises in a Swedish labour market integration programme—opportunities and challenges for social innovation	2020	*Social Enterprise Journal*
Modesti C., Talamo A., Nicolais G., Recupero A.	Social and psychological capital for the start-up of social enterprises with a migratory background	2020	*Frontiers in Psychology*
Senthanar S., MacEachen E., Premji S., Bigelow P.	Entrepreneurial experiences of Syrian refugee women in Canada: a feminist grounded qualitative study	2020	*Small Business Economics*
Calo F., Montgomery T., Baglioni S.	Marginal players? The third sector and employability services for migrants, refugees and asylum seekers in the UK	2021	*Voluntas*
Harima A., Periac F., Murphy T., Picard S.	Entrepreneurial opportunities of refugees in Germany, France, and Ireland: Multiple embeddedness framework	2021	*International Entrepreneurship and Management Journal*
Mafico N., Krzeminska A., Härtel C., Keller J.	The mirroring of intercultural and hybridity experiences: A study of African immigrant social entrepreneurs	2021	*Journal of Business Venturing*
Rantisi N.M., Leslie D.	In and against the neoliberal state? The precarious siting of work integration social enterprises (WISEs) as counter-movement in Montreal, Quebec	2021	*Environment and Planning A*
Abou Chakra, SM; Al Jardali, H; Abdallah, K	Drivers of social entrepreneurial intentions of Palestinian refugees in Lebanon	2022	*Journal of Research in Marketing and Entrepreneurship*
Chen X.	Immigrant-owned small businesses' participation in diaspora philanthropy: A case study during the COVID-19 outbreak	2021	*New England Journal of Entrepreneurship*

(*continued*)

Table 5.2 (continued)

Authors	*Title*	*Year*	*Source title*
Mittermaier, A; Patzelt, H; Shepherd, DA	Motivating prosocial venturing in response to a humanitarian crisis: Building theory from the refugee crisis in Germany	2021	*Entrepreneurship Theory and Practice*
Burrai E.; Buda D.-M.; Stevenson E.	Tourism and refugee-crisis intersections: Co-creating tour guide experiences in Leeds, England	2022	*Journal of Sustainable Tourism*
Idiakez F.J.A.; Rodríguez J.L.; Etxeberria G.M.	Workers' cooperatives as a tool to promote labour market inclusion for migrants; [Las cooperativas de trabajo como instrumento para la inclusión laboral de los migrantes]	2022	*Boletin de la asociacion internacional de derecho cooperativo*
McSweeney M.	Sport and social entrepreneurship in the base-of-the-pyramid: The institutional work of refugees and a refugee-led organization in Uganda	2022	*Sport Management Review*
Norbäck M.; Zapata Campos M.J.	The market made us do it: Public procurement and collaborative labour market inclusion governance from below	2022	*Social Policy and Administration*
Rivna A.; Gress M.	Social entrepreneurship as a new business model. The case of refugee integration	2022	*Economic Research—Ekonomska istrazivanja*
Schwabenland C.; Hirst A.	Solidarity with Soufra: Dividuality and joint action with Palestinian women refugees	2022	*Organization*
Streuli S.; Lewis T.	Shifting priorities and neoliberal ideologies in refugee health intervention design in the US	2022	*Medical Anthropology: Cross Cultural Studies in Health and Illness*
Kuckertz A.; Bernhard A.; Berger E.S.C.; Dvouletý O.; Harms R.; Jack S.; Kibler E.	Scaling the right answers—creating and maintaining hope through social entrepreneurship in light of humanitarian crises	2023	*Journal of Business Venturing Insights*
Leslie D.; Rantisi N.; Black S.	Realizing the social mandate of work-integration social enterprises through an anti-racist feminist praxis and spatiality?	2023	*Geoforum*

References

Abou Chakra, S. M., & Al Jardali, H. (2022). Drivers of Social Entrepreneurial Intentions of Palestinian Refugees in Lebanon. *Journal of Research in Marketing and Entrepreneurship, 24*(2). https://doi.org/10.1108/JRME-02-2021-0014

Ager, A., & Strang, A. (2008). Understanding Integration: A Conceptual Framework. *Journal of Refugee Studies, 21*(2). https://doi.org/10.1093/jrs/fen016

Amornsiripanitch, N., Gompers, P. A., Hu, G., & Vasudevan, K. (2021). *Getting Schooled: The Role of Universities in Attracting Immigrant Entrepreneurs* (No. w28773). National Bureau of Economic Research.

Baker, T., & Nelson, R. E. (2005). Creating Something From Nothing: Resource Construction through Entrepreneurial Bricolage. *Administrative Science Quarterly, 50*(3). https://doi.org/10.2189/asqu.2005.50.3.329

Barinaga, E. (2013). Politicising Social Entrepreneurship—Three Social Entrepreneurial Rationalities Toward Social Change. *Journal of Social Entrepreneurship, 4*(3). https://doi.org/10.1080/19420676.2013.823100

Battilana, J., & Lee, M. (2014). Advancing Research on Hybrid Organizing—Insights from the Study of Social Enterprises. *Academy of Management Annals, 8*(1), 397–441.

Bidet, E., & Jeong, B. G. (2016). Social Enterprise and Work Integration of North Korean Migrants in South Korea. *Contemporary Politics, 22*(4). https://doi.org/10.1080/13569775.2016.1175094

Bolzani, D. (2024). 15 Years of Super-Diversity Studies: What Reflections for Migrant Entrepreneurship? In B. Glinka & J. Freiling (Eds.), *Handbook of Migrant Entrepreneurship*. De Gruyter. In Press.

Bolzani, D., Fini, R., Napolitano, S., & Toschi, L. (2019, January 21). Entrepreneurial Teams: An Input-Process-Outcome Framework. *Foundations and Trends in Entrepreneurship, 15*(2), 256–258. Available at SSRN: https://ssrn.com/abstract=3308003 or https://doi.org/10.2139/ssrn.3308003

Bolzani, D., Marabello, S., & Honig, B. (2020). Exploring the Multi-level Processes of Legitimacy in Transnational Social Enterprises. *Journal of Business Venturing, 35*(3). https://doi.org/10.1016/j.jbusvent.2019.06.002

Brubaker, R. (1991). International Migration: A Challenge for Humanity. *International Migration Review, 25*(4), 946–957.

Bruton, G. D., Lewis, A., Cerecedo-Lopez, J. A., & Chapman, K. (2023). A Racialized View of Entrepreneurship: A Review and Proposal For Future Research. *Academy of Management Annals, 17*(2). https://doi.org/10.5465/annals.2021.0185

Burrai, E., Buda, D. M., & Stevenson, E. (2022). Tourism and Refugee-Crisis Intersections: Co-creating Tour Guide Experiences in Leeds, England. *Journal of Sustainable Tourism*. https://doi.org/10.1080/09669582.2022.2072851

Calò, F., Montgomery, T., & Baglioni, S. (2022). Marginal Players? The Third Sector and Employability Services for Migrants, Refugees and Asylum Seekers in the UK. *Voluntas, 33*(5). https://doi.org/10.1007/s11266-020-00306-6

Cassarino, J. (2004). Theorising Return Migration: the Conceptual Approach to Return Migrants Revisited. *International Journal on Multicultural Societies, 6*(2), 253–279.

Castles, S. (2007). Twenty-First-Century Migration as a Challenge to Sociology. *Journal of Ethnic and Migration Studies, 33*(3), 351–371.

Chen, X. (2021). Immigrant-Owned Small Businesses' Participation in Diaspora Philanthropy: A Case Study during the COVID-19 Outbreak. *New England Journal of Entrepreneurship, 24*(2). https://doi.org/10.1108/NEJE-08-2020-0033

Cheung, C. W. M., Kwong, C., Manzoor, H., Rashid, M. U., Bhattarai, C., & Kim, Y. A. (2019). The Co-creation of Social Ventures through Bricolage, for the Displaced, by the Displaced. *International Journal of Entrepreneurial Behavior and Research, 25*(5). https://doi.org/10.1108/IJEBR-03-2018-0140

Cruz, A. D., & Fromm, I. (2019). Understanding the Emergence of a Social Enterprise by Highly Skilled Migrants: The Case of Honduras Global Europa. *International Journal of Entrepreneurial Behavior and Research, 25*(5). https://doi.org/10.1108/IJEBR-02-2018-0091

Doherty, B., Haugh, H., & Lyon, F. (2014). Social Enterprises as Hybrid Organizations: A Review and Research Agenda. *International Journal of Management Reviews, 16*(4), 417–436.

Elo, M. (2016). Typology of Diaspora Entrepreneurship: Case Studies in Uzbekistan. *Journal of International Entrepreneurship, 14*, 121–155. https://doi.org/10.1007/s10843-016-0177-9

Elo, M., Täube, F. A., & Servais, P. (2022). Who is Doing "Transnational Diaspora Entrepreneurship"? Understanding Formal Identity and Status. *Journal of World Business, 57*(1). https://doi.org/10.1016/j.jwb.2021.101240

Forde, C., & Mackenzie, R. (2010). The Ethical Agendas of Employment Agencies towards Migrant Workers in the UK: Deciphering the Codes. *Journal of Business Ethics, 97*. https://doi.org/10.1007/s10551-011-1077-5

Freudenberg, J., & Halberstadt, J. (2018). How to Integrate Refugees Into the Workforce—Different Opportunities for (Social) Entrepreneurship. *Problemy Zarzadzania—Management Issues, 16*(73), 40–60.

Gaillard, D., & Hughes, K. (2014). Key Considerations for Facilitating Employment of Female Sudanese Refugees in Australia. *Journal of Management and Organization, 20*(5). https://doi.org/10.1017/jmo.2014.49

Grimm, R., Fox, C., Baines, S., & Albertson, K. (2013). Social Innovation, an Answer to Contemporary Societal Challenges? Locating the Concept in Theory and Practice. *Innovation, 26*(4), 436–455.

Guo, G. C., Ariss, A. A., & Brewster, C. (2020). Understanding the Global Refugee Crisis: Managerial Consequences and Policy Implications. *Academy of Management Perspectives, 34*(4), 531–545.

Gupta, P., Chauhan, S., Paul, J., & Jaiswal, M. P. (2020). Social Entrepreneurship Research: A Review and Future Research Agenda. *Journal of Business Research, 113*(April), 209–229.

Haines, B. C., McKay, F. H., Dunn, M., & Lippi, K. (2018). The Role of Social Enterprise in Food Insecurity among Asylum Seekers. *Health and Social Care in the Community, 26*(6). https://doi.org/10.1111/hsc.12593

Harima, A., & Freudenberg, J. (2020). Co-Creation of Social Entrepreneurial Opportunities with Refugees. *Journal of Social Entrepreneurship, 11*(1). https://doi.org/10.1080/19420676.2018.1561498

Harima, A., Periac, F., Murphy, T., & Picard, S. (2021). Entrepreneurial Opportunities of Refugees in Germany, France, and Ireland: Multiple Embeddedness Framework. *International Entrepreneurship and Management Journal, 17*(2). https://doi.org/10.1007/s11365-020-00707-5

Idiakez, F. J. A., Rodríguez, J. L., & Etxeberria, G. M. (2022). Workers' Cooperatives as a Tool to Promote Labour Market Inclusion for Migrants. *Boletin de La Asociacion Internacional de Derecho Cooperativo, 60*. https://doi.org/10.18543/baidc.2273

IOM. (2019). IOM Glossary on Migration. In *Glossary on Migration*.

IOM. (2020). World Migration Report 2020 (Full Report). *European Journal of Political Research Political Data Yearbook* (Vol. 54).

Jayawarna, D., Jones, O., & Macpherson, A. (2014). Entrepreneurial Potential: The Role of Human and Cultural Capitals. *International Small Business Journal: Researching Entrepreneurship, 32*(8), 918–943.

Kidd, S., & McKenzie, K. (2014). Social Entrepreneurship and Services for Marginalized Groups. *Ethnicity and Inequalities in Health and Social Care, 7*(1). https://doi.org/10.1108/EIHSC-03-2013-0004

Knight, M. (2016). Race-ing, Classing and Gendering Racialized Women's Participation in Entrepreneurship. *Gender, Work and Organization, 23*(3). https://doi.org/10.1111/gwao.12060

Kong, E. (2011). Building Social and Community Cohesion: The Role of Social Enterprises in Facilitating Settlement Experiences for Immigrants from Non-English Speaking Backgrounds. *International Journal of Interdisciplinary Social Sciences, 6*(3). https://doi.org/10.18848/1833-1882/CGP/v06i03/52041

Kong, E. (2019). Harnessing and Advancing Knowledge in Social Enterprises: Theoretical and Operational Challenges in the Refugee Settlement Experience.

Journal of Social Entrepreneurship, 10(2). https://doi.org/10.1080/19420676.2018.1541009

Kraff, H., & Jernsand, E. M. (2020). The Roles of Social Enterprises in a Swedish Labour Market Integration Programme—Opportunities and Challenges for Social Innovation. *Social Enterprise Journal*. https://doi.org/10.1108/SEJ-12-2019-0092

Kroeger, A., & Weber, C. (2014). Developing a Conceptual Framework for Comparing Social Value Creation. *Academy of Management Review, 39*(4). https://doi.org/10.5465/amr.2012.0344

Kuckertz, A., Bernhard, A., Berger, E. S. C., Dvouletý, O., Harms, R., Jack, S., & Kibler, E. (2023). Scaling the Right Answers—Creating and Maintaining Hope through Social Entrepreneurship in Light of Humanitarian Crises. *Journal of Business Venturing Insights, 19*. https://doi.org/10.1016/j.jbvi.2022.e00356

Lee, S. K. (2018). From Political Activists to Social Entrepreneurs: Burmese Refugees in South Korea. *Journal of Refugee Studies, 31*(3). https://doi.org/10.1093/jrs/fey011

Lee, E. S., Szkudlarek, B., Nguyen, D. C., & Nardon, L. (2020). Unveiling the Canvas Ceiling: A Multidisciplinary Literature Review of Refugee Employment and Workforce Integration. *International Journal of Management Reviews, 22*(2), 193–216.

Leslie, D., Rantisi, N., & Black, S. (2023). Realizing the Social Mandate of Work-Integration Social Enterprises through an Anti-Racist Feminist Praxis and Spatiality? *Geoforum, 138*. https://doi.org/10.1016/j.geoforum.2022.09.014

Longoni, A., Luzzini, D., Pullman, M., & Habiague, M. (2019). Business for Society is Society's Business: Tension Management in a Migrant Integration Supply Chain. *Journal of Supply Chain Management, 55*(4). https://doi.org/10.1111/jscm.12213

Madichie, N. O. (2016). The Business of Saving Lives in Sub-Saharan Africa (SSA)—A Social Imperative? Insights from "The Global Soap Project". *Journal of Enterprising Communities, 10*(3). https://doi.org/10.1108/JEC-11-2014-0025

Mafico, N., Krzeminska, A., Härtel, C., & Keller, J. (2021). The Mirroring of Intercultural and Hybridity Experiences: A Study of African Immigrant Social Entrepreneurs. *Journal of Business Venturing, 36*(3). https://doi.org/10.1016/j.jbusvent.2021.106093

Markman, G. D., Waldron, T. L., Gianiodis, P. T., & Espina, M. I. (2019). E Pluribus Unum: Impact Entrepreneurship as a Solution to Grand Challenges. *Academy of Management Perspectives, 33*(4), 371–382.

McAuliffe, M., & Triandafyllidou, A. (2021). *World Migration Report 2022*. International Organization for Migration (IOM), Geneva.

McKay, F. H., Lippi, K., Dunn, M., Haines, B. C., & Lindberg, R. (2018). Food-based Social Enterprises and Asylum Seekers: The Food Justice Truck. *Nutrients, 10*(6). https://doi.org/10.3390/nu10060756

McSweeney, M. (2023). Sport and Social Entrepreneurship in the Base-of-the-Pyramid: The Institutional Work of Refugees and a Refugee-Led Organization in Uganda. *Sport Management Review, 26*(4). https://doi.org/10.1080/14413523.2022.2148861

Mittermaier, A., Patzelt, H., & Shepherd, D. A. (2023). Motivating Prosocial Venturing in Response to a Humanitarian Crisis: Building Theory From the Refugee Crisis in Germany. *Entrepreneurship: Theory and Practice, 47*(3). https://doi.org/10.1177/10422587211025233

Modesti, C., Talamo, A., Nicolais, G., & Recupero, A. (2020). Social and Psychological Capital for the Start-Up of Social Enterprises With a Migratory Background. *Frontiers in Psychology, 11*. https://doi.org/10.3389/fpsyg.2020.01177

Murphy, P. J., Smothers, J., Novicevic, M. M., Humphreys, J. H., Roberts, F. B., & Kornetskyy, A. (2018). Social Enterprise in Antebellum America: The Case of Nashoba (1824–1829). *Journal of Management History, 24*(1). https://doi.org/10.1108/JMH-06-2017-0032

Norbäck, M., & Zapata Campos, M. J. (2022). The Market Made Us Do It: Public Procurement and Collaborative Labour Market Inclusion Governance from Below. *Social Policy and Administration, 56*(4). https://doi.org/10.1111/spol.12787

Praetorius, R. T., Mitschke, D. B., Avila, C. D., Kelly, D. R., & Henderson, J. (2016). Cultural Integration through Shared Learning among Resettled Bhutanese Women. *Journal of Human Behavior in the Social Environment, 26*(6). https://doi.org/10.1080/10911359.2016.1172997

Rantisi, N. M., & Leslie, D. (2021). In and Against the Neoliberal State? The Precarious Siting of Work Integration Social Enterprises (WISEs) as Counter-Movement in Montreal, Quebec. *Environment and Planning A, 53*(2). https://doi.org/10.1177/0308518X20948068

Rawhouser, H., Cummings, M., & Newbert, S. L. (2019). Social Impact Measurement: Current Approaches and Future Directions for Social Entrepreneurship Research. *Entrepreneurship: Theory and Practice, 43*(1). https://doi.org/10.1177/1042258717727718

Rivna, A., & Gress, M. (2023). Social Entrepreneurship as a New Business Model. The Case of Refugee Integration. *Economic Research-Ekonomska Istrazivanja, 36*(1). https://doi.org/10.1080/1331677X.2022.2120044

Ruebottom, T. (2013). The Microstructures of Rhetorical Strategy in Social Entrepreneurship: Building Legitimacy through Heroes and Villains. *Journal of Business Venturing, 28*(1). https://doi.org/10.1016/j.jbusvent.2011.05.001

Saebi, T., Foss, N. J., & Linder, S. (2019). Social Entrepreneurship Research: Past Achievements and Future Promises. *Journal of Management, 45*(1), 70–95.

Sahyoun, N. R., Jamaluddine, Z., Choufani, J., Mesmar, S., Reese-Masterson, A., & Ghattas, H. (2019). A Mixed-Methods Evaluation of Community-Based Healthy Kitchens as Social Enterprises for Refugee Women. *BMC Public Health, 19*(1). https://doi.org/10.1186/s12889-019-7950-3

Schwabenland, C., & Hirst, A. (2022). Solidarity with Soufra: Dividuality and Joint Action with Palestinian Women Refugees. *Organization, 29*(2). https://doi.org/10.1177/13505084211051046

Senthanar, S., MacEachen, E., Premji, S., & Bigelow, P. (2021). Entrepreneurial Experiences of Syrian Refugee Women in Canada: A Feminist Grounded Qualitative Study. *Small Business Economics, 57*(2). https://doi.org/10.1007/s11187-020-00385-1

Sepulveda, L., Syrett, S., & Calvo, S. (2013). Social Enterprise and Ethnic Minorities: Exploring the Consequences of the Evolving British Policy Agenda. *Environment and Planning C: Government and Policy, 31*(4). https://doi.org/10.1068/c11319

Streuli, S., & Lewis, T. (2022). Shifting Priorities and Neoliberal Ideologies in Refugee Health Intervention Design in the US. *Medical Anthropology: Cross Cultural Studies in Health and Illness, 41*(4). https://doi.org/10.1080/01459740.2022.2053965

Tracey, P., & Phillips, N. (2016). Managing the Consequences of Organizational Stigmatization: Identity work in a Social Enterprise. *Academy of Management Journal, 59*(3). https://doi.org/10.5465/amj.2013.0483

United Nations. (2020). *World Youth Report 2020.* https://doi.org/10.18356/79650d8ben

Walk, M., Greenspan, I., Crossley, H., & Handy, F. (2015). Social Return on Investment Analysis: A Case Study of a Job and Skills Training Program Offered by a Social Enterprise. *Nonprofit Management and Leadership, 26*(2). https://doi.org/10.1002/nml.21190

Xiang, R., & Luk, T. C. (2011). Friends or Foes? Social Enterprise and Women Organizing in Migrant Communities of China. *China Journal of Social Work, 4*(3). https://doi.org/10.1080/17525098.2011.620698

PART II

Case Studies and Empirical Evidence About the Policies and Practices of Social Entrepreneurship Linked to International Migration in the Adriatic-Ionian Area

CHAPTER 6

Refugees' Economic Integration Through Social Entrepreneurship: Social Plan for Bosnia and Herzegovina

Erol Mujanović, Slavko Simić, Branko Marković, and Tariku Ayana Abdi

Introduction

Bosnia and Herzegovina (BiH) is a country in the Balkans, in Southeastern Europe. After the European Union (EU)–Turkey Statement was signed in March 2016 and neighboring countries implemented new border restrictions, BiH became the main route for refugees and migrants attempting to reach Western Europe, primarily from Syria, Iraq, Afghanistan, and Pakistan, but also from North and sub-Saharan Africa (European Parliament, 2022). In recent years, BiH has been receiving thousands of

E. Mujanović
USAID Bosnia and Herzegovina, Sarajevo, Bosnia and Herzegovina
e-mail: emujanovic@usaid.gov

S. Simić
University of Business Studies of Banja Luka,
Banja Luka, Bosnia and Herzegovina
e-mail: bono@blic.net

S. Bianchini et al. (eds.), *Social Entrepreneurship and Migrants' Inclusion*, Sustainable Development Goals Series,
https://doi.org/10.1007/978-3-031-55791-0_6

migrants and refugees each year, with the tendency seeming to rise over time (Oruc et al., 2020; Poleschuk et al., 2023).

Despite an increase in the number of migrants and refugees arriving in the country, BiH's hosting practices have not been favorable or up to international standards. According to Amnesty International (2019), the legal regulatory framework in BiH, which governs issues related to refugees, asylum seekers, and migrants, was relatively poor, indicating BiH's noncompliance with best-world standards. Despite many attempts, authorities have failed to adopt the policies and legal documents necessary to establish a system to address the rights of civilian victims of war, including victims of wartime violence, following international standards and practices, according to Amnesty International's assessment report. Furthermore, international news agencies, research institutions, and independent academic researchers provide a similar assessment of the situation in BiH in terms of migration and the integration of migrants (e.g., Oruc et al., 2020; United Nations, 2020a), pointing to systemic problems.

In BiH, when migrants and refugees are granted asylum seeker status, they acquire some fundamental rights that are guaranteed to them as asylum seekers. These rights include the right to obtain residence on the territory of BiH, the right to accommodation (most often in an asylum seeker center), the right to receive primary health care, the right to attend school, get a job, receive psychosocial assistance, and follow their procedure in a language they understand. However, the formal acquisition of these rights does not necessarily imply their easy realization in practice when persons with asylum need to exercise one of these rights. There are noticeable shortcomings in terms of the integration of asylum seekers and their families, especially minors, because according to the reports of several international organizations, in BiH, many children of asylum seekers currently do not go to school, receive health care only through international

B. Marković
University UNION Nikola Tesla, FPSP, Belgrade, Serbia

T. A. Abdi (✉)
Department of Management, Alma Mater Studiorum-University of Bologna, Bologna, Italy
e-mail: tariku.abdi@unibo.it

organizations, and in practice there are no mechanisms that would ensure the registration of asylum seekers at the employment office. The consequence is that many migrants try to get involved in the economic flows through the informal, through jobs where they are not registered and taxes are not paid, and through the resale of goods at imported street stalls.

According to broader experiences at the European level, social entrepreneurship can effectively integrate refugees into the host country. In its broadest sense, social entrepreneurship refers to the application of practical, innovative, and sustainable approaches to achieving benefits for society in general, with a focus on marginalized groups (including migrants and refugees) and poor groups; a unique approach to economic and social problems, based on certain processes and values that—whether it is nonprofit or profit subject (Ninkovic-Papic et al., 2012). Moreover, social entrepreneurship is recognized as encompassing a wide range of activities, including enterprising individuals dedicated to making a difference; social purpose business ventures dedicated to bringing for-profit motivations to the nonprofit sector; new types of philanthropists supporting venture-capital-like "investment" portfolios; and nonprofit organizations reinventing themselves by drawing on lessons from the business world (e.g., Mair et al., 2006).

This chapter aims to provide an exploratory understanding of how refugees perceive their situation regarding the availability of social services and their economic integration, particularly through the potential of social entrepreneurship. To answer this research question, we first review secondary documentation about the policies for refugees' and other migrants' inclusion and social entrepreneurship in BiH, and we draw on qualitative data collected from interviews with 21 refugees in a camp.

Country Background

BiH has a complex migration policy and framework due to its location and historical context. The country serves as a transit route for migrants and refugees seeking to reach Western European countries. Neighboring Croatia is currently the Schengen zone border, and there are many tensions with migrants and refugees who are constantly trying to find ways to pass from BiH to Croatia. In the following section, we briefly provided the BiH migration contexts.

Migration Policy and Frameworks

Legal Frameworks: BiH does not have a single unified migration law but multiple laws and regulations governing different aspects of migration. The *Law on Movement and Stay of Aliens and Asylum* is the primary legislation for migration and asylum seekers.

Asylum System: BiH has established an asylum system to process asylum applications and protect refugees. The Ministry of Security is responsible for managing the asylum procedure, while the Service for Foreigners' Affairs handles the registration and documentation of migrants.

Border Control: BiH shares borders with several neighboring countries, and border control is a crucial aspect of migration management. BiH cooperates with international organizations, such as the International Organization for Migration (IOM) and the European Border and Coast Guard Agency (Frontex), to enhance border security and manage migration flows.

Reception and Accommodation: BiH has established reception centers and temporary accommodation facilities to host migrants and refugees. These centers provide basic services, including shelter, food, healthcare, and legal assistance. However, due to the increased influx of migrants, the capacity of these facilities has been strained, leading to overcrowding and challenging conditions.

International Cooperation: BiH cooperates with various international organizations, including the United Nations High Commissioner for Refugees (UNHCR) and the IOM, to manage migration and provide support to migrants and refugees. The country also engages in regional and international initiatives to address migration challenges collectively.

Bilateral Agreements: BiH has signed bilateral readmission agreements with neighboring countries to facilitate the return of irregular migrants who have transited through their territories. It is important to note that the migration policy and framework in BiH are constantly evolving due to the dynamic nature of migration flows. The country faces numerous challenges in managing migration, including limited resources, administrative capacity, and differing political interests among its constituent entities.

Socioeconomic and Political Situation

Socioeconomic Environment

The labor market situation in BiH remains very challenging, and for refugees, it is even more the case. The entire labor market faces an unprecedented shortage of skilled workforce in several professions. At the same time, that also represents a relatively unique but certainly long-lasting opportunity for refugees in BiH as this shortage affects almost all sectors of the economy (construction, IT, hospitality, etc.), and the country has started to import workforce for countries such as Nepal (construction workers). Deficient professions are various, and so are the deficient levels of skills (going from construction industry workers to doctors or IT engineers). In addition to that, the war in Ukraine, combined with a few other external shocks, significantly disturbed and increased both fixed and variable costs for almost all companies, making it more challenging for them to invest to keep creating new jobs, and even to maintain the previous level of production capacities.

In the publication "Labour Market Research in the FBiH 2021–2022,"[1] the Federal Employment Institute states, "Following a break in the multiyear growth trend of the number of persons in employment from April 2020, the growth in the number of persons in employment in the Federation of BiH resumed in 2021." According to data from the Federal Institute for Statistics, there were, on average, 525,397 workers employed in 2021 in the Federation of BiH, which is 5235 workers or 1% more compared to the 2020 average (520,162). Industries that were the most important when it came to hiring and job creation were information and communication (9.4%); administrative and support service activities (5.9%); and professional, scientific, and technical activities (4%). At the same time, the following industries registered a decrease in employment: real estate activities (-7.1%), mining and quarrying (-3.4%), and electricity generation and supply (-1.1%). Hiring needs for 2022 also look very promising and represent a considerable increase in the number of employers that reported that they plan to hire an additional workforce in 2022 compared to the previous year. In RS, trends are almost identical to trends in the FBiH. In March 2022, the RS Employment Institute announced that the number of unemployed persons decreased by 12.3% compared to

[1] https://www.fzzz.ba/ckFinderFiles/files/LABOUR-MARKET-RESEARCH-IN-THE-FEDERATION-OF-BIH-2020_2021-03-web-version_compressed-1.pdf.

the previous reporting period. Active labor market measures for 2022 exceeded 5 million convertible marks, and the employment institute of RS is currently assessing employers' needs and opinions on the workforce shortage. The results will be available in early 2023.

Political Context

According to the BTI Transformation Index data for BiH,[2] since 2019, BiH has experienced political instability, continuing dysfunctionality about large parts of state and political institutions, and a continuous undermining of democracy and the rule of law. This continuing negative trajectory is based on the continuous denial by the ruling political elites in Republika Srpska (RS) of BiH's constitutional order and statehood. Fundamental political disagreements among the main Serb, Croat, and Bosniak parties at the state and Federal BiH (FBiH) levels have for years stymied the appointment of key officials and directors of police. The BiH Parliamentary Assembly was effectively suspended until the formation of the state-level government, and both the BiH and FBiH parliaments demonstrated minimal legislative activity in 2020. The long-time RS leader, Milorad Dodik, has used his position as the newly elected Serb member of the three-member BiH Presidency to promote narrow entity-specific interests, at the expense of the interests of the state of BiH as a whole.

The COVID-19 pandemic laid bare the dysfunctionality and structural crisis of the BiH state and politics. It hit the country's weak, fragmented, and partly corrupt healthcare system hard. The economic impact of the pandemic was substantial, as gross domestic product (GDP) dropped by 5.5% in 2020, fiscal revenues decreased for the first time since 2009, and unemployment increased after several years of decrease (primarily due to mass emigration). Cooperation among the main parties and between political units initially improved; particularly within the BiH, the Presidency and the Council of Ministers worked primarily to mitigate the economic impact of the pandemic. This progress, however, was short-lived. In April–May 2020, the approval and disbursement of hundreds of millions of euros in macro-level financial support from the IMF and the EU was delayed for weeks due to disagreement over its distribution among entities and cantons. International borrowing secured fiscal stability despite the stark negative economic trends. Citizens' trust in government management has been undermined by several corruption scandals over the public

[2] https://bti-project.org/en/reports/country-dashboard/BIH.

procurement of medical supplies, with one leading to the indictment of the sitting FBiH prime minister. Some measures introduced in the entities were criticized as a misuse of the pandemic to limit freedom of expression and were partly revoked.

Very little progress has been made on key structural reforms regarding the rule of law and constitutional reform necessary for accession negotiations with the EU. Improving the fragmented and partly corrupt healthcare system remains a key priority. The organization "Friends of Europe," in its analysis titled "Understanding the Real Threats to BiH Future Stability" from April 2022, states:

> The status quo and current political crisis are fueled by the following challenges: population loss, endemic corruption, poor economic conditions, environmental concerns, and continued ethnic division. BiH is among the top 10 nations in the world with severely decreasing populations, causing a significant brain drain among talented young people who face reduced job opportunities, an insecure financial future, and distrust in the ruling politicians. Endemic corruption prevents socio-political and economic development. BiH is ranked 110th out of 180 countries on Transparency International's Corruption Perception Index. The nation's complex governance system, encouraged by a lack of enforcement of existing laws, exacerbates corruption and cronyism in both the public and private sectors to benefit those in the highest echelons of power. These are the same people who control the majority of publicly owned industries and enterprises, resulting in a lack of political will to implement effective, anti-corruption laws. BiH is also one of the poorest countries in Europe. Despite the vast financial support and aid provided since the 1990s, Bosnia still struggles with a weak social welfare system, poor infrastructure, and a large public sector. The global community blames those in power for embezzling much of the funds.[3]

Refugees' and Other Migrants' Inclusion

Despite the optimistic view regarding the decrease in the unemployment trend in BiH, immigration remains a challenge for the country's economic and human resources development. Reports show that poverty is highly concentrated among refugees in BiH (Rosas et al., 2009). According to

[3] Understanding the real threats to Bosnia and Herzegovina's future stability - Friends of Europe.

the Federation of BiH 2020/2021 labor market research and employers' survey,[4] migrants are the least favored (2%) for hiring by employers. As a result, significant efforts and initiatives are required to increase the economic integration of migrants and refugees in BiH.

In response to the socioeconomic challenges posed to BiH youth, as well as migrants and refugees, there have been some encouraging initiatives. Among such initiatives, the United Nations Development Programme (UNDP) devised a program called the "Youth Employability and Retention Program (YERP)" (Gavric, 2012). YERP strives to address high youth unemployment and irregular migrants by collaborating with the government, private sectors, and civil society to increase the employability of BiH youth while providing new entry points into the labor market. Furthermore, with the support of UNICEF, a digital learning application was implemented in schools to support integrating children of migrants and refugees in BiH (Poleschuk et al., 2023). The digital learning application, in fact, is being implemented in several migrant-receiving countries, including Italy, Greece, Serbia, and Mexico, among others, with the support of UNICEF. The program is believed to enhance the social integration, language, and communication skills of migrant and refugee students.

Social Entrepreneurship in BiH

Social entrepreneurship is viewed as a new but growing phenomenon in BiH, where it started developing more rapidly only a few years ago. Social entrepreneurship is how individuals, startups, and entrepreneurs develop and fund solutions that directly address social issues. A social entrepreneur explores business opportunities that positively impact their community, society, or the world. Social entrepreneurs tackle big societal challenges that benefit people and with sustainable business models. This rapidly growing tool against poverty also proliferates in BiH, where more and more social enterprises are launched yearly.

In BiH's national framework context, social entrepreneurship can be defined through a broader concept of social economy (e.g., Đermanović, 2019; Ninkovic-Papic et al., 2012). Social economy is an innovative and more effective way to respond to social needs compared to traditional

[4] https://www.fzzz.ba/ckFinderFiles/files/LABOUR-MARKET-RESEARCH-IN-THE-FEDERATION-OF-BIH-2020_2021-03-web-version_compressed-1.pdf.

approaches. Alongside specific actions addressed to vulnerable individuals and families, the social economy activates multilevel synergies that seek solutions to issues of collective interest. This makes it possible to go beyond the care perspective, activating reciprocity practices and, at the same time, producing both social and economic value. Social economy does more than respond to a social, economic, or environmental need. It enhances relationships between residents, the local community, and the wider society while promoting collective responsibility (Đermanović, 2019).

Analyzing the legal framework in the field of social entrepreneurship in BiH is a very complex job due to the sensitivity of the issue and the complex administrative structure of the country. According to the Constitution of BiH, the normative regulation of every form of entrepreneurship is within the competence of the entities and the district Brcko.

In the past several years, the major developments of the social entrepreneurship scene took place in BiH under the EU-funded project "Contribution of Civil Society Organizations to the Development of Social Entrepreneurship" and advancements include the creation of the definition of social enterprises in BiH, their mapping, creation of the legal framework, and, among others, creation of an association of social enterprises in each entity. Social entrepreneurship laws in both entities have been harmonized, and while the RS and district Brcko adopted the Law on Social Entrepreneurship. This process has not been finalized yet in the Federal BiH, but the relevant Ministry fully supports it. While the most significant value of laws is in their implementation, the laws are pretty modern in their approach, and they constitute an important step forward for both entities of BiH. The Law on social entrepreneurship adopted in the RS stipulates that social enterprise achieves its social mission in one of the following ways: by hiring categories of persons who are more challenging to employ, by performing work in any activity that achieves social goals, or by financing projects of legal entities that achieve social goals.

However, having a well-designed and adopted law represents just the beginning as almost all factors that compose the social entrepreneurship ecosystem are missing in both entities (adequate financing, systemic approach to social entrepreneurship development, specific learning and skills development, no laws have been adapted to the social entrepreneurship such as public procurement law for example, no special subventions to the creation of social enterprises, etc.). Overall, in BiH, the social entrepreneurship sector lacks full buy-in and support from local authorities. Thus, the development of the entire sector is still very dependent on a project funded by the international community. While social entrepreneurship has already made its proof across the EU, where more than 10 million persons work in this sector, BiH social enterprises remain very vulnerable as they lack fundamental support from all authorities. All social enterprises in BiH, although some of them do have a multimillion euros worth yearly turnover and are making a profit, still have many difficulties as they face a double challenge: the first one is related to the fact they are social enterprises and the second one is related to the fact they need to remain very competitive in order to succeed.

Regarding financing social enterprises, additional findings on the economic environment of BiH can be taken from the national state-of-the-art report on assessing the main challenges (Deliverable T1.2.1), Section 1 Questions to identify and assess the main social and economic challenges. In addition to that, there are findings from the National STA report "Assessing societal Change" (Deliverable T1.1.1), namely the chapters' "Economic and Entrepreneurship Indicators" (2010–2020) and Section III–questions 2–5. In that respect, access to finance is challenging and a significant barrier to innovation and entrepreneurship. There is a particular need for access to affordable seed capital. This is especially true for social enterprises as banks are rarely familiar with this type of company and apply the same rules and approach as ordinary companies. BiH scores very poorly on the Doing Business survey, reflected in all segments of the nascent ecosystem for social enterprises.

Social Entrepreneurship and Migrants' Inclusion

The importance of social entrepreneurship is acknowledged in the policy documents related to social inclusion, namely the *Development Strategy of BiH*, and then reflected in the Social Inclusion Strategy, which stipulates that social entrepreneurship can play an important role in the employment and social integration of socially marginalized groups (Andjelic & Petricevic, 2020). According to the document, BiH's Social Inclusion Strategy presents a clear definition (but not legal recognition) of social entrepreneurship. In addition, the last two years in BiH were very efficient and productive when it came to creating the legal framework for social entrepreneurship, with both entities and the District Brcko creating the law on Social entrepreneurship. Despite the aforementioned legal development and part of the ecosystem, the remaining parts of the social entrepreneurship ecosystem are developing more slowly. Available information is mostly based on the support organizations' databases of beneficiaries and estimates of experts.

On the other hand, the concept of social inclusion, initiated by the EU countries, looks at an individual as potential, not as an expense of the society, and it devotes attention to their social inclusion. According to the European Commission (2004), social inclusion is a process that ensures that those at risk of poverty and social exclusion have the opportunities and resources they need to participate in economic, social, and cultural life fully, as well as to enjoy a standard of living and well-being considered normal in the society they live. It ensures that individuals have greater participation in decision-making processes affecting their lives and access to their fundamental rights. Social inclusion aims to enable and return less employable categories to the lab in our market. Through active inclusion measures, which emphasize the social economy, the price that should be foreseen for the incentives for employment and education of people experiencing poverty and excluded citizens is much less than constant and unsustainable allocations for social protection. Incentivization of social inclusion of migrants and refugees, as well as vulnerable groups, through social entrepreneurship can be obtained from governmental ministries, national/federal lottery administration, civil societies, and private and non-governmental sectors in order to solve their social and economic problems of refugees, excluded and vulnerable groups (e.g., Ninkovic-Papic et al., 2012). The social inclusion and integration of these groups not only solve their social and economic problems but also allow them to participate in social and economic development, poverty reduction, and unemployment reduction in their community. Moreover, Oruc et al. (2020) argue that communities must be sufficiently equipped to receive refugees to ensure social cohesion, stability, and security. In contrast, refugees need support to realize their potential in the host country and contribute to social and economic development.

On the other hand, to comprehend the refugee integration process, we must first understand their sentiments and behaviors, the reasons and feelings that influenced them when they decided to flee and permanently move, and how they felt during the migratory journey. According to Betts (2013), the context of migration frequently suggests the following two scenarios. Firstly, these are disparities between what was claimed and what is happening in reality (activities of refugees and/or acts of governmental institutions, as well as the effects of those actions and how interested parties deal with the implications of such actions and outcomes). Secondly, shame is the dominant feeling that dominates all asylum seekers, migrants, and refugees. Shame, as a feeling anchored in the migrant's social being, has various causes and reasons and can sometimes cause anger in individuals. However, it affects in a way that significantly reduces the social ability and the ability of migrants to face the bureaucracy in institutions independently. The economic transformation we are witnessing in Europe does not affect everyone equally, and those members of society and community who are at risk and whose jobs and futures are at risk will, in principle, vote against the immigration policy that enables the broader integration of migrants from culturally different environments. It is also noticeable that the number of migrants affects the attitude toward migrants less than the state of the economy. In principle, economies that are in trouble or collapsing produce a social environment that is against migration.

In an attempt to create a negative public attitude and perception toward the possibility of migrants and refugee integration, some of the interested parties create myths about how migration works and how much the process of integrating refugees, asylum seekers, and migrants costs the national economy, beginning with the receipt of requests and ending with full integration of migrants into the local community. Betts (2013) highlighted five myths concerning migration and migrant integration.

- Refugee camps are separate and isolated from the rest of the community. However, refugees are always part of both the local and global economy.
- Refugees are a burden on the local community. However, if we allow migrants or refugees to work and open businesses, they will employ not only other migrants but also the local population and contribute to the local economy.
- Refugees are often perceived as a homogenous group, especially from the point of view of their economic position, which is far from reality and can only be reached through direct insight and fieldwork.
- Refugees are outside modern technology—this myth was established in an earlier historical period. However, it is still quite strong today, despite much evidence to the contrary. Refugees will always use the highest level of technology available whenever possible, especially to connect.
- Refugees depend on us (dependent on the aid provided by the state) and are waiting for the institutions to provide them with everything they need. This is entirely contrary to human nature and known to

anyone who has ever been a refugee—people will do everything in their power to provide everything they need precisely because of their experience of domestic institutions that collapsed. It was learned that one should trust institutions with bounds when helping and solving issues are vital.

Examples of Good Practices that Can Guide BiH in Integrating Migrants and Asylum Seekers into the Wider Social Community and Economy

As BiH attempts to build good practices in terms of a broader social and economic integration of migrants and refugees, it is vital to adapt the good practices and contextualize them in order to entertain the cultural, economic, and historical specificities of BiH. In this regard, excellent practice is observed at the level of social and institutional processes and at the level of fundamental principles on which the institutional growth of the processes of integrating migrants into social and economic reality is founded. Scholars define the successful integration of migrants and refugees as equitable access to opportunities and resources, social and economic participation in the community where they live, and feelings of security and belonging in their new homes (e.g., Hynie, 2018). Among the few available examples of good practices of social entrepreneurship that promote social inclusion and integration, Ninkovic-Papic et al. (2012) identified the following:

- *Foundation "Mozaik"*: Established in Sarajevo in 2008, the program provides youth aged 15 to 30 years an opportunity to participate in joint activities and develop skills in management and entrepreneurship. The foundation "Mozaik" implements the Youth Bank Program, which aims to increase youth participation in the local development of rural areas by allocating non-returnable funds for projects developed and managed by the youth.
- *Social enterprise "Uspon"*: Its main aim is to enable persons with disabilities to get employment and support themselves, as work engagement is the most effective approach for persons with disabilities' social inclusion and integration into society. The social enterprise began operations in 2012 in the municipality of Novo Sarajevo.
- *Organization "Bospo"*: established in 2009 in the municipality of Lukavac, it aims to support the development of greenhouse

production, which should contribute to sustainable return. Aside from the production of different agricultural products, the greenhouse will be utilized for educational purposes for the younger members of the association (who represent the minority returnee population in the area) and community, which could help the development of this agricultural branch.

- *Organization "GOPA"*: Carried out by the local unit of GOPA in BiH, based in Banja Luka, it is an entrepreneurship development project named "Women to Women." It has been implemented to support and strengthen the companies managed by women, support start-ups founded by women younger than 30, and employ young women.

Ninkovic-Papic et al. (2012) also identified additional organizations whose projects in the field of social entrepreneurship have been supported by the Inclusion Foundation in BiH *(Agency for Economic Development of Herzegovina—REDAH; Association of Agricultural Producers Poljotes—UPP Poljotes; Association of Entrepreneurs and Employers Žepče—UPIP Žepče; Foreign Chamber of Trade BiH; Institute for Education ECOS, Sarajevo; and Association of Persons with Disabilities, Berkovići)*.

However, there are scarce good practices and experiences concerning integrating migrants and refugees. Therefore, it is necessary to adapt similar laws and principles to address their inclusion and integration in the host society. For example, Ninkovic-Papic et al. (2012) noted that similar laws and regulations exist, particularly in the public sector, regarding refugees, displaced people, and sustainable return (including through establishing a fund). However, the question is whether they ensure success, transparent work, and control. Moreover, social enterprises are also in their early stages of development, mainly in the start-up phase in BiH, with a few have been very successful and are ready to scale, most of the initiatives, even though with promising initial results, are still learning the rules of the market and are working to become self-sustainable (Rosandic & Kusinikova, 2018). European Commission (2019) urges BiH to ensure its commitment to and effective implementation of laws and legal frameworks for the integration and protection of vulnerable populations such as refugees and migrants.

Methodology

Data Collection

We constructed a primary data collection tool based on a questionnaire, including open-ended, closed, and intensity estimating questions. We administered the questionnaire through one-to-one interviews at a refugee camp in Una Sana Canton, in BiH.

Sample selection is always an issue of scientific research. Thus, we carefully selected the place and number of available examiners, assuming they may give reliable answers because all of them are migrants, and the research team assisted with filling in a questionnaire. In this way, the relevance of the research participants in terms of profile and background was ensured. In this process, we interviewed 21 male migrants from different countries, most from Africa and Asia. While it would have been important to have included females' perspectives for the diversity and richness of perspectives, we could only have access to male participants. According to the International Organization for Migration (2022) report, most migrants arriving in BiH have been single men.

Data Analysis

In processing and analyzing data, we first conducted a descriptive analysis of relevant sociodemographic characteristics of the refugees through descriptive statistics and frequency distributions. Quantitative (mainly descriptive) and qualitative research methods were used to analyze current social services and activities in the economic integration of refugees and asylum seekers.

Results and Discussion

Refugees' Sociodemographic Profiles

Approximately 87% of respondents were young and between the ages 20 and 40, arrived from various countries, including Pakistan, Afghanistan, Morocco, and Syria, the majority (53%) of whom reported being Muslims. Approximately half of the respondents were 25 years old or younger. Regarding the educational level of the migrants, we found that almost half of the asylum seekers (48%) had university degrees. In comparison, the remaining 52% had a high school diploma, although most respondents did not have their diplomas available to prove they had the level of education that they claimed. In terms of age and educational level, our findings are contrary to most previous reports in Western Balkan between 2015 and 2019 migrants, stating that the profiles of the incoming migrants gradually shifted from more affluent, more educated men aged 18–35 to poorer, less educated individuals featuring a larger share of women, children, and older adults (Oruc et al., 2020). However, our findings (albeit less generalizable due to the small sample size) would have important implications for BiH's socioeconomic development. With the BiH witnessing a population decline since 2009 (International Organization for Migration, 2022), it is imperative that the BiH government design policies and regulations to address this decline to keep up its efforts in economic growth. One possible solution is effectively designing and implementing policies and regulations promoting successful refugee and migrant integration.

However, effective migrant and refugee integration is dependent on many factors, including migrants' experiences in the host country, duration in the refugee center and access to essential services and protection, willingness to reside and integrate, access to employment and education, access to employment through social entrepreneurship, access to legal representation, and access to important information among others. We presented our findings and discussed them in light of the BiH contexts as follows.

Refugees' Experiences in Accessing Basic Social Services at the Refugee Camp

We asked the refugees how long they lived in the refugee center, their refugee status, and access to essential social services in Una Sana Canton, USK, refugee camp. Refugee camps are temporary facilities built to provide immediate protection and assistance for refugees and basic social services, including food, water, shelter, medical treatment, and other essential services.[5] In this regard, our respondents indicated they had been in the refugee for several weeks or months. In terms of access to basic social services (such as social welfare, healthcare, and housing) at the Una Sana Canton (USK) refugee camp, all respondents indicated their full access to

[5] See https://www.unrefugees.org/refugee-facts/camps/.

the services, which is highly positive and consistent with international best practices. In addition, refugees also indicated that they have freedom of mobility.

Refugee Integration and the Roles of Socioeconomic and Political Environments and Social Entrepreneurship

Willingness to ask and knowledge about applying for asylum: A vast majority of respondents would like to ask for asylum in BiH, but they did not ask for it because they were unfamiliar with the procedure. The findings imply that refugee camp professionals, administrative bodies, and other concerned individuals and bodies need to teach the migrants and refugees the procedures to apply for asylum.

Knowledge of one's rights as a refugee: Most refugees (80%) reported not knowing their rights. These rights include the right to follow their legal procedures in a language they understand, the right to acquire a residence in BiH territory, the right to accommodation (most often in an asylum seeker center), the right to receive primary health care, the right to attend school, get a job, and the right get psychosocial assistance among others. In this regard, our results again indicate there is a lot to do in teaching refugees about their rights as a refugee. Moreover, it also requires political commitment to implement such rights outside of the refugee camps, for example, by allowing the refugees to work, find residences, attend schools, and have other normal rights for mainstream society.

Access to legal representation and essential information: One of the significant challenges refugees cited was a lack of access to legal representation and important information. According to our findings, the majority of the respondents (over 95%) reported that they do not have legal representation and also do not have essential information (over 60%). Although BiH has a law (United Nations High Commissioner for Refugees, 2016) requiring the government to provide legal representation and important information for the refugees it hosts, according to our results, the implementation of such a statute has been minimal.

Access to employment and education: Despite having access to social services (including social welfare, health care, and housing), all respondents indicated they do not have access to education and employment. Although the country has a legal framework (United Nations High Commissioner for Refugees, 2016) that abides the country to provide the refugees with access to education and employment, this is not the case when it comes to its implementation. Implementing the laws that oblige the country to provide education and employment requires political commitment and strong socioeconomic status. In this regard, the country has a lower socioeconomic status compared to most of its European fellow countries. Moreover, COVID-19 has also severely affected the economy, which might have exacerbated the implementation of providing education and employment to the refugees in its country.

Access to employment through social entrepreneurship: Concerning the role of social entrepreneurship in enabling refugees' access to employment, unfortunately, all the respondents stated that they do not have access to employment through social entrepreneurship. As we highlighted in our review, the role of social entrepreneurship in promoting refugees' employment in BiH is still embryonic, meaning the country must design effective policies and regulations to encourage social entrepreneurship that focuses on refugees and migrants.

Willingness to reside and integrate into BiH: Having all the aforementioned challenges, it is unsurprising that most refugees were unwilling to reside and integrate into BiH. According to our findings, most refugees (65%) were not willing to get asylum in BiH. Even among the few who wanted asylum in BiH, many would like to get citizenship to move to foreign countries. Germany is reported as the most preferred destination for the migrants, followed by France and Belgium.

In Fig. 6.1, we summarize the results of those mentioned earlier and other relevant issues we assessed in our interviews. When we asked the refugees during our interviews if they were aware of the possibility of returning to their home country if their asylum application was refused, most said they were. We also asked whether they had diplomas for their educational achievement, if relatives or friends accompanied them, if they had friends or relatives in the host country, their mother tongue, and any other information that would be useful for the integration plan.

Conclusion

In line with our research aims, we explored the current situation of the refugees' inclusion with respect to social services and socioeconomic integration, compared to the planning in BiH. Our assessment indicates refugees face poor inclusion, due to the lack of access to employment, education, and social entrepreneurship initiatives in BiH. Moreover, most refugees also lack access to legal representation and important

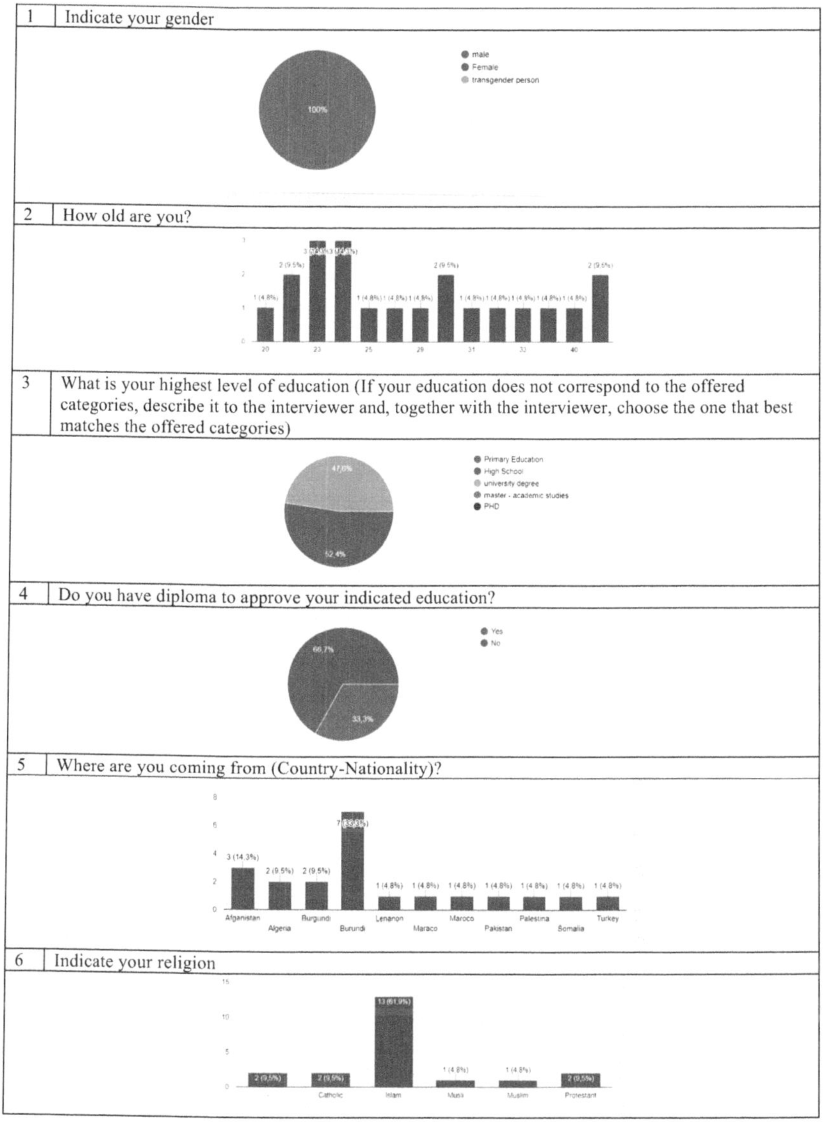

Fig. 6.1 Summary of sociodemographic characteristics and integration plan in Una Sana Canton (USK) refugee camp, BiH

7 Are you accompanied by someone?

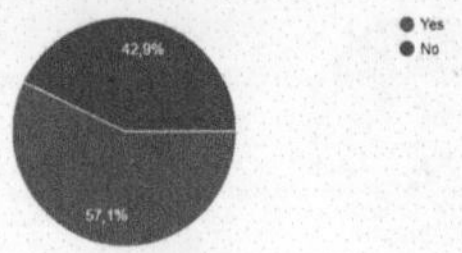

8 If your answer to the previous question is yes, give an indication of how many some relatives

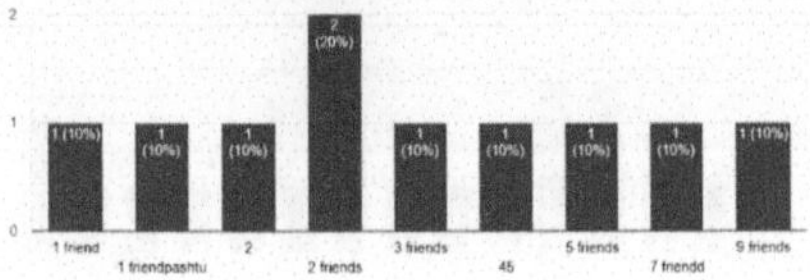

9 Please indicate your mother language

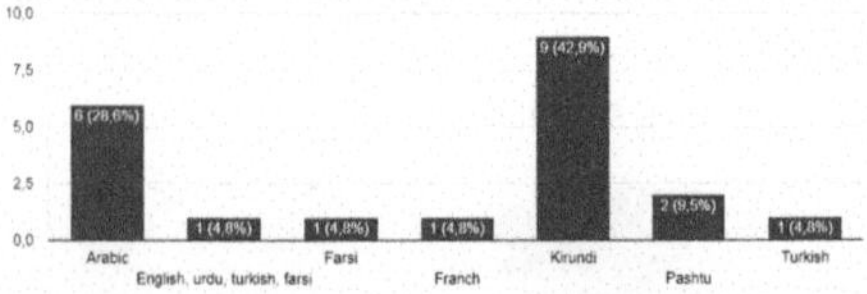

10 How long you have been in BiH as refugee, please indicate (number of days)

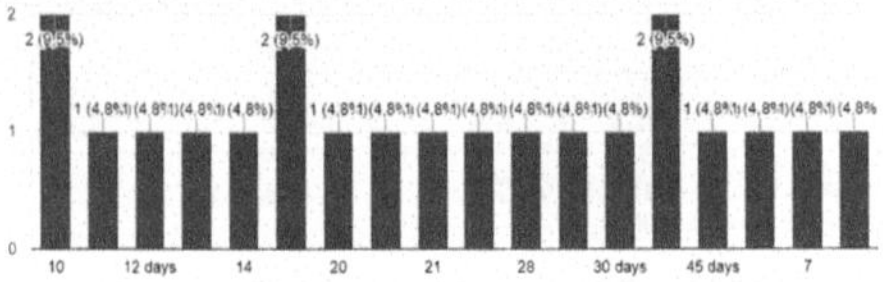

11 How long you have been in r refugee center, please indicate (number of days)

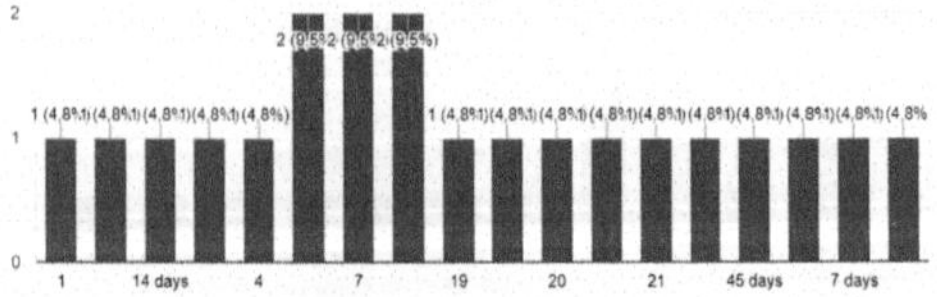

12 Did you have some support to come to BiH

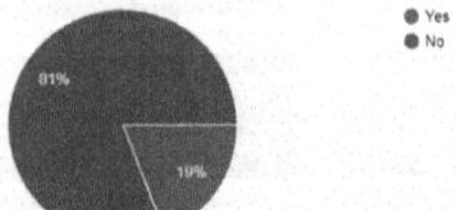

Fig. 6.1 (continued)

13 Do you know your rights as refugee in BiH

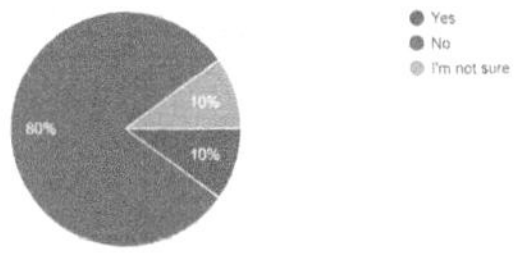

14 Would you like to get asylum in BiH

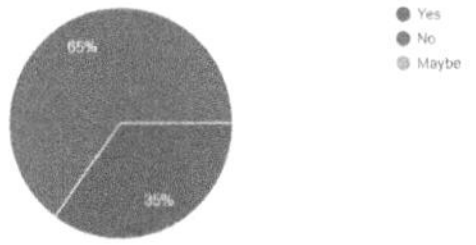

15 Did you apply to migration office to get asylum in BiH

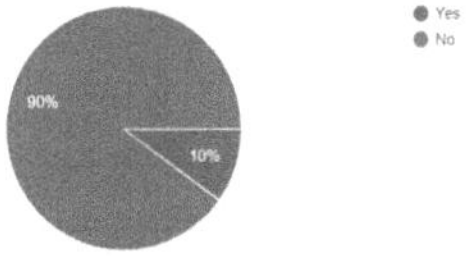

16 If you do not get asylum in BiH, are you aware that you will have to go back to your Country?

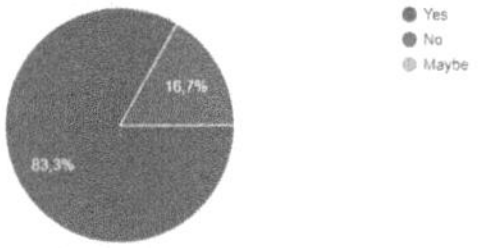

17 If you get asylum in BiH, were do you see yourself than

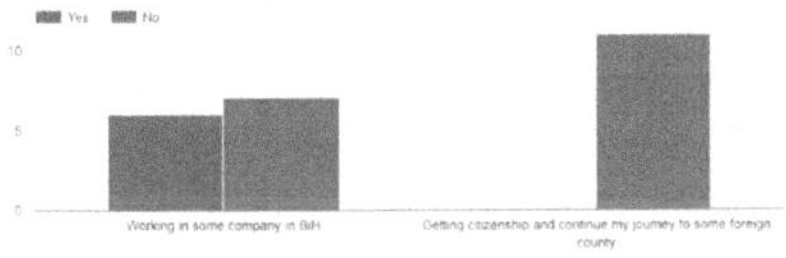

18 Are you interested to continue your journey to some of EU countries or some other if you do not get asylum?

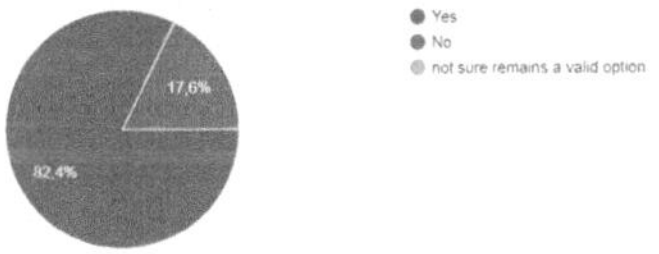

Fig. 6.1 (continued)

19	If you do not obtain asylum in BiH, are you interested to continue your journey to some of EU countries or some other?

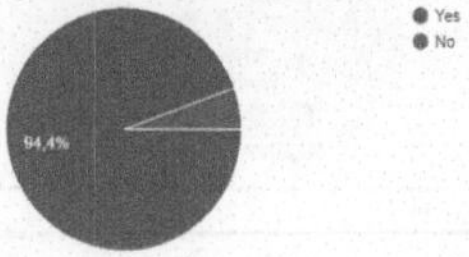

20	If BiH is not your desired destination, please indicate your desired final destination country?

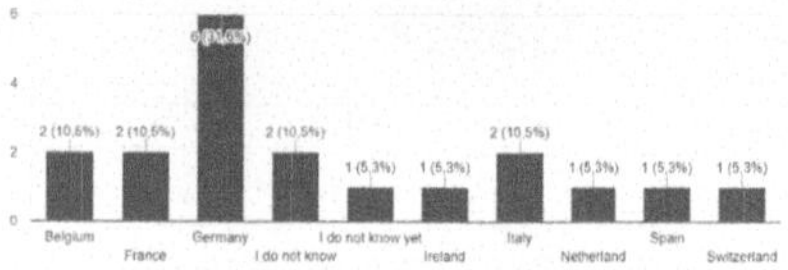

21	Do you have relatives, or friends in that county

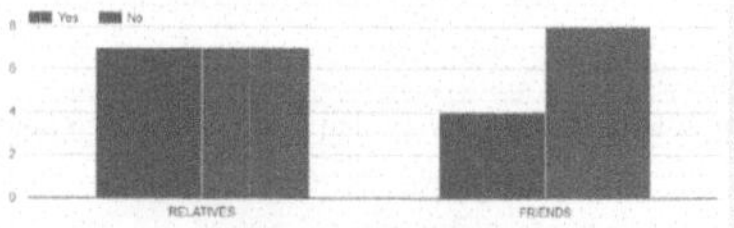

22	Do you have access to employment and education?

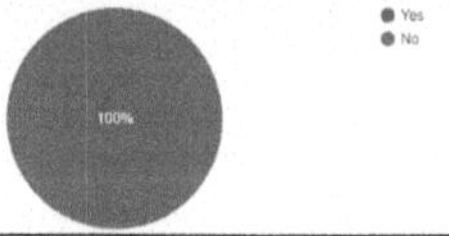

23	Do you have access to employment through social entrepreneurship?

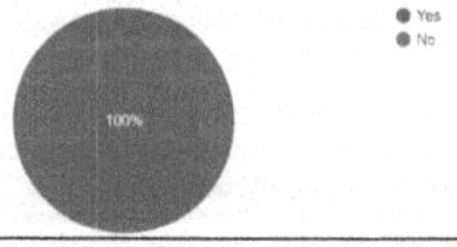

24	Are social services (social welfare, health care, housing) provided to you?

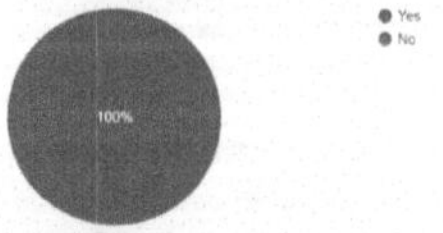

25	Can you move freely?

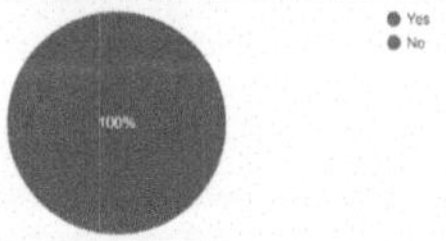

Fig. 6.1 (continued)

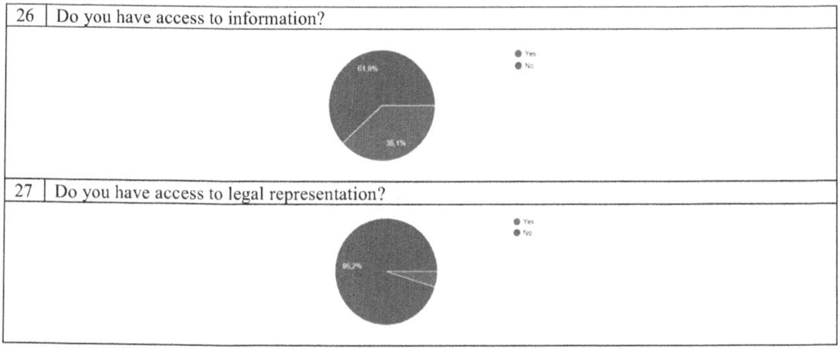

Fig. 6.1 (continued)

information, are unaware of the procedures to apply for asylum, and lack knowledge about one's rights as a refugee. Our findings confirm our initial argument that BiH generally lacks effective refugee integration policies' best practices (Amnesty International, 2019). In which might seem as a consequence, the vast majority of the refugees also reported that they do not wish to stay in the country. Instead, they reported that would like to move to other European countries mostly Germany, Belgium, and France among others. The refugees consider BiH as being just one stop on the way to the EU countries, which they see as their final destination.

Overall, our findings imply that BiH needs to set up conditions to promote social inclusion and entrepreneurship that in turn facilitate sustainable economic growth for refugees and asylum seekers, in line with Sustainable Development Goals, Goal 8 (SDG8; United Nations, 2020b). But these important socioeconomic reforms are equally urgent for the local population. Overall, the entire social economy including social enterprises is in its very early stage of development and is not yet capable of being used as a very efficient tool to provide decent work and economic growth while facilitating the refugees' integration plan. This is also being perceived and confirmed by migrants as through the interview process and the questionnaire, it is obvious they don't consider staying in BiH. In fact, studies indicate that effective refugee integration is the responsibility of both the refugees and the host country (Gulerce & Okten, 2021; Hynie, 2018).

Together, we tapped into very important information relevant to refugee integration and implementation plans in the BiH context by analyzing social entrepreneurship, socioeconomic context, and political environment. Our findings suggest that there is not much conducive environment for the integration of refugees from both sides of refugees as well as BiH. Firstly, most refugees and migrants arriving in BiH are not willing to stay and integrate into the country. Secondly, BiH also does not have a conducive environment in terms of providing refugees and migrants with education, employment, support, and important information about the rights of the refugees, as well as legal representations. If BiH wants to benefit from the migrants and refugees it hosts, it has to revisit its legal framework and political commitments.

References

Amnesty International. (2019). *Bosnia and Herzegovina: Impunity for War Crimes and Rights of Refugees and Migrants.* Submission for the UN Universal Periodic Review, 34th Session of the Up Working Group. https://www.amnesty.org/en/documents/eur63/0499/2019/en/

Andjelic, J., & Petricevic, T. (2020). *Regional Study and Guidelines on Social Entrepreneurship in the Western Balkans.* Regional Incubator for Social Entrepreneurs.

Betts, A. (2013). *Survival Migration: Failed Governance and the Crisis of Displacement* [Alexander Betts]. Cornell University Press, 10–28. Retrieved February 24, 2022, from https://www.jstor.org/stable/10.7591/j.ctt32b5cd

Đermanović, S. (2019). *Study of National Framework for Social Entrepreneurship in Bosnia and Herzegovina.* ALTER – Active Local Territories for Economic Development of Rural Areas.

European Commission. (2004). *Joint Report on Social Inclusion.* Office for Official Publications of the European Communities. https://ec.europa.eu/employment_social/social_inclusion/docs/final_joint_inclusion_report_2003_en.pdf

European Commission. (2019). *Communication from the Commission to the European Parliament and the Council: Commission Opinion on Bosnia and Herzegovina's Application for Membership of the European Union.* https://op.europa.eu/en/publication-detail/-/publication/8a338f81-8220-11e9-9f05-01aa75ed71a1

European Parliament. (2022). *EU-Turkey Statement & Action Plan, Legislative Train Schedule.* Retrieved September 7, 2023, from https://www.europarl.europa.eu/legislative-train/theme-towards-a-new-policy-on-migration/file-eu-turkey-statement-action-plan

Gavric, I. (2012). *Rethinking Active Labor Market Policies as a New Form of Aid to Bosnia and Herzegovina: The Case of Youth Employability and Retention Programme.* Master's thesis, Central European University.

Gulerce, H., & Okten, Ş. (2021). Social Entrepreneurship: Sustainable Social Development and Social Inclusion of Asylum Seekers. *Migration, Social Entrepreneurship, and Social Inclusion*, 9–21.

Hynie, M. (2018). Refugee Integration: Research and Policy. *Peace and Conflict: Journal of Peace Psychology, 24*(3), 265. https://doi.org/10.1037/pac0000326

International Organization for Migration. (2022). *World Migration Report*. https://publications.iom.int/books/world-migration-report-2022

Mair, J., Robinson, J., & Hockerts, K. (Eds.). (2006). *Social Entrepreneurship*. Palgrave Macmillan.

Ninkovic-Papic, R., Slijepčević, T., & Halepović, D. (2012). *Assessment Report on Social Entrepreneurship in Bosnia and Herzegovina*. Social Inclusion Foundation in Bosnia and Herzegovina.

Oruc, N., Raza, S., & Santic, D. (2020). *The Western Balkan Migration Route (2015–2019)*. Prague Process Secretariat International Centre for Migration Policy Development (ICMPD).

Poleschuk, S., Soldo, A., & Dreesen, T. (2023). *Unlocking Learning: The Use of Digital Learning to Support the Education and Inclusion of Refugees and Migrant Children in Bosnia and Herzegovina*. UNICEF Office of Research-Innocenti.

Rosandic, A., & Kusinikova, N. (2018). *Social Economy in the Eastern Neighborhood and the Western Balkans*. Synthesis Report from Directorate-General for Neighbourhood and Enlargement Negotiations (DG NEAR).

Rosas, G., Corbanese, V., O'Higgins, N., Roland, D., & Tanovic, L. (2009). *Employment Policy Review: Bosnia and Herzegovina*. ILO.

United Nations. (2020a, December 15). *Statement by the United Nations in Bosnia and Herzegovina on the Latest Developments with Migrant, Refugee, and Asylum-seeker in BiH* [Press Release]. https://bosniaherzegovina.un.org/en/105139-statement-united-nations-bosnia-and-herzegovina-latest-developments-migrant-refugee-and

United Nations. (2020b). *The Sustainable Development Goals Report 2020*. https://sdgs.un.org/sites/default/files/2020-09/The-Sustainable-Development-Goals-Report-2020.pdf

United Nations High Commissioner for Refugees. (2016, February 19). *Refworld | Bosnia and Herzegovina: Law on Asylum*. Retrieved September 15, 2023, from https://www.refworld.org/docid/58b575084.html

CHAPTER 7

Social Entrepreneurship for Refugees "in Transit": Opportunities and Developments in Serbia

Silvia Cittadini

Introduction

The opportunities offered by social entrepreneurship for the integration of refugees and asylum seekers, together with its challenges, have long attracted the attention of scholars and policymakers, who engaged in a debate on its effective potential to settle social injustices. On one side, it has been noted how social enterprises can address a series of challenges hindering the economic integration of asylum seekers and refugees, such as the knowledge of the language, the lack of a support networking and the discriminatory environment, by offering working opportunities combined with training within an environment sensitive to their specific conditions (Baraibar-Diez et al., 2019; Barraket, 2014; Farmer et al., 2021; Hazenberg et al., 2012; Roy et al., 2017). On the other side, it has been also noted that social enterprises might reinforce other aspects that

S. Cittadini (✉)
IECOB – Institute for Central Eastern and Balkan Europe, Forlì, Italy

S. Bianchini et al. (eds.), *Social Entrepreneurship and Migrants' Inclusion*, Sustainable Development Goals Series,
https://doi.org/10.1007/978-3-031-55791-0_7

preserve the social exclusion of these groups within the labour market, failing to address the roots of social exclusion. Cooney (2011), for instance, highlights that social enterprises mostly operate within low-skilled labour sectors, potentially hindering the possibility for asylum seekers and refugees to find better, qualified jobs and reiterating the ethnicisation of low skilled sectors.

This issue is connected with the persistence of structures and narratives informed by racism: while social entrepreneurship might offer an opportunity for racialised individuals and groups to provide for themselves and become economically independent (Hossein, 2021; Tracey et al., 2005), it must also be considered the criticism pointing to the blindness of social entrepreneurship discourses and funds towards initiatives promoted by minority groups themselves (Clarke, 2021; Hossein, 2021) and the stereotypes that might be hidden behind social enterprises' marketing strategies (Flowers & Swan, 2017). The issue is connected in general with racial privilege and the consequent risks connected to philanthropic initiatives aimed at empowering the racial subaltern, such as the reproduction of paternalistic patterns and the incapacity to question the basic structures preserving racial discrimination and exclusion. It must be considered, indeed, that although social enterprises might offer an economic income to grassroots movements and organisations, their sustainability is often dependent on public funds and support, questioning their actual autonomy (O'Shaughnessy, 2008).

Taking these criticisms in mind, however, when it comes to the integration of asylum seekers and refugees, the benefits offered by social entrepreneurship go beyond the integration in the labour market. Many authors, for instance, point to the socio-psychological benefits due to the improvement of self-confidence produced by the involvement in social enterprises, the enlargement of the social network with new friendships and improved cross-sectorial understandings (Barraket, 2014; Kummitha, 2016; Macaulay et al., 2017; Roy et al., 2014; Teasdale, 2010). Barraket (2014) also mentions the potential, although limited, impact of social enterprises in producing new narratives on the contribution of foreigners in hosting societies.

In light of these opportunities, the European Union in the last years has incentivised the development of initiatives of social entrepreneurship not only within Member States but also in its neighbouring areas, especially within EU candidate countries. Serbia, in this context, has followed the example of other Central-Eastern European countries that have fast transitioned from a socialist to a capitalist economy, marking the return to de-regularisation, privatisation and individualism. This transition has led to the dismantlement of the socialist welfare state and to the consequent necessity of developing a new system able to mitigate its direst consequences. For this reason, the EU has promoted the development of a social economy and social enterprises also in Serbia, in consideration of their contribution to economic development and inclusive growth (Defourny et al., 2021). At the same time, this country has come to address another relevant phenomenon in the last ten years, namely the transit of hundreds of thousand migrants directed to Western Europe through the so-called Balkan Route (Hameršak et al., 2020). After an initial period of chaos, Serbia organised a system of reception and humanitarian support through the establishment of reception centres aimed at controlling the new arrivals and offering basic first aid. However, with the EU-Turkey deal in March 2016 and the tightening of border controls, the relatively fast transit through the Western Balkans region has been considerably slowed down and thousands of asylum seekers remained stuck in Serbia for months or even years. For this reason, while still seeking to reach Western Europe, a good number of asylum seekers started integrating within Serbian society, despite the limited access to asylum rights and integration services (Mandić, 2021; Stojic Mitrovic, 2019; Vukcevic, 2020).

Social entrepreneurship for the specific purpose of boosting the integration of refugees and asylum seekers is an unexplored phenomenon in Serbia, while some small steps for the development of the first initiatives have been taken. This article aims to investigate the opportunities and challenges of investing into social entrepreneurship for the economic integration of asylum seekers and refugees in Serbia, departing from the experience of a social enterprise offering job opportunities to refugee women in the tailoring sector, Women on the Way. With this analysis, the study intends also to contribute to the general debate on the opportunities offered by social entrepreneurship for asylum seeker and refugee integration, focusing on the specificities of the Serbian migratory context, marked by uncertainty and the phenomenon of stranded migrants. The aim is to provide potential new insights on social enterprises and integration in a world increasingly marked by protracted im/mobilities—namely situations where migrants/refugees remain in conditions of displacement or transit for a protracted period of time that can last years (de Vries & Guild, 2019; Tobin et al., 2023). With this aim, the study is based on fieldwork and interviews conducted between December 2022 and January 2023, both onsite and online.

The selection of the interviewees departed from the founders of Women on the Way and their direct collaborators, reaching then local organisations and institutions that work in support to migrants, asylum seekers and refugees and for the promotion of social entrepreneurship. The analysis of Women on the Way required, indeed, an attentive analysis of the most recent evolutions and challenges of the integration system and social entrepreneurship environment in Serbia. All stakeholders interviewed have been contacted and informed of the aim and content of the study through email and agreed on a meeting either in presence or online. The study included a visit to the Reception Centre of Vranje, Serbia, where the women currently working for Women in the Way, Ukrainian asylum seekers and refugees, are hosted. In order to conduct the study, it was necessary to obtain the official permit by Commissariat for Refugees and Migration (KIRS), which has been informed about the study, while the women in Vranje have been informed about my arrival and study by Women on the Way. All interviews have been conducted in English, except for the ones in Vranje, due to the presence of a translator only from Ukrainian to Serbian. Here, the interviews have been supported by the collection of four written questionnaires given to women collaborating with Women on the Way that was not possible to interview. All of them have been fully informed of the aim of the study and that they will remain completely anonymous.

Social Entrepreneurship in Serbia: History and Latest Developments

The development of social entrepreneurship in Serbia followed the transition from a socialist economy, where state institutions controlled the provision of social services leaving little or no space to individual initiatives, to a capitalist one, where the return to individualism and market economy brought to the dismantle of most of the structures ensuring social support. In order to address the most dramatic consequences of mass privatisation of public services, from health to education, the Serbian government since the early 2000s enacted a series of laws and strategies for the development of alternative forms of social protection. In this context, civil society started playing an important role in the provision of social services. An example is the activation of the Social Innovation Fund that since 2003 for seven years has supported the creation of social enterprises for the provision of social services at the local level, with the idea of encouraging a plurality of service providers. This, as all other initiatives intended to support the development of a new social economy, has benefitted from the beginning of the large support of the European Union and other international organisations that played an essential role in promoting social entrepreneurship (Defourny et al., 2021; Rakić et al., 2017).

Here, although the transition has started in a later stage compared to other Eastern European countries, the adoption of a market economy and the development of an entrepreneurial mentality has been favoured by a socio-economic environment partially acquainted with the management of "social businesses". Indeed, since the 1970s, although the state continued to play a major role in the provision and control of social services and in goods production, the Yugoslav government had partially opened to the market economy and introduced the "self-management principle". In addition, agricultural cooperatives and companies for the employment of persons with disabilities were an important reality within the Yugoslav system and surely contributed to the early development of forms of social enterprises (Rakić et al., 2017). It is probably thank to this favourable socio-economic environment, that social entrepreneurship has been a growing and promising—although still marginal—economic reality for the past ten years, attracting the attention of numerous scholars and organisations (Cvejić, 2013; Defourny & Nyssens, 2021; Golubović & Muhi, 2019; Krstić et al., 2017; Rakić et al., 2017).

Although modern understandings of social entrepreneurship have been introduced in Serbia quite at the beginning of the transition, a specific law defining and regulating the creation of this kind of entities has been adopted only in 2022. However, other laws had an impact in the creation of this kind of initiatives. One of the most relevant, explicitly mentioning social enterprises in its text, is the Law on Professional Rehabilitation and Employment of Persons with Disabilities, which, among the other things, foresees state aid support for those social enterprises employing persons with disabilities. Other relevant laws are the Law on Association, establishing the conditions under which an association can engage in economic activities, the Law on Foundations and Endowments and the Law on Cooperatives. This last law establishes that social cooperatives can be created for social purposes, such as the integration of vulnerable groups, although it does not foresee tax benefits for this kind of entities (Cvejić, 2013; Golubović & Muhi, 2019).

In light of this legal framework, social enterprises in Serbia can take different institutional forms as highlighted in the studies that proposed a mapping of the social entrepreneurship environment in the country. One of the most comprehensive studies done in this sense has been published in 2014 by the Statistical Office of the Republic of Serbia. The report maps 1196 social enterprises, the majority of which take the form of Cooperatives or Associations, and are located in the region of Vojvodina. Another interesting finding is that the great majority of social enterprises in the country have "economic empowerment and employment" as main goal (61.5%), followed by "socio-humanitarian assistance" (15.4%) and "education courses and information-sharing" (7.2%) (Vukmirović, 2014, p. 44). The study also highlights that the main issues encountered by social enterprises are mostly of financial nature, as the luck of funds, the low prices of the products/services and the outstanding receivables (p. 49). Similar challenges are highlighted by another study conducted in 2016 in the region of Vojvodina, where the lack of tax benefits, funds and technical supports are identified as the main issues (Golubović & Muhi, 2019). Finally, another interesting survey conducted in 2015 on 90 social enterprises (Krstić et al., 2017) highlights how the majority of individuals establishing a social enterprise did not have previous business experience and are mostly moved by the intention of creating a personal employment opportunity and addressing social challenges. This study also points out the general dependence of social enterprises, whose majority consists of micro-companies, on external funds and grants.

The findings presented here reveal the emerging interest towards the opportunities offered by social enterprises in Serbia where this kind of social business has grown in few years, despite it still mostly consists of small companies highly dependent on external funding. The new law adopted in 2022 on social entrepreneurship, after ten years of debates that involved also the civil society sector, might prompt the adoption of further policies to support this kind of business, although the effective measures and impact are still unknown. As also highlighted during the interviews with two representatives of the Coalition for the development of solidarity economy in Serbia (KoRSE) and the Initiative for Development and Cooperation (IDC) that actively took part in drafting it, the law recognises the status of social entrepreneurship and the conditions necessary to receive this status but does not refer to specific policy measures to support social enterprises. For this reason, even the representative of IDC, who launched a number of social enterprises, declared to be unsure whether he will register them under the new law. A strategy for the implementation of measures in support to social entrepreneurship should be adopted in 2023, but it is not sure when, due also to the change of government in late 2022.

In this regard, it is also interesting what has emerged during the interviews regarding the perception of social entrepreneurship in the country. Indeed, one representative of Asylum Protection Centre (APC) was sceptical about the real potentials of social entrepreneurship in the country, stating that it is something brought from abroad, from the UN and the EU, that cannot become sustainable in Serbia. This opinion was rejected by the representative of IDC, who highlighted how social entrepreneurship is something rooted in Serbia society, although the name itself might come from abroad. However, he recognised as well that there might be some political resistance to the activities carried out by social organisations, as some political representatives currently at the government do have a negative opinion regarding the activities carried out by non-governmental organisations (NGOs). On this regard, the IDC representative said:

> I do not have this impression that people think that [social entrepreneurship] was brought from abroad from international organisations. For example, the organisations that established the coalition for solidarity economy, none of us is international organisation, all of us are local organisations, some of us are grassroot organisations, some of us are think tank organisations, some foundations but generally speaking all this concept was here for many, many years. […] I do not think that people perceive it as some sort of foreign influence or something, except maybe, our government and our law makers because we are sure that law on social entrepreneurship was pushed by EU. They said "one part of your process of joining the EU is to regulate field of SE in Serbia" Maybe they have this kind of perception and now the new minister maybe somebody told him "yes we know that you don't like this kind of social… NGOs and foreign… and who is paying them, but your role is to finish with this law and then to thick one assignment that you got from the EU". (Initiative for Development and Cooperation, interview)

The Reception and Integration of Asylum Seekers and Refugees in Serbia: Evolution and Open Issues

While social entrepreneurship in general is an emerging and quite widespread phenomenon in Serbia, social entrepreneurship for the integration of asylum seekers and refugees is still a marginal practice. This is probably due to the fact that only very recently the issue of the integration of asylum seekers and refugees in the country started to be debated, although Serbia is at the centre of the so-called Balkan Route since the early 2010s (Hameršak et al., 2020). Still now, indeed, Serbia is mostly considered a "transit country", namely a place where asylum seekers pass through but do not intend to stay for long. However, the increasing securitarisation of EU borders and the consequent difficulties to cross borders have considerably increased the number of persons and families that stay in Serbia for prolonged periods of time. As noted by some authors, despite their integration remains a marginal topic in the public debate, asylum seekers and refugees started sending their children to Serbia school, learning the local language and looking for job opportunities (Mandić, 2021; Stojic Mitrovic, 2019; Vukcevic, 2020). This process is surely hindered by a system of reception and integration constructed around the idea that Serbia is exclusively a transit, and therefore intended to simply provide basic humanitarian assistance. The access to asylum protection, indeed, remains limited: despite the legislative reforms, the process of recognition remains very long, lasting for years, as confirmed in the interviews, and the number of those who receive the status is very low (See Table 7.1).

One of the main issues for the labour integration then is the fact that access to labour market is allowed only after nine months from asylum application and asylum seekers have to renew their working permit every six months paying a fee of about 150 euros, which is a very high amount in a country where average monthly salary is between 400 and 700 euros.[1] This expense is very often covered by local NGOs supporting migrants and refugees, such as the Belgrade Centre for Human Rights, Grupa 484 and Asylum Protection Centre. These organisations support refugees and migrants in a wide series of aspects, often covering services that should be provided by state institutions. On this regard, the representative of Belgrade Centre for Human Rights said:

[1] https://www.stat.gov.rs/en-US/oblasti/trziste-rada/zarade.

Table 7.1 UNHCR data on asylum decisions in Serbia 2012–2023 (data for 2023 are available until mid-year)

Year	*Recognised decisions*	*Complementary protection*	*Rejected decisions*	*Otherwise closed*	*Total decisions*
2012	0	0	83	2751	2834
2013	0	10	20	5024	5054
2014	0	10	5	16,526	16,541
2015	22	15	0	932	969
2016	10	35	36	838	919
2017	0	10	20	330	360
2018	72	11	15	742	840
2019	49	20	78	2144	2291
2020	27	5	67	1417	1516
2021	37	5	61	748	851
2022	20	16	66	801	903
2023	28	0	16	155	199

> Commissariat [KIRS] needs to have the duty to work individually with refugees for diplomas' notifications, to support refugees in the continued education, in accessing labour market and everything but in the practise they are not doing that, we are the only one doing that [...] on the notification of diplomas, in that policy of integration there is one article that is saying that Commissariat is going to take care of that, but in practice we are paying the taxes, we are translating the documents, we are applying on behalf of the agency for the qualification and we are preparing that all documentation because if we won't do it, none would support them. (Belgrade Centre for Human Rights, interview)

This situation has been also well expressed by one of the funders of Women on the Way, who have resided in Serbia for almost four years as an asylum seeker, when she said:

> The Government does not care about you. All they care for is every six months: "Go and pay €200 and get your work permit and do whatever you want. We don't care. Where do you live? We don't care. What do you eat? We don't care". (Farimah, Women on the Way, interview)

In addition, another critical issue raised by almost all interviewees is the fact that both asylum seekers and refugees do not receive a regular ID but a handwritten document that can be easily faked, further hindering normal procedures such as opening bank accounts. Moreover, refugees that receive protection in Serbia do not have the right to move to other countries and cannot apply at any time for Serbian citizenship. These rules and procedures represent an obvious deterrent to applying for asylum in Serbia, where the number of asylum applications and decisions is still very low compared to the number of asylum seekers passing through the country (see data in Chap. 3 of this book).

Concerning possible future changes in asylum legislation in the country to address these issues, the interviews highlighted different perspectives. While the representative of the Belgrade Centre for Human Rights expressed some hopes, stating that their organisation is cooperating with the government institutions by providing recommendation to address issues such as the one of the ID through changes in legislation, the representative of the Asylum Protection Centre claimed that it is not in the interest of the government to change the legislation as the current strategy in migration and asylum management is aimed at dissuading asylum seekers to stay in the country:

> The policy will remain the same. Serbia is afraid of becoming a hotspot, a buffer zone where people will just be locked, and Serbia has this approach because of various reasons… xenophobic reasons, previous history, awareness of lack of capacity of society to change. The decision makers are adopting this approach in order to prevent new arrivals of foreigners to stay as migrants. They would rather go to the employment services to reach Bangladeshi, Pakistani to get them as labour force rather than to give a chance to anyone who is coming here as migrant on his own. (Asylum Protection Centre, interview)

This situation sums up, of course, with all other difficulties that asylum seekers encounter in their integration process in Serbia, such as the knowledge of the language, the daily acts of discrimination and the struggling economic situation of the country, where regular revenues are often insufficient to cover increasing daily expenses.

Despite these difficulties, though, the fieldwork also highlighted the possibilities offered by the employment of asylum seekers and refugees. Interestingly, most of the officers interviewed highlighted how the increasing lack of Serbian workforce, due to emigration, especially in the hospitality sector, is driving companies to look for asylum seekers. As also confirmed by the UNHCR representatives, following some good examples such as the one of IKEA that activated a programme for refugees offering an internship opportunity and then hiring a good number of asylum seekers and refugees, major companies had started reaching them to replicate the experience. The main problem here remains the fact that the number of those who possess the working permit is still very low. On this regard, the APC representative said: "We are supporting them to find employment, because we have some employers who are cooperating with us. We have a lot of options but not enough refugees to supply demands" (Asylum Protection Centre, interview).

Along with the increasing interest for local companies to hire refugees, some initiatives have tried to offer employment opportunities through social entrepreneurship, although these are still quite marginal cases. One case mentioned by everyone is Pizza Laganizza, a pizza take-away shop opened in 2019 by the Catholic Relief Services[2] and supported by UNHCR for employing asylum seekers and refugees. This case, though, was also presented as a failure due to the fact that, after some economic difficulties, it was forced to reduce considerably its employees, missing de facto its social goal. According to the UNHCR officer, this "failure" was mostly due to the COVID-19 pandemic and some poor marketing choices. However, according to the APC representative, this failure is also telling of the fact that this kind of initiative driven by international organisations proves unsustainable in the Serbian context, due to the lack of sensitivity by Serbian customers. For this reason, his organisation decided not to use the "social enterprise employing refugees" story to promote a bakery that they opened exactly with the intention of offering employment opportunities to refugees. This because they deemed it as a failing marketing strategy in the Serbian context.

Despite the difficulties here highlighted, it must be noted that the numerous grassroots and civic organisations emerged during the peak of the so-called refugee crisis in the years 2015–2017 to support asylum seekers and refugees offer the opportunity to develop potentially innovative initiatives for their integration. This emerged especially during the interview with one of the founders of Women on the Way: although in almost four years in the country she has never been accorded with international protection by Serbian authorities, going through a series of difficulties that moved her to seek asylum in France through a UNHCR

[2] https://globalcompactrefugees.org/good-practices/pizza-laganizza-pizzeria-working-space-refugees-and-asylum-seekers.

programme, she recognises and misses the spontaneous social and civic network that supported her in Serbia. In line also with the findings of a study conducted on solidarity movements along the Balkan Route by Chiara Milan (2019), her words depict a society where the negligence of the state is filled by other actors, offering less structured but, at the same time, more spontaneous opportunities of networking and solidarity. Interesting, in this sense, is her comparison with France:

> In Serbia is a bit different because the system, the government, is not really organised, is not really welcoming to people and most of projects were kind of established and supported by abroad, such as EU and America, embassies [...] But the thing I liked there actually, like the programmes or the small groups they were so organic [word used to mean "spontaneous"]!! Like people themselves are doing stuff. It wasn't the government governing and programming things like in France, because currently I'm in France and everything is like.... even the associations and NGOs, they're all funded by the central government of France and things are just so like organised. But there [in Serbia] things were more organic. So for the people, incredible people. (Farimah, Women on the Way, interview)

This aspect of spontaneity and grassroots solidarity experienced by Farimah during her stay in Serbia recurred often during the interview with her. She linked it with the negligence of state institutions, whose absence provides a space for informal action—"they (state institutions) don't care about you, so they don't put hurdles on your way", but also to the experience of war suffered by Serbian citizens during the conflicts of the 1990s—"in Serbia I could see more complicity because people are still traumatised by the war"—which still does not place them in a position of white supremacy—"here [in France] I can feel more white supremacy than in Serbia [...] they are not in a position of power, they are not the first world countries" (Farimah, Women on the Way, interview).

The vitality and solidarity of Serbian civil society experienced by Farimah surely can contribute to the flourishing of initiatives of social economy, allowing spaces for experimentation and innovation. However, the absence of the state institutions, while allowing broader spaces for informality, still represents the main burden for the meaningful integration of asylum seekers and refugees. As emerged also in other interviews, the scarce number of persons recognised with international protection in the country and the limited access to human right are probably among the main reasons that push asylum seekers passing through the country to seek for protection elsewhere. Farimah is an exemplary case, in this sense, as after almost four years in Serbia where she initiated Women on the Way, she left to France through UNHCR because she could not have access to asylum rights in Serbia. On this regard, I asked her: "What were the motivations, the main motivations for you to leave to France?"

> Ohh actually, the very first one and the most important one was that I was not recognised as a human there because.... Before I was asylum seeker, so that was a forever title to me [...] So that's just horrible and I couldn't get asylum title during four years, 3 1/2 years and I have a lot of, I had a lot of difficulties. Most importantly, like my papers, because basically I was nothing. Being a refugee is always like nothing... like the system wants to tell you that you are nothing, just migrants without paper.... even if you are killed, you are no one. And I had a lot of medical issues, so I couldn't even get a health insurance. I couldn't. Yes. So that was the motivation that I left Serbia, but I do miss Serbia. I liked my network there. I liked the people I met there. I liked my life, I mean... Although I had a lot of a lot of a lot of suffering and struggling there, but I liked my life there too because I had good friends. (Farimah, Women on the Way, interview)

The situation here outlined is quite different, though, for the Ukrainian asylum seekers fled from the conflict in their country after February 2022. Serbia, following the EU example, accorded the possibility for all Ukrainian arriving in Serbia to apply for temporary protection and have access to asylum rights through an easier and faster procedure (UNHCR Serbia, 2022). According to the estimates, by the end of June 2022, 772 persons from Ukraine (228 men, 544 women and 204 children) applied for temporary protection and 719 were granted with protection, although it is estimated that the number of arrivals is much higher (around 7000 only in the first semester of 2022) and that the great majority stays in private accommodation, hosted by relatives or friends (Belgrade Centre for Human Rights, 2022). The decision of granting temporary protection facilitated considerably the life of Ukrainian asylum seekers allowing them to access full integration services and labour market. This is also the reason why, as it is going to be explained in the next section, Women on the Way is now collaborating with Ukrainian women hosted in the newly renovated reception centre of Vranje, located about three hours by car south to Belgrade reserved to Ukrainian women and families: the main contact person there has managed to get a working permit few months after her arrival, allowing the regularisation of her working collaboration with the Serbian social enterprise.

Social Enterprise in "Transit": Women on the Way

Women on the Way is a social start-up aimed at employing refugee women in the fashion sector, established officially in September 2021 in the form of NGO. The main promoters of this initiative were two young women, an Iranian asylum seeker based in Belgrade, Farimah, and a Serbian girl, Katarina. This idea stemmed from a collective initiative launched by Farimah within a refugee women support group hosted by the local NGO Atina, back in 2019. She used her experience as artist and designer to engage her peers in artistic activities aimed at bringing them together, empowering them and earn some money, by developing a series of projects to be funded by local Foundations. The first project consisted in a training course for the decoration of denims with traditional motives from their countries of origin, ending with an exhibition of their creations. The second project funded the preparation and publication of a children book in seven different languages. In the same period, Farimah was contacted by Katarina, who she already met few years earlier during a study that the Serbian girl was conducting on refugee women. Katarina, who had specialised in political sciences, was temporarily unemployed and looking for job opportunities, showed her interest in her work and proposed her a collaboration to transform Women on the Way from an informal collective initiative into a social enterprise. With this purpose, she also applied for a macro-regional training programme for young social entrepreneurs, RISE,[3] offered by the Regional Youth Cooperation Office. This programme was essential for her to gain basic skills for launching a social enterprise, as she explained:

> That programme helped me to propel the idea and establish it as a social enterprise so I think that was the key that helped me at the beginning, otherwise I wouldn't be able to do it by myself because I didn't know anything about social entrepreneurship, nothing, and that's not something that is very….so it was 4 or 6 months of training of like basics of social entrepreneurship everything that you need to know about establishing a business, finances, marketing basically… social entrepreneurship 1.1. (Katarina, Women on the Way, interview)

The RISE programme also gave her the opportunity to present her entrepreneurial idea within a national competition and win a price of

[3] https://www.rycowb.org/?page_id=7816.

2500 euro that allowed her to buy two sewing machines, the first materials and to establish formally Women on the Way on September 2021. At the beginning, the organisation counted on the largely voluntary work of Katarina, her sister, Farimah and another Iranian girl and thanks to the contacts on the field of the NGO Belgrade Centre for Human Rights, they could start collaborating with a Nigerian refugee able to sew. Most of their products were sold online through their website and in local fairs.[4] However, after few months, Farimah took the opportunity offered by UNHCR to be transferred in France where she would be granted with full asylum rights, and the Nigerian collaborator found a job in IKEA, leaving Women on the Way.

One of the interesting aspects emerged during the interviews with Katarina and Farimah is their relationship of collaboration. As argued in the introduction, initiatives of social entrepreneurship might still be affected by unbalanced relations of power between the local promoter of the initiative and its beneficiaries/employees. In this case, the risks provoked by the different position of power/privilege were even higher, due to the fact that Farimah not only was a foreigner and asylum seekers but also never managed to receive proper protection and rights, positioning her in a further position of vulnerability. Although during the interview I did not bring out this issue explicitly, Farimah touched the topic, when I asked her what was the added value of having Katarina in Women on the Way:

> It was her who joined our group and brought her values, brought her availability, brought her, you know... Yeah, her value for us to share, to develop the idea. That's what I loved: she shared privilege to us. And that's because I have kind of political perspective usually for any programme, anything I do, but with her, I never felt that somebody's gonna save me or somebody's gonna, you know, somebody's gonna be above us or lead us or something like that. No, she was always just next to us, and just first recognising our own values, she was recognising our values and bringing her own privileges and her own values and helping to develop and to actually make the idea better. (Farimah, Women on the Way, interview)

For this reason, Farimah was happy to leave Women on the Way to Katarina, as she did not want this initiative to disappear with her departure. In fact, she expressed the intention and desire to continue

[4] https://womenontheway.co/.

developing the concept of Women on the Way, to transform it into a brand connecting an international network of women that can use it to develop and promote their arts and ideas: "women on the way could be an umbrella idea to cover us, and to actually to empower each other, to learn from each other, and to serve the next coming women who are desperate" (Farimah, Women on the Way, interview).

Intentioned to continue with this experience, in 2022, Katarina started looking for new collaborators and opportunities to develop more Women on the Way. It was always thanks to Belgrade Centre for Human Rights that she came into contact with Natalia [invented name], a Ukrainian refugee arrived in Serbia at the end of February 2022 and hosted in the Reception Centre of Vranje, who was working as a professional tailor also in Ukraine. After meeting, they started collaborating: Natalia could apply for working permit and be then regularly paid by Women on Way. At the same time, Katarina started transforming Women on the Way from a business-to-consumer enterprise to a business-to-business one, also thanks to the consultancy services offered by UNHCR, which started supporting her. In this way, she started receiving larger orders from companies and embassies that are then forwarded to Natalia, who receives by post the material to work on. At the Reception Centre, Natalia is helped by other four to six women, although she remains the main contact person. Katarina, then, interacts directly with Natalia and never had any contact with the authorities managing the centre of Vranje.

In December 2022, I visited the Reception Centre of Vranje, after asking and obtaining with no difficulties the permit by the local authorities. Here I found a welcoming and relaxed environment both from the side of the local KIRS officers and the asylum seekers and I had the opportunity to interview Natalia and one of her collaborators, with the mediation of a Ukrainian to Serbian translator, and a local officer. I then distributed and collected four questionnaires from other informal collaborators of Women on the Way in Ukrainian language. Most of the interviews took place within the sewing laboratory where the women gather to work, chat and make projects. In fact, they sew not only for Women on the Way but also for themselves, thanks to the local organisation Sigma Plus, which organised a sewing workshop and gave to the Reception Centre the sewing machines and material. In this way, also those women who did not have experience in sewing could get some basic skills and start collaborating with Natalia and Women on the Way. This activity is evidently perceived as a pleasant diversion: the environment within the laboratory is very cheerful—the interviews were often interrupted because of the laughs and jokes between each other, including the translator and the KIRS officer (all women)—and they immediately showed me the pictures of the fashion parade they had organised the night before my arrival within the Centre with the clothes they had created.

In the laboratory, Natalia, a middle-aged woman that proved a little shy at the beginning but revealed to be very cheerful, is presented by the others as a woman with many talents and the main motivator and driving force of the laboratory. At the beginning of the interview with Natalia, the KIRS officer and the translator intervened:

KIRS officer	Natalia knows everything, she know how to sew, how to knit, how to cook, how to make cakes.... [they all laugh together]
The translator	she has 10 million talents!
KIRS	yes!
Natalia	my husband says "I have a universal woman!" [they all laugh]

The other Ukrainian woman interviewed in the laboratory immediately started talking how Natalia motivated her to start sewing:

> I am happy because Natalia came to pick me up [convince her] that I could sew and gain some money... she gave me the motivation. And I am happy that she motivated me because of my psychological well-being, because before I was just continuously thinking about Kherson [the region she comes from], looking at the news... what and how... the husband. (Women on the Way's collaborator, interview)

In this quote, the Ukrainian woman starts mentioning the main positive aspect of being engaged with Women on the Way, as expressed by all other who have been surveyed: this activity gives them something to do, in a situation of psychological distress due to the war and the displacement, bringing them together, creating a group of support and occupying them with an activity that makes them proud. In fact, on this regard, she also added:

> Now we are busy, we do not have time to look at the news. The time passes faster, we gather together, positive emotions, interesting things, yesterday night we had this fashion catwalk. And we have a result, a finished work, we are proud of what we do, that people wear and like it. Every day, she asks

"what did we do today?" and there is always something that we did. (Women on the Way's collaborator, interview)

Natalia, when asked whether her life improved since she started working with Katarina, replied:

> Yes, of course. You have something to do, you don't seat all time in the room… we gather here with the women, we talk, we laugh… it is interesting… Women on the Way, Sigma and Kommissariat, we are happy that we can do this here and receive everything and you do not think too much of the situation… and you get money! This is the best motivation [they laugh] This is necessary… here everything is fine, the services are great, but you need the money, you have the kids, and maybe the kids want something. This is a motivation… for money, all women want to work for money. (Natalia, Women on the Way, interview)

Having an occupation and gaining some money were then the main positive aspects of Women on the Way. This was also confirmed in the questionnaires, filled by other women who not in all cases work with Natalia full time as some managed to keep their Ukrainian job online and collaborate with Women on the Way as a hobby. On this collaboration, they wrote: "It is a pleasant thing. It proved to be something that calms me down" (1); "I can earn some money and learn something new" (2); "you earn some money doing what you like and you do not think of the bad situation" (3); "it is nice that a group of persons with common interests and passions gathered. Sewing united us" (1).

The psychological benefits of working in an activity as sewing, together with other women in similar situation, were also well expressed by Farimah, who talked about the deep depression she fell during the first months of her stay in Serbia and how gathering with other women with a common purpose helped her. On this regard, she said:

> So yeah, that's my biggest part of the benefit for me and everybody I guess, and it was true, we found… we got friends, we found each other in a very difficult time. When one of us was feeling bad, we could join each other, we could find each other and get more close to each other. […] Just to be able again to dream. That was what I needed: just to be able again to dream. And just to hand it over to each other, you know, just to spread it over and I guess that collective energy is the biggest benefit we could get. First, like virtually I would say and the second was the money. (Farimah, Women on the Way, interview)

A third benefit of working with Women on the Way emerged during the study was the flexibility allowed by this kind of activity that does not require fixed hours and allow women to work from home. This emerged especially when I asked to Natalia and her collaborator whether they would prefer doing another job. They both replied that they would prefer a stable job, but given the current situation, the job with Katarina is more than fine. On this regard, Natalia added:

> what is good of working with Katarina is that we do not go anywhere, here there is everything and we look after the kids... we can do everything here and then we can quickly go for lunch, everything is here. If we had a stable job we would need to go somewhere, so for now this is very good. Because like that we can stay with family, the family is here, and we can do things here... Katarina empowered up! For these conditions that we can stay with the family, this is a big plus. (Natalia, Women on the Way, interview)

Conclusion

Despite being a newly opened business with still limited capacity and resources, the study here presented highlights the potential of the idea behind Women on the Way within the Serbian context. On the one hand, it provides a much-needed occupation and diversion to refugee women who are living a condition of great psychological distress, bringing them together for a common purpose and developing informal networks of support. On the other hand, this activity allows them to earn some money that can be used for extra-expenses not covered by the state's basic assistance. In addition, this kind of business proved to be quite flexible and adaptable to the situation: it does not require big economic investments, it can be carried out in different locations, and it brings to a finished product in a short period of time. For these reasons, it better adapts to the instable conditions of displacement or prolonged transitions compared to other jobs.

In addition, the experience of Women on the Way shows how social entrepreneurship can represent an opportunity of employment and economic empowerment not only for refugees or other vulnerable groups, but for the Serbian population in general. Indeed, the main motivation that moved Katarina, a highly educated young Serbian, to engage in Women on the Way was the necessity to create a job opportunity for her. This is not an isolate case, as the intention of creating a personal employment opportunity has been identified as the main driver for establishing a social enterprise in the country (Krstić et al., 2017). This aspect can represent an opportunity also for asylum seekers, refugees and migrants in general, because a common necessity might boost bottom-up networks of solidarity and collaboration between locals and foreigners where relations of power are not so marked as it might be in the case where this collaboration is moved by the intention of the local to help the foreigner. Indeed, the skills and competences of the foreigners might be more valued as they might become an asset for the economic empowerment of both locals and migrants.

The experience of Women on the Way also shows how the success of such initiatives relies much on a series of factors and on the collaboration of different actors. The support of the Belgrade Centre of Human Rights was essential to connect Katarina with Natalia and start their collaboration. This was also favoured by the presence in the Reception Centre of Vranje of the NGO Sigma Plus, which organised a sewing workshop and gave to the Ukrainian women the sewing machines. In this way, Natalia could easily engage other women in her work with Women on the Way. Moreover, the establishment of Women on the Way as a social enterprise was made possible thanks to the RISE programme that provided Katarina with basic business management skills and its sustainability is now supported by UNHCR that provides her with free business consultants. This network of different actors reveals the presence of an emerging eco-system which is favourable to the development of social enterprises in Serbia.

However, the potential of initiatives like Women on the Way is surely hindered by the current conditions of asylum seekers and refugees in Serbia, where the obstacles to access asylum rights severely affect their possibilities not only to establish their new life in Serbia but also to find a temporary job and an income while being displaced or transiting in the country. It is indeed not a coincidence that Women on the Way is now engaged with refugees from Ukraine, as they could access temporary protection within a relatively short time and therefore apply for working permit, although they still do not know if in the future they will remain in Serbia or go back to Ukraine. To asylum seekers entering the country from other contexts this possibility is very often precluded, while being engaged in an occupation may help them to overcome the traumas related to the displacement and earn some money that can be used to continue the trip.

References

Baraibar-Diez, E., Odriozola, M. D., Llorente, I., & Fernández Sánchez, J. L. (2019). Evaluating the Business Model of a Work Integration Social Enterprise in Cantabria. In V. Ratten, P. Jones, V. Braga, & C. S. Marques (Eds.), *Subsistence Entrepreneurship: The Interplay of Collaborative Innovation, Sustainability and Social Goals* (pp. 51–67). Springer International Publishing. https://doi.org/10.1007/978-3-030-11542-5_5

Barraket, J. (2014). Fostering Wellbeing of Immigrants and Refugees? Evaluating the Outcomes ofWork Integration Social Enterprise. In S. Denny & F. A. Seddon (Eds.), *Social Enterprise: Accountability and Evaluation Around the World.* Routledge.

Belgrade Centre for Human Rights. (2022). *Right to Asylum in the Republic of Serbia. Periodic Report for January–June 2022.* http://azil.rs/en/wp-content/uploads/2022/08/Right-to-Asylum-in-the-Republic-of-Serbia-Periodic-Report-for-January-June-2022.pdf

Clarke, K. (2021). Addressing Systemic Racial Injustice in the United States from the War on Poverty to Social Enterprise to Black Lives Matter. *The Journal of Social Policy Studies, 19*(1), 143–154. https://doi.org/10.17323/727-0634-2021-19-1-143-154

Cooney, K. (2011). The Business of Job Creation: An Examination of the Social Enterprise Approach to Workforce Development. *Journal of Poverty, 15*(1), 88–107. https://doi.org/10.1080/10875549.2011.539505

Cvejić, S. (Ed.). (2013). *Cooperatives and Social Enterprises in Europe and in Transitional Contexts.* The Institute for Sociological Research, University of Belgrade.

de Vries, L. A., & Guild, E. (2019). Seeking Refuge in Europe: Spaces of Transit and the Violence of Migration Management. *Journal of Ethnic and Migration Studies, 45*(12), 2156–2166. https://doi.org/10.1080/1369183X.2018.1468308

Defourny, J., & Nyssens, M. (Eds.). (2021). *Social Enterprise in Central and Eastern Europe: Theory, Models and Practice* (1st ed.). Routledge. https://doi.org/10.4324/9780429324529

Defourny, J., Mihály, M., Nyssens, M., & Adam, S. (2021). Introduction: Documenting, Theorising, Mapping and Testing the Plurality of SE Models in Central and Eastern Europe. In J. Defourny & M. Nyssens (Eds.), *Social Enterprise in Central and Eastern Europe: Theory, Models and Practice* (pp. 1–19). Routledge; Scopus.

Farmer, J., De Cotta, T., Kilpatrick, S., Barraket, J., Roy, M., & Munoz, S.-A. (2021). How Work Integration Social Enterprises Help to Realize Capability: A Comparison of Three Australian Settings. *Journal of Social Entrepreneurship, 12*(1), 87–109. https://doi.org/10.1080/19420676.2019.1671481

Flowers, R., & Swan, E. (2017). Seeing Benevolently: Representational Politics and Digital Race Formation on Ethnic Food Tour Webpages. *Geoforum, 84*, 206–217. https://doi.org/10.1016/j.geoforum.2016.07.012

Golubović, D., & Muhi, B. (2019). Social entrepreneurship in Serbia: The state of play. *Revija Za Socijalnu Politiku, 26*(3), 359–378. https://doi.org/10.3935/rsp.v26i3.1564

Hameršak, M., Hess, S., Speer, M., & Mitrovic, M. S. (2020). The Forging of the Balkan Route. *Movements, 5*(1), 9–29.

Hazenberg, R., Seddon, F., & Denny, S. (2012). Investigating the Outcome Performance of a WISE Delivering Employability Programmes to the Unemployed. *Journal of Leadership, Accountability and Ethics, 9*(6), 40–50.

Hossein, C. S. (2021). Racialized People, Women, and Social Enterprises: Politicized Economic Solidarity in Toronto. *Feminist Economics, 27*(3), 21–50. https://doi.org/10.1080/13545701.2020.1821078

Krstić, G., Mirić, A. A., & Rakić, J. Ž. (2017). Profil socijalnih preduzetnika u Srbiji: Motivacija i socio-demografske karakteristike. *Sociologija, 59*(1), 62–80. https://doi.org/10.2298/SOC1701062K

Kummitha, R. K. R. (2016). Social Entrepreneurship as a Tool to Remedy Social Exclusion: A Win–Win Scenario? *South Asia Research, 36*(1), 61–79. https://doi.org/10.1177/0262728015615485

Macaulay, B., Roy, M. J., Donaldson, C., Teasdale, S., & Kay, A. (2017). *Conceptualizing the Health and Well-being Impacts of Social Enterprise: A UK-based Study. Health Promotion International.*

Mandić, D. (2021). A Migrant "hot potato" System: The Transit Camp and Urban Integration in a Bridge Society. *Journal of Urban Affairs, 43*(6), 799–815. https://doi.org/10.1080/07352166.2018.1490153

Milan, C. (2019). Refugees at the Gates of the EU: Civic Initiatives and Grassroots Responses to the Refugee Crisis Along the Western Balkans Route. *Journal of Balkan and Near Eastern Studies, 21*(1), 43–60. https://doi.org/10.1080/19448953.2018.1532686

O'Shaughnessy, M. (2008). Statutory Support and the Implications for the Employee Profile of Rural Based Irish Work Integration Social Enterprises (WISEs). *Social Enterprise Journal, 4*(2), 126–135. https://doi.org/10.1108/17508610810902011

Rakić, J. Ž., Mirić, A. A., Lebedinski, L., & Vladisavljević, M. (2017). Welfare State and Social Enterprise in Transition: Evidence from Serbia. *VOLUNTAS: International Journal of Voluntary and Nonprofit Organizations, 28*(6), 2423–2448. https://doi.org/10.1007/s11266-017-9844-2

Roy, M. J., Donaldson, C., Baker, R., & Kerr, S. (2014). The Potential of Social Enterprise to Enhance Health and Well-being: A Model and Systematic Review. *Social Science & Medicine, 123*, 182–193. https://doi.org/10.1016/j.socscimed.2014.07.031

Roy, M. J., Baker, R., & Kerr, S. (2017). Conceptualising the Public Health Role of Actors Operating Outside of Formal Health Systems: The Case of Social Enterprise | Elsevier Enhanced Reader. *Social Science & Medicine, 172*, 144–152. https://doi.org/10.1016/j.socscimed.2016.11.009

Stojic Mitrovic, M. (2019). The Reception of Migrants in Serbia: Policies, Practices, and Concepts. *Journal of Human Rights and Social Work, 4*(1), 17–27. https://doi.org/10.1007/s41134-018-0077-0

Teasdale, S. (2010). How Can Social Enterprise Address Disadvantage? Evidence from an Inner City Community. *Journal of Nonprofit & Public Sector Marketing, 22*(2), 89–107. https://doi.org/10.1080/10495141003601278

Tobin, S. A., Etzold, B., Momani, F., Adel Al Yakoub, T., AlMassad, R. F. S., & Shdefat, A. G. (2023). Ambivalent Entanglements: Syrian Refugees' Network Relations and (Im)mobilities in Protracted Displacement. In J. Ahrens & R. King (Eds.), *Onward Migration and Multi-Sited Transnationalism* (pp. 99–119). Springer International Publishing. https://doi.org/10.1007/978-3-031-12503-4_5

Tracey, P., Phillips, N., & Haugh, H. (2005). Beyond Philanthropy: Community Enterprise as a Basis for Corporate Citizenship. *Journal of Business Ethics, 58*(4), 327–344. https://doi.org/10.1007/s10551-004-6944-x

UNHCR Serbia. (2022). *Temporary Protection in Serbia*. UNHCR Serbia. https://help.unhcr.org/serbia/temporary-protection-in-serbia/

Vukcevic, N. (2020). Eventual Integration or Delayed Transit: Interaction of Residents in Reception Centres with Their New Environment in Serbia. *Stanovnistvo, 58*(1), 1–23. https://doi.org/10.2298/STNV191017003V

Vukmirović, D. (2014). *Economic Impact of Social Enterprises in the Republic of Serbia*. Statistical Office of the Republic of Serbia.

List of Interviews

Katarina Ejdus, Women on the Way, Belgrade, 05/12/2022.
Belgrade Centre for Human Rights, Belgrade, 06/12/2022.
Grupa 484, Belgrade, 07/12/2022.
Asylum Protection Centre (APC), Belgrade, 07/12/2022.
Coalition for Solidarity Economy Development, Belgrade, 07/12/2022.
Natalia, Women on the Way, Reception Centre of Vranje, Vranje, 09/12/2022.
Women on the Way's collaborator, Reception Centre of Vranje, Vranje, 09/12/2022.
KIRS officer, Reception Centre of Vranje, Vranje, 10/12/2022.
Initiative for Development and Cooperation, online, 23/01/2023.
UNHCR Serbia, online, 24/01/2023.
Farimah, Women on the Way, online, 27/01/2023.

CHAPTER 8

Augusto Boal in the Asylum Home: Theatre of the Oppressed for Social Entrepreneurship

Jure Gombač

Introduction

At the beginning of September 2020, my colleague and I were knocking on the (too) many doors in a multilevel asylum home on Kotnikova Street in Ljubljana, the capital of Slovenia, offering "social entrepreneurship courses" to the residents. Most of the asylum seekers were reluctant to participate, and some were even openly sceptical about the value of such courses. We received many "no thanks" or "get out" responses on several occasions. Indeed, the situation was a peculiar one: a group of activists, researchers, cultural mediators and translators, asylum seekers, and two theatres of the oppressed facilitators met daily in a room that was otherwise used as a gym. The idea of this undertaking was twofold: first, to offer a course in social entrepreneurship to a population otherwise not

J. Gombač (✉)
ZRC SAZU ISIM, Ljubljana, Slovenia

Faculty of Arts, University of Nova Gorica, Nova Gorica, Slovenia
e-mail: jure.gombac@zrc-sazu.si

S. Bianchini et al. (eds.), *Social Entrepreneurship and Migrants' Inclusion*, Sustainable Development Goals Series,
https://doi.org/10.1007/978-3-031-55791-0_8

considered ready to integrate, since most integration programmes target individuals with an official refugee status,[1] and second, to use the methods of the theatre of the oppressed to research the experiences of a population that is not only difficult to access, especially within institutional confines, but also a thoroughly overlooked one. In general, there is a strongly held idea that most, if not all, asylum claims in Slovenia are bogus, that they are simply a tactical move to ease the path across the Balkan Route heading towards Trieste and not expressions of a genuine intention to stay and "make a life" in the country. This conviction is shared by a variety of actors, from asylum officers at the Ministry of the Interior to the social workers, guards and language teachers who encounter migrants daily in their work (Bučar Ručman & Šulc, 2019; Abdou Hadj & Pettrachin, 2021). While it is rarely overtly expressed, it shows in a variety of measures: asylum seekers are not allowed to work for the first nine (now three) months following their arrival, they have to renew their temporary documents every three months, their movement is restricted to a given municipality, and they have to request permission to leave the asylum home overnight. These measures—which work both to control and to repel asylum seekers—often turn out to be a self-fulfilling prophecy with regard to such people not attempting to settle in Slovenia. After some days or weeks of "rotting away" in an overcrowded facility, asylum seekers receive the message that they are in an inhospitable environment and then, in most cases, leave (Vianelli, 2021).

Therefore, the aim of this article is to explore the situation of social entrepreneurship in Slovenia with regard to asylum seekers and refugees, as well as the methods that were used to gain information and create content for a social entrepreneurship workshop curriculum for their possible future education and training in this field. First, we examine the situation in the field of social entrepreneurship in relation to asylum seekers and refugees in Slovenia. We then present the theoretical framework, which applies theoretical approaches from social entrepreneurship and the theatre and pedagogy of the oppressed, with reference to the concept of border struggles and the literature on the making of migrations. We then briefly present the situation of asylum seekers and refugees in Slovenia and analyse the reality of their plight. Finally, we end this text with conclusions and recommendations for future work in this area.

[1] We use the term "refugee" when speaking about people with international protection status and "asylum seeker" when speaking about people who have submitted a request for such status, but have not yet been recognized as forcibly displaced.

Social Entrepreneurship and Migration in Slovenia

The integration of asylum seekers and refugees into the Slovenian labour market presents a constant challenge for all the actors and stakeholders involved, even though this market has continued to improve after 2014 as a result of strong economic growth following the 2008 economic crisis. For instance, at the end of April 2018, a total of 243 refugees were registered with the Slovenian Employment Service (ESS), claiming unemployment benefits and receiving assistance in finding employment, and "this number represented more than two thirds of the refugee population" (Vončina & Marin, 2019). Between January and August 2018, however, only 21 refugees were deregistered from the ESS database because they had found employment (Employment Service of Slovenia—ESS, 2018a, 2018b). The situation did not improve in the following years, and during the COVID-19 crisis, it actually dramatically deteriorated (Ladić & Alali, 2021). As asylum seekers in Slovenia were then not allowed to work legally for their first nine months in the country—now reduced to three months—most of them were unemployed or worked illegally and/or experienced extreme poverty, being dependent on humanitarian aid and other forms of charity.

According to various official reports, asylum seekers and refugees still face both systematic and practical obstacles in Slovenia, such as language and cultural barriers, lack of work experience, low levels of education or no evidence of education, medical problems, discrimination and structural imbalances in the labour market. The NIEM[2] Report from the Peace Institute in Ljubljana, which examined ways of improving the integration of people with recognized international protection, also stated that refugees report that they repeatedly receive the same job offers, regardless of their actual education or experience Ladić et al., 2020).

As Government Office for Support and Integration of Migrants (GOSIM) together with the ESS was looking for new solutions to this problem, the International Organization for Migration (IOM) suggested

[2] NIEM stands for National Integration Evaluation Mechanism. It is an Asylum, Migration and Integration Fund (AMIF) EU-sponsored project. Find more on http://www.forintegration.eu/

promoting self-employment and social entrepreneurship among asylum seekers and refugees. The ESS responded to this suggestion by noting that "no support is currently being provided for self-employment or social entrepreneurship (for asylum seekers and refugees), but it may be a suitable solution for some refugees" (Vončina & Marin, 2019).

This response was unsurprising, since the OECD's 2022 social entrepreneurship policy review[3] praised Slovenia for solid economic growth and good performance on its Sustainable Development Goals, while highlighting considerable challenges in the economic and social context, since the country had been hit hard by the 2008 global financial and economic crisis, as well as the COVID-19 pandemic, with GDP contracting by 4.2% in 2020. The authors of the report agreed that social enterprises could address some of the social issues that emerged after cuts in public services and social transfers were promoted by the EU "*troika*"[4] and carried out by every member state from 2011 on. However, before such measures could be taken, several challenges with regard to the development of social entrepreneurship and social enterprises would have to be resolved. The OECD report mentions the fragmentation of the institutional and legal landscape for social enterprises and the limited coherence of the support frameworks, which together create inconsistent operating environments for social enterprises.[5] The report also noted that the capacity of such enterprises to thrive was constrained by limited access to financing, as well as to public and private markets, while impact measurements were still rare despite preliminary public and private efforts in this regard. Finally, the report mentioned that confusion and limited awareness remained in Slovenia around the concepts of social enterprise, social entrepreneurship, the social economy and social innovation, terms that were often used interchangeably (OECD, 2022).

[3] "Boosting social entrepreneurship and social enterprise development in Slovenia—In-depth policy review".

[4] The troika is a term used to refer to the single decision group created by three entities, the European Commission (EC), the European Central Bank (ECB) and the International Monetary Fund (IMF). It was formed in the aftermath of the European debt crisis 2008–2011 as an *ad hoc* authority with a mandate to manage the bailouts of Cyprus, Greece, Ireland and Portugal.

[5] The main foundations for social entrepreneurship in Slovenia were the adoption of the Social Entrepreneurship Act in 2011 and its revision in 2018. Moreover, the transfer of the responsibility for social enterprises from the Ministry of Economic Development and Technology to the Ministry of Labour, Family, Social Affairs and Equal Opportunities meant a reinforcement of the business orientation in social enterprises.

The political ambition to support the social economy gained momentum in 2018, when the city of Maribor was made the European Capital of the Social Economy and a strategy for the development of the social economy was promised. However, enthusiasm for this ambition decreased rapidly in the following years (OECD, 2022).

Nevertheless, some of the asylum seekers and refugees in Ljubljana started to look for opportunities to open their own businesses. These efforts were mainly driven by their own entrepreneurial backgrounds and mostly positive experiences with one of the very few social enterprises run by a team of Slovenian citizens and migrants in the country, a restaurant called Skuhna on Trubarjeva Street in Ljubljana. Trubarjeva is a rather special street in the centre of Ljubljana with a high proportion of migrant enterprises, which are constantly looking for more affordable staff. It is also not far from the asylum home on Kotnikova Street, while until the complex's recent redevelopment, Trubarjeva itself was home to the "Autonomous Zone" of the abandoned Rog Factory, which housed many alternative culture enterprises and initiatives, including some aimed at migrants, such as Second home and Ambasada Rog.

However, the asylum seekers and refugees in Ljubljana probably only saw one side of the complicated story of Skuhna, as they were not aware of or had not taken into consideration the hardship that the owners and employees of this social enterprise experienced. In an interview carried out in 2018, before COVID-19, Teja, the founder of this restaurant and social enterprise along with her husband Max, stated that "time is a problem because I am supposed to do more than a million things aside. [...] I am writing now on a project (funding application), and I don't even sleep" (Booth et al., 2019). She also mentioned that the heavy workload both she and her husband faced had burned them out psychologically and physically and that they were considering closing the business due to a combination of health problems and unmanageable stress.

It was thus clear that more information and assistance should be offered to asylum seekers and refugees with aspirations to open an enterprise and potentially a social enterprise, especially after the 2015–2016 border crisis in the EU, when the number of asylum seekers increased dramatically (Gombač & Pehar, 2021), and the subsequent COVID-19 pandemic that officially began in early 2020. While some support was offered by different civil society organizations such as Zavod Global (Skuhna);[6] trade

[6] Cultural association, https://zavodglobal.si/

unions such as NSDS,[7] Svetovalnica za migrante[8] and the ZSSS;[9] NGOs such as Gmajna,[10] Odnos[11] and Slovenska Filantropija;[12] and grassroots organizations such as Second Home[13] and Ambasada Rog,[14] this was not done in a systematic or sustainable way. There was a need for a project or programme that would have a longer-term orientation, with results that would help both the official integration system and potential migrant social entrepreneurs.

Due to the increased number of undocumented migrants, asylum seekers and refugees after the crisis of the EU border regime in 2015–2016 and the EU's solidarity measures in the form of the European Return and Reintegration Network (ERRIN) initiative, a team from ZRC SAZU expanded its migration research. We became increasingly interested in the social and labour market integration of asylum seekers and refugees to learn about the challenges they faced while at the same time testing different approaches, interventions and pilot programmes to assist them and the institutions involved. Due to the good relationship with the ESS, with whom we have been working on the Danube Region Information Platform for Economic Integration of Migrants (DRIM) project,[15] we also wanted to offer some support in trying out new and more effective concepts and approaches to address the focal issues. Employers were also very important stakeholders in this process, as they were looking for workers with certain kinds of education, skills and competences, although they tended to avoid employing asylum seekers and refugees and instead hired workers from other nations in the former Yugoslavia. In our search for possible solutions during the Urban Diversity project,[16] we also became acquainted with the

[7] Independent Trade Union of Workers in Slovenia, https://nsds-sindikat.si/

[8] Workers Advice Center Trade Union, https://delavskasvetovalnica.si/

[9] Slovenian Association of the Free Trade Unions, https://www.zsss.si/

[10] Cultural Association Gmajna, https://www.facebook.com/kdgmajna/

[11] Odnos (relationship) association, involved in orientation and integration programs for the migrants, https://www.odnos.si/

[12] Slovene Philanthropy, Association for Promotion of Volunteering, https://www.filantropija.org/en/migration/

[13] Migrant collective, continuation of the Second home, https://www.facebook.com/infokolpa/?locale=sl_SI

[14] Migrant collective, https://ambasada-rog.si/

[15] Danube Region Information Platform for Economic Integration of Migrants, https://www.interreg-danube.eu/approved-projects/drim

[16] The Urban Diversity project addressed the themes of migrant entrepreneurs, creativity and cross-border cooperation. http://www.urbandiversity.eu/

concepts of social entrepreneurship and social innovation in the field of labour market integration of migrants, which showed great promise in theory and worked partially in practice, as in the case of the Skuhna restaurant; therefore, we wanted to further test such approaches.

For our research group, this became possible after receiving grants from two projects sponsored by the EU. The SiforREF[17] project was aimed at searching for grassroots-level social innovations for the employment of asylum seekers and refugees and putting them in practice, while the BEST[18] project was sponsored by the Asylum Migration and Integration Fund (AMIF) in 2019 and was aimed at improving the possibility of employment of asylum seekers and refugees through self-employment and social entrepreneurship. It offered the possibility to create a 100-hour blended learning programme with 30 hours of face-to-face workshops and then test it in practice. Four sets of lectures/workshops were organized with different groups of migrants, with a special emphasis on those living in the asylum home on Kotnikova Street in the centre of Ljubljana.

Our research was guided by the following questions: Can we use participatory approaches with asylum seekers and refugees to (1) define the main challenges of their integration into the Slovenian labour market; (2) design a social entrepreneurship course in a way that will address these challenges and enable people to use their newly acquired skills, knowledge and information to emancipate themselves from situations they perceive as oppressive, exploitative, discriminative and leading to poverty—by influencing legislation, employers, organizations and other stakeholders?

We mainly referred to the literature on the social entrepreneurship of asylum seekers and persons with international protection, which explores the possibility of self-employment or employment in the social economy sector, participatory practices of the theatre of the oppressed and the "migrant struggles" (Mezzadra & Neilson, 2013) and "making of migration" approaches (Tazzioli, 2020).

[17] Social Innovation for Refugees (SIforREF) improved policies for the inclusion of refugees into society and labour market through socially innovative policies and practices. https://programme2014-20.interreg-central.eu/Content.Node/SiforREF.html

[18] Boosting Entrepreneurial Skills as Tool of Integration of migrants to labour market (BEST), https://www.facebook.com/project.BEST.amif/

Theoretical Framework: Social Entrepreneurship, Theatre and Pedagogy of the Oppressed

It comes as no surprise that several authors agree there is no definitive consensus on what the term "social enterprise" actually means. It is an essentially contested concept, which explains why it is so difficult to find a universal definition of social entrepreneurship and why it is used with different meanings by different parties. However, if we want to find some common ground, it can be argued that a social enterprise is commonly defined as a hybrid organization built on an explicit social objective (for segments of the population who are excluded, marginalized or suffering), striving to create social value while securing profits and doing this in an entrepreneurial and innovative way (Zahra et al., 2009, p. 519). This includes the "innovative use of resource combinations (Saebi et al., 2019) to pursue opportunities aiming at the creation of organizations and/or practices that yield and sustain social benefits" (Mair & Noboa, 2003).

Social entrepreneurship thus denotes an "innovative, social value creating activity that can occur within or across the nonprofit business or government sectors" (Saebi et al., 2019). Finally, it provides an umbrella term for all "activities and processes undertaken to discover, define and exploit opportunities in order to enhance social wealth by creating new ventures or managing existing organizations in an innovative manner" (Zahra et al., 2009).

While some social entrepreneurship initiatives have had a considerable social impact in Slovenia, focusing on the needs of asylum seekers and refugees was and still is particularly challenging for several reasons. First, asylum seekers and refugees are a highly heterogeneous group, and thus, their challenges could be extremely diverse, so potential social entrepreneurs are required to address many varied and specific needs as well as the usual and common ones. Access to and local interaction with asylum seekers and refugees can also be difficult and very limited. The social networks established by asylum seekers and refugees tend to be informal, which makes it difficult for social entrepreneurs to acquire information from and gain legitimacy with the refugee community (Miller, 2004). Asylum seekers and refugees face numerous linguistic, legal and cultural obstacles in their host countries. They also experience liminality (Bendixen & Eriksen, 2018), their statuses are temporary (non-status, asylum seeker, asylum seeker with (multiple) negative responses to their claim and family reunification status, which is mainly for women), and their position on the labour market is precarious.

As such, the potential of involving disadvantaged target groups such as asylum seekers and refugees in the social business development process as entrepreneurial actors is yet to be fully realized, although studies have shown that social entrepreneurship can be a way to integrate minority groups (Dana, 2007) and other disadvantaged people (De Clercq & Honig, 2011).

To make the process possible for our target group in the asylum home in Ljubljana, we wanted to use participatory practices with emancipatory results, inspired by Paulo Freire and his pedagogy of the oppressed, as he realized that "marginalized people possess sharp analytical skills as long as they are provided with opportunities to investigate their own realities and reflect upon their living conditions" (Freire, 1996). We also wanted to use some of the methods developed by Augusto Boal's theatre of the oppressed as a set of dramatic techniques whose purpose is to bring to light systemic exploitation and oppression within common situations and to allow spectators to become actors (Boal, 2006).

We could say that we explored the transformative potential of participatory theatre methods for democratizing social research, as we utilized participatory theatre techniques (Fritz, 2020) with a group of asylum seekers in Ljubljana—who were mainly unemployed or working without papers, were marginalized, discriminated against and racialized—to reframe their efforts in an emancipatory intervention to enter the Slovenian labour market legally and remain there officially with papers as a critical intervention on the path to citizenship (Erel et al., 2017).

During our workshops, our two tutors on the pedagogy of oppressed and the theatre of the oppressed used several techniques from the former, such as image theatre, forum theatre, newspaper theatre, legislative theatre, analytical theatre and breaking repression. The experts together with participants decided that they would not use individual techniques but combine them with their prepared workshop materials to facilitate a discussion and enrich the learning process in a more active and critical way. This mixture of techniques was very well suited to work with asylum seekers and refugees, since we were also trying to bring attention to "how some people are racialized, governed and labelled as 'migrants' both individually and as part of a multiplicity" (Tazzioli, 2020).[19]

Research Methodology

How could we create a course on social entrepreneurship in Slovenia with minimal experience and no support from the governmental institutions responsible for supporting the social economy, with people who have experienced not only the hardship of the Balkan Route but now find themselves in a very specific and rigid labour market, often with exploitative employers? The answer was to be found in the rich history of anti-racist or "border struggles" in Slovenia, such as the struggles of Bosnian refugees between 1992 and 1995, the Erased of Slovenia (*izbrisani*), migrant workers and asylum seekers. These struggles illuminate and challenge the violence of border control and selection, while at the same time, they also have "consequences and resonances that extend into and even manifest themselves at the very centre of formally unified political spaces" (Mezzadra & Neilson, 2013). They involve ongoing work with and by migrants, such as monitoring, advocacy, the development of social spaces, research, media and cultural interventions, volunteering and political campaigns (Beznec & Gombač, 2022).

During our preparations, we put together a group consisting of a (social) entrepreneurship expert who already had experience using the pedagogy of the oppressed during his workshops with various SMEs, social enterprises and NGOs; another person with more than 15 years of experience with the theatre of the oppressed who was responsible for adapting the related methods to the realities of the workshops/courses; three people with international protection status who served as cultural mediators/translators from Arabic and Persian; two researchers from ZRC SAZU; and an activist in the field of freedom of movement. Later, during the course, which lasted approximately four hours a day for ten days, we expanded the group to include 15 asylum seekers to facilitate "horizontal, non-hierarchical subject-to-subject relationships among the group members, wherein all participating parties were held in equal importance and were interchangeable as problem-solvers, thinkers and learners" (Boog, 2003).

[19] The daily workshops lasted between four and five hours, depending on the mood of the group and the interest expressed by the asylum seekers.

The workshops began in September 2020, during the COVID-19 pandemic but between two lockdowns, and we collected data by organizing a series of participatory reflection sessions with the participants after every workshop and conducted interviews to collect various information, including the participants' opinions, and then used this information to prepare new or additional materials, cases and documents. Individual participants also wrote their own field diaries. We collected all of these materials, transcribed them and created a repository where we could use simple coding for the most pressing issues. As our goal was not a scientific book or article but a support tool to improve our activities, simple coding for day-to-day challenges during the project was sufficient.

The workshops and their results benefited all the participants, since the use of participatory practices with emancipatory aspirations provided information that would otherwise be difficult or impossible to obtain. Nevertheless, the process was complex and the progress was slow since there were continuous methodological, theoretical and content disagreements among all those involved.

Target Group: Asylum Seekers and People with International Protection in Slovenia

People who decided to cross into the EU without papers using the Balkan Route first met with the EU border regime in Turkey (Hess & Kasparek, 2017), where they experienced its externalization policies (Rumford, 2006) when forced to cross the border between Turkey and Greece on land or sea, and then tried to gain asylum status in the latter. They thus became familiar with militarization of the borders with fences, forced and intentionally produced liminality in refugee camps, squats, shelters and other types of temporary accommodation, working precarious jobs and looking for opportunities to continue their journeys.

On their way across the Balkan peninsula—with the exception of the "long summer of migration" in 2015–2016, when the "Balkan humanitarian corridor" (Beznec & Kurnik, 2020) allowed people to legally and quickly move into the EU—most migrants, according to various reports, experienced unprecedented violence, humiliation, harsh conditions and situations of protracted/stranded migration (Collyer, 2010), being stuck in individual countries for different periods of time, working precarious jobs, living in official and unofficial camps, squats, shelters, or private forms of accommodation, preparing for their next step—the undocumented crossing of another heavy militarized border on their way to the EU. These journeys could take months or even years (Minca & Collins, 2021).

One of the first EU Schengen border countries on this journey is Slovenia, which is quite protective towards its sovereignty, borders and nation, constantly living in a "state of exception" because of the "waves" of migration that began in October 2015 (Beznec & Gombač, 2022). Slovenia's border regime and integration system are intentionally constructed around a narrative about being a "transit country", based on the idea that most people on the move want to reach one of the "richer" EU countries and would not ask for asylum in Slovenia. This narrative was enforced by police violence on the borders and "pushbacks"[20] to Croatia and Bosnia and Hercegovina (Black Book of Pushbacks, 2020) on the one hand and an *ad hoc*, temporary, weak and short-term orientated integration system with unattractive opportunities with regard to social and labour market integration on the other. While the first of these was designed to either push migrants away from the EU or force them to cross and leave Slovenia as fast as possible, the second was designed to persuade asylum seekers that their lives in Slovenia will be hard and they should move on as soon as possible, with the hope that the Dublin[21] system would not send them back (Beznec & Gombač, 2022). This was enforced by a very strict asylum policy that has allowed only approximately 0.02% of asylum seekers to gain refugee status in Slovenia over the years (Ladić et al., 2020). Many asylum seekers thus either left for other EU countries or were stuck in prolonged legal battles after receiving a negative response from the Slovenian authorities and appealing their cases in a court of law. Their situation was mainly one of constant poverty, insecurity and liminality, as they had to live in overcrowded, outdated and understaffed asylum homes, receiving support of just 18 euros per month and being allowed to work only after spending nine months in the country. They received no or little psychological support, language classes were not adapted to their needs (mostly being aimed at those who could already speak a Slavic

[20] Illegal group expulsion across a border.

[21] The EU Dublin Regulation provides the legal basis and procedural rules for establishing the criteria and mechanisms for determining the state responsible for examining an application for international protection made in one of the participating states by a third-country national or a stateless person.

language), their qualifications were not recognized, and they experienced difficulties in finding and keeping a job (Alali et al., 2022). In several cases, they were approached by "employers", offering them illegal or problematic work arrangements without insurance, sometimes with very creative payment deals in which they were usually exploited. Some private labour agencies also offered jobs, which were sometimes problematic or were physically very demanding, with high possibilities of injuries.

Equality Bites, or Working in the Field

It was this group of mostly young people who was targeted, as we started our workshops on social entrepreneurship in the asylum home on Kotnikova Street in Ljubljana on 1 September 2021, after we received official permission from the head of GOSIM. We started at 14:00 right after lunch when most of the residents were present but also early enough to catch them before they went out to work in order to be back by 22:00, the time of the *hora legalis* (curfew) imposed by the private security company working at the building. We were instructed to do this by our cultural mediators—people with international protection—who had previously lived at the same asylum home. Agamben describes a "camp" as a permanent state of exception on a certain territory inside the nation state with its own facilitators, rules and regulations, and the possibility to "kill with impunity" (Agamben, 1998). In line with the securitization of migration discourse, which Slovenia was enforcing at the time, it was no surprise that a strong security force was present at all times in the asylum home, with the staff sometimes being quite harsh towards anyone entering or exiting the building. Certain rules in contravention of the asylum law were imposed, such as restrictions on movement at night (especially after 22:00 and during the COVID-19 period), and police officers were often present. Social workers who were employed on a temporary basis by the GOSIM were also working under strict rules and not allowed to make independent decisions concerning day-to-day running of the home without guidelines from the central asylum home, which was in a different location. This meant that the usual programme at the asylum home on Kotnikova Street was rather modest, with minimum interventions from the outside, as every NGO had to obtain approval from GOSIM before starting work, which took some time. Therefore, even if the asylum home was in the centre of the city, it was rather isolated from the outside world, as is often the case with such facilities in EU cities (Bulent & Laustsen, 2005).

We also found this asylum home to be a "non-place", an outdated partly abandoned ex-police cadet dormitory in the centre of Ljubljana that was turned into a "home" for young male asylum seekers, where they waited either for refugee status or their appeal against such status being rejected to be resolved. It had no history as an asylum home and had never hosted asylum seekers before (Auge, 1995).

For our lessons/performances, we were offered a large room that had been turned into an *ad hoc* gym. This turned out to be a good solution, as the room also served as a community space and had a small stage and some sofas and chairs. As we wanted to create a relaxed and safe environment, we provided some coffee and biscuits. No whiteboard was available, so we regularly taped our materials and posters to the walls. All this worked very well, as it made the room look familiar, informal and comfortable. It was still a strange and temporary solution for a place that was supposed to act as something permanent in the Slovenian integration system, but we were used to seeing this method used in makeshift and temporary camps along the Balkan Route.

Our first challenge was how to get asylum seekers to attend the lectures. We asked our cultural mediators—people with international protection—to contact their friends in the asylum home and inform all potential attendees about the benefits of our programme on social/migrant entrepreneurship. However, this, together with posters and handouts, created little response. In later discussions, we found that most asylum seekers had already attended several courses that they felt they did not need during their stays in different camps on the way from Turkey to Slovenia, and they did not trust us enough to spend their time on another "worthless course that teaches us nothing and ten receiving a useless certificate which no employer takes seriously" (Alali et al., 2022). Moreover, some of them had already participated in various theatres of the oppressed with foreign volunteers on their journey across the Balkan Route, with quite mixed (and often negative) experiences.

We thus asked social workers for help, and they provided us with a list of potential students who had participated in previous activities organized by other organizations and NGOs. Armed with this list, we went from one room to another, asking people if they would like to attend. This was perhaps our first theatrical performance, as some of them decided to attend and others expressed their autonomy by saying no, or even literally kicking us out of their rooms. On the first day, we had more than 15 asylum seekers from Iraq, Iran, Syria, Kosovo, Pakistan, Afghanistan and elsewhere attending, but in the following days, this number varied according to the content, presenters, topics and so on. Additionally, because we were not able to provide a translator for Albanian, lacking the budget for it, we lost an entire group of very active asylum seekers from Kosovo who were very experienced in catering.

The participants from different countries had very different educations, experiences and skills but were willing to participate because of our methods, which were viewed as something different. We quickly learned that the lectures alone did not produce results, but instead came from the discussions and various theatre techniques that allowed the asylum seekers to express their concerns, needs, experiences and fears. If we allowed this process to take place, then people would come and participate because they had a feeling they were in charge of the process. If we insisted on our curriculum, however, no matter if it was agreed upon the day before, people just left if they felt their concerns were not addressed.

We were not completely aware of the difficulties that asylum seekers face because of their status, especially during the COVID-19 pandemic. In fact, they felt oppressed by various actors, such as security staff, employers, police, human traffickers, social workers, NGOs, lawyers, doctors, people employed by various governmental offices, banks, language teachers and sometimes us.

Asylum seekers in Slovenia experienced many obstacles in everyday life. Instead of freedom, they were put in a "prison", as one of the participants described it. Their situation was insecure because they were waiting for a positive answer from the authorities with regard to their asylum status, but several of them already had one or two negative responses and were suffering severe stress and sometimes depression because they feared deportation. As Nicolas de Genova put it, they wore the border on their faces, carried it on their backs (De Genova, 2013). They also experienced severe poverty, as they were not allowed to work for the first nine months but could not survive on the 18 euros of pocket money they received each month, so some of them were involved in illegal drug and pharmaceutical markets inside and outside the asylum home, while others worked illegally, risking punishment by the financial inspectors or police and even deportation. As some of the employers were aware of their difficult situations, they took advantage and exploited them in different ways (Mezzadra & Neilson, 2013). Such asylum seekers worked overtime, without the necessary protection or tools, sometimes receiving less money in return than agreed upon. Moreover, their obligatory social contributions were not paid, and they were not insured against injuries. Their employment agreements were precarious, and they were fired if demand for their labour decreased, periodically putting them back in a difficult situation of poverty and dependency. They also complained about the low wages in Slovenia compared to Germany, Sweden and the UK. Sometimes there was an intersection of issues, such as being seen as too old, coming from a "safe" country not being entitled for refugee status, a medical condition, lack of qualifications, lack of language abilities (Slovenian or English), addiction, psychological issues (PTSD, anxiety, depression), and so on.

As we were gathering more and more information by using methods from the theatre of the oppressed and other techniques, such as conversations, improvisation and roleplay, we also adapted the learning curriculum on social entrepreneurship with the participants' support. Several learning techniques and materials were removed for being too hierarchical, and others were added to address the asylum seekers' immediate needs. Together, we managed to create some content that served as a tool for challenging the different forms of oppression. There were already existing materials that addressed some forms of exploitative practices on the Slovenian labour market. Some of these came in the form of a comic strip to simplify the message in case the reader was not fluent in Slovenian or English. There are also institutions that could be contacted if a violation was found, such as labour inspectors and labour courts. There was a list of employers that were not to be trusted. There were NGOs, grassroots movements and individuals who offered informal language lessons, psychological support and dancing classes. All the information on these services and opportunities was collected and made available to everyone.

Moreover, when we were searching for the asylum seekers' business experiences and skills together, looking for new business ideas, developing business plans, discussing the best way to present your CV, exploring Slovenian working etiquette and other things that would benefit asylum seekers with regard to operating a social enterprise, we found that no matter how experienced and innovative asylum seekers were, Slovenian legislation prevented most of the participants from opening and running a business. Even if they had official documents proving their education, these were not recognized, and the same barriers were faced if they possessed skills such as working under pressure, police/security work, marketing, nursing, textile work, taxi driving, selling cars or real estate, advertising, dry-wall installation, organizing of warehouses, grass cutting, translation, power-plant engineering, professional photography, managing stock exchange trades, carpeting, hairdressing, painting and setting of wallpaper, working with refugees, electric repairs, cooking, administration, interior design, or selling car parts, and had been already working or wanting to work in cafés, restaurants, domestic services, sports shoe companies, mini markets, online stock exchange houses, import-export offices, refugee consulting, animal shelters, the military, as a businessman, accountant, entrepreneurship expert, communications manager, international cuisine cook, teacher, airplane electrician, handyman, certified technician and so on.

This situation was especially difficult to understand for our (social) "entrepreneurship guru", who, in addition to following the ideas of Paulo Freire, also believed in free and open markets and opportunities for everyone. He was already aware that non-citizens face different challenges than citizens in the field of self-employment, but during the presentations, he became frustrated as he had the feeling that he was destroying people's ideas, dreams and hopes because of the ways in which strict legislation and lack of support first created anomalies with regard to asylum seekers and refugees and then tended to eliminate this "problem" through negative responses to their claims and deportations. He described this as follows:

> *You were a policeman in Pakistan. Unfortunately, in Slovenia, you can only be a security guard. In addition, you cannot open your own security firm as you are an asylum seeker.*
>
> *Do you want to open a restaurant? What about the initial finances? Renting a space? What about the hygiene standards? Bank account?*
>
> *Have you decided to make sneakers? How will your production be competitive? Do you even know that Slovenian companies are moving their factories to Bangladesh? Who will make the model of your shoe? Will they copy it?*
>
> *Do you want to make bags? What kind of bags? How are you going to sell them? How will you be the cheapest? What will you be better at? Where is the social part of your enterprise?*

Moreover, sometimes the solutions he offered "from the top" were discussed by the asylum seekers and dismissed as irrelevant. He thus had to adapt his approaches and sometimes also admit defeat.

> *In the end, I did not feel sorry for anyone anymore. I understood that we were all just hanging out at the station where no one would stay. We exchanged a few words and said goodbye. I went back to lecture the privileged white Europeans, they went on to find their place under the sun. Will it be any better, any easier*

for them after my interventions? Are they more confident? Did they get anything useful from my workshops? I wonder if I will ever know….

This process was also quite informative for asylum seekers, as one of cultural mediators/translators pointed out:

Finally, there is a course, so asylum seekers and refugees became aware that entrepreneurship in Slovenia (and the EU) can be something quite different than their experiences at home.

Some of the asylum seekers already had a business at home but found it impossible to open and run something similar in the EU. The main obstacle was that as asylum seekers, they could not legally open an enterprise in Slovenia, although they could do so in Austria, which they knew and were frustrated about it. While they could start a business with refugee status, banks were reluctant to open accounts for people on the move from the Middle East and former Soviet states. Finally, the rules and procedures for operating as an SP (*samostojni podjetnik*, the simplest form of self-employment in Slovenia) are rather complicated even for citizens, especially with regard to taxes and social contributions, and most foreign companies use Slovenian accountants to help manage their businesses, but this is also expensive.

While we found many of the ideas of our participants interesting and realistic, this actually made our work more difficult in some ways. As the activist who was part of the team stated in her interview:

In fact, it was nice to see how many people had ideas—good ideas, perfectly feasible ideas, based on existing competences. However, that makes it even harder. Because one can SEE that all these ingenious plans will not come to fruition. Not here, not in Slovenia. Maybe in Austria. Maybe in Germany. Maybe at another time…

Thus, from patenting a potential perpetual motion machine and the making of shoes, bags and sweets to operating party boats, restaurants, security firms and so on, as well as engaging in role-plays, forums, juggling, playing cricket, physical exercises and dance, this social entrepreneurship course simply inspired visions of a utopia waiting for its conclusion after the end of the project.

Conclusions

In this chapter, we wanted to answer our research question: Can we use participatory approaches with asylum seekers and refugees to (1) define the main challenges of their integration into the Slovenian labour market; (2) design a social entrepreneurship course in a way that will address these challenges and enable people to use their newly acquired skills, knowledge and information to emancipate themselves from situations they perceive as oppressive, exploitative, discriminative and leading to poverty—by influencing legislation, employers, organizations and other stakeholders? We can draw on the following experiences gained as part of this project.

As our ten-day series of workshops came to an end, we began to think about the impact of the course and materials on the participants, the sustainability of the results and possible recommendations for the stakeholders. We were also thinking about the support offered to the participants interested in (social) entrepreneurship. We shared our concerns with the participants themselves, and the final session on Friday afternoon was organized as an evaluation of the course, materials and results. We summarize the responses and comments that we received with the help of the various forums and theatre methods that were used both before and during an indoor cricket game in the following conclusions.

A social enterprise is a "hybrid organization, based on an explicit social objective to help segments of the population that are excluded, marginalized or suffering, with the aim to create social value while securing profits and doing this in an entrepreneurial and innovative way" (Zahra et al., 2009), and this idea was perceived as something possible and helpful by our participants. They found the idea of a social enterprise useful as a possible intermediate state between unemployment and employment. It could also serve as an educational unit to make asylum seekers and refugees aware of the knowledge, skills and working habits that are perceived as necessary by (Slovenian) employers. The related labour legislation and protection of workers' rights could also be addressed in this context. Future (social) entrepreneurs could thus learn most of the skills and information needed to open and manage their own (possibly social) enterprises. They could also gain experience and skills, learn the language, create social and professional networks and develop their business ideas further, as well as become familiar with the institutions that are involved in social entrepreneurship support, programmes and projects.

With regard to problems with the idea of social entrepreneurship in this context, we must consider the already mentioned day-to-day challenges faced by asylum seekers and refugees, complicated legislation for opening a company in Slovenia, lack of support from the ministries in charge of supporting social entrepreneurship, and fading political will to support such activities, especially for asylum seekers and refugees, who are seen as "problematic migrants" by some political parties, parts of the media and some of the population, all of which were noted by the participants. Despite this, in general, the asylum seekers felt that they obtained a better view of what it means to open a (social) business in Slovenia and the EU with regard to specific demands, rules and regulations.

The educators who took part in this project tested their pedagogy of the oppressed and theatre of the oppressed methodologies and tools with the asylum seekers to understand and possibly challenge the "invisible" barriers and obstacles such individuals face and thus empowered them in such a way that they could address the challenges themselves and/or with support of already existing institutions, such as official institutions (ministries, labour inspectors, courts, employment services, centres for social affairs), third sector organizations such as trade unions, NGOs, chambers of trade and commerce, various municipal structures and grassroots organizations. They stated that they obtained valuable data and experience from working in this way but noted that it is still early days with regard to creating a curriculum that would be able to cover such a broad and challenging field.

The researchers who participated in the project gained further information about the influences of the so-called Balkan Route and the EU border regime (De Genova, 2018) on people on the move (Beznec & Kurnik, 2020) and obtained fresh insights into asylum seekers' social and labour market integration in Slovenia, where exploitation, precarity, illegality, solidarity and deportation play an important role.

Overall, we tried to prove that it is possible to build a community where we share our experiences, skills and knowledge and create concrete pedagogical and informative content with potentially emancipatory results in the field of self-employment and social entrepreneurship for asylum seekers in Slovenia and the EU with a combination of methods and approaches. This was particularly significant for those whose marginalization is partly constituted by their social isolation and the idea that their experiences are not a subject worthy of politics. The participants made visible experiences of oppression and became more conscious of the power relations at work. They were also able to explore and analyse how these power relations operate in concrete, embodied situations. A variety of techniques were used to rehearse different options for intervening, challenging and changing these situations, and thus, a course of action was developed.

All the participants collaborated in sharing "subjugated knowledge" (Foucault, 1980), and developing, making explicit and sharing such knowledge is an important part of social transformation. We were also able to disseminate knowledge to wider audiences through our networks, challenging social exclusion and the hegemonic construction of citizenship. This made visible social injustices and claimed legitimacy for the participants' "acts of citizenship", which challenged some of the injustices (Isin, 2002). The reason and motivation for this was the fact that for many asylum seekers, their situation did not improve even if they were granted refugee status. As one of the cultural mediators, as a person with such status, said of his current situation in Slovenia and the EU:

> *I fell into the abyss of 'refugee status'—into the tortuous search for accommodation, the scraping by of living paycheck to paycheck, into precarious work, exploitative working relationships, constant fear, anxiety, a daily life on the edge of poverty. Experiencing discrimination at every turn. Because that is where they need us—on the margins. As a 'reserve' in case someone has to fix the potholes in their roads or pick up their vegetables.* (Hasan, Interview, November 2021)

When we went back to the asylum home just one week after the end of the workshops to deliver certificates of participation, we found that many of the asylum seekers had already left. The narrative of Slovenia as a transit country was obviously very effective with regard to presenting Slovenians as territorially bounded, culturally distinct imagined communities. However, some of our "graduates" later managed to open their own small enterprises in food transportation (Wolt, Glovo) and catering, their success this opposing the majority narrative and creating new possibilities for themselves and their (future) employees.

References

Abdou Hadj, L., & Pettrachin, A. (2021). *From "Bogus" Asylum Seekers to "Genuine" Refugees; Shifting Discourses and Attitudes Towards Afghan Migrants.* Retrieved April 12, 2023, from https://www.compas.ox.ac.uk/2021/from-bogus-asylum-seekers-to-genuine-refugees-shifting-discourses-and-attitudes-towards-afghan-migrants/

Agamben, G. (1998). *Homo Sacer: Sovereign Power and Bare Life.* Stanford University Press.

Alali, A., Klun, L., & Gombac, J. (2022). Vključevanje v vzgojno-izobraževalni sistem iz perspektive staršev in otrok beguncev. *Dve domovini/Two Homelands, 56*, 149–168.

Auge, M. (1995). *Non Places. An Introduction to Supermodernity.* Verso.

Bendixen, S., & Eriksen, T. H. (2018). Time and the Other: Waiting and Hope Among Irregular Migrants. In K. J. Manpreet et al. (Eds), *Ethnographies of Waiting, Doubt, Hope and Uncertainty.* Bloomsbury Publishing PLC.

Beznec, B., & Gombać, J. (2022). New Migration Policies and Innovative Practices: Slovenia Between Bordering and Inclusion. *Innovation: The European Journal of Social Science Research.* https://doi.org/10.1080/13511610.2022.207124016.pg

Beznec, B., & Kurnik, A. (2020). Old Routes, New Perspectives: A Postcolonial Reading of the Balkan Route. In: B. Beznec et al. (ur.), The Frontier Within: The European Border Regime in the Balkans. *Movements, 5*(1), 33–54. https://movements-journal.org/issues/08.balkanroute/02.beznec,kurnik%2D%2Dold-routes-new-perspectives.pdf

Black Book of Push-Backs. (2020). Volume 1 and 2. Compiled by Border Violence Monitoring and Published by the Left (GUE/ANGL). https://left.eu/issues/publications/black-book-of-pushbacks-volumes-i-ii/

Boal, A. (2006). *The Aesthetics of the Oppressed.* Routledge.

Boog, B. W. (2003). The Emancipatory Character of Action Research, its History and the Present State of the Art. *Journal of Community & Applied Social Psychology, 13*(6), 426–438.

Booth, M., Hyemi, S., & Slavec Gomezelj, A. (2019). Challenges in a Social Enterprise from the Case of a Social Enterprise in Slovenia. *Proceedings of the 2019 International Conference on Global Entrepreneurial Talent Management & Social Collaboration.* http://researchportal.northumbria.ac.uk/ws/portal-files/portal/27035293/BoothShinGomezel_ICGETMSC_2019.pdf

Bučar Ručman, A., & Šulc, A. (2019). Medijsko (so)ustvarjanje »begunske in varnostne krize« in njen odsev na državni in lokalni ravni. *Revija za kriminalistiko in kriminologijo, 70* (1), 5–20.

Bulent, D., & Laustsen, C. B. (2005). *The Culture of Exception. Sociology Facing the Camp.* Routledge.

Collyer, M. (2010). Stranded Migrants and the Fragmented Journey. *Journal of Refugee Studies, 23*(3), 273–293.

Dana, L.-P. (2007). *Handbook of Research on Ethnic Minority Entrepreneurship: A Coevolutionary View on Resource Management.* Elgar Publishing.

De Clercq, D., & Honig B. (2011). Entrepreneurship as an Integrating Mechanism for Disadvantaged Persons. *Entrepreneurship & Regional Development, 23*(5–6), 353–372.

De Genova, N. (2013). Spectacles of Migrant "Illegality": The Scene of Exclusion, the Obscene of Inclusion. *Ethnic and Racial Studies, 36*(7), 1180–1198.

De Genova, N. (2018). The 'Migrant Crisis' as Racial Crisis: Do Black Lives Matter in Europe? *Ethnic and Racial Studies, 41*(10), 1765–1782.

Employment Service of Slovenia—ESS. (2018a). Stopnja registrirane brezposelnosti [Registered Unemployment Rate]. Retrieved August 30, 2022, from https://www.ess.gov.si/trg_dela/trg_dela_v_stevilkah/stopnja_registrirane_brezposelnosti

Employment Service of Slovenia. (2018b). Registered Unemployment Rate. Retrieved April 11, 2023, from https://ess.gov.si/trg_dela/trg_dela_v_stevilkah/stopnja_registrirane_brezposelnosti

Erel, U., Reynolds, T., & Kaptani, E. (2017). Participatory Theatre for Transformative Social Research. *Qualitative Research, 17*(3), 302–312. https://doi.org/10.1177/1468794117696029

Foucault, M. (1980). *Power/Knowledge: Selected Interviews and Other Writings.* Pantheon Press.

Freire, P. (1996). *Pedagogy of the Oppressed.* Penguin Books.

Fritz, B. (2020). *InExActArt.* Trasformator.

Gombač, J., & Pehar, A. (2021). "It Is Not Too Bad in Slovenia, But It Could Be Much Better": Inclusion of Asylum Seekers and Refugees at the Borders of Europe. In M. Bufon, T. H. Malloy, & C. H. Williams (Eds.), *Societies and Spaces in Contact: Between Convergence and Divergence* (pp. 169–182, Vol. 11.). Berlin: P. Lang, Cop. Studies in European Integration, State and Society.

Hess, S., & Kasparek, B. (2017). De and Restabilizing Schengen. The European Border Regime After the Summer of Migration. *Cuadernos Europeos de Deusto, 56*, 47–78.

Isin, E. F. (2002). *Being Political. Genealogies of Citizenship.* University of Minnesota Press.

Ladić, M., & Alali, A. (2021). The Influence of Covid-19 Pandemic and Preventive Measures on Lives of Refugees in Slovenia. *Mirovni Institut.* https://www.mirovni-institut.si/wp-content/uploads/2015/11/the-covid-19-influence-on-refugees-in-Slovenia-report.pdf

Ladić, M., Bajt, V., & Jalušič, V. (2020). *National Integration Evaluation Mechanism. Slovenia. Report for year 2018.* Mirovni inštitut.

Mair, J., & Noboa, E. (2003). Social Entrepreneurship: How Intentions to Create A Social Enterprise Get Formed. *IESE Working paper No. D/521*. https://ssrn.com/abstract=462283

Mezzadra, S., & Neilson, B. (2013). *Border as Method, or, The Multiplication of Labor*. Duke University Press.

Miller, K. (2004). Beyond the Frontstage: Trust, Access, and the Relational Context in Research with Refugee Communities. *American Journal of Community Psychology, 33*(3–4), 217–227.

Minca, C., & Collins, J. (2021). The Game: Or, 'the making of migration' Along the Balkan Route. *Political Geography, 91*, 1–11. https://doi.org/10.1016/j.polgeo.2021.102490

OECD. (2022). *Boosting Social Entrepreneurship and Social Enterprise Development in Slovenia*. OECD Local Economic and Employment Development Papers.

Rumford, C. (2006). Theorizing Borders. *European Journal of Social Theory, 9*(2), 155–169.

Saebi, T., Foss, N. J., & Linder, S. (2019). Social Entrepreneurship Research: Past Achievements and Future Promises. *Journal of Management, 45*(1), 70–95. https://doi.org/10.1177/0149206318793196

Tazzioli, M. (2020). *The Making of Migration: The Biopolitics of Mobility at Europe's Borders*. Sage.

Vianelli, L. (2021). Warehousing Asylum Seekers: The Logistification of Reception. *Environment and Planning D: Society and Space, 40*(1), 41–59. https://doi.org/10.1177/02637758211056339

Voncina, V., & Marin N. (2019). What Issues do Refugees Face in Integrating into Labour Markets? Evidence from Slovenia. *Transfer: European Review of Labour and Research, 25*(1), 101–102.

Zahra, S. A., Gedajlovic, E., Neubaum, D., & Joel, S. M. (2009). A Typology of Social Entrepreneurs: Motives, Search Processes and Ethical Challenges. *Journal of Business Venturing, 24*(5), 519–532. https://doi.org/10.1016/j.jbusvent.2008.04.007

CHAPTER 9

Social Entrepreneurship and Refugee's Employment: The Case of Slovenia

Ksenija Perković, Blaž Lenarčič, and Maja Zadel

Introduction

The chapter addresses the complex topic of the employment of refugees in the context of social entrepreneurship. Initially, it is important to highlight that this is an under-researched topic in Slovenia. In the existing studies on refugees and the employment, this issue has been addressed only indirectly, namely highlighting that refugees are a vulnerable group which should be given special attention in this context, while none of the studies addressed the narrow area of their employment in the context of social entrepreneurship. The aim of the chapter is thus to present the broader socio-economic environment in Slovenia, focusing on legal, systemic, practical, cultural, and economic barriers and drivers to refugee employment in the social enterprises.

It is relevant to mention that employment of refugees in social enterprises goes beyond purely economic benefits for both entrepreneurs and

K. Perković (✉) • B. Lenarčič • M. Zadel
Science and Research Centre Koper, Koper, Slovenia
e-mail: Ksenija.Perkovic@zrs-kp.si; Blaz.Lenarcic@zrs-kp.si; Maja.Zadel@zrs-kp.si

S. Bianchini et al. (eds.), *Social Entrepreneurship and Migrants' Inclusion*, Sustainable Development Goals Series,
https://doi.org/10.1007/978-3-031-55791-0_9

refugees, and for this reason, this is important from the broader perspective of integration of refugees into the host societies. Therefore, we argue that engagement of refugees into the social enterprises can help towards popularization of this sector and consequently change general (public) opinion that refugees do not contribute to host societies.

Defining Social Economy and Social Entrepreneurship

Social economy, which also includes social entrepreneurship, is comprised of different forms and legal entities and is operating in a variety of fields. Following policy documents and legislation, both social economy and social entrepreneurship also presuppose democratic (and participatory) management principles as well as reinvestment of profits,[1] being it either in the "collective interest", that is, in the interest of its members or users, or in "general interest", that is, society at large (European Commission, 2021). Accordingly, social entrepreneurship, like social economy, is first and foremost defined by its purpose, namely a social and/or environmental purpose.[2]

However, as the concept and field of enquiry, social entrepreneurship is rather new (Mair et al., 2006; Martí, 2006; Perrini & Vurro, 2006; Mair & Noboa, 2006; Rakar & Kolarič, 2019) and also considering the multiple disciplines that study social economy and social entrepreneurship, it is not surprising that multiple definitions coexist. Even though defining social economy—and social entrepreneurship as its part—is not an easy task and scholars are still trying to find the optimal definition, different authors in general emphasize the combination of the social and business elements (e.g., Dees, 2001; Mair, 2006; Robinson, 2006; Austin, 2006; Perrini & Vurro, 2006; Mair & Noboa, 2006; Katzenstein & Chrispin, 2011; Haugh, 2006; Desa & Kotha, 2006; Mair et al., 2006). Among these definitions, the most suitable for the topic that we are dealing with

[1] This is also reflected in the Slovenian legislation, Social Entrepreneurship Act (ZSocP) 2011 (2018), Article 23.

[2] Accordingly, since their aim is to serve the community in which they are located, social economy entities are very much connected to their local environment (European Commission, 2021). The impact of their work and actions also leads to the reinvigoration of their local areas, including the retention of population, the provision of local products and (social) services, the shortening of the supply (and consumption) chain and the retention of local revenues (European Commission, 2021).

is the one proposed by Robinson (2006), which defines social entrepreneurship as a "process that includes: the identification of a specific social problem and a specific solution (or set of solutions) to address it; the evaluation of the social impact, the business model and the sustainability of the venture; and the creation of a social mission-oriented for-profit or a business-oriented nonprofit entity that pursues the double (or triple) bottom line" (p. 95).[3]

Kickul and Lyons (2020) stress the relative ease to define the "social" in "social entrepreneurship"—especially, in their view in relation to "entrepreneurship": starting from the Latin meaning of the world *socialis* (associate, ally, or companion) they understand it as "the organization of people [...] that lives and works together cooperatively—a community or society" and thus "social" refers to "anything that pertains to a community or society. By definition, it puts society ahead of the individual" (Kickul & Lyons, 2020, p. 12) and stress the normative propensity to separate the economic aspect from the social, for example, *laissez-faire* policy, while, in their view, this is an artificial division (Kickul & Lyons, 2020, pp. 12–13). Conversely, Cho (2006) tries to define the "social" of "social entrepreneurship" more thoroughly and argues even that the definitions of social entrepreneurship "leave 'social' undefined", which is "a surprising lapse given that the social dimension of SE [social entrepreneurship] is, in large part, responsible for the concept's inherent complexity" (Cho, 2006, p. 35). Cho (2006, pp. 35–36) explicitly points to the tautological and monological issue of previous definitions of social entrepreneurship, which juxtapose the social value with the business pursuit. The author questions the "social" in "social entrepreneurship" and rightly presents Milton Friedman's view of "social" and "social good", who understands "the welfare optimum" as arising "from the free operation of market forces" (Cho, 2006, p. 37). In this sense, Milton Friedman, as one of the most prominent advocates of *laissez-faire* policy, equates the social good to the economic good, but, of course, this may not be the case. In his paper, Cho thus proposes a working, open-ended definition of social entrepreneurship: "a set of institutional practices combining the pursuit of financial objectives with the pursuit and promotion of substantive and terminal values" (2006, p. 36). Likewise, the author cautionary warns us not to romanticize the benefits of social entrepreneurship as it usually arises in areas where structural problems have not been tackled and thus social

[3] In the third aspect, authors' emphasise is the environmental aspect.

entrepreneurship "may privilege addressing symptoms over resolving more fundamental root causes" (Cho, 2006, p. 50) and emphasizing the need for structural (governmental) change. Nevertheless, he also stresses the importance to meet social needs with social entrepreneurship "and assist those in need rather than to sacrifice them for the sake of attracting attention to the need for social change" (Cho, 2006, p. 52).

In this sense, we can welcome the fact that the potential of the social economy—and social entrepreneurship with it—has been acknowledged in the EU for some time. The most recent Social Economy Action Plan, "Building an economy that works for people: an action plan for the social economy", of December 2021, recognizes the social and solidarity economy as an untapped potential for the economies of the European Union and beyond. As the Action Plan for Social Economy points out, there are approximately 2.8 million social economy entities in Europe, and social economy employs some 13.6 million people in EU Member states. In the European Union, social economy represents 8% of the GDP (European Commission, 2021). However, the situation in Slovenia is quite different. As stated in the Draft of the Social economy development strategy for the period 2022–2032 in Slovenia (*Svet za socialno ekonomijo = Council for social economy*, 2022), the study of European Commission reveals the Slovenia's lack in this field, and thus the untapped potential is even greater: only 0.2% of working population is employed in social economy and social economy contributes only 0.2% to Slovenian's GDP.[4]

The social economy creates jobs while also taking into account, or rather prioritizing, people and local communities, social concerns and the environment. The Action Plan also emphasizes that the social economy can help to implement the principles of the EU Pillar of Social Rights: increasing employment rates and reducing the number of people at risk of poverty and social exclusion. Likewise, it highlights the complementary role of the social economy to countries' policies for integrating young people and disadvantaged groups—including persons with a migrant background—into the labour market as well as into society in general (European Commission, 2021, p. 3).

Taking this into consideration, it is not surprising that within one of the four pillars of the European Commission's "Action Plan for Integration

[4] However, there are many organisation types in Slovenia that correspond to the EU operational definition; the number of *de facto* social enterprises thus exceeds the number of *ex lexe* (Rakar & Kolarič, 2019).

and Inclusion 2021–2027" (2020), namely employment, social economy is also mentioned. Social economy—alongside civic society organizations, educational institutions and others as well as migrants themselves—plays a crucial role in fostering social cohesion and building inclusive society. Namely, social economy can build "strong partnerships for a more effective integration process" and promote "participation and encounter with the host society" (European Commission, 2020, pp. 15–21). Social economy is, hence, very important in "building strong partnerships for a more effective integration process" and "promoting participation and encounter with the host society" (European Commission, 2020, pp. 15–21). Furthermore, social economy and social entrepreneurship with it have also been emphasised by various authors as a crucial domain of integration: Ager and Strang (2008), for example, highlight employment as one of the ten domains of integration, and stress that employment, education health and housing are not merely "marker" of integration (they nevertheless may serve as such), "but they also clearly serve as potential means to support the achievement of integration" (Ager & Strang, 2008, p. 169). The latter is also evident from several empirical studies dealing with the topic (e.g., Beznec & Gombač, 2022; Rivna & Gress, 2022; Freudenberg & Halberstadt, 2008).

The National Context of Social Entrepreneurship and Migration in Slovenia

Historically, Slovenia, as part of the former socialist Yugoslavia and even before, had a tradition of a social economy. As mentioned earlier, the "social" in "social entrepreneurship" presupposes a positive social aim, positive social impact, positive social change (Dees, 2001 [1998]; Mair, 2006; Robinson, 2006; Austin, 2006; Haugh, 2006; Desa & Kotha, 2006; Katzenstein & Chrispin, 2011; Babič & Dabič Perica, 2018; Rihter, 2018; Rakar & Kolarič, 2019); however, in Slovenia, this may not be a straightforward case as the term has a strong connotation to its welfare system, "social work" ("social aid", including "social monetary aid") (Svet za socialno ekonomijo = Council for social economy, 2022, moderated discussion, 2022, see chapter results) as well as to socialist Yugoslavia. As Rihter (2018) notes, when Slovenia was still part of Yugoslavia, "all enterprises had at least some of the characteristics of social enterprise" (e.g., democratic management in the form of self-governing and enhancement of social well-being), but as Slovenia gained independence in 1991 and consequently with the transition to market-oriented model "these goals were to some extent neglected as the heritage of the socialist's era, carrying many negative attributes that needed to be collectively rejected and abandoned as soon as possible" (Rihter, 2018, p. 288). Rakar and Kolarič (2019) similarly note that there are certain political connotations regarding social entrepreneurial discourses, however, the long (socialist Yugoslav) "history of the cooperative movement, the Yugoslavian self-management model and the well-developed policies protecting citizens with disabilities offer" "fertile ground for the development of social enterprises" in Slovenia (Rakar & Kolarič, 2019, p. 17), however, in their opinion "social enterprise" is a new concept. Namely, the legal framework for social entrepreneurship in Slovenia, the Social Entrepreneurship Act (Social Entrepreneurship Act [ZSocP], 2011), was adopted only in 2011, and it was complemented in 2018 (Act on Amendments to the Act on Social Entrepreneurship, 2018). This is also reflected in the statistics, as there were no social enterprises before 2011 therefore at the data was not collected and the legal status did not exist. As of 2012 there were five and their number is rising steadily to 17 in 2013, 49 in 2014 and 95 in 2015. In 2016 they exceeded to 200, and by 2020, there were 270 social enterprises in Slovenia; in 2022, the number decreased to 261 (OPSI—Odprti Podatki Slovenije, n.d.). However, there are many organization types in Slovenia that correspond to the EU operational definition; the number of de facto social enterprises thus exceeds the number of *ex lexe* (Rakar & Kolarič, 2019). According to the Ministry of economic development and technology's study (Babič & Dabič Perica, 2018), the main reasons for the increasing number of social enterprises are high unemployment rate among vulnerable groups,[5] need for social services, privatization of companies, rise of

[5] Already at the general level, the employment rate was the lowest in 2013 (63.27%) and 2014 (63.9%)—as compared to 66.2% in 2010 and from 2015 when it was gradually increasing up to 71.88% in 2019. In 2020, it was just slightly lower (70.85%), undoubtedly linked also to the consequences of Covid-19 restrictions (OECD, 2022). The Slovenian economy has been fairly hurt by the European economic crisis, which occurred in the late 2000s. This is visible also in GDP data: from the year 2000, GDP was rising until 2008 (29.595$), but after that it is declines and only in 2013 surpasses the amount of 2008 (29.931$). Since 2013 began rising again, but due to the Covid-19 crisis gradually decreases in 2020. In 2021 it was 43.767$ (OECD, 2022).

"green economy", rural development, access to credit and empowerment of professional and self-employed workers.

Therefore, even though the growth of (official) numbers of social enterprises is encouraging, there is still a lot of untapped potential in Slovenia. Especially relating to larger number of refugees and asylum seekers that came to Slovenia in recent years and whose integration into the labour market and wider society remains a challenge. Historically, economic immigration to Slovenian—and thus the mere presence and consequently integration of migrants—was fundamentally related to the economic needs of the state, and, more precisely, to individual needs of specific industries. Economic migrants from the republics of former Yugoslavia started coming already from the 1950s, but (especially) since Slovenia gained independence, the inflow of migrant workers was related to specific sectors, industry needs and shortages of specific professions.[6] As it is also stressed in the Strategy of Economic Migration for the period 2010 to 2020 (Ministry of Labour, Family, Social Affairs and Equal Opportunities, 2010), and especially in the Strategy of the Government of the Republic of Slovenia in the area of migration (Vlade Republike Slovenije/Government of Republic of Slovenia, 2019), Slovenia must respond thoughtfully to the challenges posed by the ageing population and the growing volume of emigration of the active population. On the other hand, Slovenia has not been a particularly desirable destination country for refugees and asylum seekers with the exception of 1990s with the aftermath of the war in Balkans after the split of SFRY; besides lacking proper integration programmes, Slovenia is a relatively small and unknown country. Furthermore, as Beznec and Gombač (2022) stress, there is a discrepancy in between the political action and Slovenian immigrational reality, as, even though Slovenia "is a net immigration country, it has not made significant progress in terms of integration policies and participation practices of migrants. Slovenia still considers itself a 'transit' country in regard to asylum procedures and a 'temporary county' in regard to labour migration, and consequently, there are minimal or no efforts to find new and durable solutions to migrant inclusion" (2022, p. 13). As other countries in Europe, Slovenia also encountered a rise in asylum application in

[6] Foreign citizens could get employment based on the work permission issued (personal work permit, work permit and permit for employment, seasonal work, etc.).

the second half of the 2010s, after the closure of the refugees' Balkan route through Hungary.[7] In this regard, for the integration of refugees and asylum seekers into larger society, social entrepreneurship and social economy in general can play a crucial role. In the first instance, for employing the vulnerable group of persons with international protection and asylum seekers, and later offering a viable option to create their own enterprise.

To reiterate the Action Plan for Integration and Inclusion's proposed actions, social economy is very important in "building strong partnerships for a more effective integration process" and "promoting participation and encounter with the host society" (European Commission, 2020, pp. 15–21).

Research Methodology

Based on the existing literature (Vončina & Marin, 2019; Beznec & Gombač, 2022; Shin et al., 2019; Robinson, 2006), available statistical data and legislation review, qualitative part of the study was designed. Namely, first, the search for best practices in national environment was implemented. With the purpose of obtaining data on existing social enterprises, we searched for information on the internet using various combinations of the following keywords: refugees, asylum seekers, migrants, integration with social enterprise, social innovation and employment. The results showed that there is no social enterprise that fits our criteria exactly (i.e., employing only refugees and/or asylum seekers), and thus we widened our search including also associations and projects that employ

[7] In the beginning of the decade, 2010–2012, for example, there were around 300 asylum application per year, but the number rose to 1300 and 1400 in 2016 and 2017, and to almost 3000 in 2018, and then to more than 3.500 in 2019 and 2020. This is reflected also in the number of recognised asylum decisions, that was steady between 15 and 20 recognised asylum decisions in years 2010 to 2013, 28 in 2014, but rose to 136 in 2016 and 141 in 2017. After that, it was below 100 a year, but substantially higher that in the beginning of the decade. The countries of origin of asylum applicants have also shifted in the last decade; however, Afghanistan is among the top three countries almost all years. In the first half of the decade, Serbia and Kosovo are present every year among the top three countries, from 2012 there is also Syrian Arab Republic, gaining presence until 2016. Since 2017 there are noticeable numbers also from applicants from Algeria and Pakistan, in the last two years also from Morocco (see UNHCR Refugee Data Finder and Migration Directorate, Ministry of the Interior, 2021).

immigrants[8] (in general). What follows is brief presentation of these enterprises/initiatives.

Skuhna is a social enterprise whose aim is to increase the employability of migrants through culinary work (is actually employing migrants, including refugees) as well as to bridge the understanding gap between migrants and locals who live in Slovenia.

Revealed Hands is a project which engaged a group of immigrant women from different cultural environments that are extremely rich in the field of textile cultural heritage (mainly former Yugoslavia). The goal was to design a collection of contemporarily designed hand-made textile products, which on the aesthetic and content basis relied on textile cultural heritage of the vulnerable group and benefited from Slovenian tradition.

"*Active relations II—Empowerment and social activation of migrant women*" is a pilot project which aimed to develop social competences of migrant women, social skills, rising functional competences in order to solve social problems and to enter the labour market.

Migrantour is a project that in Slovenia is coordinated by NGO Terra Vera, transferred to Slovenia from Italy. It provides city tours focused on migration in Ljubljana and thus aims to provide a new instrument for integration that promotes the cultural heritage brought by migrant citizens, asylum seekers and refugees as well as it contributes to the development of a new narrative on the phenomenon of migration.

Akupara: The Incubator of Handicrafts, Social Cooperatives and Cultural Productions was a project that connected immigrants and refugees with prominent Slovene creators, the project promotes methods of co-creation and exchange of skills that came to exist as a result to past and present migration.

After identification of best practices, we conducted semi-structured in-depth interviews with five actors responsible for the initiative/project/enterprise. The interviews were conducted in July and August 2021 via ZOOM and on average lasted for an hour. All interviews were

[8] We use the umbrella term of "migrant" to indicate a person who moves from one place to another, and more specifically, from another state to Slovenia. Economic migrant and economic migration, although sometimes hard to distinguish from forced migration, is understood as a person coming from other countries for work-related purposes. Refugees, on the other hand, are people who applied for asylum and were granted international protection. Refugees "cannot return to their country of origin because of a well-founded fear of persecution" and represent an especially vulnerable and protected group (see UNHCR: https://www.unhcr.org/asylum-and-migration.html).

implemented with prior personal consent and recorded, transcribed, and anonymized. Research topics addressed in the interviews were focused mainly on gaps and constraints regarding establishing social enterprises and employment of refugees and migrants.

Based on the obtained results, we prepared starting points for discussion with experts from migration and social entrepreneurship fields. The moderated discussion was implemented for the purposes of the REInSER project in November 2022 with eight participants, namely five experts from the migration and integration fields and three from the field of social entrepreneurship, and the moderator. It lasted for six hours.[9] The aim of the discussion was the identification of the main gaps and constrains in (1) the field of refugees' employment in the social enterprises and (2) stimulating environment for social entrepreneurship. For the purposes of this study, the outcomes of the discussion were organized in general topics, their further elaboration derive from interviewees from the practice and available literature.

In identifying the main gaps, we followed Robinson's (2006) types of entry barriers for the social sector markets. He refers to the traditional entry barriers described by Bainand Porter as economic barriers. Economic barriers are related to market structure (i.e., the concept of structure-conduct performance). Social entry barriers such as the lack of resource networks and access to suitable labour, are related to the social structure of the market. There are at least five categories of social networks that can be barriers to business entry: business owners, business organizations, civil society organizations, political infrastructure and attractive labour markets. It is through these networks that information is shared, and resources are made available. Lack of access to these social networks can be a significant barrier to market entry, especially for new businesses. Institutional entry barriers prevent an entrepreneur from knowing or adapting to the rules, norms and values that contribute to the culture, order and practices of a market. They occur at multiple levels in a market and dictate the relationship between a firm and the consumer, and between the firm and the community. Robinson also addresses formal (or public) institutional barriers, which relate to government systems, laws, financial markets and credit institutions, as well as cultural entry barriers such as informal institutions. Language, slang, dress and etiquette are part of cultural norms, which include attitudes, beliefs and expectations of behaviour in a market. For

[9] The long duration resulted in taking only the main points and not recording the sessions.

our research institutional, formal and cultural entry barriers turned out to be the most relevant for Slovenian national context and they are analysed below.

Results

The results are jointly presented in this subchapter under relevant topics. At this point, it is necessary to explain that although the results of our study refer to refugees as a particularly vulnerable group, which needs special treatment in the field of employment, we must not perceive them as a homogenous group. It must be stressed that refugees are highly heterogeneous group, also according to characteristics that influence the level of their employability. In this manner, it is also necessary to understand presented outcomes.

Institutional and Formal Entry Barriers: Refugees' Employment in the Social Enterprises

Based on the results of the interviews and discussion with the experts, we note that there are quite large discrepancies between the rights of refugees in Slovenia and the actual practice. Namely, according to the legislation (Act Amending the International Protection Act [2021] and Employment, Self-Employment and Work of Foreigners Act [2015] and subsequent amendments), beneficiaries of international protection and their reunited family members have free access to the labour market and may be employed or self-employed or work without needing a special work permit or meeting other requirements.[10] Their access to the labour market is also not subject to a market labour test. There is no difference between refugees and beneficiaries of subsidiary protection. The identity documents issued to beneficiaries of international protection include a reference to the right to work, same as IDs for other foreigners with this right, thus avoiding misunderstandings in practice. Beneficiaries also enjoy equal treatment as nationals with respect to "active employment policy" programmes and other rights as unemployed persons.

As indicated in Nabergoj and Regvar (2021) ECRE report, asylum seekers acquire the right to free access to the labour market nine months

[10] Article 102 of Act Amending the International Protection Act (2021) and Article 6(2) of Self-Employment and Work of Aliens Act, and subsequent amendments.

after filing their application, if the decision in their procedure has not yet been made by the Directorate of Migration and the delay is not attributable to the asylum seeker (Article 87) (Act Amending the International Protection Act, 2021). Once asylum seekers have the right to free access to the labour market, they can be self-employment, employment and work without having to meet any other requirements, such as consent to the single residence permit and work permit or the EU Blue Card or seasonal work permit. The Ministry of the Interior simply issues them a notice stating that they meet the above conditions (Employment, Self-employment and Work of Foreigners Act, 2015).

The reoccurring and main obstacle that was identified in interviews as well as by experts relates to the project-based and consequently also short-term financing of the social initiatives which means that the refugee cannot be fully employed.

> *The main drawback is that the user is clearly told that you can be here for 6 months, but we have no chance of hiring you.* (Representative of the project Revealed Hands)

Short-term financing is a wider problem, which is also exposed in the Action Plan for Social Economy (European Commission, 2021) saying that the access to funding must be improved (although also through other means than project funding, for example, (ethical) bank loans.

Cultural Entry Barriers: Lack of Knowledge and Learning Opportunities of Slovenian Language and Intercultural Differences

The second major obstacle identified is lack of knowledge of the Slovenian language, which encompasses more than just the practical obstacle of being unable to communicate. In general, Slovenian employment legislation—the Employment, Self-employment and Work of Foreigners Act (ZZSDT) (2015) and the Foreigners Act (ZTuj-2) (2011)—does not require the knowledge of Slovenian language for the employment.[11]

[11] There are, of course, specific fields and job position that do require the knowledge of Slovenian language, for example, teachers and educational workers, doctors, dentists, and so on.

However, the Public Use of the Slovene Language Act(ZJRS), 2004) in Article 14 (business with customers) foresees that the Slovenian language must be used when communicating with end customers. To this end the Employment Agency of the Republic of Slovenia (ZRSZ) may also require a certain level of knowledge of the Slovenian language, furthermore the new Act Amending the Labour Market Regulation Act (ZUTD-E) from December 2019 foresees that third-country nationals which are registered in the Unemployment Register and access to social assistance must pass the Slovenian language exam (level A1) within 12 months of registration in the Unemployment Register.

If refugees do not obtain a certificate of successful examination, they are removed from the register of the unemployed and consequently do not have access to social assistance, except in exceptional cases. Furthermore, the implementation of language courses is also a major problem, as individuals with different knowledge or understanding of the language are unable to learn the language in an appropriate way. According to the information obtained from discussion with experts, the lack of language knowledge extends to various areas, such as employment (finding a job and performing certain professions that require the use of the Slovene language), training and education. As Beznec and Gombač (2022) argue, on the basis of their empirical study among migrants in Slovenia, the language barrier is important factor that makes the life of asylum seekers and refugees difficult in all spheres of integration—including employment.

The issue with the knowledge of Slovenian language was mentioned by the representative of the Revealed Hands project, who highlighted that during implementation of their activities, they faced translation problems in certain language.

> *As said at the beginning, 'we were faced' with mistrust and the departure of the younger generation, with problems for translation into the Albanian language.* (Representative of the project Revealed Hands)

On the other hand, the representative of the Migrantour project made use of different strategy, namely she engaged in tours with individuals who have knowledge of English if not Slovene language as narration is crucial part of tourist tours. The ones that did not master the language enough were part of other activities.

> *We found that it is better to appoint people who have been here for some time and who already have certain language skills, least know English, if not Slovenian.* (Representative of the project Migrantour)

In certain cases, the lack of language knowledge can be overcome by orientation of the social enterprise in specific services and differentiation of labour tasks. This was explained in a very good way by the manager of Skuhna social enterprise.

> *And an important element of Skuhna itself is the idea that we are looking for ways—or we found them very easily—where migrants are active and realize some of their goals, while at the same time all these classic shortcomings, such as language, lack of education, ignorance of the system, social network … They fall off. They are not in the foreground; they do not occupy a very important role, when they perform activities in Skuhna.* (Representative of the social enterprise Skuhna)

During the discussion with experts, intercultural differences—informal institutions of cultural entry barriers as delineated by Robinson (2006)—were also identified as important gaps. Although, as already mentioned, according to the legislation, refugees have the right to free access to the labour market, different concerns regarding their employment may appear among potential employers. In this context, experts mentioned following issues: lack of work experience, health problems, discrimination, structural imbalances in the labour market, and lack of trust from employers. At this point, it is important to mention that during the interviews, no one of these issues appeared.

The Importance of (Supporting) Environment for Social Entrepreneurship

Social entrepreneurship in Slovenia (still) faces challenges due to social and legal environmental barriers. As it was emphasised during our discussion with experts, the crucial barrier lies in fundamental understanding of social entrepreneurship in general society. Namely, social entrepreneurship in Slovenia seems to be comprehended much more as "social" than "entrepreneurship", whilst "social" also bearing a negative connotation. Two implications follow: the first is the lower recognition of social entrepreneurship on the market. In this context is social entrepreneurship understood as a type of entrepreneurship which is not serious business and therefore does not have good market products. Therefore, it is more understood as a charity and does not gain broader public support. The second implication is a lack of business and management knowledge among providers, which often leads to an unsuccessful business model and underestimates the requirements of a successful social business. In relation to that, it is important to stress that most social enterprises in Slovenia are established by NGOs, who do not have a business mindset, and they rely more on creating social impact than financial stability. The latter causes a lot of problems for every enterprise as well as for the whole sector. Business models are often too weak to sustain the organization, and many social enterprises live on the edge of collapse. This is also reflected in some of the best practices collected, but we must keep in mind that not all are social enterprises. For example, the primary aim for Revealed Hands project was socialization, and the financial aspect was just a bonus, which allowed for more socialization (e.g., trips). The project Akupara acknowledged the financial security: even though it was a project implemented also during Covid-19 times, they pointed out they are working on this aspect. Finally, it must be noted that interviews with representatives of the projects and enterprises were conducted in summer of 2021, during Covid-19 times, which also affected the business part of the initiates. Some initiatives' financial stability suffered, as there are dealing with clients, for example, the restaurant and catering Skuhna and tourist tours Migrantour.

The main issue that was highlighted by both interviewees and experts was that there is the lack of supporting environment for social entrepreneurship:

> *There is no best supporting environment for social enterprises in Slovenia.* (Representative of the social enterprise Skuhna)

As our research of best practices revealed, most of the activities connected with refugees and migrants in the social enterprise field are project based, which causes certain issues mainly from the financial and sustainable points of view.

> *We know, there are always limitations in project work, because it is limited in time and so on.../... Because this is in the non-governmental sector, which does not have regular financing.* (Representative of the project Revealed Hands)

In practice, this means that after the duration of the project financing is over, project managers must search for new funds, which means preparation of new application and waiting for evaluation.

> *It is very tiring to search for funds again and again, and it is also the case that when you already have something well planned, well executed, well implemented, even if you are an example of good practice, no one will say yes, we will support this, let's change the project into program, here are program assets that you can rely on and that will fuel this program for years to come.* (Representative of the project Akupara)

At this point, it is necessary to highlight that Babič and Dabič Perica (2018) divide the support environment for the social economy in Slovenia into two parts, namely the organizations of the support environment and the support environment or ecosystem formed by the state. Regardless of the perceived increase in the number of support organizations, they note that the support environment is not satisfactorily developed as well. They mainly highlight the lack of comprehensive support for social economy entities, outlining non-systemic financing or dependence on project financing, disjointedness of the support environment and the absence of professional standards as the reason. OECD (2022) also finds that the supporting environment is not connected and does not form an adequate support network for improving the ecosystem. The improvement of the ecosystem of the social economy and the development of representative actors in this field, in their opinion, would also lead to the formation of a constructive dialogue between various subjects of the social economy and beyond, and at the same time, it would facilitate consultation with public authorities.

According to discussion with experts, the other major consequence of presented condition is the lack of financial support from different sources in Slovenia, most social enterprises use public funding sources. Public funding sources are available at national, regional and local levels. The public resources available to social enterprises are divided into national resources and resources of the European Cohesion Policy (primarily the European Social Fund and the European Fund for Regional Development). In addition, public resources are divided into non-returnable and returnable funds. Private resources or social financing are limited in Slovenia. Also, commercial banks recognize social enterprises as risky clients, so lending is limited. Combination of limited interest of commercial banks in social enterprises and the lack of established social investors or investors emphasizing (social) impact, means that social enterprises are, according to the OECD, difficult to sustain financially and are consequently relatively dependent on grant funding. In addition, social enterprises mostly choose to apply for grants that allow for 100% reimbursement, which leads to a heavy dependence on public resources (OECD, 2022).

During the discussion with experts, the confusion about the terms social enterprise, social entrepreneurship, social economy and social innovation was also mentioned, which are in the Slovenian context often used interchangeably. The OECD in its study notes that it would be useful if the strategy in preparation by Council for Social Economy[12] helped to define in more detail the terms used in Slovenia and to define connections between them. OECD (ibid.) outlines that the official definitions of the terms in the Social Entrepreneurship Act do not need to be changed, but the Council for Social Economy or the relevant departments could provide greater clarity in the use and promotion of the development and use of these terms. As discovered, confusion in the understanding of the mentioned concepts is present both in the general and professional public. In addition, the fragmentation of the institutional and legal landscape for social enterprises and the limited coherence of support frameworks create an inconsistent operating environment for social enterprises.

An important finding is also that Slovenian legislation[13] is not harmonized with all forms of social enterprises. The OECD (2022) notes that, despite the relative pre-normation of the legal framework in Slovenia, it is not properly harmonized, or the legal acts are not consistent. In addition, the wide range of legal and status forms that can be acquired by entities wishing to operate in the social economy sector presents a challenge. The consequences of the established inconsistency of the legal framework also

[12] The Council for Social Economy, headed by the Minister of Economic Development and Technology, ensures the coordination of policies in the field of social economy with ministries, government departments, municipalities, social partners and civil society organizations. Among the council's key tasks is the preparation of the ten-year Social Economy Development Strategy for the period 2022–2032.

[13] The social economy and social enterprises in Slovenia are defined by the Social Entrepreneurship Act, whereby the status of a social enterprise is a sub-form that can be obtained by an individual private legal organizational entity. The registration of the basic form depends on the individual field law, for example, acts on societies, cooperatives, commercial companies, and so on, while the social economy is not defined as a status or subform, but is defined as a way of performing activities.

led to the fragmentation of measures for the development of an all-encompassing support system that would cover all areas of activity of social enterprises, and the inconsistency of policy formulation. According to the OECD, the multitude of choices increases the volume of bureaucracy and leads to the pursuit of benefits and analysis of costs for an individual entity (2022).

Discussion and Conclusions

The integration of refugees into the labour market in general remains a challenge in Slovenia. As noted by Beznec and Gombač (2022) in Slovenia it is quite hard for refugees to open and run enterprise, since they face several systemic and practical obstacles, or institutional and formal as well as informal cultural entry barriers, as presented above. One of the reasons for this condition is that Slovenia is primarily considered a transit country and has relatively small number of refugees and asylum seekers. But despite this argument, we are facing the challenge of introducing new measures to promote the integration of refugees into the labour market and society in general. One of the crucial measures that Vončina and Marin (2019, p. 108) outline to be useful would be offering individually tailored literacy or special language courses, combined with vocational training. Furthermore, organizations within well-developed non-governmental sector play crucial role, above all, by providing support in all areas that the state does not fully provide for.

According to a recent in-depth study by the OECD (2022), social enterprises are important tools for labour market integration and rural and regional development, which have received increasing and more active support from policymakers since the adoption of the Social Entrepreneurship Act in 2011. Awareness of the importance of social entrepreneurship is increasing, but nevertheless, there are some challenges that hinder the development of social entrepreneurship and social enterprises. As mentioned, there is still confusion about the use of terms related to social entrepreneurship, social economy and social innovation. In addition, the fragmentation of the institutional and legal landscape for social enterprises and the limited coherence of support frameworks creates an inconsistent operating environment for social enterprises. Another major obstacle is the lack of financial support from various sources. Financing from EU funds and sometimes national funds is occasionally available, but there is no financial infrastructure for investment money from the private sector.

Based on the findings from the study, we provide possible solutions and recommendations for improvements of identified gaps. Quite a few recommended possible improvements are given in the Action Plan (European Commission, 2020), which conducted an in-depth study in Slovenia in 2020 and 2021 and also gave its relevant targeted recommendations for Slovenian context. In this regard, we would like to point out that the solutions that we present below rely on the findings and recommendations presented in this Action Plan by the European Commission and the OECD.

As noted by Babič and Dabič Perica (2018), the collection of data on subjects of the social economy in Slovenia is impossible due to the absence of statistical monitoring, which lead to the fact that analysis and studies are based on the assessments of individual authors as the concept of social economy is not included in statistical and analytical monitoring in Slovenia. For various entities, such as social enterprises, non-governmental organizations, companies that include people with disabilities and employment centre's, the data are provided by individual line ministries and support organizations. In addition, the crucial problem is that the basic definitions of the terms differ between the records, and that in the case where the data is collected by both competent ministries and civil associations, terms differ from each other. Since the data are the basis for conducting studies and the preparation of appropriate policies and necessary measures, the necessity of statistical collection of data on the social economy and methodological and technical harmonization at the national level is essential.

As the OECD (2022) suggests policymakers should try to eliminate the fragmentation of institutional and legal environments. They also suggest simplifying the legal environment in which social enterprises operate and strengthening coherence between support programmes, including tax benefits, as they believe that these could help eliminate the current fragmentation of the legal environment. In the long run, they also suggest the possibility of reducing the various statuses to one common denominator.

Securing long-term systematic funding mechanisms and financial incentives (public and private at transnational, national and regional/local level) for empowerment and action of all relevant actors is crucial. Furthermore, OECD (2022) proposes to increase the availability of financial resources for all social enterprises, regardless of their legal organizational form. In addition, it proposes the empowerment of local intermediaries and the adaptation of current entrepreneurship support networks to the specific needs of social enterprises, which, in their opinion, would lead to an expansion of the range of support mechanisms for developing their capacity. In the long term, however, they propose improvements to the financial mechanisms available to social enterprises, or the development of a consistent strategy of public financing of social enterprises, primarily by harmonizing public procurement procedures in the state administration, which help ensure that social enterprises have access to all public procurement and financial support regardless of to its legal organizational form. One of the areas of action in the field of financing the social economy, which the OECD recognizes as key, is a coordinated tax system, or a set of tax incentives to promote the operation and development of social economy entities. The European Commission also highlights the importance of taxation policy for the development of the sector and notes that only a few countries have developed a specific and consistent taxation framework for social enterprises.

Increasing the visibility of social enterprises among the general public as well as professionals is needed in the short run, which is one of the development guidelines that has been set through discussions with experts. Similarly, OECD recommends enhancing the visibility of social enterprises and promote the social economy as an overarching concept (OECD, 2022).

What should be considered as necessary according to findings within discussions is also development of a supportive environment with needed infrastructure within relevant fields, which include education system; establishment of training, mentoring, consulting programmes and access to relevant information; infrastructure facilities and business toolkits as well as established networks of relevant stakeholders that could enable connections at different levels.

Despite the challenges listed, good practices from Slovenia and broad show that social entrepreneurship can be an opportunity for integration, especially for vulnerable groups, including refugees and asylum seekers. The Slovenian government has recently considered two laws that will allow for faster issuance of residence permits and reduce the workload of administrative units, as well as simplify the employment of foreigners. According to new law proposal for the Foreigner Act (in parliamentary procedure) asylum seekers would be able to work in Slovenia after only three months, instead of the previous nine months. This would enable easier employment of foreigners for many employers who are currently facing shortage of labour.

Acknowledgements This chapter was published with the financial support from the project "REInSER—Refugees' Economic Integration Through Social Entrepreneurship" (INTERREG V-B Adriatic-Ionian ADRION Programme 2014–2020) and the Slovenian Research Agency through the research programme "Constructive Theology in the Age of Digital Culture and Anthropocene" (P6–0434) and the research project "A Child-Centred Approach to Integrating Immigrant Children: The Role of School in Integration with Regard to the Parents' Aspect" (Z5-3219).

References

Act Amending the International Protection Act (ZMZ-1A). (2021). http://www.pisrs.si/Pis.web/pregledPredpisa?id=ZAKO8192

Act Amending the Labour Market Regulation Act (ZUTD-E). (2019). http://pisrs.si/Pis.web/pregledPredpisa?id=ZAKO8078

Act amending the Act on Social Entrepreneurship (ZSocP-A). (2018). https://pisrs.si/pregledPredpisa?id=ZAKO7175

Ager, A., & Strang, A. (2008). Understanding Integration: A Conceptual Framework. *Journal of Refugee Studies, 21*(2), 166–191. https://doi.org/10.1093/jrs/fen016

Austin, J. (2006). Three Avenues for Social Entrepreneurship Research. In J. Mair, J. Robinson, & K. Hockerts (Eds.), *Social Entrepreneurship* (pp. 22–33). Palgrave Macmillan. https://doi.org/10.1057/9780230625655_3

Babič, K., & Dabič Perica, S. (2018). *Aplikativna analiza stanja na področju socialne ekonomije v Republiki Sloveniji (s smernicami za pripravo dolgoročne Strategije razvoja socialne ekonomije v Sloveniji 2019–2029 ter Programom kratkoročnih ukrepov—Akcijski načrt 2019–2020)*. CAAP, so.p. http://socialnaekonomija.si/wp-content/uploads/Analiza_stanja_na_podrocju_socialne_ekonomije_v_Sloveniji.pdf

Beznec, B., & Gombač, J. (2022). New Migration Policies and Innovative Practices. Slovenia between Bordering and Inclusion. *Innovation: The European Journal of Social Science Research*. https://doi.org/10.1080/13511610.2022.2071240

Cho, A. H. (2006). Politics, Values and Social Entrepreneurship: A Critical Appraisal. In J. Mair, J. Robinson, & K. Hockerts (Eds.), *Social Entrepreneurship* (pp. 34–56). Palgrave Macmillan. https://doi.org/10.1057/9780230625655_4

Dees, J. G. (1998; Reformatted and Revised 2001). The Meaning of 'Social Entrepreneurship'. Https://centers.fuqua.duke.edu/case/wp-content/uploads/sites/7/2015/03/Article_Dees_MeaningofSocialEntrepreneurship_2001.pdf

Desa, G., & Kotha, S. (2006). Ownership, Mission and Environment: An Exploratory Analysis into the Evolution of a Technology Social Venture. In J. Mair, J. Robinson, & K. Hockerts (Eds.), *Social Entrepreneurship* (pp. 155–179). Palgrave Macmillan. https://doi.org/10.1057/9780230625655_11

Employment, Self-Employment and Work of Foreigners Act (ZZSDT). (2015). http://www.pisrs.si/Pis.web/pregledPredpisa?id=ZAKO6655

European Commission. (2020). *Action Plan on Integration and Inclusion 2021–2027*. Communication from the Commission to the European Parliament, the Council, the European Economic and Social Committee and the Committee of the Regions. COM(2020) 758 Final.

European Commission. (2021). *Building an Economy that Works for People: An Action Plan for the Social Economy*. Communication from the Commission to the European Parliament, the Council, the European Economic and Social Committee and the Committee of the Regions. COM(2021) 778 final.

Foreigners Act (ZTuj-2). (2011). http://www.pisrs.si/Pis.web/pregledPredpisa?id=ZAKO5761

Freudenberg, J., & Halberstadt, J. (2008). How to Integrate Refugees Into the Workforce—Different Opportunities for (Social) Entrepreneurship. *Management Issues—Problemy ZarzÈdzania, 16*(1(73) part 2), 40–60. https://doi.org/10.7172/1644-9584.73.3

Haugh, H. (2006). Social Enterprise: Beyond Economic Outcomes and Individual Returns. In J. Mair, J. Robinson, & K. Hockerts (Eds.), *Social Entrepreneurship* (pp. 180–205). Palgrave Macmillan. https://doi.org/10.1057/9780230625655_12

Katzenstein, J., & Chrispin, B. R. (2011). Social Entrepreneurship and a New Model for International Development in the 21st Century. *Journal of Developmental Entrepreneurship, 16*(1), 87–102. https://doi.org/10.1142/S1084946711001720

Kickul, J., & Lyons, T. S. (2020). *Understanding Social Entrepreneurship: The Relentless Pursuit of Mission in an Ever Changing World* (3rd ed.). Routledge.

Mair, J. (2006). Introduction to Part II—Exploring the Intentions and Opportunities Behind Social Entrepreneurship. In J. Mair, J. Robinson, & K. Hockerts (Eds.), *Social Entrepreneurship* (pp. 89–94). Palgrave Macmillan. https://doi.org/10.1057/9780230625655_6

Mair, J., & Noboa, E. (2006). Social Entrepreneurship: How Intentions to Create a Social Venture are Formed. In J. Mair, J. Robinson, & K. Hockerts (Eds.), *Social Entrepreneurship* (pp. 121–135). Palgrave Macmillan. https://doi.org/10.1057/9780230625655_8

Mair, J., Robinson, J., & Hockerts, K. (Eds.). (2006). *Social Entrepreneurship*. Palgrave Macmillan. https://doi.org/10.1057/9780230625655

Martí, I. (2006). Introduction to Part I—Setting a Research Agenda for an Emerging Field. In J. Mair, J. Robinson, & K. Hockerts (Eds.), *Social Entrepreneurship* (pp. 17–21). Palgrave Macmillan. https://doi.org/10.1057/9780230625655_2

Ministry of Labour, Family, Social Affairs and Equal Opportunities. (2010). Strategija ekonomskih migracij za obdobje od 2010 do 2020 = Strategy on Economic Migration for the Period from 2010 to 2020.

Nabergoj, M. & Regvar, U. (2021). *Country report: Slovenia*. PIC (Legal Centre for the Protection of Human Rights and the Environment) and edited by ECRE. https://asylumineurope.org/wp-content/uploads/2022/05/AIDA-SI_2021update.pdf

OECD. (2022). *Boosting Social Entrepreneurship and Social Enterprise Development in Slovenia: In-Depth Policy Review*. OECD Local Economic and Employment Development (LEED) Papers, No. 2022/02, OECD Publishing, Paris. https://doi.org/10.1787/8ea2b761-en

OPSI—Odprti podatki Slovenije. (n.d.). Podatki.gov.si. https://podatki.gov.si/

Perrini, F., & Vurro, C. (2006). Social Entrepreneurship: Innovation and Social Change across Theory and Practice. In J. Mair, J. Robinson, & K. Hockerts (Eds.), *Social Entrepreneurship* (pp. 57–85). Palgrave Macmillan. https://doi.org/10.1057/9780230625655_5

Public Use of the Slovene Language Act (ZJRS) (2004). http://www.pisrs.si/Pis.web/pregledPredpisa?id=ZAKO3924

Rakar, T., & Kolarič, Z. (2019). *Social Enterprises and Their Ecosystems in Europe, Country Report Slovenia*. https://doi.org/10.2767/203806

Rihter, L. (2018). Social Entrepreneurship in Slovenia: An Opportunity for Sustainable Development? *Revija Za Socijalnu Politiku, 25*(3), 285–302. https://doi.org/10.3935/rsp.v25i3.1492

Rivna, A., & Gress, M. (2022). Social Entrepreneurship as a New Business Model. The Case of Refugee Integration. *Economic Research-Ekonomska Istraživanja, 36*(3), 1–19. https://doi.org/10.1080/1331677X.2022.2120044

Robinson, J. (2006). Navigating Social and Institutional Barriers to Markets: How Social Entrepreneurs Identify and Evaluate Opportunities. In J. Mair, J. Robinson, & K. Hockerts (Eds.), *Social Entrepreneurship* (pp. 95–120). Palgrave Macmillan. https://doi.org/10.1057/9780230625655_7

Shin, H., Booth, M., & Gomezel, A. S. (2019). Challenges in a Social Enterprise from the Case of a Social Enterprise in Slovenia. In *Proceedings of the 2019 International Conference on Global Entrepreneurial Talent Management & Social Collaboration* (pp. 13–21). Chonnam National University.

Social Entrepreneurship Act. (2011). Social Entrepreneurship Act. http://www.pisrs.si/Pis.web/pregledPredpisa?id=ZAKO6175

Svet za socialno ekonomijo (2022). Strategija razvoja socialne ekonomije za obdobje 2022–2032—Osnutek = Social economy development strategy for the period 2022–2032 in Slovenia—Draft.

UNHCR. (2021). UNHCR Refugee Data Finder. https://www.unhcr.org/refugee-statistics/download/?url=2bxU2f

Vlada Republike Slovenije/Government of Republic of Slovenia. (2019). *Strategija vlade RS na področju migracij*. Portal GOV.SI. https://www.gov.si/novice/2019-07-18-strategija-na-podrocju-migracij/

Vončina, B., & Marin, N. (2019). What Issues Do Refugees Face in Integrating into Labour Markets? Evidence from Slovenia. *Transfer: European Review of Labour and Research, 25*(1), 101–112. https://doi.org/10.1177/1024258918807388

CHAPTER 10

Social Entrepreneurship and Migrants' Inclusion in Albania

Imelda Sejdini and *Bederiana Shyti*

Introduction

Enhancing migrants' integration through all forms of entrepreneurship including "social entrepreneurship" for increasing their independence and financial security has been in focus of many EU programs over the years.

The term "social entrepreneurship" was first used in the literature in 1953 in the book "Social Responsibilities of the Businessman" by Howard R. Bowen. We find the term "social entrepreneurship" later used as a way to illustrate administrative skills and as a solution to solve different social problems, in the book "Sociology of movements" by Joseph Banks in

I. Sejdini (✉)
Faculty of Economy, University of Elbasan "Aleksandër Xhuvani", Elbasan, Albania
e-mail: imelda.sejdini@uniel.edu.al

B. Shyti
Faculty of Natural Sciences, University of Elbasan "Aleksandër Xhuvani", Elbasan, Albania
e-mail: bederiana.shyti@uniel.edu.al

S. Bianchini et al. (eds.), *Social Entrepreneurship and Migrants' Inclusion*, Sustainable Development Goals Series,
https://doi.org/10.1007/978-3-031-55791-0_10

1972. This term became familiar in the 1980s, advancing further in the 1990s, promoted by Bill Drayton,[1] Charles Leadbeater[2] and others. In the 2000s, with the increase of the concern about social problems, social entrepreneurship became known as a separate part of academic research connecting better the theory with practice. As social entrepreneurship continued to gain more visibility and traction from practitioners, it triggered a wave of academic analysis of the concept and marked a sharp increase in research and publications (Bacq et al., 2022). More research is conducted in the coming years, for developing theories in 2010 and after and today we have a lot of books written about social entrepreneurship (e.g., Sinek, 2009; Yunus, 2010).

Social entrepreneurship is an activity that generates incomes by supporting a social mission. Solving effectively social problems is the approach of social entrepreneurship. Social entrepreneurship in many countries is believed to be a contributor in solving individuals with fewer opportunities and marginalized groups (as well as refugees and migrants) inclusion, especially with a focus on unemployed and low-income people. People who have different experiences and come from different realities; people with a cultural diversity belonging who are subject to discrimination, exclusion and marginalization; and people with lack of opportunities and future perspectives, even because of their personal development, need to have a chance. Social entrepreneurship is a good opportunity to increase inclusion of these people of above-mentioned categories and to give them the chance of being part and belonging to the society.

In the very beginning, when this concept was first introduced in the USA and then expanded all over the world, social enterprises reference was only for non-profit organizational forms. Later on, for-profit organizations with a social aim were included in this reference, expanding further this approach. They can perform the same activities in both forms, for-profit or non-profit, enough that they pursue a social goal. This broadens the possibilities of inclusions and increases the chances for a better future of people with social problems.

There are many considerations about social entrepreneurship, and we can find different definitions in the literature. An interesting one is the

[1] Considered the pioneer and the father of social entrepreneurship in the literature about social entrepreneurship.

[2] Leadbeater, Ch. (1997). *The Rise of the Social Entrepreneur*. London, UK. Demos report.

definition by that "all entrepreneurship is social",[3] which means that by production of positive outcomes through job creation, building the economy and advancing human capacity, unless through legal or illegal activities, all entrepreneurship has a social impact. Still there is no unique social entrepreneurship model that can solve all the problems society is facing today all over the world. Through studding different practices and contributing to the literature, we can raise new questions and find new ways of improving things in this path.

At the center of all consideration on social entrepreneurship is the satisfying of unmet needs by using underutilized resources, through creation of new products and services, new ways of dealing with problems, bringing transformation into the communities through new opportunities of self-development and addressing social and environmental challenges through the creation of new organizations or initiatives. So, social entrepreneurship is pioneering in all these directions.

Connecting social entrepreneurship to migration means that there are issues and concerns with inclusion and acceptance of diversity among local communities, resulting in lack of opportunities. The creation of new economic opportunities for all by leaving no one behind is among the priorities of the UN 2030 Agenda for Sustainable Development. One mechanism to achieve this is consequently through the promotion of entrepreneurship. Entrepreneurship has a significant role in enhancing the positive effects of migration on economic growth and development. Entrepreneurship can be an effective way of migrant's inclusion in local economies, by sharing their knowledge and entrepreneurial spirit, and creating new market opportunities and networking.

Despite the difficulties and barriers such as cultural, operational and financial ones, governments and public institutions, NGOs and migrants themselves need to find opportunities and take measures to support social entrepreneurship and to maximize the potential of migrant's communities in countries of origin and in countries of destination. For countries of origin, return migration can contribute to entrepreneurship development by capitalizing on resources, skills, networks and knowledge that they acquire through migration, by acting as mentors for local entrepreneurs or facilitators of cross-border trade and marketing.[4] It is important to note

[3] Chanine, T. (2016). *Introduction to Social Entrepreneurship* (1st ed). CRC Press.

[4] UN (2018). Policy guide on entrepreneurship for migrants and refugees. https://www.unhcr.org/5bd31fd67.pdf

that although entrepreneurship is an important factor in advancing migrant integration, it should be viewed as complementary to a more inclusive involvement on their socio-economic integration that includes access to services, legal protection and cultural orientation if the opportunities and benefits are to be maximized. This means that the government approach is important to ensure the right responses in all aspects. There is evidence from EU countries like Greece, Italy, etc. that considering the facilitation of integration to work of marginalized groups, social enterprises resources are private and public, having the support of respective states in obtaining more than 50% of their funds through contracts, agreements and public procurement.[5]

Government approach must also consider the effects of entrepreneurship in economic growth. Urbano et al. (2019) found in their study about 25 years of research on institutions, entrepreneurship and economic growth that the relationship between entrepreneurship and economic growth differs depending on the stage of a country, and the diversity in entrepreneurship is particularly important for economic growth, among others including social entrepreneurship and immigrant's transnational entrepreneurship. Wang (2022) in her study concluded that social entrepreneurship is a phenomenon that effects the economic growth of a country, and higher economic growth leads to a higher rate of employment and better living standards for the people in the society.

Albanian migration background is progressively being considered as an effective approach to overcoming some of the challenges of integration by providing employment possibilities for individuals with restricted access to the labor market. Despite this prospective, Albanian migrants face barriers to engaging in entrepreneurial activities, that can be related to their legal status or regulations that may prevent them from working and accessing essential services, as well as difficulties in accessing funds and financing. Migrants are considered minorities in the countries they migrate. In all studies about discrimination, minorities result as one of the most discriminated categories along with women. According to Barjaba (2018), many scholars (Labrianidis & Lyberaki, 2001; Hatziprokopiou, 2003; Lyberaki & Maroukisa, 2005) reinforce the idea that the overall work experience of Albanians is improving and that they are becoming increasingly integrated within local communities, shifting toward more diversified sectoral

[5] Haska, E. & Hoxha, J. (2020), *Characteristics and challenges of social enterprises in Albania, Baseline Study*. Partners Albania.

employment and social mobility. Empirical evidence suggests many cases of positive effects of migration in the country development through remittances, job creation, human capital accumulation, etc. as some of the ways of contribution of migrants in the country's development.

The Albanian Government's approach is also important with policies, strategies, legislation and measures for a better integration of migrants, considering the increasing figures of net migration during the last years. But yet, there is no much evidence and studies on Albanian migrants in social entrepreneurship, and the existing research is mainly focused on characteristics and challenges of social enterprises in Albania in general. Social entrepreneurship sector in Albania is still in the early stage of development, considering that the first social enterprises were created in 2000 with the financial contribution of donors from other countries or nonprofit activities. In the existing research results that the access to financial mechanisms that is critical for social enterprises is complex in Albania. Investors and other entities such as banks or other intermediaries in financing, consider social enterprises of high risk and low return on investment, according to EC, 2020.[6]

Concerning the methodology, the research in this study is mainly based on the descriptive method. First, a literature review is conducted by selecting and analyzing journal articles, papers and books related to this topic and secondary data from official sources of information are gathered and analyzed for a better understanding of migrants in social entrepreneurship in the Albanian context. Secondary data are also obtained by national and international reports on the topic and the discussion is oriented according to thematic analysis. The findings from the research are presented and integrated in each section.

Country Background: Social Enterprises and Migration Context

Albanian Environment and Migration Data

Albania, as a country in development, is characterized by many disparities and social challenges. Considering unemployment rates and poverty level in Albania, the migration rates toward European countries are high, as a result of lack of opportunities especially for young generations.

[6] Haska, E. & Hoxha, J. (2020), *Characteristics and challenges of social enterprises in Albania, Baseline Study*. Partners Albania.

Albania has a population of 2,793,592 inhabitants as of 1 January 2022, according to INSTAT (2022),[7] which is 1.3% lower than the same period of the previous year. The net migration is increased during 2021, by 16,169 inhabitants. International migration is an important component, which has an impact on changing population numbers. INSTAT estimates the annual number of immigrants and emigrants based on the integrated migration module in the Labor Force Survey, since 2015 (INSTAT, 2022).

According to INSTAT (2022), statistics on foreigners with residence permits and asylum seekers in Albania have been included for the first time in the Official Statistics Program 2017–2021. At the end of 2021, the number of foreigners with a residence permit in Albania was 14,921 inhabitants, increasing by 9.6%, compared to 2020 (Table 10.2). Resident foreigners originating from Iran, Italy and Kosovo constitute the largest number of foreigners with residence permits in Albania in 2021, respectively, with 2586, 2324 and 1869 inhabitants.

Foreigners originating from Europe, in 2021, result in 8812 inhabitants and make up 59.1% of foreigners in total against the 56.8% they accounted for in 2020. According to INSTAT figures referring to the previous year 2021, 59.1% of them are from Europe, 28.3% from Asia, 8.5% from USA, 3.8% from Africa and 0.3% from Oceania.

In 2021, 10,062 irregular foreigners were recorded in the territory of the country, where most of them, foreigners originating from Syria and Afghanistan, occupy 67%. The reason for employment is the main reason for the residence permits of foreigners in Albania in 2021, with 47.7% (Table 10.1).

Figures in Table 10.1 also show that the number of foreigners in Albania has a slight increase. Figures show that the main reason for this flow is employment, being followed by the reason of reunification with family members who have been employed previously in Albania. There are also migrants who have chosen Albania for humanitarian reasons and a few of them for study reason.

Data in Table 10.2 show that net migration of Albania is negative, and these figures in the recent years have been growing in absolute value. So, Albania is not yet an immigration country.

[7] INSTAT (2022). *Albanian Population, 1 January 2022*. INSTAT. http://www.instat.gov.al/media/9828/popullsia-me-1-janar-2022_final-15-04-2022.pdf

Table 10.1 Foreigners with residence permits in Albania according to the reason for the application, 2017–2021

Years	*2017*	*2018*	*2019*	*2020*	*2021*
Total	**12,906**	**14,162**	**13,507**	**13,609**	**14,921**
Employment	6334	6950	7432	6465	7124
Family Reunification	2982	3303	3696	3334	3602
Study	656	633	750	277	413
Humanitarian	2381	2558	820	2679	2656
Other	553	718	809	854	1126
In %					
Total	**100**	**100**	**100**	**100**	**100**
Employment	49.1	49.1	55.0	47.5	47.7
Family Reunification	23.1	23.3	27.4	24.5	24.1
Study	5.1	4.5	5.5	2.0	2.8
Humanitarian	18.4	18.0	6.1	19.7	17.8
Other	4.3	5.1	6.0	6.3	7.6

Source: INSTAT (2022)

Table 10.2 Number of immigrants, emigrants and net migration in Albania 2017–2021

Year	*Immigrants*	*Emigrants*	*Net migration*
2017	25,003	39,905	**−14,902**
2018	23,673	38,703	**−15,030**
2019	20,753	43,835	**−23,082**
2020	7170	23,854	**−16,684**
2021	9195	42,048	**−32,853**

Source: INSTAT (2022)

Related to this study, employment of emigrants is an important tool to show how this is related to social entrepreneurship. For this is important to analyze the historical background of social entrepreneurship in Albania, the changes and challenges and how this is connected with migrant's employment in and out Albania.

Social Entrepreneurship Background in Albania

Social entrepreneurship in Albania dates back during the communist regime. We already have a history of social enterprises in the form of agricultural cooperatives[8] completely owned by the state since 1946 when the first agricultural cooperative has been created and this process ended in 1979 with the new constitutional changes, when the process has been completed for the whole agriculture in the country. During this period, the state's attention was focused on setting up scientific institutions for preparing specialists, managers and scientists to deal with soil, production, increasing the yield of agricultural crops, livestock, etc. Plants were built for producing chemical fertilizers, supportive structures such as cars and tractors stations were built as well, and funds through the agricultural bank were provided to finance the production. The main reason promoted for these developments was a social one: *the employment of the entire rural population*. Because of their work, agriculture would reach high production levels, including improvements in mechanization, chemistry, transportation and processing of agro-food products, management strategies, etc.

As centralizing economic policies were closely followed, the impact they had over the population after the failure was very negative because of the lack of autonomy, lack of property right and production use. After the regime changed, the negative perception of the concept on social enterprises also changed along with it. Non-profit organizations, supported and guided from foreign donors, started to focus on delivering social services, being the initiators of social entrepreneurship in the democracy after the 90s. Later on, these activities expanded and started to be delivered also by other kind of enterprises, developing the social economy and getting the government's attention. Most of social enterprises established during the last five years have been registered as for-profit entities in order to overcome some of the legal and operational barriers and to be more flexible in the type of economic activity they chose to conduct. The main characteristic of social enterprises is the low number of employees, at a maximum of five full-time engaged staff, and the main reason for this is the low income and the lack of fiscal incentives. Most of for-profit social enterprises do not engage in social services and these services are provided by non-for-profit

[8] Agolli, A., Haska, E. & Hoxha, J. (2019). *Social enterprises and their ecosystems in Europe; Country fiche Albania* (1st edition). *EU*. https://doi.org/10.2767/418617

organization, targeting focus groups that are at the bottom line. For-profit social enterprises operate mainly in the food services, hotel services, tourism, agriculture and farming, manufacturing, healthcare and educational services.

There is a difference in the funding of non-profit organizations and for-profit organizations. The most common incomes in Albanian for-profit organizations are incomes provided by the activity's products and services sale, while non-profit organizations are funded by grants and donations by foreign programs or donators. There is little support by the state for social enterprises, and this makes the Albanian social enterprises differ from EU enterprises that are supported by state, with public contracts.[9] In general, only a few for-profit organizations make profits and these profits are reallocated in employment, new purchases of equipment, marketing or new ideas development. They can barely manage to distribute a small percentage of dividends for the shares.

One specific characteristic of for-profit organizations is the employment of marginalized group's members at large, targeting unemployed, youth and the poor, and this leads to the need for support by the government as the actual legal framework does not include this category of social enterprises.

Legal Framework and Recent Changes

The legislative framework on social entrepreneurship and social economy in Albania is still incomplete. The main reason may be that social entrepreneurship in Albania is not well established yet. However, the development of social economy has increased the focus of Albanian Government by approving the law No. 65/2016[10] "For Social enterprises in the Republic of Albania" from the Albanian Parliament. This law regulates the organization and functioning of social enterprises and defines the conditions and criteria that subjects must fulfill in order to gain the status of social enterprise.

The purpose of this law is to regulate the activity of social enterprises, in order to protect and social inclusion of vulnerable groups, through:

[9] Haska, E. & Hoxha, J. (2020), *Characteristics and challenges of social enterprises in Albania, Baseline Study*. Partners Albania.

[10] The Official Journal of Albanian Republic, No.118/2016, pp.8312–8318

(a) employment, within the recognition of the fundamental right of the individual to have sufficient resources for living, in accordance with human dignity;
(b) providing employment opportunities for people whose age, health and family condition do not allow them an active availability in the labor market;
(c) offering goods and services in diverse forms and with good quality, while providing appropriate and accessible opportunities for individuals with special needs, as well as mark an essential step toward gender equality, as these services facilitate the participation of women in the labor market;
(d) economic and social integration of groups in need, encouraging the spirit of responsibility, solidarity and social cohesion in the community.

One of social criteria that a social enterprise must fulfill is that at least 30% of employed staff must belong to disadvantaged groups that, according to this law among others, include displaced people. The juridical form of a social enterprise is non-profit according to this law, operating according to the legislation for non-profit organizations. Only non-profit organizations in Albania have the right to apply for the status of social enterprise to the Ministry of Health and Social Protection. The current law does not allow distributing any kind of profit, even though in other countries, it is recognized by law that a certain percentage of profits could be distributed to the social entrepreneurs. The distribution of any kind of profit, even indirectly, in favor of the members, employees or associates of the social enterprise is prohibited in Albania.

The Ministry responsible for social protection is charged with the drafting of policies for promotion and development of social enterprises, and it is also in charge for performing controls, in order to ensure compliance with the legislation for social enterprises on social enterprise entities, according to DCM No.716 dated 01 December 2017 "For determining procedures of performing control on social enterprises activity".

In 2018, it was issued Directive No. 607 dated 01 August 2018 "On procedures and necessary documentation for gaining the status of social enterprise" by the Ministry of Health and Social Protection. Later on, a DCM No.789 dated 26 December 2018 "On creation of the fund to support social enterprises and forms of support through subsidies for social enterprises" provides support for social enterprises through subvention up to 70% of the costs but not more than 1,500,000 ALL, if the entity is able to finance the remaining of 30% of the investment according to the business plan applied to be supported. This law does not have a broad view. It recognizes the non-profit organizations such as foundations, centers and associations as a legal form of social enterprises but does not include other existing types of enterprises that generate incomes by supporting a social mission.

Non-profit organizations in Albania are also supported by law No.10 093, dated 9 March 2009 on "Organization and Functioning of the Agency for Supporting Civil Society", that includes providing financial assistance for programs that promote and strengthen the sustainability of non-profit organizations, international and inter sectors cooperation, civil initiatives, philanthropy, volunteerism, as well as other programs, that facilitate the fulfillment of Agency's mission. There are 675[11] registered non-profit organizations at the Agency for Supporting Civil Society in Albania, until December 2022. There is no available data on how migrants are supported by these organizations and how many of them are totally engaged in social entrepreneurship by emigrants.

Albanian Migrant's Social Entrepreneurship Potential and Contribution

Connecting social entrepreneurship with migration is not so easy in Albania, because it is difficult to distinguish these enterprises whether according to the aim of their activity or according to the status of social enterprise gained according to law. Albania is a country with high emigration rates in ascending figures during the recent years. This phenomenon initiated in the early 1990s, as a job-seeking effort toward countries with more promising and better opportunities, after political system and economical situation changed. Due to changes from the centralized economy to capitalism, the difficulties afforded by Albanian emigrants were doubled. Their lack of knowledge and experience with the capitalism rules and the need to be integrated in the new environment is seen as an obstacle to developing entrepreneurships in the host countries. They have succeeded over the years, and some of them are now engaged in a wide range of entrepreneurial activities. According to Albanian Ministry of Europe and

[11] AMSHC, (2023). *Database of registered NGO-s in Albania*. AMSHC web. https://amshc.gov.al/ojf-qe-veprojne-ne-shqiperi/

Foreign Affairs, in Italy there are about 500.000 Albanian emigrants. In Italy, there are also about 32,000 emigrant's entrepreneurship activities until 2021. Albanian community is ranked the third in Italy for entrepreneurship on the overall non-EU population. Moreover, an analysis of the evolution of Albanian entrepreneurship in Italy from a long-term perspective shows how entrepreneurship has grown constantly in the last decades. The majority of companies are in the construction sector; in terms of geographical distribution, data show that these enterprises are widely distributed in the Italian territory.[12]

According to ILO, most of Albanian migrants have migrated toward European countries, especially in Italy and Greece and recently in Germany, the USA and Canada. Many social and development theories have considered different phases of migration, development and contribution in the economy, starting with better work opportunities abroad and remittances flow in the country of origin, continuing with brain-drain and shifting recently to brain-gain policies by home countries. From the positive side of consideration, migration is an added value to both host countries and home countries. In the host country, they contribute to the labor market as an asset, and in the home countries, they contribute to poverty reduction and economic growth with the inflow of remittances they send. This is true for Albanian migrants as well. Remittances are significant part of the Albanian economy since they contribute to the GDP by 9%–15%, and they make 15% of family incomes, considering also an extra 10% in informal remittances.[13] Migrants also contribute to their home countries by transferring new skills and knowledge they have improved abroad. This is a key tool in entrepreneurship development by returned migrants. There are many studies that address the discussion of return migration from the point of view of reintegration. For Albania, this phenomenon is not massive and is quite recent. Figures show that return migration in Albania is very low. Some of them try to be self employed and start their own activity.

[12] CESPI (2021). *Mapping and Profiling of Albanian Diaspora.* Mapping and Profiling of Albanian Diaspora. *An economic and social survey in five Italian regions. Overview of the situation in France and Belgium. International Organization for Migration (IOM), Geneva.* IOM Albania. ISBN 978-92-9268-106-7 (PDF) https://albania.iom.int/sites/g/files/tmzbdl1401/files/documents/mapping-and-profiling-of-albanian-diaspora.pdf

[13] Musabelliu, M. (2019). Albania social briefing: Albanian diaspora—an essential social stronghold for the entire nation. China CEE-Institute. 15(3). 1–5. https://china-cee.eu/2019/03/20/albania-social-briefing-albanian-diaspora-an-essential-social-stronghold-for-the-entire-nation/

There are two ways of return migrant's integration through social entrepreneurship: being employed in existing social enterprises that follow an inclusion of returnees' path or investing in a social enterprise as an employment in following a social goal. In Albania, the first way is possible through non-profit organizations and their inclusion programs, and the second one is possible by using remittances in a productive way or by using credit. Guiding remittances which are private into productive uses is a government issue. Through training programs on entrepreneurship and information on priority sectors and business potentials, government can channel remittances in a better use other than consumption and savings. In March 2022, a new law "For the support and development of start-ups" was approved in Albania, and now start-ups can apply for grants according to the government priorities, including initiatives with a positive environment impact, increase of social inclusion, diversity and social impact.[14] This is a positive step by the government and a very good opportunity for return migrants to be involved in entrepreneurship activities.

Policy Framework of Social Enterprises in Albania

In Albania, there is no clear classification or division of social enterprises, which makes it almost impossible to accurately determine the number of social businesses that develop activity in our country. These businesses have different legal forms and can be non-profit organizations, commercial companies, agricultural cooperation societies, or even savings-credit societies for financial activity. As we mentioned above, by law, only non-profit organizations are recognized and can be registered as social enterprises in Albania. These enterprises must be registered in a dedicated register[15] that is not available yet, even that it is recognized by law. In general, from the Albanian practice, social enterprises have to do with the job rehabilitation of marginalized groups, or with the provision of services for these groups. A non-profit organization can develop economic activity, as long as its income does not exceed 20% of the total income, which generally comes from international projects or donations. EC is the most important funder of non-profit sector in Albania, through grant schemes like IPA Cross Border, Regional Grant Scheme, etc. Developing an eco-

[14] Law no.25/2022 on "Support and development of start-ups"

[15] Directive no. 2, dated 04 January 2019 "On the creation of the register of social enterprises and the rules for its maintenance".

nomic activity gives the non-profit organizations the opportunity to not be completely dependent on grants and donations, but to be able to provide their own incomes, through the provision of goods, services or others. But this is limited by law, and if the income from the economic activity exceeds the limit of 20%, then the non-profit organization must be registered as a business. Some of non-profit organizations in Albania offer free services, but recently, there is an increased number of non-profit organizations that offer services by payment in order to support their activity.

Social enterprises in Albania are considered as opportunities for social inclusion and employment for disadvantaged and marginalized categories, as the law implies and still are not seen at large by public authorities as means to encourage innovation and to establish an entrepreneurship mindset.

If we refer to the official data from INSTAT,[16] by the end of 2021 in Albania operate 181,599 entities, distinguished by the legal form of organization. A total of 2370 of them are non-profit organizations and international organizations. No data about the number of social enterprises exists from official sources of information. According to a study conducted by Partners Albania in 2020, only six NGOs obtained the status of social enterprise until March 2020. It is supposed that many of them in Albania have decided to operate as businesses, due to the restriction by law in using the funds even at the benefit of marginalized categories included in their activity. For-profit legal form is considered as the most convenient form of registration to operate as social enterprise due to the flexibility in terms of the type of economic activities conducted and less operational barriers compared to the other legal forms.[17]

Another form of social entrepreneurship in Albania are microfinance institutions. These institutions provide banking services to unemployed or low-income individuals or groups who otherwise would have no other access to financial services. They provide funds for return migrants as well by applying simple procedures and helping them to start entrepreneurship activities.

[16] Çapo, O. Dala, F. & Haxhillari, K. (2022). *Business Registers 2022*. INSTAT. https://www.instat.gov.al/al/temat/industria-tregtia-dhe-sh%C3%ABrbimet/regjistrat-e-biznesit/#tab2

[17] Haska, E. & Hoxha, J. (2020), *Characteristics and challenges of social enterprises in Albania, Baseline Study*. Partners Albania.

Socio-economic Integration of Migrants in Albania

Social entrepreneurship focuses on solving social problems all around the world, provides support for migrants and supports the efforts made by international organizations, the state and civil society. They can develop solutions that relate to their employment, education, training and other needs to enhance their quality of life. All over the world, there are many social enterprises that support migrants and change their future for better.

Social entrepreneurship and entrepreneurship in general are not the first choice of migrants, but it depends on the circumstances they find in the host country. Financial support is the first reason for other more immediate income-providing sources. There are also other barriers such as language knowledge, lack of market knowledge, unfamiliarity with regulations, laws, taxation, along with the limited access to finance and credits that have resulted in different studies about migration. Many countries almost do not offer support for migrant's entrepreneurship. Even that there are many programs financed by the EU to identify the needs and characteristics of migrants and to explore new opportunities for them, there is little knowledge among migrants for the access they can have due to low networking. The decision to start a business may be driven more often by necessity than by the identification of opportunities, but entrepreneurship may offer migrants an important route to financial security and self-reliance.

However, it is still not clear the extent to which returned migrants invest in Albania and even more difficult to identify and to provide data about Albanian migrant's social entrepreneurship. There is little research done on this topic as well. The most recent research conducted by Partners Albania (2020) shows that only 21% of refugees benefit from social enterprises in Albania.

Albania has some evidence for social entrepreneurship such as the paper-recycling project started in 2008 in Tirana from the non-profit organizations "Terre des Hommes" and "Common Actions Against Poverty (CAAP)" by supporting the local non-profit Romani Baxt to set up a paper collection team, renting a warehouse and establishing a collection point. By also providing a crushing/pressing machine and a truck they helped to create this social enterprise as a business that employed low-skilled Roma people and generated income to fund summer camps and a kindergarten for Roma children. This recycling activity had also a positive impact in the environment for a long time even after the program ended.[18]

Another social entrepreneurship with the same aim was funded in Korça in 2006 by the same non-profit organizations, including Roma mothers in handicraft productions to provide incomes for their families. These women were also part of an active community in discussion of children protection issues. These activities were better than what they had done before to provide incomes for their families.

There are some programs that are active now in Albania, for example the program "Migration and Diaspora"[19] financed by German Government and implemented by GIZ (German Society for International Cooperation) that assists in leveraging the benefits of regular migration and engaging Diaspora for sustainable development. Among other approaches of this program, promoting investment, knowledge exchange and innovation in partner countries by supporting Diaspora in Germany and fostering circular migration by placing skilled workers with a migration history with employees active in development issues in countries of origin is a very wide inclusive approach and support for Albanian migrants.

Another project aiming to evaluate the engagement of professionals in Diaspora is the project "Scientific Diaspora as a factor of change in the process of Albania's integration to the European Union," approved by Decision no. 321, dated 15 May 2019 of the Council of Ministers "On the financing of the project 'Scientific Diaspora as a factor of change in the process of Albania's integration to the European Union' and its implementation by the Albanian Fund for the Development of Diaspora".[20]

RE-IN-VEST is another project implemented in Albania in 2019 for the integration of returned migrants through employment and business ideas development, financed by German Government, supported by GIZ Albania and implemented by World Vision Albania in partnership with Diakonia Agapes. This project helped several families in 13 municipalities of Albania to improve their living conditions, access in qualitative social services, as well as opportunity to generate income for child and family

[18] Vendresha, A. & Sinani, I. (2014). *Supporting Social Entrepreneurship in Albania to Better Protect Children*. Report for Albania. Terre des Hommes.

[19] GIZ (2021). *Programme Migration and Dispora*. GIZ. https://www.giz.de/en/downloads/giz2021-en-programm-migration-diaspora.pdf

[20] Council of Ministers (2020). *Albanian National Diaspora Strategy 2021–2025*. https://diaspora.gov.al/wp-content/uploads/2020/12/STRATEGJIA-KOMBETARE-E-DIASPORES-2021-2025-ENG.pdf

well-being. 254 Albanian returned families have been supported through capacity building to develop their ideas for start-ups.[21]

Since 2012, also Nobel Laureate, Professor Muhammad Yunus started a social business development project in Albania and then was formally registered in February 2013 as an NGO, named Foundation "Yunus Social Business Fund Albania." With the mission to bring significant positive change to the society by enterprising people and equip entrepreneurs with the knowledge, skills, tools and means to design, test, build and grow entrepreneurship initiatives that have the potential to create positive impact for the society, YSB started supporting local social entrepreneurs to develop their social business initiatives. In few years YSB has supported more than 200 entrepreneurs with various entrepreneurial services and has deployed about USD 700,000 to social businesses in Albania. Also, 11 start-ups out of 26 that have fully completed the Accelerator Program have gone to market, newly established or sustained their businesses.[22]

Considering these endeavors, still social entrepreneurship in Albania is underdeveloped as a sector, especially when we consider migration and Diaspora inclusion in social entrepreneurship activities. The Albanian National Diaspora Strategy 2021–2025 will conduct a reassessment of the cooperation between the donors and the "Brain Gain" model programs with the aim of creating institutional structures that enable the attraction of Diaspora professionals for short- and long-term engagements.[23]

Some of Best Practices in Albania

Entrepreneurial activity in Albania is mainly organized in micro-enterprises with an average number of three employees, and this has been the most common business where return migrants typically invest their savings. In these activities usually are committed to work family members or relatives and this micro-enterprises in general are easy to start with a very small

[21] World Vizion (2022). *RE-IN-VEST Project helps families returning from migration.* World vison Albania Web. https://www.wvi.org/stories/albania/re-vest-project-helps-families-returning-emigration

[22] Marku, Sh. (2015). *Interview with Shkelzen Marku, Director of Yunus Social Business Balkans.* IIA. https://invest-in-albania.org/interview-with-shkelzen-marku-director-of-yunus-social-business-balkans/

[23] Council of Ministers (2020). *Albanian National Diaspora Strategy 2021–2025.* https://diaspora.gov.al/wp-content/uploads/2020/12/STRATEGJIA-KOMBETARE-E-DIASPORES-2021-2025-ENG.pdf

capital from own resources, some skills gained in migration and work. Even though emigrants do different jobs abroad and sometimes their previous qualification is not useful, when they return, they are more skilled and have acquired more useful experience and expertise. In their return in many cases, migrants open the same enterprise they have worked in the host countries. As a result of these experiences, in Albania there are many "souvlaki" shops from emigrants returned from Greece or "pizza" shops from emigrants returned from Italy in every city of Albania.

Recently returned migrants can apply for support and funds at the state agencies when their remittances are not enough to develop a new activity. One of these agencies is AARD (AZHBR is the acronym in Albanian) Agency for agricultural and rural development. As an institution accredited for the administration of funds from the EU, AARD is focused on the development of a sustainable agriculture and the diversification of the rural economy, through grants obtained from the State Budget, the European Union, the World Bank and the Swedish Government. We already have some good examples of migrants in entrepreneurship who obtained support from this agency.

"RIVIERA" is an entrepreneurship created by investing remittances in a gathering point for farmer's products from all over Albania, storing them in freezers and selling them in the market in low seasons as frozen products. This enterprise already employs ten employees. The government supported this entrepreneurship through IPARD program with 20% of the investment (ATA, 2022).[24]

Another entrepreneurship by return migration is "SOFJANI", an investment of remittances for the activity of collection, processing and sale of livestock sub-products. With the support of the government through IPARD program, this entrepreneurship is now operating and expanding (Ministry of Agriculture and Rural Development, 2021).

AARD also offers support for investments in Agro-tourism through IPARD II program, supporting up to 50% of the investment but not more than 10,000,000ALL for subject. To date, 52 start-ups have been supported through IPARD program. There is no data from official sources of information about how many return migrants are supported by this program or other programs, such as Albanian Agribusiness Support Facility

[24] ATA(2022). https://ata.gov.al/2022/12/14/rama-pika-e-grumbullimit-ne-kamze-me-12-dhoma-frigoriferike/

(AASF), which is another program financed by European Bank for Reconstruction and Development and supported by Albanian Government that is active since 2016.[25] But these supporting programs show that the government endeavors are increased and are in a positive path for supporting new ideas of entrepreneurship and start-ups.

Discussion and Conclusions

Albanian migration is considered a continuous and dynamic process since the 90s, showing fluctuations over the years. At the very beginning of economic transition in Albania, due to the opening of the country and the transition's reforms in Albania, the rate of migration was very high especially toward Italy and Greece, lasting for more than one decade. There was a stabilization of migration rates after the 2000s, due to the increased economic and social stabilization in the country, migration continued with a lower intensity and mainly in legal forms.[26] After the global economic crisis of 2008 with an increased number of returned migrants in Albania, there was a revival of Albanians migration in 2015 toward other EU countries and toward USA, reveling for a high migratory potential of Albanian population, driven mainly by economic indicators such as unemployment, underemployment, low wages, low living standards, etc. But still one-fourth of migration is also pushed by other factors such as education and professional career (Gedeshi & Xhafaj, 2016). In this situation of migration, we must consider that the multitude of different resources, such as cultural, social and professional, compound a capacity to see migrants in entrepreneurship activities, but there is not much evidence for connecting migrant entrepreneurs with social entrepreneurship. Empirical studies show that the probability of entrepreneurship activities is higher for return migrants, and state policies on return migration should focus on the facilitation of reintegration and incentives to develop social entrepreneurship, as migration is considered to have the major contribution to the country's economic development through remittances.

[25] AASF (2020). *Supporting program of Albanian Agribusiness; Newsletter 4*. AASF. https://aasf.com.al/wp-content/uploads/2020/11/web_newsletter_4_shqip.pdf

[26] King, R., Uruci, E., Vullnetari, J. (2011). *Albanian migration and its effects in comparative perspective*. Journal of Balkan and Near Eastern Studies, 13(3).

Challenges for the Future of Social Entrepreneurship in Albania

Even though Albania has an improved HDI value for 2021 in 0.796 which puts the country in the high human development category, positioning it at 67 out of 191 countries and territories[27] still has many social problems such as unemployment, low income, poverty and social exclusion of minorities (mainly Roma), and these problems are challenges in the social, healthcare and environmental area of Albanian environment. Addressing all these problems through social businesses would be a challenge for our country.

Broadening the view of legal framework of social enterprises in Albania, by including all social types of enterprises, providing incentives and support for them, as a way to improve the Albanian economy, is one of the main challenges for the future of social enterprises.

Migrant's entrepreneurship requires an approach from many actors, starting with government and respective ministries, chambers of commerce, entrepreneurship incubators, financial service providers, such as banks or microfinance institutions, research institutions and universities, non-profit organizations and international agencies, but first of all, there is a need for will and commitment. All these actors can assist in offering mentorship and training, identifying opportunities, offering expertise, facilitating access to funds, including them in existing services and programs, reducing barriers and changing policies.

Data show that there are 1,641,354[28] Albanian living in migration and there is a considerable remittance flow that supports the Albanian economy that could also use the knowledge and know-how of these migrants to expand the start-ups and social enterprises environment as well.

The 2030 Agenda for Sustainable Development has confirmed migration as an important global priority which, if properly governed, can bring positive benefits to migrants and their families, host and sending societies and countries in general.

[27] Merino, M. (2022). *With the Human development index in reverse: why are we ignoring a world at breaking point?* UNDP Albania. https://www.undp.org/albania/blog/human-development-index-reverse-why-are-we-ignoring-world-breaking-point

[28] I NSTAT (2019). *Albanian Diaspora in Figures.* INSTAT. http://www.instat.gov.al/media/6547/diaspora-2019.pdf

Conclusions

Entrepreneurship may, in many perspectives, offer migrants better economic prospects such as obtaining a higher social status, as well as achieving independence and autonomy. The social entrepreneurship path is a way of merging their social and working lives. Pursuing entrepreneurship as an alternative employment strategy can also support psychological health as well as economic welfare. Migration policies, especially those focused on return migration should attract migrants to return to the native countries and facilitate their social-cultural and economic reintegration. Origin countries can facilitate returnees' engagement in entrepreneurial activity by helping them settle back home; in this way, states implement these policies as a tool for economic development of the country.

By supporting inclusion of vulnerable returned migrants in the labor market through entrepreneurship, start-ups can serve as an effective tool for their socio-economic reintegration into the community. Supporting economic empowerment and autonomy through entrepreneurship is one of the ways to help returned migrants secure the living in their home countries and keep them invested in their domestic economies. There is a variety of activities such as agriculture and livestock, hairdressing, crafts, car wash, car mechanic, tire repairing services, clothing repair, grocery shops and other start-up ideas that can be developed as entrepreneurships by returned migrants and help them reintegrate and earn their living. State incentives such as competitions for start funds are important to stimulate the returnees' engagement in these autonomous activities. Aspirant entrepreneurs also need to receive training in entrepreneurship and business development, and mentoring support before and after the initiation of their business.

Entrepreneurship is a significant support for the society as well. Generating employment and reducing poverty are the main challenges to be addressed in Albania as a developing country, and social entrepreneurship indicates opportunities to improve the lives of marginalized population. Innovative ideas of social entrepreneurs are beneficial to the society because through these ideas at least there is a positive impact on employment.

Social entrepreneurs in general bring their ideas to serve to the communities and to address social challenges among them. Looking for opportunities in this sector is related to innovation in the social path, including actors important to the environment. The collaboration with the community and the government makes funds and expertise worth in creating the value and increasing the impact of the investment. Maximizing economic growth along with social progress will result in a mutual gain. Social entrepreneurship is also important in defining career paths of the youth by offering better possibilities for creative roles and better rewards.

This means that there is still a lot to be done in this direction, including all actors of the social enterprises' ecosystem.

References

AASF. (2020). *Supporting Program of Albanian Agribusiness; Newsletter 4.* AASF. https://aasf.com.al/wp-content/uploads/2020/11/web_newsletter_4_shqip.pdf

Agolli, A., Haska, E. & Hoxha, J. (2019). *Social Enterprises and Their Ecosystems in Europe; Country Fiche Albania* (1st edn). EU. https://doi.org/10.2767/418617

AMSHC. (2023). *Database of Registered NGO-s in Albania.* AMSHC Web. https://amshc.gov.al/ojf-qe-veprojne-ne-shqiperi/

ATA. (2022). https://ata.gov.al/2022/12/14/rama-pika-e-grumbullimit-ne-kamze-me-12-dhoma-frigoriferike/

Bacq, S., Wasieleski, D. M., & Weber, J. (2022). Preface—Social Entrepreneurship: Origins, Trends, and Future Directions. In D. M. Wasieleski and J. Weber (Eds.), *Social Entrepreneurship* (Business and Society 360, pp. xi–xviii), Emerald Group Publishing Limited. Retrieved September 27, 2023, from https://www.researchgate.net/publication/353482890_Social_Entrepreneurship_Origins_Trends_and_Future_Directions

Barjaba, J. (2018). *Exploring Transnational Entrepreneurship among Albanian Migrants and Returnees* (pp.75–83). PhD thesis in Migration Studies. University of Sussex. https://sussex.figshare.com/articles/thesis/Exploring_transnational_entrepreneurship_among_Albanian_migrants_and_returnees/23468141

CESPI. (2021). *Mapping and Profiling of Albanian Diaspora.* Mapping and Profiling of Albanian Diaspora. *An Economic and Social Survey in five Italian Regions. Overview of the Situation in France and Belgium. International Organization for Migration (IOM), Geneva.* IOM Albania. ISBN 978-92-9268-106-7 (PDF). https://albania.iom.int/sites/g/files/tmzbdl1401/files/documents/mapping-and-profiling-of-albanian-diaspora.pdf

Chammartin, G.-M., & Fernando, C.-B. (2005). Identification of Potential for Increasing Employment and Productive Investment in Albania, Moldova and Ukraine based on Remittances. *ILO Working paper (International Migration Papers),* No. (74).

Chanine, T. (2016). *Introduction to Social Entrepreneurship* (1st ed). CRC Press.

Council of Ministers. (2020). *Albanian National Diaspora Strategy 2021–2025.* https://diaspora.gov.al/wp-content/uploads/2020/12/STRATEGJIA-KOMBETARE-E-DIASPORES-2021-2025-ENG.pdf

Directive no. 2, dated 04.01.2019 "On the Creation of the Register of Social Enterprises and the Rules for its Maintenance".

Gedeshi, I., & Xhafaj, E. (2016). *Social and economic profile of the return migrants in Albania.* Report, IOM (2016).

GIZ. (2021). *Programme Migration and Dispora.* GIZ. https://www.giz.de/en/downloads/giz2021-en-programm-migration-diaspora.pdf

Haska, E., & Hoxha, J. (2020). *Characteristics and Challenges of Social Enterprises in Albania, Baseline Study.* Partners Albania. https://childhub.org/sites/default/files/library/attachments/final_earb_assessment_eng.pdf

Hatziprokopiou, P. (2003). Albanian immigrants in Thessaloniki, Greece: Processes of economic and social incorporation. *Journal of Ethnic and Migration Studies, 29*(6),1033–1057.

INSTAT. (2019). *Albanian Diaspora in Figures.* INSTAT. http://www.instat.gov.al/media/6547/diaspora-2019.pdf

INSTAT. (2022). 2021 *Business Registers.* INSTAT. https://www.instat.gov.al/en/themes/industry-trade-and-services/business-registers/publication/2022/business-registers-2021/

King, R., Uruci, E., & Vullnetari, J. (2011). Albanian Migration and Its Effects in Comparative Perspective. *Journal of Balkan and Near Eastern Studies, 13*(3), 269–286.

Labrianidis, L., & Lyberaki, A. (2001). Back and forth and in between: Returning albanian migrants from Greece and Italy. *Journal of International Migration and Integration, 5*(1), 77–106.

Law No.10 093, dated 9.3.2009 on "Organization and Functioning of the Agency for Supporting Civil Society".

Law No.25 dated 10/03/2022 on "Support and Development of Start-ups".

Leadbeater, C. (1997). *The Rise of the Social Entrepreneur.* Demos Report.

Lyberaki, A., & Maroukis, Th. (2005). Albanian immigrants in Athens: New survey evidence on employment and integration. *Journal of Southeast European and Black Sea Studies, 5*(1), 21–48.

Marku, Sh. (2015). *Interview with Shkelzen Marku, Director of Yunus Social Business Balkans.* IIA. https://invest-in-albania.org/interview-with-shkelzen-marku-director-of-yunus-social-business-balkans/

Merino, M. (2022). *With the Human Development Index in Reverse: Why Are We Ignoring a World at Breaking Point?* UNDP Albania. https://www.undp.org/albania/blog/human-development-index-reverse-why-are-we-ignoring-world-breaking-point

Ministry of Agriculture and Rural Development. (2021). "Poliçan, në baxhon moderne të familjes Sejdini", YouTube, 2 Apr. 2021. https://www.youtube.com/watch?v=rZH6uA8-lHw&t=68s

Musabelliu, M. (2019). Albania Social Briefing: Albanian Diaspora—An Essential Social Stronghold for the Entire Nation. *China CEE-Institute, 15*(3), 1–5. https://china-cee.eu/2019/03/20/albania-social-briefing-albanian-diaspora-an-essential-social-stronghold-for-the-entire-nation/

Sinek, S. (2009). Start with why: How great leaders inspire everyone to take action. Portofolio.

The Official Journal of Albanian Republic. (2016). QBZ, *118*, 8312–8318.

UN. (2018). Policy Guide on Entrepreneurship for Migrants and Refugees. https://www.unhcr.org/5bd31fd67.pdf

Urbano, D., Sebastian, A., & Audretsch, D. (2019). Twenty-five years of research on institutions, entrepreneurship, and economic growth: What has been learned? *Small Business Economics, 53*(1), 21–49. Springer.

Vendresha, A., & Sinani, I. (2014). *Supporting Social Entrepreneurship in Albania to Better Protect Children*. Report for Albania.

Wang, W. (2022). Toward Economic Growth and Value Creation Through Social Entrepreneurship: Modelling and Mediating Role of Innovation. *Frontiers in Psychology, 13.* https://doi.org/10.3389/fpsyg.2022.914700

World Vizion. (2022). *RE-IN-VEST Project Helps Families Returning from Migration*. World Vison Albania Web. https://www.wvi.org/stories/albania/re-vest-project-helps-families-returning-emigration

Yunus, M. (2010). *Building social business: The new kind of capitalism that serves humanity's most pressing needs*. PublicAffairs.

CHAPTER 11

Social and Solidarity Economy in Greece: European, National and Local Perspectives

Konstantinos Mantzos, Aspasia (Sissie) Theodosiou, and Achilles Kameas

Introduction

It has been noted that during times of crisis economic practices organized on principles of reciprocity often arise (Papadaki & Kalogeraki, 2018: 39). In the last decade, in Greece, social economy has seemed to gain a momentum under the shadow of the debt crises which struck the country from 2009 onwards. This momentum included both grassroots movements in the form of civic association and institutional changes that attempted to tune in with a European trend towards social economy. In this chapter we

K. Mantzos (✉) • A. Kameas
DAISSy Research Team, HellenicOpen University, Ioannina, Greece
e-mail: kmantzos@daissy.eap.gr; kameas@eap.gr

A. (Sissie) Theodosiou
DAISSy Research Team, HellenicOpen University, Ioannina, Greece

University of Ioannina, Ioannina, Greece
e-mail: stheodosiou@eap.gr

S. Bianchini et al. (eds.), *Social Entrepreneurship and Migrants' Inclusion*, Sustainable Development Goals Series,
https://doi.org/10.1007/978-3-031-55791-0_11

review the social and institutional changes that resulted in a social economy 'big bang' during the previous decade.

We argue, in our contribution, that this genealogy of Social and Solidarity Economy (SSE) shows that the so-called third sector has not yet solidified its position in the general financial and entrepreneurial landscape of Greece. It remains at an ideological fringe still seeking to carve an independent trajectory of its own. A case in point in relation to this claim is the detailed description of the formation of a local association of social enterprises in northwest Greece. Through this case study we attempt to show the ideological premises and the practical difficulties that the Social and Solidarity Economy landscape face, especially in the Greek periphery, and its relation to a more traditional entrepreneurial and economic activity.

Social and Solidarity Economy

In the last decade of the twentieth century and the first decades of the twenty-first century, Social and Solidarity Economy (SSE) has emerged, capturing a vast number of economic activities that appear worldwide. However, SSE is not a new concept; it embraces both the social economy and the solidarity economy. The former, which has its roots mainly in the cooperative movement, is understood as the group of entities where members are shareholders and amongst whom the profits are distributed (Kousis & Paschou, 2017: 150). In relation to the solidarity economy, it is derived from social movements and promotes both political and economic goals for socio-economic transformation (Adam, 2016). The combination of these concepts, which does not always work in a complementary way, results in different understandings and definitions of what SSE is.

In a broad sense, SSE defines a group of institutions with explicit social (in many cases environmental as well) objectives—and is not just creating profit—working on the principles of solidarity, participation and democratic governance (Fonteneau et al., 2010; Utting, 2015). International agencies, such as the International Labour Organisation (ILO) and the Organisation for Economic Co-operation and Development (OECD), define SSE entities based on legal status, including cooperatives, mutual societies, foundations and social enterprises (TFSSE, 2014). An alternative definition by RIPESS[1] points to SSE as the productive space that includes both formal organizations and informal initiatives and citizen's

[1] https://www.ripess.org/.

movements that hold as their central aim the transformation of the economy through its democratization. Research into SSE traces its development to the revitalization of new forms of cooperatives and social enterprises, as well as in various formal and informal groups, including exchange networks, fair trade networks, solidarity-based credit organizations and groups, solidarity networks, alternative food networks and time banks, to give just a few examples (Utting et al., 2014; Sahakian, 2016). Thus, SSE reaches far more than traditional social economy organizations, such as cooperatives, or the more recent model of social enterprises, including numerous bottom-up alternative initiatives and practices (Amin et al., 2002; Marques, 2013).

Recently, the SSE has affected a larger number of citizens since the sector is constantly expanding (Utting, 2015). Several scholars come to the same conclusion that this expansion of SSE is mainly related to increased social needs connected to unemployment and poverty (Morais & Bacic, 2013; Utting, 2015; Meglio & Zandonai, 2015). Sahakian (2016) highlights the fact that the interest in SSE is linked to the recent economic crisis and widening inequalities. The recent financial crisis has led people to turn to different types of cooperative economic activity and alternative ways of accessing goods and services in order to cope with daily difficulties and overcome challenges (Nardi, 2016; Kousis & Paschou, 2017).

Experiences from previous recessions verify these tactics. Indeed, the SSE works as a tool to fight poverty. The SSE was born and initially developed as a necessity and its main objective was to actively respond to the social problems associated with unemployment, poverty and social exclusion (Neamtan, 2002). Empirical studies around the world highlight its importance as a basis of anti-poverty action (Kay, 2006; Klein et al., 2009). The SSE practices that support such objectives include the provision of services to meet needs excluded by the welfare state (e.g. homeless shelters, collective kitchens etc.), as well as economic activities promoting the integration of people excluded from the labour market (e.g. social enterprises, women's cooperatives etc.) (Levesque, 2003; Fontan et al., 2003; Levesque & Mendell, 2005). These practices mostly attract—as users, clients and beneficiaries—the most vulnerable members of society, that is, those who have limited or no access to employment or to certain goods, products and knowledge (Fonteneau et al., 2010).

However, SSE despite its potential to offer relief in difficult times cannot be limited to this alone. It also serves as an alternative economic model, placing people at the centre of economic and social life (Sahakian

& Dunand, 2015; Calvo et al., 2017). As Papadaki and Kalogeraki point out (2018), from the perspective of a radical social movement, the SSE is a project for the development and improvement of the economy, for the benefit of people and communities, but also a tool for empowerment, transformation and social change, a form of resistance and emancipation from neoliberal domination, a path to a more equal and sustainable society and a viable economic alternative to capitalism (Arruda, 2004; Marques, 2013; Saguier & Brent, 2017). In this sense, the SSE is at the heart of the anti-capitalist global movement and local social movements (Dinerstein, 2014).

Social and Solidarity Economy as a Social Movement: The Greek Case

Greece has been at the epicentre of the 2008 global economic crisis, facing the deepest recession in its modern history. Since early 2009, the country has entered a prolonged and sustained economic downturn, captured in the declining trends of its Gross Domestic Product (GDP) and escalating general government gross debt (as a percentage of GDP) (Featherstone, 2011). Unavoidably, SSE genealogy has to be described in terms of pre- and post-crisis. Thus, SSE before 2009 financial collapse was composed of formal institutions, such as cooperatives and social enterprises, and was less developed compared to other European countries (Adam & Papatheodorou, 2010). Also, the insufficient policy frameworks, lack of official register data and limited scientific research resulted in our modest knowledge of the sector (Tsobanoglou, 2012). Nevertheless, Adam (2012) focuses on the importance of women's cooperative in the sustainability of local communities, as well as the importance of European Union (EU) and state funding for social enterprises that support the employment and education of people with mental disorders.[2] In addition, Nasioulas (2012) explores, until 2011, the cooperative field in Greece and points out its underdevelopment, despite the positive potential for the economy. According to Nikolopoulos and Kapogiannis (2013), the weak expansion of the Greek SSE sector is related to the anaemic civil society and the prevailing distorted image of cooperativism and volunteerism in public

[2] KOISPE, Social Cooperatives of limited liability were introduced in 1999 (Law 2716) and were the first form of social enterprises introduced in Greece, as part of the psychiatric reformation that was initiated during the 1990s.

opinion. Similarly, Tsobanoglou (2012) pointed out that the low prevalence of volunteerism and self-organization act as key components of the poor development of SSE in Greece.

The beginning of the financial crisis was about to change all this. The austerity politics and the recession effects have been related to an increase in formal and informal SSE initiatives and institutions (Kavoulakos, 2015; Vathakou, 2015; Adam, 2016). SSE activities and services, that were initiated during this period, differ from the creation of social kitchens and free medical examinations (e.g. social clinics) to networks of cooperatives, exchange networks, time banks etc. (Bekridaki & Broumas, 2017). A celebrated example has been the VIOME factory in Thessaloniki (https://viomecoop.com/), which was closed due to the crisis, and now operates as an example of a cooperative and solidarity economy, based on self-management and participatory approach of former employees and citizens to produce natural cleaning agents and environmentally friendly products.

Similarly, several studies have focused on the ways that the economic crisis has acted as the main trigger for the spread of SSE in the country as a way to redress the effects of the crisis (Kousis et al, 2018). For example, Adam and Teloni (2015) examine the numerous social clinics that emerged during the crisis in response to the increased number of citizens excluded from the National Health System (NHS). In addition, Gritzas et al. (2015) investigate the time banks created in Athens which not only aimed to help citizens cope with the consequences of the recession but also critically questioned capitalist values and practices. The authors argue that time banks usually operate in weekly meetings open to all members, and their core principles include Equality, Democracy and Transparency (Gritzas et al., 2015).

Rakopoulos (2015) explored the characteristics of about eighty initiatives that seek to overcome middlemen which have been launched in Greece since 2010. In his view, SSE in Greece was not only a strategy to deal with the crisis but also a politicized response to austerity, arguing that it was initiated by the rupture created by the financial crisis followed by a consequent political radicalization (Rakopoulos, 2015: 179). Moreover, local exchange systems, such as the exchange network of Chanià in Crete, were examined by Sotiropoulou (2015). Research on such SSE initiatives points to the fact that their everyday practices are mainly based on the growing needs of people in times of crisis, promoting at the same time a distinctive shift in everyday practices and relationships based on solidarity (Petropoulou, 2013).

In addition, by interviewing members of SSE grassroots organizations established in Athens after 2011, Bouziouri and Pigou-Rebousi (2014) conclude that the main principles and values involve citizens' empowerment so that they may contribute to their community, supporting an anti-capitalistic way of living by focusing on recycling and exchanging products and services, as well as promoting respect towards the environment and biodiversity.

The Institutional Take: The State and Social and Solidarity Economy

Although the above studies have contributed significantly to the understanding of the development of SSE in Greece, they are geographically limited and/or focus on specific types of SSE and activities. In this context, as the advancement of SSE in Greece is analysed mainly as a bottom-up process, the relationship between the SSE entities and the state is generally insufficiently explored. The main emphasis has been on the informal status of certain practices, their innovative character and the strong link to new forms of political action (Adam & Kavoulakos, 2020). However, contributions from international institutions and organizations underline the importance of a favourable institutional environment for the flourishing of SSE (GECES, 2016; CIRIEC, 2017; European Commission, 2021). Furthermore, a strand of contributions on state-SSE relations highlights the possibility of a fruitful interaction through the co-design of public policies (Vaillancourt, 2009; Hazenberg et al., 2016). Public policies constructed in this way are expected to address the challenges of today's societies by supporting positive aspects of both poles of the equation: that is, the universal interest expressed by the state planning with the innovative flexibility expressed by the active participation of citizens (Fontan & Lévesque, 2023).

The lack of focus on the role of the state is not specific to the Greek case. It is also true for the international literature. Jonas (2010) points out that there is still much work to be done to understand the relationships between alternative social structures, power relations and institutions. As a result, he argues that there is a need to link the issues of an alternative economy to the state and progressive policies. The appeal of SSE to researchers is largely due to its creativity, innovation and preparatory politics at the grassroots level. Historically, some parts of SSE have developed against the state or by neglecting state policies. Particularly so in the case of informal ventures, this is largely justified by the lack of institutionalization. However, it should be borne in mind that state policies still determine what is formal and what is informal. Informal ventures can be an important part of the solidarity economy and sometimes with radical tendencies, but another equally important part is struggling for institutional recognition to ensure sustainability and further dissemination. Therefore, the debate on the relationship between the state and SSE is inevitable.

Until 2011, Greek Law on traditional cooperatives was characterized by the institutional inconsistency manifested by the fragmented cooperative legislation (Douvitsa, 2019). With the exception of the first cooperative law that concerns all types of cooperatives (Law 602/1915), all subsequent cooperative laws address a specific subset and delineate different competent ministries and supervisory bodies. The result of this legislative process is the proliferation of cooperative laws with divergent provisions in regarding fundamental functional aspects (e.g. number of founding members, establishment procedures, distribution of surplus and profits, dissolution) which do not reflect the different needs in the sector, but simply the institutional fragmentation at the level of government and public administration (Adam & Kavoulakos, 2020).

The development of the SSE legal framework against the aforementioned fragmentation was heavily influenced by international institutions. At this point we need to consider the role of the European Union's attempt to institutionalize civil society and social economy actors.

For example, the proliferation of NGOs in the 1990s is attributed to the inclusion of Greece to the Development Assistance Committee and the availability of relevant funds to support such organizations (Afouxenidis, 2006). As far as social enterprises are concerned, the impetus comes mainly from the European Union (Adam, 2009). While the pioneering social enterprises of labour integration were those developed in continental Europe in the 1970s and 1980s in response to intense social problems (Lemaitre et al., 2006, p. 279), efforts towards similar initiatives in Greece can be attributed mainly to structural funds (and in particular the European Social Fund).

The first time the term social economy was explicitly addressed in the Greek Legal context was Law 4019/2011 on "Social Economy, Social Entrepreneurship, and other provisions". This law was coupled with a Strategic Plan for the Development of the Social Entrepreneurship Sector in Greece (February 2013). This strategic plan linked social economy, unemployment and social inclusion with a sole focus on social enterprises. In this way, social enterprises were mainly seen as a tool for the (re-)integration into the labour market of those facing the strongest barriers and as an alternative to state provision of social services (Adam, 2016).

After the political shift in government that occurred in 2015, the coalition government that was formed insisted on the priority agenda assigned to the Social and Solidarity Economy. The search for a new national strategy and a favourable legal framework for SSE practices were identified as a priority for the newly elected government. This remained so even after the referendum (July 2015) and the final signing of a new Memorandum between the government and international lenders. After this signing the SSE remained an important priority, albeit under the so-called parallel programme for two main reasons: (a) the need to restore trust with the social movements at the grassroots level and (b) the given space to move, given the fact that this policy area was not explicitly affected by the conditions imposed by the new Memorandum (Howarth & Roussos, 2023).

The result of this political process was Law 4430/2016 titled Social and Solidarity Economy and the Development of its Actors which constituted the general legal framework over all legal entities registered as Social and Solidarity Economy Actors in Greece.

The Law adopted a normative approach that intended to incorporate the policy objectives set out from recent developments in the SSE movement in Greece and abroad. In this context, the Social and Solidarity Economy was seen as a means for both the productive reconstruction of the Greek economy and for the development of the Social and Solidarity Economy as well as for socio-economic transformation. This is due to its inherent characteristics that distinguished the SSE practices from typical private for-profit enterprises that aim at the reproduction of their capital base and the maximization of profit. As such, the law intended to diffuse SSEs practices to all potential sectors of economic activity and to support productive initiatives based on self-management and collective social entrepreneurship. In particular, the law preface endorsed a number of values related to solidarity economy, given that the SSE is expected to promote the democratization not only of the economy, but also of society in general, by creating institutions for social provision for all, irrespective of their economic situation, based on different principles from the market price mechanism (Adam, 2019).

The law distinguished between legal persons introduced under the framework of Law 4430/2016, which are automatically considered as SSE entities, and other legal persons who may be registered after fulfilling specific criteria set out in the law. In the first category were included:

- Social Cooperative Enterprises-SCEs (Articles 14–23)
- Social cooperatives with limited liability[3]
- Workers' cooperatives (Articles 24–33)

In the second category, the law makes clear that any other legal person consisting of more than one member may be registered if it fulfils the following criteria (Article 3 § 1, point d):

i. it explicitly pursues both collective and social benefit.
ii. it takes due care for the exchange of information and the participation of its members and applies a democratic decision-making system based on the principle of 'one person-one vote', irrespective of the financial contribution.
iii. provides for a limited distribution of profits in accordance with the following rules: (a) 5% of the profits shall be kept in reserves; (b) up to 35% is distributed among employees; and (c) the remainder is used to create employment opportunities within the enterprise and to expand production capacity.
iv. it implements convergence payment systems whereby the highest wage cannot be higher than three times the minimum wage within the same enterprise, unless otherwise decided by 2/3 of the enterprise of the members of the general meeting.
v. it shall seek to strengthen its economic activities and maximize the social benefits generated through horizontal networking with other bargaining units.
vi. it is not established and/or managed directly or indirectly by a legal entity of the strict or broader public sector and/or first/second level local authorities.

As per these criteria, the institutional framework of SSE as it is formulated in the Law 4430/2016 stresses a series of principles that follow the SSE perspective both in Greece and in Europe. These include the pursuit of a broader social benefit and not only focus on the collective benefit of

[3] A pre-existing work integration social enterprise for people with mental health problems based on Law 2716/1999, art. 12.

members. The second criterion also extends the specificity of cooperative identity (i.e. democratic decision-making) to all actors in the SSE. The third criterion requires limited profit-sharing systems to all members of the SSE. The fourth criterion aims to ensure fair payment systems. The fifth criterion promotes networking between the SSEs as a constitutional objective. The last criterion defines the independence of SSEs from the wider public sector (Adam, 2019).

Within this context it is important to try to assess quantitatively the result of the state's attempt to introduce a unified framework for the SSE. In the most recent annual report of the Directorate (previously General Secretariat) for Social Solidarity Economy (Directorate for Social Solidarity Economy 2023), information on various types of mainly formal and active SSE entities across the country are included. The report shows that, from 2012 to 2018, there has been a continuous increase in the number of new registering SSE institutions in the country, while the tendency is reversed in the following years (Fig. 11.1).

Underpinning the report is that the registered SSE entities in the country are mostly concentrated in the region of Attica and are active in a wide range of sectors of activity, primarily associated with education, catering, wholesale and retail trade. Moreover, SSE entities mostly operate locally, have diverse staffing and management structures, as well as clear social

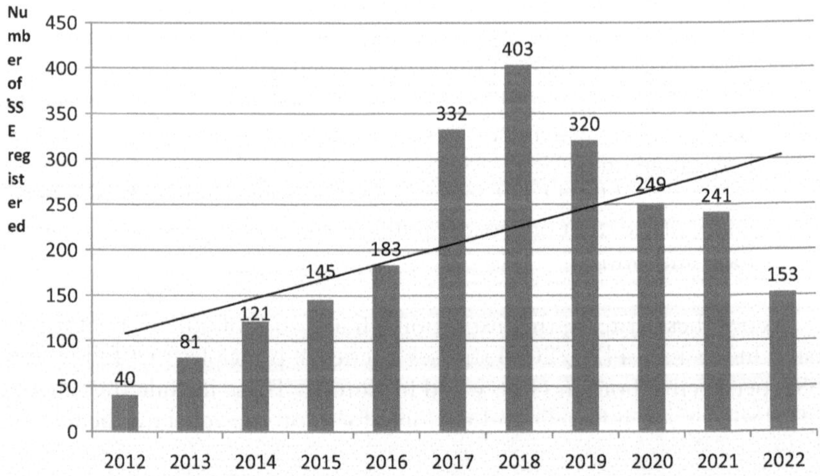

Fig. 11.1 Number of new entries of SSE organizations per year

goals, and provide assistance to those in need. Despite the potential merits of the Report by the SSE Directorate, empirical quantitative evidence that captures a broader portrait of the wider SSE sector and its main attributes across the country remains scarce.

Methodology

In the previous sections we tried to sketch out the intersection between the SSE-as-a-social movement, that blossomed parallel to the financial crisis of the previous decade and the political/institutional attempt to solidify a clear reference framework aiming to further enhance, but also normalize, the SSE ecosystem. In the following part, we attempt to bridge these two strands by giving a detailed account of the creation of a Social Enterprise Association in a specific local context in the northwest of Greece. We should note here that our interest lies solely on the novel actors in SSE in the area.[4] Our methodological argument has been that research on SSE can benefit considerably if we grant ethnographic approaches a proper place in our research agenda. The main points on this are the following: (1) Studying social enterprises ethnographically complicates simple reductions to socio-economic tensions, by enriching the set of differences through which practitioners make sense of their work-world. (2) Ethnography provides a tool for unravelling how practitioners engage with discourse(s) of power, thus marking the concrete results of intervention (to some degree at least) as not being able to be planned and yet effective. (3) Ethnographic examples signal the merits of moving beyond leaders towards more collective representations and in-depth accounts of (self-)development. (4) Reflexive ethnographies demonstrate the heuristic value of accepting the self as inevitably part of research and exemplify insights won through a thoroughly bodily and emotional commitment to sharing the lifeworld of others (Mauksch et al., 2017). Thus, our methodological take included participant observation during the process of the local association creation in addition to a series of open-ended interviews

[4] Despite the fact that we look into the development of Social and Solidarity Economy through the prism of the aforementioned developments in the field in the last decade, we cannot ignore that social economy in the form of cooperatives has a long history in Greece and more specifically in the area we focus on, Epirus. Although a detailed history of cooperatives in the area runs far beyond the scope of this paper we cannot avoid to mention that cooperatives in the local context, mainly in the form of local unions of producers in the primary section, follow the fate of cooperatives in the Greek context (Vetsopoulos, 2018).

with the key actors in the above-mentioned process. The data collected was either in the form of field notes or as transcriptions of the interviews.

The Social and Solidarity Economy Ecosystem in a Local Context

Social enterprises in the Epirus region represent a small fraction of the total number within the Greek ecosystem of SSE. According to data from the annual report of the Directorate for the Social and Solidarity Economy, the number of registered social enterprises in the Epirus region range from 15 in 2008 to 23 in 2021, representing an approximate 3% of the total number at the national level.

"When in Athens mainly but in Thessaloniki also, several social enterprises were blossoming, in Epirus we were the only one, and it was by no lack. We both (the interviewee and his associate) knew many people that have attempted such, still the law was problematic and we had to work with a law firm in the Thessaloniki, however this is how we started, and no one could understand locally. Some were saying 'but you know, co-operations are dead', we were faced constantly with a lack of understanding, a lack of knowledge of the administration. It was mainly ideological, our starting point, we wanted to bring a social air of some kind". This account from one of the first attempts to create a social enterprise locally, a media cooperative, paints with vivid colours the initial phase of the creation of social enterprises locally. In fact, the main drive besides don-quixotic attempts as the one described was the availability of European funds channelled locally. For example, in 2014 an open call by the local prefecture for the creation of a peripheral social economy observatory including a social business incubator brought together an array of local institutions (the local university, the municipality, the chamber of commerce etc.) trying to combine their forces in order to create a novel ecosystem. We should keep in mind that at the time there were eight registered enterprises in the whole region of Epirus, which covers an area of 9203 km^2 with a population of around 320,000. This initiative collapsed for the same reasons it came into action in the first place. The governmental shift of 2015 brought the whole project under scrutiny by the new administration leading eventually to its cancellation.

The issue of the availability of European funds, to which we will return, either to create supportive institutions as the one mentioned above, or in the form of hand outs, or even lately as funded projects (through Erasmus+, Creative Europe etc.) remains central in the sustainability of social enterprises in the region. Another important factor is the personnel of the SSE locally. If we try to sketch a rough profile, we would come across highly educated individuals in their mid-thirties to early forties who attempt to balance their ideological dispositions with their professional life.

Turning now to the association in point, it is quite important to give a brief sketch on the actual reasons that this initiative came to life. The aforementioned project of creating a peripheral observatory of SSE was replaced by the creation of an institution that was supposed to support and provide consultation to SSE agents. This was one out of 13 corresponsive structures that were created in each Greek region in order to locally support SSE. "When it was created, we thought things would become easy, however the way they worked was old fashioned clientelism, they wanted everything to work through them, and for sure we had not chosen them. They had relations with all the politicians and had no actual interest in anything social". The point in this comment cannot be overstressed, and was repeated in several of our interviews pointing out a gap between the agents of the institutional interventions in SSE (the project was funded through the European Social Fund) and the actual social enterprises already in place.

Thus, in 2021 the attempts to "create our own voice" saw its fruition in the establishment of Association "ΚοινόΚαλό" ("Common Good")[5] consisting of 13 social enterprises, 2 energy communities and 1 urban cooperative. Their scope is quite diverse, ranging from agricultural production, to psychological counselling, to market branding, to cultural tourism and to energy self-production. All these organizations seem to share, at least nominally, the aim to "Create the conditions for a sustainable development in Epirus". At this point it is quite important to present the ideological premises of the Association.

To do so we will investigate two specific initiatives that preceded the creation of the Association and the personnel of which were at the forefront of its creation. We believe that both point clearly to the ideological premises supporting the creation of the Association. The first initiative P2P lab,[6] itself a founding member of the Association, is an academic collective aiming at: "designing and implementing projects using participatory

[5] https://koinokalo.gr/.

[6] https://www.p2plab.gr/en/.

and community-based methods and practices. We forward research and knowledge through the creation of spaces for creative resistance and common-based alternatives". Although the collective has its headquarters in Ioannina, its members (most of them born in the area) are scattered in academic institutions all over Europe.

The second one is the Tzoumakers Open Lab initially a project of the P2P lab. Tzoumakers in their own words are "an open lab for communities to cooperatively design and manufacture tools for small-scale agricultural production. Our vision is to create such sites in both villages and cities where citizens may seize technology into their own hands. These sites may be supported by municipalities and/or by multi-stakeholder cooperatives".[7] The main idea of the initiative was to use open-source technologies to create agricultural tools and structures that would meet the needs of the inhabitants of semi-deserted mountainous communities. The lab itself is situated in such a community and was initiated by the p2p lab and doctoral students of the local university that saw an opportunity both in the open-source technologies (connecting with similar initiatives in France and the USA) and in the mountainous terrain of Epirus.

These initiatives seem to be at the opposite ends of a symbolic continuum that attempts to define SSE as a 'glocal' (Swyngedouw, 2004) fact. However, the 'local' part of the synthesis is clearly rooted in a specific understanding and interpretation of the Epirotic landscape, idealized in the mountainous community.

"What is at stake here is to try to support the rebirth of a kind of culture of production that was based on cooperation and not on profit". What is proposed here, in the words of Sotiris, one of the central figures in the creation of the association, is an alternative understanding of development that attempts to bridge a so-called traditional economic ethos based on the idea of the community as a self-sufficient economic unit (Nitsiakos, 2015). Thus, there is a strong local interpretation of social and solidarity not simply as an alternative to the mainstream economic model based on democratic management and equal share of the economic profit but as an heir to a long but somehow forgotten line of descent that actively attempts to connect itself not to the cooperative movement (itself discredited as part of the pre-crisis management). As another of our interlocutors pointed out "in the past (non-defined) communities were offering collective work to each one of their members without expecting this to produce

[7] https://www.tzoumakers.gr/.

any profit, these ways have been here for a long-long time and we need to remind people about them". However, this reminding is not an easy task.

To understand why, we need to move beyond the seemingly consistent premises of the (ideological) intentions and move towards the ruptures created through everyday practice. The main issue around which such ruptures revolve is sustainability of the individual social enterprises. Despite the fact that all members of the Association aim to create marketable products and services, most of them (apart from two) base their day-to-day financial existence from projects funded by European Union. Especially those who proclaim to offer long-term sustainable solutions in mountainous areas, taking into consideration the actual needs of local communities, are partners in several such projects that in some cases enhance the transformation of the mountain space into sites of cultural consumption,[8] which in turn can fuel local conflicts on the appropriation of space (Schirpke et al., 2020). Thus, the need to align with the priorities of European funding mechanisms creates the need for SSE actors to constantly invent projects that do not necessarily align with the needs of local populations.

Furthermore, those members of the Association that have managed to succeed and become financially viable without the need of a constant external flow of capital have to come to terms with the institutional limitations of the SSE legal framework. "You see, being a KOINSEP (social enterprise) creates several problems, if we were a normal enterprise we would be easily earning 20% more, to be honest one has to have a normal (mainstream) enterprise in order to create surplus and then have the luxury to create a social enterprise", our interlocutor here refers to the strict rules on allocation of the social enterprises' profits, foreseen in the law, which makes it compulsory that profits should pay the wages up to a 40% of the social enterprise, leaving the remaining 60% to be reinvested in the social enterprises' activities. The strict limitations imposed by the 4430/2016 law concerning re-investment of profit and fare distribution of wages made one of the working members of a social enterprise (member of the Association) to express the view that one should have a 'normal' (i.e. mainstream) company and have a social enterprise as a 'side project'. In a way such views reflect concerns of those who are more 'organically' connected to the larger market of the area. However, what remains unsaid

[8] A case in point is the project Incultum (https://incultum.eu/pilots/7-aoos-the-shared-river/).

here is that part of that success is that social enterprises seem to carry a de facto symbolic capital that in a sense gives them a potential advantage against mainstream competition.

This brings forward yet another important aspect of the development of SSE locally, that of local government and its position towards SSE. For the purpose of this paper we interviewed several public officials who expressed mixed opinions towards social enterprises. In one case, it was clearly expressed that choosing a social enterprise as a sub-contractor carried a 'feeling' that this was an investment in the community as a whole: "we need social economy, and we need to channel funds towards social economy as they bring a breath of fresh air into the economy in general and they give back to the local [people], the European Union knows that and is going to continue supporting social enterprises". On the other hand, SSE Association was seen more as a potential political player in local politics than an actual economic actor. However, looking into the specificities and the different levels of the entanglement of local political actors with SSE goes far beyond the scope of this chapter, opening up a whole new area of research.

Concluding Remarks

In our chapter we attempted to sketch out the development of SSE in Greece as both a social movement and its institutional framing. The conjecture of the socio-economic crises that Greek society has been going through since 2009 brought these two sides of the development of SSE on intersecting trajectories. However, despite the declared intention of all sides to create a common framework that will support the development of SSE, it is quite clear that the attempt to create a stable institutional/legal framework is heavily influenced by decisions that are taken at a European level. SSE actors attempt as well to align with the European priorities in order to be able to secure funds that will guarantee their sustainability.

Through our case study analysis, we attempted to show how the aforementioned trajectories intersect locally. Following the formation of a local Association of SSE entities we tried to point at how the members of this Association attempt to balance between the ideological premises that in a sense define the limits of and up to a point brought it to existence, with concerns on their sustainability, that seems to be constantly under threat. The outcome of this struggle cannot be foreseen.

It is our opinion that in order for SSE to continue being both ideologically attractive, social effective and at the same time viable there needs to be a creation of more stable lasting relations with local societies (including local markets) moving out of the fringes of being an interesting exception.

References

Adam, S. (2009). Social Economy and the Greek Welfare State: Can Polanyi Help Us? Paper presented at the *2nd EMES International Conference on Social Enterprise*, Trento, Italy. http://emes.net/content/uploads/publications/ECSP-T09-05_Adam.pdf

Adam, S. (2012). Social Economy and Active Inclusion Policies. Results from Field Work in Work Integration Social Enterprises in Greece. *Athens: Observatory of Economic and Social Developments.* Labor Institute, Greek General Confederation of Labor, Athens, Greece [in Greek].

Adam, S. (2016). Social and Solidarity Economy and the Crisis: Policy Challenges and Opportunities. Paper presented at the *First International Conference in Contemporary Social Sciences*, Rethymno, Greece.

Adam, S. (2019). Legal Provisions for Social and Solidarity Economy Actors. The Case of Law 4430/2016 in Greece. *International Journal of Cooperative Law, I*(2), 97–110.

Adam, S., & Kavoulakos, K. I. (2020). State and Social Solidarity Economy: Friends or Foes? The Potential for Co-construction of Public Policies for Social Solidarity Economy in Greece. *The Greek Review of Social Research, 155*, 121–150. https://doi.org/10.12681/grsr.24829

Adam, S., & Papatheodorou, C. (2010). The Involvement of Social Economy Organisations in the Fight Against Social Exclusion: A Critical Perspective. *Athens: Observatory of Economic and Social Developments.* Labor Institute, Greek General Confederation of Labor. Athens, Greece [in Greek].

Adam S., & Teloni, D. (2015). Social Clinics in the Crisis-ridden Greece: The Experience of Healthcare Services When the National Healthcare System Drawbacks. *Athens: Observatory of Economic and Social Developments.* Labor Institute, Greek General Confederation of Labor. Athens, Greece. [in Greek].

Afouxenidis, A. (2006). Facets of Civil Society in Greece. *Science and Society, 16*, 163–178. [in Greek].

Amin, A., Cameron, A., & Hudson, R. (2002). *Placing the Social Economy.* Routledge.

Arruda, M. (2004). Solidarity Economy and the Rebirth of a Matristic Human Society. Paper presented at the panel *Towards People's Economy: Realities and Strategies from Local to Global.* World Social Forum, Mumbai, India.

Bekridaki, G., & Broumas, A. (2017). Greek Society in Crisis and in Motion: Building the Material Bases for an Alternative Society from the Bottom up. *Interface: A Journal for and About Social Movements, 9*(1), 230–255.

Bouziouri M., & Pigou-Rebousi, M. (2014). Structures and Practices of Solidarity in the Urban Web: New Aspects of Citizenship in Athens During the Crisis. *Report for Solidarity Networks Project.* http://solidaritynetworks.gr/project/description/

Calvo, S., Morales, A., & Zikidis, Y. (2017). *Social and Solidarity Economy. The World's Economy with a Social Face.* Routledge.

Commission Expert Group on Social Entrepreneurship (GECES). (2016). Social Enterprises and the Social Economy Going Forward. https://gsgii.org/reports/social-enterprises-and-the-social-economy-going-forward/

Dinerstein, A. (2014). The Hidden Side of SSE: Social Movements and the Appropriation and 'Translation' of SSE into Policy. *Potentials and Limits of Social and Solidarity Economy, Occasional Paper* No. 9, UNRISD, Geneva. www.unrisd.org/dinerstein

Douvitsa, I. (2019). The New Law on Energy Communities in Greece. *Cooperativismo e Economía Social.* https://doi.org/10.35869/ces.v0i40.1385

European Commission. (2021). *Building an Economy that Works for People: An Action Plan for the Social Economy.* Publications Office of the European Union.

European Economic and Social Committee (CIRIEC). (2017). Recent Evolutions of the Social Economy in the European Union. https://www.ciriec.uliege.be/en/publications/etudesrapports/recent-evolutions-of-social-economy-study/

Featherstone, K. (2011). The Greek Sovereign Debt Crisis and EMU: A Failing State in a Skewed Regime. *Journal of Common Market Studies, 49*(2), 193–217.

Fontan, J. M., Klein, G. L., & Lévesque, B. (2003). *Reconversion économique et Développement Territorial: Le Rôle de las Société Civile.* Presses del'Université du Québec.

Fontan, J.-M., & Lévesque, B. (2023). The Institutional Ecosystem of the Social and Solidarity Economy. In I. Yi et al. (Eds.), *Encyclopedia of the Social and Solidarity Economy.* Edward Elgar Publishing Limited in partnership with United Nations Inter-Agency Task Force on Social and Solidarity Economy (UNTFSSE).

Fonteneau, B., Neamtan, N., Wanyama, F., Pereira, M. L., de Poorter, M., & Carlo, B. C. (2010). Social and Solidarity Economy: Our Common Road Towards Decent Work. Paper in support at the *Social and Solidarity Academy,* Montréal, Canada.

GECES (2016). Social Enterprises and the Social Economy Going Forward. https://gsgii.org/reports/social-enterprises-and-the-social-economy-goingforward.

Gritzas, G., Tzekou, E., & Pazaitis, A. (2015). Forms of Alternative Spaces. In K. Kavoulakos & G. Gritzas (Eds.), *Alternative Economic and Social Spaces.* Kallipsos Publications. [in Greek].

Hazenberg, R., Bajwa-Patel, M., Mazzei, M., Roy, M. J., & Baglioni, S. (2016). The Role of Institutional and Stakeholder Networks in Shaping Social Enterprise Ecosystems in Europe. *Social Enterprise Journal, 12*, 302–321.

Howarth, D., & Roussos, K. (2023). Radical Democracy, the Commons and Everyday Struggles During the Greek Crisis. *The British Journal of Politics and International Relations, 25*(2), 311–327. https://doi.org/10.1177/13691481211067147

Jonas, A. (2010). 'Alternative' this, 'Alternative' that...: Interrogating Alterity and Diversity. In R. Lee, A. E. G. Jonas, & D. Fuller (Eds.), *Interrogating Alterity: Alternative Economic and Political Spaces* (pp. 3–27). Ashgate Publishing, Ltd.

Kavoulakos, K. (2015). Social Movements, State and Alternative Spaces. In K. Kavoulakos & G. Gritzas (Eds.), *Alternative Economic and Social Spaces*. Kallipsos Publications.

Kay, A. (2006). Social Capital, the Social Economy and Community Development. *Community Development Journal, 41*(2), 160–173.

Klein, J. L., Fontan, J. M., & Tremblay, D. G. (2009). Social Entrepreneurs, Local Initiatives and Social Economy: Foundations for a Socially Innovative Strategy to Fight Against Poverty and Exclusion. *Canadian Journal of Regional Science, 32*(1), 23–42.

Kousis, M., Kalogeraki, S., Papadaki, M., Loukakis, A., & Velonaki, M. (2018). Confronting Austerity in Greece: Alternative Forms of Resilience and Solidarity Initiatives by Citizen Groups. In J. Roose, M. Sommer, & F. Scholl (Eds.), *Europas Zivilgesellschaft in der Wirtschafts- und Finanzkrise. Bürgergesellschaft und Demokratie*. Springer.

Kousis, M., & Paschou, M. (2017). Alternative Forms of Resilience: A Typology of Approaches for the Study of Citizen Collective Responses in Hard Economic Times. *Partecipazione e Conflitto, 10*, 136–168. https://doi.org/10.1285/i20356609v10i1p135

Law 2716. (1999). Development and Modernisation of Mental Health Services and Other Provisions. *Government Gazette* A' 96/17.5.1999. https://www.kodiko.gr/nomothesia/document/194703/nomos-2716-1999. [in Greek].

Law 4019. (2011). Social Economy and Social Entrepreneurship and Other Provisions. *Government Gazette* Á 216/30.9.2011. https://www.kodiko.gr/nomothesia/document/63473/nomos-4019-2011. [in Greek].

Law 4430. (2016). Social and Solidarity Economy Development of Its Institutions and Other Provisions. *Government Gazette* 205/31.10.2016. https://www.kodiko.gr/nomothesia/document/242234/nomos-4430-2016. [in Greek].

Lemaitre, A., Laville, J.-L., & Nyssens, M. (2006). Public Policies and Social Enterprises in Europe: The Challenge of Institutionalization. In M. Nyssens (Ed.), *Social Enterprise* (pp. 259–271). Routledge.

Levesque, B. (2003). Mondialisation, Démocratie Plurielle, économie Sociale et Solidaire. *Économie et Solidarités*, 103–121.

Levesque, B., & Mendell, M. (2005). The Social Economy: Approaches, Practices and a Proposal for a New Community-University Alliance. *Journal of Rural Cooperation, 33*(1), 21–45.
Marques, S. J. (2013). Social and Solidarity Economy Between Emancipation and Reproduction. Paper presented at the UNRISD Conference *Potential and Limits of Social and Solidarity Economy*, UNRISD, Geneva.
Mauksch, S., Dey, P., Rowe, M., & Teasdale, S. (2017). Ethnographies of Social Enterprise. *Social Enterprise Journal, 13*(2), 114–127. https://doi.org/10.1108/SEJ-03-2017-0019
Meglio, R. D., & Zandonai, F. (2015). The Role of Social and Solidarity Economy in Employment Generation. Concept Note. Paper presented at *the III World Forum of Local Economic Development*, Torino.
Morais, L. P., & Bacic, M. J. (2013). Social and Solidarity Economy, Youth Employment and the Fight Against Poverty: The Case of Public Works and Employment Programmes in Brazil. Paper presented at *4th CIRIEC International Research Conference on Social Economy*, University of Antwerp.
Nardi, J. (2016). Solidarity Economy in Europe: An Emerging Movement with a Common Vision. Paper presented at *European Summer School*, Prague.
Nasioulas, I. (2012). Social Cooperatives in Greece. Introducing New Forms of Social Economy and Entrepreneurship. *International Review of Social Research, 2*(2), 141–161.
Neamtan, N. (2002). The Social and Solidarity Economy: Towards an 'Alternative' Globalization. Paper presented at the symposium *Citizenship and Globalization: Exploring Participation and Democracy in a Global Context*, Carold Institute for the Advancement of Citizenship in Social Change, Langara College, Vancouver.
Nikolopoulos T., D. Kapogiannis (2013). Introduction to Social and Solidarity Economy. Athens: Ekdoseis ton Synadelfon. [in Greek]
Nitsiakos, V. (2015). *Peklari: Small Scale Social Economy.* Isnafi Publishing.
Papadaki, M., & Kalogeraki, S. (2018). Exploring Social and Solidarity Economy (SSE) During the Greek Economic Crisis. *Partecipazione e Conflitto, 11*, 38–69. https://doi.org/10.1285/i20356609v11i1p38
Petropoulou, C. (2013). "Alternative Networks of Collectivities" and "Solidarity-Cooperative Economy" in Greek Cities: Exploring Their Theoretical Origins. *Journal of Regional & Socio-Economic Issues, 3*(2), 61–85.
Rakopoulos, T. (2015). Solidarity's Tensions: Informality, Sociality, and the Greek Crisis. *Social Analysis, 59*(3), 85–104.
Saguier, M., & Brent, Z. (2017). Social and Solidarity Economy in South American Regional Governance. *Global Social Policy, 17*(3), 259–278.
Sahakian, M. (2016). The Social and Solidarity Economy: Why Is It Relevant to Industrial Ecology? In R. Clift & A. Drukman (Eds.), *Taking Stock of Industrial Ecology* (pp. 205–227). Springer.

Sahakian, M., & Dunand, C. (2015). The Social and Solidarity Economy Towards Greater 'Sustainability': Learning Across Contexts and Cultures, from Geneva to Manila. *Community Development Journal, 50*(3), 403–441.

Schirpke, U., Tscholl, S., & Tasser, E. (2020). Spatio-temporal Changes in Ecosystem Service Values: Effects of Land-use Changes from Past to Future (1860–2100). *Journal of Environmental Management, 272*. https://doi.org/10.1016/j.jenvman.2020.111068

Social Solidarity Economy Directorate General. (2023). Annual Report 2021–22 & Action Plan for the Development of the Ecosystem of the Social and Solidarity Economy and Social Innovation. Hellenic Ministry of Labour, Social Security and Social Solidarity: Athens. https://drive.google.com/file/d/1pcGurRPlYALpENqSC1J8wm6okfWU2Jvb/view. [in Greek].

Sotiropoulou, I. (2015). Prices in Parallel Currency: The Case of the Exchange Network of Chania, Crete. *International Journal of Community Currency Research, 19*, 128–136.

Swyngedouw, E. (2004). Globalisation or 'Glocalisation'? Networks, Territories and Rescaling. *Cambridge Review of International Affairs, 17*(1), 25–48. https://doi.org/10.1080/0955757042000203632

TFSSE. (2014). *Social and Solidarity Economy and the Challenge of Sustainable Development*. A Position paper by the United Nations Inter-Agency Task Force on Social and Solidarity Economy, Geneva.

Tsobanoglou, G. (2012). Barriers to Participation in the Social Economy in Greece. *OñatiSocio-Legal Series, 2(2)* Available at https://ssrn.com/abstract=2055697

Utting P. (2015). Social and Solidarity Economy: Beyond the fringe. Zed Books.

Utting, P., van Dijk, N., Matheï, M.-A. (2014). Social and solidarity economy: Is there a new economy in the making?, *UNRISD Occasional Paper: Potential and Limits of Social and Solidarity Economy* No. 10. United Nations Research Institute for Social Development (UNRISD), Geneva. https://hdl.handle.net/10419/148793

Vaillancourt, Y. (2009). Social Econonomy in the co-construction of public policy. *Annals of Public and Cooperative Economics, 80*, 275–313. https://doi.org/10.1111/j.1467-8292.2009.00387

Vathakou, E. (2015). Citizens' Solidarity Initiatives in Greece During the Financial Crisis. In J. Clarke, A. Huliaras, & D. Sotiropoulos (Eds.), *Austerity and the Third Sector in Greece: Civil Society at the European Frontline*. Ashgate.

Vetsopoulos, A. (2018). The History of Cooperatives in Greece. Messolonghi: Gramma.

CHAPTER 12

Social Incubators and Accelerators for Migrant Entrepreneurs: Exploratory Insights From Italy

Giulia Martinelli, Greta Serpente, and Daniela Bolzani

Introduction

There has been an increasing scholarly interest in entrepreneurial ecosystems, due to their potential role in sustaining the establishment and growth of enterprises and the development of local socio-economic contexts (for a review, Alvedalen & Boschma, 2017). Recently, scholars and policy-makers have started to worry about the under-representation and marginalization of some social groups in entrepreneurship, such as women

G. Martinelli
Gran Sasso Science Institute, L'Aquila, Italy
e-mail: giulia.martinelli@gssi.it

G. Serpente • D. Bolzani (✉)
Department of Management, Alma Mater Studiorum-University of Bologna, Bologna, Italy
e-mail: greta.serpente2@unibo.it; daniela.bolzani@unibo.it

S. Bianchini et al. (eds.), *Social Entrepreneurship and Migrants' Inclusion*, Sustainable Development Goals Series,
https://doi.org/10.1007/978-3-031-55791-0_12

or ethnic entrepreneurs, noting the persistent biases that replicate social categorizations and social structures in entrepreneurship (e.g., Bruton et al., 2023; Essers & Benschop, 2009; Ozkazanc-Pan & Muntean, 2021). Therefore, a pressing issue is linked to critically examining the assumptions about the homogeneous nature of entrepreneurial ecosystems and their inclusiveness in equitable access to resources, networks, and related power for all entrepreneurs (e.g., Krueger, 2021; Neumeyer et al., 2019).

Migrant entrepreneurs are one of the social groups that need particular consideration in terms of inclusion into local entrepreneurial ecosystems, due to their potentially different cultural understanding of entrepreneurship and local institutions, and their "outsiderness" with respect to social networks and other pillars of the local ecosystems, such as advisors, investors, clients, suppliers, qualified workers, and universities (Bolzani & Mizzau, 2019). Specific support in this regard can be provided by entrepreneurial support organizations, such as pre-incubators, incubators, or accelerators (Serpente et al., 2023). While the concept of entrepreneurial support remains ambiguous in literature, it generally regards providing information, facilities, materials, and networks to entrepreneurs or aspiring entrepreneurs (Bergman & McMullen, 2022).

As testified to the growing academic and policy literature (e.g., Solano et al., 2019; van Rijs et al., 2021; Serpente et al., 2023), many support programs have recently been launched by several types of actors, ranging from mainstream incubators/accelerators (i.e., open to all entrepreneurs) to migrant-specific programs (i.e., explicitly targeting migrants), operated by a variety of actors, such as private for-profit companies, social enterprises, civil society organizations, or public institutions. However, while growing, our knowledge about these programs still needs to catch up because the literature is mainly taking the entrepreneurs' perspective, focusing on the benefits and costs of participating in entrepreneurial support programs. Therefore, we still lack knowledge about the "supply side," i.e., entrepreneurial support providers' motivations, organizational arrangements, competencies, and their match with the needs of entrepreneurs, which represent key conditions for support effectiveness.

Among the significant shortcomings in the available literature is the lack of studies about social incubation and acceleration programs, which are currently understood as either programs that support entrepreneurial initiatives carried out by vulnerable individuals (e.g., Aernoudt, 2004) or entrepreneurial initiatives targeting social challenges through innovative and market-oriented solutions (e.g., Casasnovas & Bruno, 2013). Given the potential of social incubation and acceleration programs in increasing social impact and entrepreneurs' human capital development (Sansone et al., 2020), there is a need to further study this type of entrepreneurial support in the context of migrant entrepreneurship. Therefore, this chapter aims to provide evidence to answer the following research question: *How do social incubators and accelerators support migrant entrepreneurs?* We aim to provide an understanding of how different social incubators and accelerators approach migrant entrepreneurs, in particular, looking at the relationship among their governance and organizational structures, their targeting and selection procedures, and the competencies and approaches applied to provide different services.

This work is based on explorative, qualitative research based on interviews with the managers of two social incubators implementing initiatives targeting migrant entrepreneurs in Italy. We explored the extent to which their governance and organizational structures are related to the targeted entrepreneurs and businesses, and how their selection processes and services are decided, designed, and managed to be more or less inclusive towards migrant entrepreneurs. Our analyses provide several insights about the importance of a critical approach towards recognizing patterns of privilege in decision-making about incubation and acceleration organizations at the top management and staff/partners levels. We discuss the implications in terms of theory and practice to sustain migrant entrepreneurship.

Literature Review

Social Incubators and Accelerators

Various types and models of incubation and acceleration have been recently examined in the entrepreneurship and management literature (Mian et al., 2016; Ratinho et al., 2020). Incubators and accelerators fall within the broader organizations dedicated to entrepreneurial support (Bergman & McMullen, 2022). They might be understood as providers of all-rounded help for entrepreneurs, including providing facilities, materials, and network access (Ratinho et al., 2020). As several authors have pointed out, adequate entrepreneurial support builds upon the interests, goals, and expectations of the two main involved parties—entrepreneurs and the incubator/accelerator (Ellerman, 2009)—and thus entrepreneurial support can be understood as a dynamic, relational process (Ratinho et al., 2020; Bergman & McMullen, 2022).

Social incubation and acceleration represent specific contexts, where it is crucial to frame entrepreneurial support as a relational process, as it targets entrepreneurial initiatives with a social impact as well as marginalized or vulnerable entrepreneurs. In this perspective, Sansone et al. (2020) found that social incubators emphasize the services related to social impact and human capital development rather than providing physical and financial support. However, to date, limited research has been dedicated to exploring social incubators or accelerators, both from a theoretical and an empirical point of view.

At present, a definition of a social accelerator is missing in the literature, and a precise definition of a social incubator remains elusive. The first author who introduced this concept was Aernoudt (2004), who stated that the primary objective of social incubators is "to stimulate and support the development, growth, and continuity of companies employing people with low employment capacities" (p.129). This definition sets the primary goal of social incubators as addressing social disparities by enhancing employment opportunities for individuals facing various employment challenges, including but not limited to disabled individuals, recipients of minimum guaranteed income, low-skilled workers, or those who have been unemployed for an extended period. Social incubators are perceived as organizations providing services, including business development, support, accommodation, and operational assistance to nascent ventures. The definition proposed by Aernoudt (2004) is akin to the one used by Etzkowitz et al. (2005).

Later, Sonne (2012) adopted a broader perspective, defining social incubators as assisting social entrepreneurs. Similarly, Casasnovas and Bruno (2013) described social incubators as "*programs that support the scaling process of organizations that target social challenges through innovative and market-oriented solutions*" (p.180). Under this definition, social incubators distinguish themselves from other support organizations by providing a comprehensive range of services, including training, mentoring, networking, and funding. An important aspect to note is that, within this framework, social incubators can encompass both for-profit and nonprofit organizations, in addition to being affiliated with universities or governments. Few empirical studies prove how these social incubators operate (e.g., Bank et al., 2017).

Overall, the limited theoretical and empirical development suggests that social incubators and accelerators, like other incubators/accelerators, are organizations that provide various types of support and resources to entrepreneurs. However, the target beneficiaries can be defined as social entrepreneurs introducing innovative solutions with a social impact, or as individuals in need, marginalized, or deserving of a type of support that can be defined as a social mission.

Social Incubators and Accelerators for Migrants

The literature about social incubators and accelerators targeting migrant entrepreneurs can be considered part of the broader literature dealing with entrepreneurial support for migrants (e.g., Solano et al., 2019; Serpente et al., 2023). To date, the empirical studies on this topic are relatively scant. They mainly focus on analyzing and supporting incubation for migrant entrepreneurs who seek to start or develop businesses in host countries (Jones et al., 2008). Social incubators targeting migrants have been mainly characterized as having similar strategies to generalist social incubators, which frequently concentrate on empowering a specific population (Harima et al., 2019). Consequently, the primary objective of social incubators for migrants is not only to foster entrepreneurship among migrants, but also to empower them and facilitate their socio-economic integration, especially by providing self-employment opportunities that could match their skills (Brock, 2008; Freudenberg & Halberstadt, 2018).

Literature is generally consistent in finding that social incubators to support migrant entrepreneurs are designed to provide targeted support, considering the participants' cultural, linguistic, social, and financial barriers (e.g., Brock, 2008; Kushnirovich & Heilbrunn, 2008). Support might take place through different activities and services, such as entrepreneurship training and capacity-building courses to help migrants develop entrepreneurial skills and knowledge of the local market (Nicolopoulou et al., 2017); access to external services, such as translation assistance (Gonzales et al., 2013); access to credit and financing (Jones et al., 2008; Nayak et al., 2019); and networking with local professionals or mentoring from experienced entrepreneurs (Freudenberg & Halberstadt, 2018).

Methodology

This exploratory work is focused on the social incubators and accelerators targeting migrant entrepreneurs in Italy,[1] which is an important context to study contemporary migration and entrepreneurship patterns (for a review, see Bolzani, 2021). The diffusion of social incubators is still limited across Italy (Social Innovation Monitor, 2022, 2023): in 2022, there were 13 social incubators, constituting 15% of the overall incubators' population.

The data collection started by developing a list of 39 Italian incubators/accelerators targeting migrants, based on desk research and contacts with policy-makers, practitioners, and experts in the field as of April 2021. The research team identified six different social incubators or accelerators that could be analyzed in detail based on secondary data about the targeted entrepreneurs, sponsorship, geographical location, and types of offered services. Four specifically targeted migrants, while the other two were generalists, i.e., not explicitly focusing on migrant entrepreneurs (and therefore potentially open to any entrepreneur). For this chapter, we focus on the last two, which we name Incubator#1 and Accelerator#1, to preserve the anonymity of participants. Through secondary data collection and in-depth interviews, the research team explored the two organizations' history, business model and governance, programs and activities, the organization and competencies of the staff, the methodological approach to incubation support, the perceived barriers and needs of migrant entrepreneurs by different incubators, and the competencies needed by incubation professionals to tackle them. In addition, in order to understand specificities in supporting migrant entrepreneurs compared to local entrepreneurs, 14 generalist incubators and accelerators were interviewed.

The interviews were carried out online and were recorded and transcribed. The interviewees were the startup program coordinator and the

[1]The chapter hinges on the data collected by the University of Bologna during the development of MIG.EN.CUBE, a project funded by the EU Erasmus+ program, focused on enhancing the knowledge and competencies of diverse incubation professionals who deal with current or aspiring migrant entrepreneurs. The University of Bologna led the project, whicht involved university and incubation partners from France, Italy, and the Netherlands and lasted from November 2020 to April 2023. In this chapter, we only focus on some findings about the Italian context. However, a more comprehensive understanding of the types of incubation initiatives specifically targeting migrant entrepreneurs can be found in the two reports released by the project (van Rijs et al., 2021; Martinelli & Bolzani, 2021).

startup acceleration specialist. The transcriptions of the interviews were analyzed through text analysis to answer our research question comprehensively. Specifically, by reading and re-reading the transcriptions, we highlighted the recurrent words and identified key sentences to create a first-order coding structure. Then, by comparing the two interviews and reconsidering the first-order codes in light of our research question, we clustered them into higher-order categories that represented three blocks of issues that influence how social incubators/accelerators provide support to migrant entrepreneurs: governance and organizational structure, approach and selection of the target group, and type of incubation services provided. In forming these second-order categories, we used the work by Bergman and McMullen (2022) as a sensitizing framework to analyze incubators' and accelerators' activities.

Findings

The findings are organized into three sections—governance and organizational structure, target and selection, and services—to provide a detailed description of similarities and divergences between the two case studies, and to compare and contrast the findings with those emerging from the interviews with generalist incubators.

Governance and Organizational Structure

In this analysis, we follow Bergman and McMullen (2022), who look at the dichotomy between for-profit and not-for-profit incubators and accelerators, and at the structure of shareholders and sponsors, such as universities, corporations, governments, non-profit organizations, financial institutions, and entrepreneurs.

INCUBATOR#1 was founded in 2011 as a spin-off of an existing social enterprise. It was established as a certified incubator and accelerator of ideas and businesses with high social, cultural, and environmental value. In 2020, it was re-branded to strengthen its objective to "encourage and support the creation and development of impactful businesses in order to generate innovation and social transformation"[2] as well as to reinforce its relationship with the mother company and its network. This change was accompanied by the transformation into a benefit corporation, further

[2] INCUBATOR#1's website.

specifying the importance of sustainability in its mission. Being an incubator and accelerator, it can cover and be present across the entire life stages of enterprise development, from the idea development to the launch and growth on the market. In addition, INCUBATOR#1 serves as an advisor for the venture capital fund of the mother company "*for which it performs analyses and selects companies to be assisted in the preliminary stages of investment.*" The transformation to cover this role "*[…] reinforced the startup supply chain […] because with the high-impact investment fund in the social business sphere, we go from the informal, pre-constitution groups to the accelerated startups looking for an investment.*"

For this incubator, the relationship with the mother company is significant: "*We realized that one of the strengths of INCUBATOR#1 is […] the fact that we have an internal network, […] that is the colleagues working in the open innovation area, who in turn work with companies willing to invest in startups.*" The role of the mother company is manifest in the composition of the board. Indeed, the website lacks a clear description of the power structure of INCUBATOR#1, but the role of the mother company appears instead.

The interview revealed the weight of external partners for INCUBATOR#1, which continuously works in partnership with corporate businesses as partners or clients, to ensure revenues and resources to sustain its activities in the domain of social entrepreneurship: "*In the perspective of entering in the impact value chain and citizens' advocacy—especially concerning urban regenerations from the bottom together with corporate business […] our model is almost entirely based on the call, partner, and business we intersect. […] basically startups have zero money, especially if they want to work in social impact projects.*"

INCUBATOR#1's team comprises five men and three women with a high level of education, among which seven out of eight are Italians from the largest Italian cities. The team is supported by the employees of the mother company, who can provide specific knowledge and competencies. Italian men occupy the top and senior positions.

ACCELERATOR#1 is a not-for-profit company functioning as a center for social innovation, specializing in designing and supporting innovative ideas and solutions that tackle contemporary societal challenges. It comprises two units, i.e., impact design and startup acceleration. For our chapter, we focus on the acceleration activities. The accelerator aims to foster the growth of social impact startups, helping them to attract investments. This function is eased thanks to its private seed investment vehicle, which invests in startups selected and accelerated by ACCELERATOR#1 since 2017. According to them, "*having an investment vehicle changes the approach completely. [...] the selection is different, there are some reasons to be done related to the return of the investments as well.*"

The investment vehicle is a private, for-profit company owned by family offices, banking foundations, and business angels. It is a distinct entity with respect to ACCELERATOR#1, yet closely linked because it invests only in the startups accelerated by ACCELERATOR#1, and because ACCELERATOR#1 also invests equity in the startups. Such choices signal the intense focus on social impact entrepreneurship: ACCELERATOR#1 has no interest in making a profit and, therefore, relies on an independent vehicle fund. The presence of the investment vehicle is considered in the composition of the accelerator board. The independence of ACCELERATOR#1 from any company or foundation is mirrored in the participation, but not affiliation, to networks and the small and selected number of venture partners interested in social issues.

The six members of the acceleration team are Italian, four women and two men, having different education and disciplinary backgrounds yet interested in the startup world.

According to the classification proposed by Bergman and McMullen (2022), the cases under analysis show that social incubators and accelerators can be either for-profit or not-for-profit. Nevertheless, they pursue a social objective and want to impact society positively. They rely on external yet related investment vehicles and a sound network of investors and partners to have a sustainable business model. Their governance structures reflect their efforts to balance independence and reliance on external partners aligned with their social mission. Their organizational structures could appear more diverse regarding race and culture because they rely on Italian team members.

Target and Selection Process

The literature distinguishes incubators as targeting pre-venture and infant entrepreneurial projects, and accelerators as addressing infant and early-growth entrepreneurs (Bergman & McMullen, 2022). Such a distinction is satisfied in the case of INCUBATOR#1 and ACCELERATOR#1. As seen previously, INCUBATOR#1 can be present along the entire lifecycle of a startup project, from the entrepreneurial idea to early- and later-stage startups. ACCELERATOR#1, on the other hand, looks for "early-stage startups with a tested prototype or a market product" willing to scale up and have an impact, either established or in the founding phase.

However, as social incubators and accelerators, the central defining feature for their selection processes should be the incubated/accelerated startups. As discussed in the literature review, there are two main approaches to defining the target of social incubators: a focus on social startups or a focus on vulnerable/marginalized entrepreneurs. In our interviews, we confirmed both these approaches.

INCUBATOR#1 looks for "*[…] businesses that should be economically sustainable and […] scalable as well, and maybe scalability in this case is not scale economy in the sense of production and lower costs […] my value is in the perspective of impact, integration, community […] scalable because people are part of the value.*" In other words, this incubator promotes businesses whose mission is to improve the local context where they are established. In particular, it looks for entrepreneurial projects from those territories that might be more fragile, underdeveloped, and disadvantaged.

INCUBATOR#1 runs several programs, all characterized by being oriented towards social innovation and creating social value. The heterogeneity in programs and the broad target audience generate some complexity in summarizing the selection processes. Each program has specific requirements that are defined together with the partners, corporates, or foundations willing to invest: "*[…] we work in a B2B perspective then we have partners and clients who might be corporations, foundations […] that have a sum of money to invest in incubation programs […] so we co-design the incubation program with them, then select the startups they are interested into.*"

When defining selection criteria around the goal of the entrepreneurial team to address the needs of Italian territories, there is no specific need to focus on attracting or selecting entrepreneurs based on their migratory background. However, migrants could fall under the recipients of a call or project developed by INCUBATOR#1 if they "*live the context and are willing to improve the context where they live. […] The place doesn't change if a private citizen builds a building, the place changes if people change and their businesses change with them, but these individuals are fragile.*" In other words, migrants might be fragile individuals and, in this capacity, they can join and benefit from the programs. In such cases, even though the business might not be innovative or of social impact, "*the fact that the entrepreneur is a migrant has a social impact per se, because the beneficiary [of the project] is the entrepreneur herself.*" The interviews, therefore, reveal that

INCUBATOR#1 also adheres to the definition of "social incubators" by focusing on including marginalized or vulnerable entrepreneurs. The interview revealed that migrants can become specific target groups for incubation support if external partners are willing to invest in them.

Similarly, ACCELERATOR#1 admits that "*[the] standardization of the evaluation of early-stage startups in social impact is impossible.*" Nevertheless, the identification of some parameters is possible thanks to the narrow scope of the accelerator: "*[…] there are two basic parameters… if the startup is not social impact-focused we cannot consider it. And if the startup is too late or too early stage we cannot consider it.*" Therefore, ACCELERATOR#1 targets only startups—"*not small or medium enterprises*"—with a social or environmental impact. In particular, selected startups should tackle global environmental, health, education, and social cohesion challenges, specifically targeting Italy. In this regard, the focus on Italy might seem limited. Nevertheless, in the interview, ACCELERATOR#1 pointed out that the margins are flexible since the fundamental criterion is the social or green impact: "*The investment vehicle was born with the objective of accelerating Italian startups […] For example, the startups that are born in Italy with the aim of improving life conditions in Tanzania are not in our target. Then there are exceptions. We accelerated a terrific startup with a very interesting social impact. […] the social impact is on Syrian refugees in Jordan, but they sell to the Western and European market, so it seemed worth investing in it.*"

To be considered for the acceleration program, the entrepreneurs should have a minimum viable product to be presented to the accelerator's team members and the investment vehicle's board during the selection process. At that stage, the entrepreneurial team should convince the accelerator that their business makes an intentional, additional, measurable social impact and stands out for being highly innovative. To do so, in the application process, the entrepreneurs are required to present a pitch deck and answer some questions regarding their competencies and commitment, the quality of the product/service, the dimensions of the market, the competitive advantage, the value proposition, the scalability, the innovativeness, and the strength of the brand. If the first screening is passed, the startups go through a series of interviews with the accelerator's team and the investment vehicle's board, who try to "*look beyond appearances*" and understand whether the business is truly valuable and whether the entrepreneurial team is enough motivated, committed, and presents the desire to work intensively, scale up, and exit their comfort zone.

Compared to INCUBATOR#1, ACCELERATOR#1 has a clearly defined selection process and relatively homogeneous target startups, which resemble the practices followed by generalist incubators or accelerators. Such a clearly defined selection process, which was developed based on the goals and needs of the accelerator, is intended to be open to any entrepreneur, among which migrant ones who are fluent in English. In fact, the application form can either be filled in Italian or English. While several projects presented by migrants hosted in Italy were received by ACCELERATOR#1, none met the minimum requirements to enter the acceleration program to date.

Services

Incubators' defining services are physical space and networking opportunities, while accelerators tend to offer curriculum/mentoring activities, financial capital, and a graduation event (Bergman & McMullen, 2022). Nevertheless, these organizations could provide physical resources, administrative support, and workshops (Bergman & McMullen, 2022).

Given its role in all startups' life stages, INCUBATOR#1 offers several services beyond incubators' specific features. Before describing the services, it is important to clarify the approach employed by INCUBATOR#1. As the interview reveals, across the diverse range of programs offered, a common thread can be discerned in the applied methodology that "*enables competencies, so not only we support and accompany the teams in developing their idea but through a hybrid methodology we enable them to develop their own skills in order to use them autonomously […] We teach them […] to develop an entrepreneurial mindset. […] The enabling process is beyond facilitation, because to facilitate is to make something easier, instead we teach them to do something, we make them able to do it.*" The services and the approach of the team are therefore to be read under this lens: they try to enable the competencies of the entrepreneurs to develop further and strengthen specific skills and to allow entrepreneurs to continue their business development trajectory autonomously.

The services include training sessions, workshops, administrative support, ad hoc consulting, and networking. Indeed, "*there is an initial part of training […] but being in an incubation program, we try to make it more interactive, more practical, giving the theoretical concepts but focusing a lot on sharing the tools.*" In addition, in the case of businesses in an advanced stage of development, it provides a sort of coaching tailored to the specific needs of the business idea and entrepreneurial team, and integrated with the network of experts they might need. The principles and tools of design thinking, lean startup, and change theory help entrepreneurs develop business ideas to impact their target society and context.

As explained in the governance paragraph, INCUBATOR#1 tailors its programs to the needs and requests of external partners willing to invest in sustainable and social-impact startups, and it aims to bridge startups' and investors' needs through its activities and network. The services provided to entrepreneurs are free: the partners, corporations, and foundations sponsoring the program fund it and cover the expenses.

INCUBATOR#1's programs are delivered by the internal team, which is supported by specialized activities carried out by the employees of the mother company. The offered training and activities are in Italian, limiting the accessibility to Italian-speaking entrepreneurs only. When specifically inquired about the potential participation of migrant entrepreneurs in their program, the interviewee at INCUBATOR#1 stated that working with migrants requires specific soft skills, which currently the staff is not endowed with: "*for sure, migrant entrepreneurs require more attention, for example in functional support [...] because obviously coming from contexts where certain opportunities are more feasible [...] There are expectations also on the human side which falls outside the scope of incubation.*"

ACCELERATOR#1's services match the defining characteristics of Bergman and McMullen (2021): provision of spaces, administrative support, one-to-one mentoring, support to accessing financial capital, and a graduation event. The 4-month acceleration program is "*composed of theoretical and practical modules, taught by the team but also external experts who discuss various themes, from product/service/market validation to the proposition target, etc. [...] let's say all those fundamental themes that make the startup investment ready.*" The generalist theoretical-practical side is complemented by tailor-made mentoring for the single startup, evolving around the specific industry or specialization. Mentorship, tutoring, and consultancy activities are carried out by the internal staff or external professionals who are part of the network of ACCELERATOR#1. The theoretical modules are taught in Italian, even if the team could easily switch to English; the practical activities are also carried out in Italian, and switching to English would depend on the knowledge of the internal or external professional in charge of the service.

When selected, startups are recommended to move to ACCELERATOR#1's co-working spaces: "*We warmly invited startups and entrepreneurs to move to our city [...] the program was never online before Covid-19,*" the main reason being that in-presence training and mentoring activities are a valuable source of networking with other startups, investors, and the accelerator's team as well. Networking per se is not listed as a service, yet it is intrinsic and of crucial importance for startups' growth: "*in the case you move in our co-working space, you work three times faster because you see each other almost every day, you work together almost every day [...] it's a completely different quality.*"

When applying for ACCELERATOR#1's acceleration program, entrepreneurs expect to receive training and administrative and financial support. The program has a fee intended as an investment to make the startup grow. This initial investment is expected to be compensated in terms of training, acquisition of skills for business development, and access to networks. In terms of financial support, not all accelerated startups are funded by the investment vehicle: "*the investment vehicle decides on the startups to be accelerated and on the investments in them [...] because there is always a relationship between risk and return [...] we are still talking of returns on investments in social impact, so it is clear that it is different from the classical finance [...] but we are convinced there is an interesting investment opportunity so a potential investment return.*"

Discussion

The interviews with INCUBATOR#1 and ACCELERATOR#1 bring to the forefront several discussion points. For consistency, they are dealt with in the same order as above: governance and organizational structure, target and selection process, and services.

Both INCUBATOR#1 and ACCELERATOR#1 are social enterprises having a not-for-profit nature. However, they rely on a for-profit investment fund, connected by being part of the same group of companies or functionally related to implementing incubation/acceleration services. The selected organizations can maintain a strong focus on the social objectives, thanks to such decoupling of the profit and not-for-profit structures.

The boards and teams of INCUBATOR#1 and ACCELERATOR#1 display different stakeholders who can bring to the forefront different interests that characterize the size and scope of the programs. However, stakeholders directly linked to or representing migrant entrepreneurship are not represented in these organizations, which instead appear governed and managed by a relatively homogeneous group of Italian, highly-skilled professionals with an interest and experience in social or scalable entrepreneurship. As testified by prior literature, organizations might replicate racialized social systems, by reinforcing and replicating categories of identity, privilege, and oppression (Ray, 2019). Therefore, the two organizations studied in this work might not be aware of the risks linked to the absence of racial, ethnic, or cultural diversity across their internal and external human resources and consultants. The lack of diversity is also referred to here as an intersectional issue, for instance, reinforced by the male-dominated decision-making structures in top and senior positions.

There are no programs specifically targeting the category of migrant entrepreneurs in INCUBATOR#1 and ACCELERATOR#1. On the one hand, this approach is beneficial to avoid categorizations based on essentialistic assumptions—such as culturalism or racialization—to identify the beneficiaries of incubation programs. Such programs might be designed and run with a welfaristic approach, rather than a business development/growth approach, also providing sponsors and investors with the opportunity to gain a reputation based on the association with marginalized/fragile target entrepreneurs. On the other hand, this approach might be blind to existing diversity and needs, such as migrants' liability of outsiderness in local entrepreneurial ecosystems, discrimination from host countries' social structures, or lack of resources to attend the incubation/acceleration program full-time.

The design of a call for entrepreneurial ideas or startups following the requests of partners, clients, and sponsors—as in the case of INCUBATOR#1—might appear as a top-down approach replicating existing socioeconomic privilege and logics. Therefore, local entrepreneurs might perceive they are not listened to, especially in the case of migrants. ACCELERATOR#1's request to entrepreneurs to physically move to the accelerator's co-working spaces might appear insensitive about the implied economic and personal consequences and costs—for instance, relocation and moving costs, loss of side income-generation activities, psychological costs for re-socialization, or management of family ties. This type of request seems to follow the idea of a privileged, rootless, disembodied entrepreneur who should only focus on his/her business idea. Given their potential for impact, social incubators and accelerators should be more reflexive about the social, economic, and historical sources of power and privilege.

Our study has found that both INCUBATOR#1 and ACCELERATOR#1 offer their services in Italian, thus excluding those migrant entrepreneurs who do not speak the language. In the approach of INCUBATOR#1, such a choice seems logical as the incubator invests in the territory to solve local social challenges, assuming that migrants are part of the territory and could equally participate. However, we know that some groups of migrants are not ready to engage in entrepreneurial practices using the host country's language (e.g., recently arrived migrants or disconnected from employment or socialization networks) or might be somewhat interested in addressing relevant social challenges by focusing on international or transnational business ideas. Once again, the definition of incubation/acceleration services can replicate top-down logics based on the interests of the privileged groups represented in decision-making structures. The issue of which language is adopted to deliver support programs is essential, as it has wide-ranging practical and logistic implications. For instance, while ACCELERATOR#1 declared being able to provide the training and tailored support in English to be consistent with the application phase, this might become unfeasible or too costly when facing entrepreneurs from different linguistic groups with different levels of mastery of English.

Our interviewees suggested that migrant entrepreneurs require additional services, such as cultural mediation, introduction to the Italian administrative system, and other tools to navigate the Italian context. Providing these services implies having dedicated infrastructure, skills and knowledge, and dedicated personnel, which both INCUBATOR#1 and ACCELERATOR#1 lack. The soft skills necessary in incubation and acceleration programs do not suffice to cover all the needs of migrant entrepreneurs. One possible solution would be to add a staff member specialized in these issues to support migrants in developing the entrepreneurial path and the personal side. However, the working and personal profile of this expert should aim at preventing the othering of entrepreneurs with a migrant background, the creation or replication of stereotypical assumptions about their needs and behaviors, or their infantilization through the establishment of charitable practices.

Conclusions

This chapter aimed to shed light on the entrepreneurial support that social incubators and accelerators can provide migrant entrepreneurs. Leveraging primary data collected from semi-structured interviews with incubation specialists working in one social incubator and one social accelerator in Italy, we find that the governance and the organizational structures adopted by these organizations play an indirect yet meaningful role in shaping support initiatives for startup entrepreneurs. The diversity in the background of the incubator's team, top management team members, and external partners, together with equity and inclusion policies at the broader organizational level, can introduce meaningful opportunities for migrant entrepreneurs' participation in entrepreneurial support programs. There is a trade-off between designing and delivering programs dedicated to migrants vs. open to everyone, which is important to be acknowledged and reflected upon by social incubators and accelerators—as specific skills and mindsets are required.

The insights this chapter provides are useful general indications that could be applied beyond social incubators and accelerators. However, the study suffers from some limitations. First, the external validity could be challenged, as the explorative findings relate strictly to the Italian context and may not be directly applicable to other geographical contexts or similar programs. Additionally, there is a risk of selection bias that could influence the perceptions gathered from the interviews, as they were based on the accounts provided by program managers in selected organizations, and may only partially represent other experiences. To address these limitations, future research could examine a broader and more representative sample of social incubation programs in various geographical and cultural contexts and consider the evolution of programs longitudinally.

Based on the findings of this chapter, a set of practical recommendations can enhance the role of social incubators in supporting migrant entrepreneurs. First, diversifying the governance, internal organizational structures, and external partners' network of social incubators, by including individuals with diverse cultural, ethnic, or racial backgrounds, can lead to more effective programs tailored to the needs of migrant entrepreneurs. Second, language inclusivity, such as offering services in multiple languages, or program flexibility, such as allowing personalized schedules and locations, could increase equity in selection, access, and retention in the programs. Moreover, social incubators for migrants should engage with governmental bodies and local organizations to promote inclusion and raise awareness about the potential of migrant entrepreneurs, challenge stereotypes, and encourage their economic and social integration. These recommendations can create more inclusive and effective support systems for migrant entrepreneurs within social incubation programs, fostering their success and broader inclusion in host country societies and entrepreneurial ecosystems.

References

Aernoudt, R. (2004). Incubators: Tool for Entrepreneurship? *Small Business Economics, 23*(2), 127–135.

Alvedalen, J., & Boschma, R. (2017). A Critical Review of Entrepreneurial Ecosystems Research: Towards a Future Research Agenda. *European Planning Studies, 25*(6), 887–903.

Bank, N., Fichter, K., & Klofsten, M. (2017). Sustainability-profiled Incubators and Securing the inflow of Tenants–The Case of Green Garage Berlin. *Journal of Cleaner Production, 157*, 76–83.

Bergman, B. J., & McMullen, J. S. (2022). Helping Entrepreneurs Help Themselves: A Review and Relational Research Agenda on Entrepreneurial Support Organizations. *Entrepreneurship Theory and Practice, 46*(3), 688–728.

Bolzani, D. (2021). *Migrant Entrepreneurship.* Emerald Publishing Limited. https://doi.org/10.1108/978-1-83867-491-520211003

Bolzani, D., & Mizzau, L. (2019). Supporting Migrant Entrepreneurs in Entrepreneurial Ecosystems: Insights from Milan. *Piccola Impresa/Small Business, 3*, 78–105.

Brock, D. (2008). *Social Entrepreneurship: Teaching Resources Handbook for Faculty Engaged in Teaching and Research in Social Entrepreneurship.* Ashoka's Global Academy for Social Entrepreneurship.

Bruton, G. D., Lewis, A., Cerecedo-Lopez, J. A., & Chapman, K. (2023). A Racialized View of Entrepreneurship: A Review and Proposal for Future Research. *Academy of Management Annals, 17*(2), 492–515.

Casasnovas, G., & Bruno, A. V. (2013). Scaling Social Ventures. *Journal of Management for Global Sustainability, 1*(2), 173–197.

Ellerman, D. (2009). *Helping People Help Themselves: From the World Bank to an Alternative Philosophy of Development Assistance.* University of Michigan Press.

Essers, C., & Benschop, Y. (2009). Muslim Businesswomen Doing Boundary Work: The Negotiation of Islam, Gender and Ethnicity Within Entrepreneurial Contexts. *Human relations, 62*(3), 403–423.

Etzkowitz, H., De Mello, J. M. C., & Almeida, M. (2005). Towards "meta-innovation" in Brazil: The Evolution of the Incubator and the Emergence of a Triple Helix. *Research Policy, 34*, 411–424.

Freudenberg, J., & Halberstadt, J. (2018). How to Integrate Refugees into the Workforce–Different Opportunities for (Social) Entrepreneurship. *Problemy Zarządzania, 1*(73), 40–60.

Gonzales, V., Forrest, N., & Balos, N. (2013). Refugee Farmers and the Social Enterprise Model in the American Southwest. *Journal of Community Positive Practices, 4*, 32–54.

Harima, A., Freudenberg, J., & Halberstadt, J. (2019). Functional Domains of Business Incubators for Refugee Entrepreneurs. *Journal of Enterprising Communities: People and Places in the Global Economy, 14*(5), 687–711.

Jones, R., Latham, J., & Betta, M. (2008). Narrative Construction of the Social Entrepreneurial Identity. *International Journal of Entrepreneurial Behavior & Research, 14*(5), 330–345.

Krueger, N. (2021). Beyond "getting asked to dance": Inclusive Entrepreneurial Ecosystems. In T. M. Cooney (Ed.), *The Palgrave Handbook of Minority Entrepreneurship* (pp. 117–135). Palgrave Macmillan.

Kushnirovich, N., & Heilbrunn, S. (2008). Financial Funding of Immigrant Businesses. *Journal of Developmental Entrepreneurship, 13*(2), 167–184.

Martinelli, G., & Bolzani, D. (2021). *Incubators' Training Needs to Serve Migrant Entrepreneurship.* Report of the MIG.EN.CUBE Project. https://site.unibo.it/mig-en-cube/en/results

Mian, S., Lamine, W., & Fayolle, A. (2016). Technology Business Incubation: An Overview of the State of Knowledge. *Technovation, 50*, 1–12.

Nayak, G., Salovaara, I. M., & Wade, J. (2019). Self-regulated Learning in Refugee Entrepreneurship Education: A University-based Program for Tibetan Entrepreneurs in India. *Diaspora, Indigenous, and Minority Education, 13*(2), 81–96.

Neumeyer, X., Santos, S. C., Caetano, A., & Kalbfleisch, P. (2019). Entrepreneurship Ecosystems and Women Entrepreneurs: A Social Capital and Network Approach. *Small Business Economics, 53*, 475–489.

Nicolopoulou, K., Karataş-Özkan, M., Vas, C., & Nouman, M. (2017). An Incubation Perspective on Social Innovation: the London Hub–a Social Incubator. *R&D Management, 47*(3), 368–384.

Ozkazanc-Pan, B., & Muntean, S. C. (2021). *Entrepreneurial Ecosystems: A Gender Perspective.* Cambridge University Press.

Ratinho, T., Amezcua, A., Honig, B., & Zeng, Z. (2020). Supporting Entrepreneurs: A Systematic Review of Literature and an Agenda for Research. *Technological Forecasting and Social Change, 154*, 119956.

Ray, Victor. (2019). A Theory of Racialized Organizations. *American Sociological Review, 84*(1), 26–53. https://doi.org/10.1177/0003122418822335

Sansone, G., Andreotti, P., Colombelli, A., & Landoni, P. (2020). Are Social Incubators Different from Other Incubators? Evidence from Italy. *Technological Forecasting and Social Change, 158*, 120132.

Serpente, G., Martinelli, G., & Bolzani, D. (2023). Entrepreneurial Support for Migrant Entrepreneurs: A Systematization of a Growing Stream of Literature. In B. Glinka & J. Freiling (Eds.), *Handbook of Migrant Entrepreneurship.* De Gruyter.

Social Innovation Monitor. (2022). Report Incubatori 2022. Retrieved September 29, 2023, from https://socialinnovationmonitor.com/italy-incubators/

Social Innovation Monitor. (2023). Report sulle Startup Innovative a significativo impatto sociale. Retrieved September 29, 2023, from https://socialinnovationmonitor.com/startup/report-sulle-startup-innovative-a-significativo-impatto-sociale-2/

Solano, G., Wolffhardt, A., & Xhani, A. (2019). Measures to Support early-stage Migrant Entrepreneurs. *MEGA Handbook*. http://migrant-entrepreneurship.eu/wp-content/uploads/2019/05/A.1.b-1.pdf

Sonne, Lina. (2012). Innovative initiatives supporting inclusive innovation in India: Social business incubation and micro venture capital. *Technological Forecasting and Social Change, 79*, 638–647, https://doi.org/10.1016/j.techfore.2011.06.008

van Rijs, S. B., Scalera, V. G., & Lupoi, O. (2021). *Incubation Services for Migrant Entrepreneurship*. Report of the MIG.EN.CUBE Project. https://site.unibo.it/mig-en-cube/en/results

CHAPTER 13

Economic Integration of Refugees: A Cross-country Comparison of Slovenia, Spain and Austria

Anja Zafošnik and Simona Zavratnik

Introduction

The 'refugee crisis' of 2015 has re-opened several issues concerning people on migratory routes to Europe, including access along different paths into Europe like, for example, the Western Balkan route, policies of reception and the various ways refugees are perceived by the public across the EU. The war conflict in Syria and broader crisis in the region have triggered important mobility shifts, with Europe thus being faced with a demographic expansion. Balibar (2015) described this expansion as not

This research is part of M.A. thesis of Anja Zafošnik. (Integration policies in the field of refugee employment: a comparative analysis of Slovenia, Austria and Spain, 2021).

A. Zafošnik (✉) • S. Zavratnik
Faculty of Social Sciences, University of Ljubljana, Ljubljana, Slovenia
e-mail: zafosnikanja@gmail.com; simona.zavratnik@fdv.uni-lj.si

S. Bianchini et al. (eds.), *Social Entrepreneurship and Migrants' Inclusion*, Sustainable Development Goals Series,
https://doi.org/10.1007/978-3-031-55791-0_13

being caused by the movement of national boundaries or the inclusion of countries, but in the wider mobility of people. The fact that migration is an integral part of human societies, in both the present and the past (e.g. see: Bade, 2005; De Haas et al., 2014; Goldin et al., 2012; King, 2007), led to the need to determine appropriate integration policies and long-term migration strategies on both national and EU levels.

Although considerable data reveal the importance of integrating refugees and migrant workers more widely into the European Union,[1] the fact remains that public policies covering this issue vary quite strongly from country to country. Since an extensive review of academic literature in this field lies beyond the scope of this article, just one of the latest studies, *Anxieties of Migration and Integration in Turbulent Times* (2023) edited by Mari-Liis Jakobson, Russell King, Laura Moroşanu and Raivo Vetik, is mentioned here. The mentioned editors write: "The effects of turbulent times on migration and integration are thus manifold and complex and are often a poor fit with the formal regulations or informal traditions governing the field. This raises the question of how to cope with turbulent times" (2023, 15). They refer to the broader dimension of migration policies, world changes and migration following social crises. Alongside the migration crisis and border management, central place is clearly still held by integration, even if likely somewhat reframed and adapted to the new dynamics of mobility after major social crises, such as the 2015 refugee crisis and COVID-19, as may be deduced from Spencer and Charsley's (2021) in-depth critique of the concept of integration.

Solidarity, inclusion and social cohesion doubtlessly continue to be a central topic in the integration paradigm. In the analysis presented in this article, we focused on a much narrower aspect of migration policies, namely, integration policies that affect the employment of refugees in three countries: Slovenia, Austria and Spain. The aim was to analyse similarities and differences, traditions in migration management, approaches in refugee employment policies and potentially identify common characteristics that could lead to a cross-country practice. Our starting assumption was that entering the labour market and the consequent access to income are important factors that allow refugees to live independent lives

[1] See more at EUROSTAT—publications, data base, migrant integration statistics etc. https://ec.europa.eu/eurostat/web/migration-asylum/migrant-integration/publications.

in new societies. The latter is understood as the central point and principal intention of integration policies. Three research questions guided our investigation:

RQ1: What are the situation and the trends regarding the employment of refugees in Slovenia, Spain and Austria in the changed migration realities following the 2015 refugee crisis? A starting point here is that the chances of refugees becoming employed are limited by their legal and social status despite them legally holding equal rights under the Geneva Convention Relating to the Status of Refugees.

RQ2: On which type of employment is the integration policy focused and what is the relationship between employers and the state? We assume that integration policy concentrates chiefly on quickly finding work for refugees, not the jobs for which they have been educated. Further, employers show a reluctance to employ refugees, which is based on a lack of information on employment opportunities, prejudice and stereotypes about refugees in broader society.

RQ3: How effective are public policies in the field of refugee employment? We assume that bigger differences are an outcome of different policies, experiences and traditions. In general, countries with a long tradition are more successful, achieve better results from their integration policy and employ larger numbers of refugees.

With respect to the methodology used, we adopted a qualitative approach by collecting data in the field, entailing 25 semi-structured interviews with refugees. Several topics were enquired into and the responses analysed: (1) arrival in new societies (reasons and motivation), (2) employment (access to employment, support mechanisms), (3) interactions at work (with employers) and (4) integration into the new environment (including plans for future). The majority of the interviewed refugees had arrived in Slovenia, Austria and Spain after 2015 and had already integrated into the labour market (namely, they had/have experience of working in the new environment). The fieldwork in the three countries was conducted between 2019 and 2021.

First, we note that no specific focus was given to the issue of migrant/refugee entrepreneurship during the field research. Nevertheless, this issue arose later in the implementation phase in the field when in a few cases (admittedly rarely) interviewees, especially those who already had done so in their country, mentioned the possibility of running one's own company. This means that in the article the topic is framed based on data obtained in a wider field where refugee entrepreneurship was more randomly mentioned, not systematically discussed. We are aware that this amounts to a shortcoming of the presented research and hope that from the broader perspective of integration into the field of work our contribution brings at least partial insights into the topic of refugee entrepreneurship.

Country Background: Migration Context and Labour Market Integration

"Work is key for integration into work" is what is stated in the preface of the extensive policy analysis "From Refugees to Workers, Mapping Labour-Market Integration Support Measures for Asylum Seekers and Refugees in EU Member States" prepared by the Migration Policy Centre at the European University Institute in Florence and Bertelsmann Foundation. Challenges facing the common European (policy) level, nine detailed country studies and a discussion of the prospects of integrating migrants in the European context give valuable insights into the dynamic migration situation.

> One conclusion stands out clearly from the comparative analysis of the nine country case studies: despite the differences in social contexts, labour market structures and support measures, the challenges, policy trade-offs and choices involved in the labour market integration of refugees and asylum seekers (the key questions emerging from the country case studies) are pretty similar across countries. This hints at a certain scope for mutual learning, cooperation and even Europe-wide solutions. (2016: 43)

Extensive academic literature (e.g. Grzymala-Kazlowska & Phillimore, 2018; Fasani et al., 2018; Vogiazides & Mondani, 2020) together with policy papers on refugee integration by EU institutions, civil society organisations and other relevant stakeholders identify refugees as an important social group in need of targeted programmes to integrate them into the labour market. Their often-traumatic experiences mean that refugees require a strong support system and transparent policies for improved economic integration, given that this constitutes a basis for a decent life.

In the next chapter, we analyse policy frames and selected historical features that significantly influence and create new realities for refugees in the labour market of the three countries.

Austria: A Long Tradition of Immigration to the Country

Since the Second World War, Austria has been among the Western countries that have become typical destinations for immigration. The latter applies to both economic migrants and refugees who come to the country to seek protection. Large migrations occurred in response to several war conflicts, including the Hungarian Revolution of the 1960s, the wars in former Yugoslavia, Afghanistan, Iraq and also in Russia, e.g. primarily the conflict in Chechnya. In recent years, people have fled to Austria mostly from the Arabian Peninsula, notably Syria, Afghanistan, Iran and Iraq. Austria has been a protagonist not only by accepting refugees, but has also played a valuable role as a transit country. In 2020, the country experienced yearly population growth of 6.6% and 95% of that growth came from migration. Data from 2019 reveal that 23.7% of the total population is first- or second-generation people with a migrant background. In 2019, 12,886 refugees (The Expert Council for Integration, 2020) applied for international protection in Austria.

A study by Leitner and Landesmann (2020) investigated the dynamics of the mismatch of occupational mobility and decent work and showed that careers follow the expected U-shaped pattern marked by an initial loss and a subsequent mild recovery. Although most refugees experienced a considerable reduction in their professional level or type of work between their last country of employment and their first employment in Austria, some refugees were later able to improve their professional status and work according to their qualifications and experience. The biggest drops in the rate of working in one's vocation are experienced by refugees who had previously worked in highly skilled occupations. The greatest reduction was seen among those who had worked as legislators, managers and senior officials in their country of origin. In Austria, refugees generally worked as service or sales workers during their first employment, some in agriculture and fisheries. The occupational mobility of refugees in Austria is limited to particular occupations requiring a medium or low education. The higher the level of education, the more pronounced the U-shaped career path, with the fall from employment in the country of origin and growth in a second or third job in the new country.

One of the more important programmes available in the country is learning German. The German language course is organised by the Employment Service for persons with international or subsidiary protection. A course on Austrian values and culture is also offered, albeit participation is conditional on the payment of a minimum income. Stakeholders believe that learning German is the most important qualification for the future, and is also important for continuing learning after completing the course and obtaining new skills. Integration projects need realistic objectives and the cooperation between service providers has to be improved while the support of civil society must also be maintained. The Employment Service states that persons with international and subsidiary protection should not be seen as lower-skilled workers (as has already happened with many refugees) simply because of their poor German language skills, but that attention should be paid to their previous work experience, education and actual abilities.

The qualification check carried out by the Employment Service is important because it allows the qualifications held by refugees to be categorised and hence provides information on where to continue with additional training and qualification. As a good practice, "A year of voluntary integration" also demonstrated ways in which young refugees can gain insight into the functioning of the labour market and thus find it easier to integrate into jobs later" (Martín, 2016).

Stakeholders are calling for more effective labour market access for asylum seekers by removing the current restrictions, facilitating access to all economic sectors and reducing the time limits for being able to enter the labour market. Employers propose allowing asylum seekers to enter the labour market 6 months after their asylum application has been submitted. For persons with a high likelihood of gaining status, this period could be reduced to 3 months. Employers stress that successful integration and rapid integration into the labour market depend on companies being willing to recruit refugees (Martín, 2016). Such measures would also significantly help to reduce work in the 'black market' or without an employment contract and fixed pay, thereby improving refugees' employment situation.

Spain: Shifting Roles from Emigration to Immigration

Spain has changed since 1980 from being a country of people emigrating to a country that receives migrants. For most of the twentieth century, Spain was an expatriate country with around 6 million citizens having emigrated to America and North and Western Europe. With the end of the Franco regime in 1975, Spain joined the then European Economic Community. By 2009, 4.79 million foreigners with a residence permit were living in Spain. In 2008, 13.4% of the population was foreigners, with this statistical trend Spain became one of the largest countries for accepting immigrants (Hooper, 2019).

According to a report on integration in Spain (Martín, 2016), there are frequent bureaucratic hurdles and delays in deciding on protection, with applicants waiting on average 1.5 years for a response. Legal access to labour markets is often identified as a key factor in the integration of refugees and asylum seekers into new societies (Martín, 2016, pp. 108–111).

Asylum seekers should have the right to enter the labour market 6 months after having applied for international protection. When they enter the labour market, they are given 'red card' that allows them to work in Spain for a period of 6 months. When the red card's duration expires, asylum seekers can reapply for an extension (AIDA, 2020). Further, vocational and linguistic training is organised for applicants in reception centres. The three main NGOs manage reception centres: Accem, the Spanish Red Cross and CEAR. They have an action plan which offers the following integration and job-search support programmes: personal counselling, pre-employment training, vocational training and job-search support. However, in practice, asylum seekers encounter several difficulties trying to enter the Spanish labour market. Many do not yet speak Spanish upon obtaining a red card and the time limits for the recognition of qualifications are very long, complex and entail considerable expense. Many refugees also experience discrimination on the grounds of their nationality and religion.

In 2020, the Secretary of State for Migration adopted guidelines for autonomous community authorities (which are responsible for the custody of unaccompanied migrant children) to provide work permits to young people aged 16–18. The aim of the measure is to improve the situation of young people and ensure their access to the labour market on the same conditions as Spanish citizens. The government also announced an automatic extension of the 6-month work permit during the COVID-19 pandemic at the time of the state of emergency. Individuals who receive positive refugee or subsidiary protection status and are still within the 18-month integration process may continue to participate in the mentioned programmes and job-search assistance, CV preparation and vocational training. Yet, despite their recognised status, beneficiaries in practice face barriers to entering the labour market because of language, qualifications and discrimination. This situation is exacerbated by the fact that the Spanish economy has been experiencing a long economic crisis, including a high unemployment rate for the national population (AIDA, 2020) (Fig. 13.1).

The lack of funding for implementing programmes is a great problem affecting the sustainability of the national integration system in Spain. There have also been significant decreases in the number of financial transfers and support in the second and third stages. In general, the Spanish model seems more inclined to provide occasional services rather stable and predetermined policies. While the country specialises politically in the reception phase, this is not the case with the integration of refugees and asylum seekers into the labour market. Such integration is perceived more as a cost and an investment. According to the survey, the biggest difficulties for refugees and applicants seeking employment arise in the

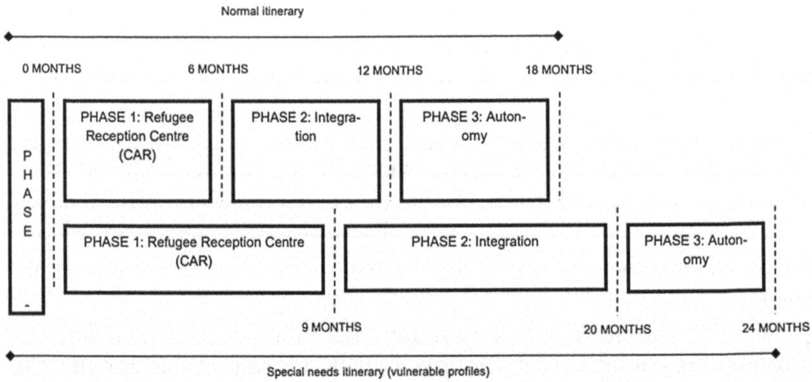

Source: Own illustration.

Fig. 13.1 Structure of Spain's national system of reception and integration. (Source: Martín, 2016, p. 112)

recognition or approval of educational qualifications and in the procedure for checking and recognising professional skills (Martín, 2016, pp. 112–113).

The survey established that the majority of asylum seekers and refugees are employed in tourism and hospitality, the second-most important sector being agriculture, followed by supply and sales.

We highlight the most promising factor of the Spanish system: connection with and integration into the labour market with networking between the actors involved that are collaborating on implementing the support measures. The exchange of information makes the management of the available resources more efficient, which ultimately also affects the quality of the support. All information and main user characteristics collected by each organisation are centralised in the in-app database. Therefore, one organisation can deploy its user to another organisation, which is more appropriate in terms of user education and the need for specific programmes. As a good practice, the use of information technologies for active job searching on LinkedIn in Spain was also pointed out since NGOs there can raise employers' awareness of the different ways in which refugees and asylum seekers can be recruited. This is a good example of a low-cost initiative able to reach a larger audience.

The integration scheme, on the other hand, also has several shortcomings. One of the most fundamental is the lack of a clear and long-term labour market integration strategy that is more or less resource-dependent. Another drawback is that the asylum system is over-centralised and ignores the fact that integration into the labour market is essentially a local process. On top of all the problems mentioned above concerning implementation of the measures, administrative delays and a reduction in the level of protection which bring consequences for integration into the labour market remain. Inefficient legal procedures, particularly extension of the red card, have a negative impact on both supply and demand in the labour market. Employers frequently offer a fixed-term job to applicants still waiting for the decision on their application (Martín, 2016).

Slovenia: In Between the Balkans and the EU

Slovenian migration is defined today by two major features: historical trends of immigration from the republics of the former common state of Yugoslavia and international migration as part of global migration flows from the South and East. The independent Slovenia already encountered forced migration in the 1990s when refugees from war-conflict zones in Bosnia, Serbia and Croatia fled to safe countries across Europe (Zavratnik & Cukut Krilić, 2020, p. 115). According to a UNHCR report for 2001, over 72,000 people sought international protection in Slovenia, mostly women with children and the elderly fleeing the war in Bosnia and Herzegovina. To date, the majority of these have returned and a minority have remained and are integrated into their new society. Further, the year 2000/2001 marks a change in migration dynamics since migration to Slovenia became increasingly diverse relative to the country of origin while ever more migrants started to arrive from more distant non-European countries such as Iran, Pakistan, China, Bangladesh, Algeria and others (Zavratnik, 2004 in Zavratnik & Cukut Krilić, 2020, p. 120). Called the "Balkan route", the third major migration path to Slovenia commenced in 2015–2016 and migration along this route continues today.

Refugees obtain access to the labour market 9 months after they have applied for international protection and can perform work under the same conditions as citizens. After 9 months, they also have access to vocational training courses and all active employment policy measures organised by the Employment Service of Slovenia. Persons granted with subsidiary protection status or refugee status may access the labour market and can be employed, self-employed and work on the same conditions as citizens. If they are unemployed, they can also exercise the same rights as citizens of the Republic of Slovenia. Family members of persons holding international protection also have the right to freely access the labour market (IOM, 2017, p. 27).

Beneficiaries of international protection have the right for their education to be recognised. The costs shall be borne by the competent authority and shall cover the costs where persons with international protection are unable to prove their formal qualifications and skills by presenting documents. Asylum seekers must regulate and fund their own education. The ENIC-NARIC Centre at the Ministry of Education, Science and Sport is responsible for the recognition of education/skills in Slovenia. In 2015, only five people with refugee status applied for the recognition of skills/education in Slovenia, although refugees can also arrange recognition in other educational institutions. It is often the case that persons are unable to provide the documentation required for successful recognition and therefore do not apply for nostrification at all. In turn, this means they carry out lower-paid and physical work despite the professions they previously acquired (Ladić et al., 2018, pp. 43–46).

It is important that people looking for a job become involved in counselling programmes. In Slovenia, an on-the-job training programme that lasts 6 months is available for persons with international protection. As part of the programme a beneficiary receives food, transport and a payment of EUR 3.30 per hour. Companies are reimbursed EUR 373.00 by way of monthly training costs for a participant and the cost of a transitional medical examination (ZRSZ, 2021). In 2016, the Employment Service of Slovenia recruited two specialised persons to work with persons holding international protection in Ljubljana and Maribor.

The state's funding for NGOs changes annually, with little funding being allocated to the provision of job-search assistance. The Attitudes Association provides integration assistance in general, while another non-governmental organisation, Slovenian Philanthropy, runs an orientation programme that has historically been funded for a period of 3 months and is now reduced to 1 month. Part of the funding can also be earmarked to help find a job, yet the systematic introduction of such a programme should be nationwide. The Cene Štupar Institute allows persons with international protection to attend 300 hours of a Slovenian language course and, with the consent of the state office for integration, they can obtain additional hours in a Slovenian language course (MNZ, 2021).

In the report National Integration Evaluation Mechanisms (Ladić et al., 2018, pp. 48–49), researchers emphasise the biggest challenges concerning the employment of refugees. One of the greatest problems with finding a job is poor knowledge of the Slovenian language. If refugees or applicants for international protection do not speak Slovenian, their chances of finding a full-time job are very low. It is also difficult for applicants for international protection to find employment themselves without the help of institutions. As a second challenge, the researchers note that most employers do not want to hire a refugee, and they encounter racism and discrimination while looking for a job.

Finding and Discussion: Narratives Concerning Integration into the Labour Market Across Europe

The presented policy frames and data show that the systems in the three countries vary considerably due to a range of factors, such as historical circumstances, geographical position of the country, linguistic situation etc. To sum up, all three countries have in place certain programmes for integration and specifically for the integration of refugees into the labour market. In the chapter below, we consider the effectiveness of these programmes through the experience of refugees in their day-to-day lives.

One of the principal aims of our research was to investigate the day-to-day situation and policy framework in the area of refugee employment in Slovenia, Spain and Austria in the period following the refugee crisis. We found that systems in certain areas in all three countries vary widely. In Spain and Slovenia, we established that a clear and long-lasting strategy of integration policies and labour market integration is missing. In Austria, we detected, inter alia, the high refugee intake, along with a clear and long-term strategy for integration into both society and the labour market. The experts for Spain stress that the country specialises in the reception phase, but not in the integration of asylum seekers and refugees into the labour market. The lack of funds to finance integration programmes is also the biggest reason for failure, which depends not so much on the country's financial situation, but on the importance of integration policies and the current politics establishment, which is now most visible in Austria as programmes are being cut. Asylum seekers have access to the labour market in Austria 3 months after applying for international protection, albeit these are short-term jobs in a particular sector and are available if no EU citizen has registered for these posts. In Spain, asylum seekers can enter the labour market 6 months after having applied for international protection and can obtain a 'red card', which must be renewed after 6 months. In Slovenia, asylum seekers are free to access the labour market 9 months after the time they submitted an application for asylum.

A social worker from Austria underscored that the first problem is the long asylum procedures. In the time applicants are waiting for the decision, they do not have an opportunity to further educate and improve their knowledge of the German language. When they obtain a status, they often have other problems such as illness, a lack of energy and hope, making it harder to find a job (Social worker 2, personal interview, 7 March 2021):

> Many people who come to us are full of energy in the first few months, optimism, they're very happy to be in this country, and to be safe. Then a lot of times there's a depressing phase where they think they must sit here and not do anything. Experience shows that as soon as you start with the daily structure, educate them, give them the opportunity to work as quickly as possible, the integration is faster and more successful… Because nothing's better integration than being in an environment, meeting the local population, encountering local customs, the way you work etc. Integration is much more successful.

A problem also arises with the recognition of education and qualifications since persons are unable to provide proof of the required education. In Slovenia, the recognition of qualifications for refugees is free of charge, in Spain and Austria it involves payment of a fee, which further deters individuals from going into the lengthy process of having their education recognised or diplomas nostrified. A social worker from Austria explained that they have an organisation which helps people with their nostrification, but they must possess enough financial means to do the nostrification. When it comes to recognising education, there is also a significant part of the Austrian population that wants to make it more difficult to recognise because they fear competition. Professional criteria are additionally required for recognition, the process is quite difficult and individuals who choose to do so must have sufficient will, be persistent and have an adequate financial basis. One expert from Austria also noted that it is very difficult to achieve nostrification, you must be very ambitious and young and very rarely does anyone decide to have their education recognised. The interviewee stated that WAFF (Wiener adequate Förderungsfonds) also bears some of the nostrification costs for those who already have a job or are close to employment and finances certain schooling (Social worker 2, personal interview, 7 March 2021). Further, a social worker in Spain explained: “This only happens to some refugees with a higher education. Most are forced to retrain professionally in lower-skilled occupations in order to find a job as soon as possible, for example in hotels and hospitality, house cleaning or home care” (Social worker 3, personal interview, 16 September 2019). Both migration experts and refugees stressed that, despite refugees having the right to enter the labour market, they miss out on job opportunities due to not knowing the language of the new country.

Analysis showed that the most important qualification for the future of refugees and successful integration is knowing the language of the host country. In Austria, the Employment Service provides language learning to refugees and asylum seekers, whereas in Spain and Austria this role is largely taken up by NGOs, and in Slovenia a Slovenian language course is organised at the Cene Štupar public education centre. An interviewee from Iraq also highlighted the importance of knowing the country’s language: “Frankly speaking, I have no expectations at all. All that I wanted is to be in a safe place and to protect my family. But I knew that I must learn the German language so I can communicate with others” (Interviewee 14, personal interview, 5 February 2020).

With respect to the first research question regarding the situation and trends in refugee employment in Slovenia, Spain and Austria following the changed migration realities after the 2015 refugee crisis, we can especially identify the insufficient knowledge of the language, the recognition of education and experience and the lack of job-search assistance programmes. This allows us to confirm our assumption about refugees having limited access to the labour market due to their legal and social status. Despite being protected by the Geneva Convention, they are generally excluded from the main employment opportunities and sectors and are typically employed in precarious work conditions.

Further, in line with research question 2 we investigated the type of employment the integration policy is focused on and the relationship between recruiters and the state. We assumed that the integration policy largely focuses on quickly finding jobs for refugees, not jobs for which they have been educated. Moreover, that employers are reluctant to employ refugees, with this outcome being due to a lack of information on employment opportunities, prejudice and stereotypes about refugees in wider society.

The data show a common aspect in all three countries, namely, that refugees are highly represented in lower-skilled jobs. However, in Austria it soon became clear that refugees should also be assigned to higher-skilled jobs according to their experience and education. Too many people in the country were doing lower-skilled jobs and the pool was therefore overfilled and, on the other side, the restructuring from lower- to higher-skilled jobs has positively contributed the economy. Interviewees were asked what work refugees are doing in their new countries. One interviewee explained that there are many people in Slovenia doing construction work, including at the Knauf company (Social worker 1, personal interview, 24 August 2020):

> Welders were very desirable, many of them are now taking exams for welders. Catering. Many of them are tying social entrepreneurship in this area. You've probably heard of Skuhna, at the beginning it was a social enterprise, where they include many migrants who then gain knowledge from them, and then also became employed there. Refugees often work through agencies or have short-term contracts and are often paid less. There are also cases where employers take advantage of them. However, on the other hand, some employers act perfectly correctly.

The interviewees—social workers and consultants at the Institutes—also confirmed that the vast majority of refugees work in lower-skilled jobs. Refugees often have fixed-term contracts and precarious jobs, while others also reported working on the 'black market', without a proper employment contract, and typically have lower-paid jobs. In Slovenia and Spain, no interviewed refugee had a permanent contract. One interviewee from Syria who had his own small business making handbags before arriving in Slovenia stated:

> I started in February 2020 and now I have a contract until February 2021, and a contract for only 4 hours a day. If I could work for 8 hours, that would be much better. If I had my own company it would be better and I could have more work and I could also export products to other countries. (Interviewee 7, personal interview, 27 August 2020)

In Austria, some interviewees have permanent contracts and, above all, work in jobs largely in line with their prior education and experience. One interviewee who lives in Austria, has a degree in literature and English and works as a social worker at the Employment Service stated: "Yes, it is now almost 3 years since I have been working and I have a permanent contract" (Interviewee 9, personal interview, 30 July 2019).

We note that the interviewees in Spain were able to enter the labour market the fastest, as explained by their previous knowledge of the Spanish language. Social workers in all three countries pointed out that refugees chiefly work in construction, tourism, cleaning services and sales. The analysis of the interviews partly confirms the assumption that the integration policy is focused primarily on quickly finding jobs for refugees, not on the jobs for which they have been educated. Some deviation from this is seen in Austria, which is a result of a long tradition in this respect.

Asylum seekers in Slovenia can only enter the labour market 9 months after making an application, yet it is rare for them to find any employment. They point to knowledge of the Slovenian language as being the greatest obstacle. Barriers to integrating into the labour market led to the Employment Service of the Republic of Slovenia specifically recruiting two consultants for persons with international protection and introducing a workplace training programme for refugees in which they can acquire practical skills and experience. Training also improves their chances of further employment, while employers learn about refugees and can see how they work. The programme's flexibility means that it is not mandatory to employ a trainee and, accordingly, many employers do not decide to hire them once the training has ended. Instead, they take on another trainee again, noting that the cost of the worker is paid by the Employment

Service. Further, those refugees wishing to start their own business in the new country also encounter problems, typically being hampered by ignorance of the language and administrative barriers (Interviewee 7, personal interview, 27 August 2020):

> Ok, I was thinking about employment before, but since I started my S.P. (sole proprietorship), everything has changed. I pay much more money, but I am my own boss. I don't have anybody over my head. I can do anything I like. I'm supported by my Slovenian partner, who supported me to make the S.P. and everything, with the language, with bureaucrat things, it's much easier and, of course, I'm my own boss, and I'm connected a lot with people. I have a really wide network, which gets me work in many places. And because of my skills, that I speak English, I speak Arabic, a bit of Slovenian, this helps a lot.

Employers often lack information regarding who these people are and why have they come to their country, the rights they hold and, in particular, how the employment process proceeds. The lack of information, prejudice and unfounded assumptions lead them to not choose to recruit asylum seekers and refugees. Social workers described how in some cases employers exploit refugees. Refugees work illegally for businesses, or sign contracts in which they renounce their rights and have no rights should their contract be terminated. However, the lack of information is also a concern for refugees who are unaware of their rights under the labour law that provides them with the right to a vacation, payments according to the law, the right to sick leave etc. This allows us to confirm the third hypothesis that employers are not in favour of employing refugees.

Only two interviewees in Spain had a good experience with employers. One interviewer from West Africa explained (Interviewee 18, personal interview, 15 August 2019):

> It's not the same, it's not the same at all, since you're not a Spanish man, you're a foreigner. They call you a friend, you're different. The leaders are also Spanish and do not work like us. We do hard work, all bad work is done by foreigners, in hotels, restaurants. People from Venezuela, Africa … I haven't seen anyone here working at a bank or being a bus driver. We only do physical work or cleaning. … If you want to be well accepted here, a lot of time must pass, the mentality has to change. … There are also language barriers, if you want to work, you have to educate yourself or go to a course here.

In answering research question three, we analysed the effectiveness of public policies in the area of employing refugees. We assume that the biggest differences are the outcome of different policies, experiences and traditions. In general, countries with a long tradition are more successful, achieve better results with their integration policy and employ more refugees. A social worker from Slovenia highlighted the initial support for persons who are eligible for financial assistance with housing, but only provided that they are not employed. If they have a job, even if it is not full time or not well paid, they lose their financial support. This method demotivates people to find a job within the period they are receiving assistance. In addition, improved access to Slovenian language courses is required for different groups according to their language skills and predisposition: for instance, on-the-job training could be provided in combination with a language course. In this regard, the interviewees in Spain stressed it is necessary to improve the process of nostrification, the recognition of work experience, and access to housing opportunities and to raise awareness of refugees among the organisations that will work with them in the future. Although many measures exist that are well placed in theory, in practice their results are insufficient. The analysed countries share in common the fact that they have long-established procedures to obtain status that in some cases can take many years, during which time applicants are living amidst uncertainty and the fear of deportation, which further negatively impacts their integration and mental health.

One positive measure in Austria is the quota system under which each federal state or region must take in a certain percentage of refugees. Beside reception across the states, the quota system regulates access to housing and education in each federal state. Our data confirm the starting assumption that countries with years of experience with employing refugees are more successful and achieve better results from their integration policies for refugee employment. A good indicator of this is Austria, which is 'the leader' in migration policy and refugee employment among the three countries analysed. This is seen in the availability of various programmes, long-term employment and the satisfaction of refugees living and wishing to remain in the country permanently.

Migration processes across Europe are also changing in the aftermath of the 2015 refugee crisis and Russia's war in Ukraine that started in February 2022, and thus the integration policies of countries and policies on the level of the European Union. In general, migration policies have been restrictive in the last few decades, paying most attention to the question of the security of the EU's external borders, illegal entries into EU territory and deportations. Refugees have frequently been labelled a security threat to the state and society and act as 'on-call culprits' or 'scapegoats' for gaining political power and the grounds to implement 'security' measures. One example of the latter we observed is the razor wire along the Kolpa River along the Slovenian–Croatian border (Zavratnik & Cukut Krilić, 2020, p. 127).

In the discussion part, we note that the data from the field research permit the conclusion that the integration systems in the countries under analysis vary considerably in some aspects, yet are similar in others. In Slovenia and Spain, a clear and long-term employment strategy for refugees is missing compared to Austria, which has a well-defined strategy. In all countries, implementation of the strategies in integration policy documents depends on annual funds earmarked for various integration programmes. An important finding is that the most important way to integrate successfully is to learn local language, which is also the key to rapidly integrating into the local/national society. These mean language skills are crucial and constitute the backbone of refugee integration support systems. The research findings further show that the refugees' opportunities to enter the labour market are initially minimal and limited by their refugee status, despite the otherwise declared equal rights they enjoy.

The fact is that in all three countries refugees are overrepresented in lower-skilled jobs. Yet, Austria is an exception since it assigns many people to higher-skilled jobs according to their education and experience. It is also interesting that Austria is the only country in which the interviewees had permanent employment contracts, some in line with their education and experience. We also found that employers are reluctant to hire refugees due to a lack of information, prejudice and unfounded assumptions.

In Slovenia, access to Slovenian language courses for different groups with various degrees of language skills should also be improved, and as a suggestion, on-the-job training could be provided in combination with a language course. In Spain, the interviewee stressed the need to improve the process of recognising qualifications and work experience, as well as access to housing. Like in Spain, the recognition of one's qualifications also requires the payment of a fee in Austria. A social worker from Austria also pointed out the quota system which allows refugees to be distributed across the country as a localisation solution. Such dispersion has a significant impact on integration, job search and housing. On the local level,

Table 13.1 Selected characteristics of the integration process of refugees

Country	*Access to the labour market (months)*	*Contract for permanent/ temporary work*	*Finding jobs according to education/skills*	*Long-term experience with employing refugees*
Slovenia	9	Temporary	No	No
Austria	3	Permanent	Yes	Yes
Spain	6	Temporary	No	Yes

Source: Field work data

refugees find it easier to connect with the local population, which prevents ghettoisation (Table 13.1).

What the analysed countries share in common are the long procedures for recognising refugee and subsidiary protection status, which in some cases take several years. Refugees live amidst uncertainty and a fear of rejection, which in turn negatively impacts their integration, labour, decent livelihood and mental health.

Conclusion

Migration is an integral part of human societies of both the present and the past. This makes it important to adopt effective integration policies and long-term migration strategies on the national and EU levels alike. Refugees are one of the most vulnerable groups of migrants due to their often-traumatic experiences and marginal position in new societies generally. A good support system and clear policies are therefore required to make their arrival in the host country easier and to build a bridge leading towards their inclusion in new environments. In our comparative research on integration policies in the field of working life, i.e. refugee employment and integration into labour markets in Slovenia, Austria and Spain, we tried to collect the voices of newly arrived refugees and the evaluations of experts in the area of refugees' employment.

We can only declare that a policy for integrating refugees into the labour market is successful when it allows refugees to gain economic independence and, further, when their position is comparable to that of the majority population. In this respect, differences between the targeted population, for example refugees or social minorities, and the majority population should be as small as possible. Certain measures in countries with a long tradition and extensive experience, in our analysis Austria, show that experience and tradition play an important social role, whereas countries that are newer to immigration may be characterised not only by negative public opinion, but by fragile or even non-existent public policy instruments and practices as well.

In summary, our research findings show that the analysed countries face similar barriers such as language obstacles and negative public attitudes towards migrants in new countries, but that these are lower in countries with greater experience dealing with the migration phenomenon. The possibility of rapid integration into countries, namely, the existence of comprehensive integration policies, has a significant impact on the timing of entry into the labour market. The employment of refugees no doubt has a central role in the overall process of integration and entry to the labour market, while the consequent access to income importantly contributes to the autonomous life of refugees in their new societies.

As partly identified in the field research, an important part of the integration process is the possibility of migrants being able to establish their own companies. Even though we did not deal with this issue in detail in the study, nor was it a central research question, a few interviewees nonetheless emphasised that they would like to engage in entrepreneurship, notably those who had already a small business in their country of origin. Here, it should be stressed that the entrepreneurship of migrants and/or refugees is a relatively overlooked topic since integration into the labour market is primarily understood as employment with a domestic employer and less as the possibility of individual entrepreneurial projects run by the refugees themselves.

References

AIDA. (2020). Country Report: Spain. https://asylumineurope.org/wp-content/uploads/2021/03/AIDAES_2020update.pdf

Bade, K. J. (2005). *Evropa v gibanju. Migracije od poznega 18. stoletja do danes.* Založba /*cf.

Balibar, É. (2015). Evropa in begunci: Demografska širitev. *Časopis za kritiko znanosti, 43*(262), 207–215.

De Haas, H., Castles, S., & Miller, J. (2014). *The Age of Migration. International Population Movements in the Modern World* (5th ed.). Palgrave Macmillan.

European Commission. (2016). Measures for Asylum Seekers and Refugees in EU Member States. Volume I: Comparative Analysis and Policy Findings, Migration

Policy Centre European. University Institute, Florence, Bertelsmann Foundation. https://ec.europa.eu/migrant-integration/library-document/refugees-workers-mapping-labour-market-integration-support-measures-asylum-seekers_en

Fasani, F., Frattini, T., & Minale, L. (2018). *Refugee Integration into the Labour Market: Evidence from Europe*. Centro Studi Luca d'Agliano Development Studies Working Paper No. 435. https://doi.org/10.2139/ssrn.3180206

Goldin, I., Cameron, G., & Balarajan, M. (2012). *Exceptional People: How Migration Shaped Our World and Will Define Our Future*. Princeton University Press.

Grzymala-Kazlowska, A., & Phillimore, J. (2018). Introduction: Rethinking Integration. New Perspectives on Adaptation and Settlement in the Era of Super-diversity. *Journal of Ethnic and Migration Studies, 44*(2), 179–196. https://doi.org/10.1080/1369183X.2017.1341706

Hooper, K. (2019). *Spain's Labour Migration Policies in the Aftermath of Economic Crisis*. Migration Policy Institute Europe. http://migrationpolicy.org/

IOM. (2017). https://publications.iom.int/books/migration-health-annual-report-2017

Jakobson, M. L., King, R., Moroşanu, L., & Vetik, R. (2023). Migration and Integration in Turbulent Times. In M. L. Jakobson, R. King, L. Moroşanu, & R. Vetik (Eds.), *Anxieties of Migration and Integration in Turbulent Times*. IMISCOE Research Series. Springer. https://doi.org/10.1007/978-3-031-23996-0_1

King, R. (2007). *Atlas of Human Migration*. Firefly Books.

Ladić, M., Bajt, V., Jalušič, V., & Kogovšek Šalamon, N. (2018). *Nacionalni mehanizmi za evalvacijo integracije: poročilo za leto 2016*. Mirovni inštitut.

Leitner, S., & Landesmann, M. (2020). *Refugees Integration into the Austrian Labour Market: Dynamics of Occupational Mobility and Job-Skills Mismatch* (Working Paper 188). The Vienna Institute for International Economic Studies. https://wiiw.ac.at/refugees-integration-into-the-austrian-labour-market-dynamics-of-occupational-mobility-and-job-skills-mismatch-dlp-5425.pdf

Martín, I. (2016). From Refugees to Workers: Mapping Labour Market Integration Support Measures for Asylum-Seekers and Refugees in EU Member States. Volume II: Comparative Analysis and Policy Findings. *Bertelsmann Stiftung (HRSG.)*. https://ec.europa.eu/migrant-integration/library-document/refugees-workers-mapping-labour-market-integration-support-measures-asylum-seekers_en

Ministrstvo za notranje zadeve [MNZ]. (2021). *Integracija oseb s priznano mednarodno zaščito*. https://www.gov.si/teme/integracija/

Spencer, S., & Charsley, K. (2021). Reframing 'Integration: Acknowledging and Addressing Five Core Critiques. *Comparative Migration Studies, 9*. https://doi.org/10.1186/s40878-021-00226-4

The Expert Council for Integration. (2020). *Integration Report 2020: 10 Years Expert Council for Integration—10 Years Integration Report*. https://www.bundeskanzleramt.gv.at/service/publikationen-aus-dem-bundeskanzleramt/publikationen-zu-integration/integrationsberichte.html

Vogiazides, L., & Mondani, H. (2020). A Geographical Path to Integration? Exploring the Interplay Between Regional Context and Labour Market Integration Among Refugees in Sweden. *Journal of Ethnic and Migration Studies, 46*(1), 23–45. https://doi.org/10.1080/1369183X.2019.1588717

Zavratnik Zimic, S. (2004). *Migration trends in selected EU applicant countries. Slovenia: The perspective of a country on the 'Schengen periphery'*. Dunaj: International Organization for Migration.

Zavratnik, S., & Cukut Krilić, S. (2020). *Digitalni begunci: transformacija migracijskih poti ali ko pametni telefon nadomesti kovček*. Fakulteta za družbene vede, Založba FDV: ZRC SAZU, Založba ZRC.

ZRSZ. (2021). https://www.ess.gov.si/delodajalci/zaposlovanje-delavcev-iz-evrope-eures/zaposlitev-delavca-iz-evrope/integracijatujega-delavca/

Index[1]

[1] Note: Page numbers followed by 'n' refer to notes.

S. Bianchini et al. (eds.), *Social Entrepreneurship and Migrants' Inclusion*, Sustainable Development Goals Series,
https://doi.org/10.1007/978-3-031-55791-0

SPRINGER NATURE

GPSR Compliance

The European Union's (EU) General Product Safety Regulation (GPSR) is a set of rules that requires consumer products to be safe and our obligations to ensure this.

If you have any concerns about our products, you can contact us on ProductSafety@springernature.com

In case Publisher is established outside the EU, the EU authorized representative is:

Springer Nature Customer Service Center GmbH
Europaplatz 3
69115 Heidelberg, Germany

The manufacturer's authorised representative in the EU is Springer Nature Customer Service Centre GmbH, Europaplatz 3, 69115 Heidelberg, Germany. If you have any concerns regarding our products, please contact ProductSafety@springernature.com

Printed and bound by CPI Group (UK) Ltd, Croydon, CR0 4YY

01/10/2026

02225903-0013